Speaker's Library *of* BUSINESS

STORIES, ANECDOTES —AND— HUMOR

Speaker's Library *of* BUSINESS

STORIES, ANECDOTES AND HUMOR

JOE GRIFFITH

PRENTICE HALL
Paramus, New Jersey 07652

Library of Congress Cataloging-in-Publication Data

Griffith, Joe, [date]
    Speaker's library of business stories, anecdotes, and humor / by
Joe Griffith.
        p.   cm.
    Includes index.
    ISBN 0-13-826975-0—ISBN 0-13-826983-1 (pbk.)
    1. Business—Anecdotes.   2. Business presentations.   3. Oral
communication.   I. Title.
    HF5351.G69   1990   90-37525
    650—dc20   CIP

Printed in the United States of America

10   9   8

ISBN 0-13-826975-0   ISBN 0-13-826983-1(PBK)

 PRENTICE HALL
Career & Personal Development
Paramus, NJ 07652
A Simon & Schuster Company

On the World Wide Web at http://www.phdirect.com

Prentice-Hall International (UK) Limited, *London*
Prentice-Hall of Australia Pty. Limited, *Sydney*
Prentice-Hall Canada Inc., *Toronto*
Prentice-Hall Hispanoamericana, S.A., *Mexico*
Prentice-Hall of India Private Limited, *New Delhi*
Prentice-Hall of Japan, Inc., *Tokyo*
Simon & Schuster Asia Pte. Ltd., *Singapore*
Editora Prentice-Hall do Brasil, Ltda., *Rio de Janeiro*

Dedication:

To all the people who have had to learn to cope with dyslexia.

INTRODUCTION

Have you ever stood before a sales group or a business meeting and given a speech that fell flat?

Was it a speech that was well researched and thoughtfully presented but that sank like a stone in a broad pool of audience apathy?

Have you ever wished for a good motivational or inspirational story that could shake your employees awake and translate their apathy into action?

Have you ever searched for references that would give you the power to grab your colleagues' attention, only to find no effective source book available?

Wish no more. Search no more. You hold in your hands a treasury of material carefully collected and chosen by Joe Griffith, one of the top professional speakers in the business today, to help you turn your best thoughts about business into memorable messages.

It is no secret that leadership gravitates to the person who can present an effective speech. People love leaders who can keep them on the edge of their chairs. Some, like Chyrsler chief executive Lee Iacocca, are known for their enthusiasm. Others, like President John F. Kennedy, were statesmen. Whatever their field of influence, gifted communicators have one common denominator: They can tell a story. More to the point, they can use a good story to make a point and to fix that point firmly in their listeners' minds.

The Speaker's Library of Business Stories, Anecdotes and Humor offers you access to the techniques enjoyed by great speakers. It will become an integral part of your own development as a skilled communicator. At your fingertips rests a collection of more than 3000 stories, anecdotes, quotations, examples, comparisons, illustrations, and sayings applicable to the needs of executives, salespeople, and managers alike. Many of them are already podium tested by professionals. What does this mean to you? It means that for the investment of a few dollars, you have the services of America's premier professional communicators at your disposal. It's the next best thing to hiring a professional speechwriter. In several important ways it's even better.

With this book you tailor your own speeches to your own needs. Better yet, you might eventually quit writing speeches altogether and start giving them instead. Just remember the points you want to make and select from these pages the anecdotes or analogies that best illustrate them. These techniques work anytime, anywhere. These analogies are applicable to any business situation from an informal "talk" with your sales staff in the morning to the annual report to the stockholders at noon and including a majority industry address at dinner.

Inspired by more than 20 years spent at some of the world's most prestigious podiums, this volume is filled with effective communications aids, catalogued by subject, along with the suggested point that each illustration can make.

Here's how to use it.

Suppose you are to make a speech before your peers. Make a list of the points you want to make. Now refer to the alphabetized categories and to the index in this book for stories and quotes that apply.

Let's say you are concerned about getting your employees to face the coming changes in your industry as a team. Read the stories and anecdotes in the section labeled TEAMWORK. Since many stories make more than one point you might also check the sections that are comparable with teamwork such as Achievement, Commitment, Competition, and Delegation. Explore these sections until you have found at least 10 stories you like that relate to the message you want to present.

Now *you* become the editor.

You may use a half-dozen stories, or all of them, in your presentation. You may personalize them to fit your own specific situation. How many you use and how you use them is up to you. For example, if one of the points you want to reinforce is the idea that we need to react to the signs of change, your remarks might be something like this:

> "We need to react to the signs of change or else we could end up like the man who bought a barometer and when he hung it on his den wall it predicted a hurricane. He took it back complaining that it was broken. There had never been a hurricane in New England before. The next day his house was blown away by the great hurricane of 1939. We too could be blown away if we don't react to the changes that are coming."

By sprinkling illustrations like these throughout your presentation, you will grab the imagination of listeners in a way that films or television are hard pressed to duplicate. Never forget that as a communicator you are appealing to the most powerful image-producing mechanism on earth . . . the human mind. It thrives on images. Good stories are a trigger that release an explosive, powerful, positive form of communication energy. To quote the late Dr. Carl Winters, for years a popular member of the prestigious General Motors speaking staff, "If you want to be a successful speaker, you've got to have a messsage with stories for people to remember your message by."

The use of these techniques is effective for everything from minor points to blockbuster presentations. Best of all, the stories come directly from you because you have chosen them specifically for the message you intend to deliver. Just remember to use only those stories you feel comfortable telling and that make a specific point more memorable. And make sure you use stories that are not only good but also tell your point of view.

An ample supply of proven speech openings and closes is included to get you started and finished with impact. There are also valuable categories such as *Commencement Speech* and *Fund-Raising*, speeches any executive can be called on to deliver.

The Speaker's Library places the raw materials—the stories, anecdotes, and the illustrations—here at your fingertips.

The choices are yours.

Joe Griffith

CONTENTS

ABILITY

"Men habitually use only a small part of the powers they actually possess."

William James

□ Our happiness depends on using all of our abilities.

"If you deliberately plan to be less than you are capable of being, then I warn you that you'll be unhappy for the rest of your lives."

Abraham Maslow

□ We need to stretch ourselves.

"You have enormous untapped power that you will probably never tap, because most people never run far enough on their first wind to ever find they have a second."

William James

□ You are never a failure as long as you recognize your own abilities.

When the singer Bob Dylan performed at a high school talent show, his classmates, failing to realize he was a kid bound for glory, booed him off the stage.

□ Always perform to reach your abilities.

"Playwright Noel Coward reached his mid-sixties. Though he had suffered for years from gastritis, Coward stubbornly refused to slacken his pace. Noting his activities on the stage and television, the London *Times* wrote: 'Here is a craftsman who has remained at the top of his profession . . . simply because he has dedicated his life not to attitudes or to transient movements but to getting on with his work to the best of his ability.' "

Mortimer R. Feinberg, Effective Psychology for Managers

☐ Some people can't recognize ability.

Bill Walsh, former head coach of the San Francisco 49ers, is recognized today as an offensive wizard.

So how come pro football, with all its finesse and intelligence, allowed Bill Walsh to grow gray before recognizing his skills? How come he had to serve an apprenticeship of twenty-one years as pro assistant coach, in the colleges, in the semi-pros before there was a head NFL job for him? How come he was forty-seven years old before a rookie owner named Edward J. DeBartolo Jr. rejected the counsel of other owners and hired Bill Walsh?

It is one of the most curious accidents in a sport that is devoted to the perfection of its coaches.

Walsh said, "I was forty-five before I even had an interview for a head coaching job in the NFL."

And then he didn't get it. He was turned down. He was told he and his unorthodox ideas weren't wanted.

He was interviewed by the Bengals. Rejected.

He was interviewed by the Jets. Rejected.

He was interviewed by the Rams. Rejected.

The pros had Bill Walsh labeled: "Good technician. Not a head coach."

☐ Three Super Bowl victories later, Bill Walsh proved that we need to recognize people's unique abilities, not compare them to others.

☐ Ability has to be proven everyday. No matter how successful we are, we have to prove ourselves everyday.

Once there was a college running back who everyone agreed had the ability to be the best in the business. He was drafted early by the pros. Sadly, he never really performed up to his ability. His coach finally released him in favor of a player who had much less ability. Asked how he could do such a thing, the coach said the decision had been relatively simple: "That man has all the ability in the world, but the one I kept has all the touchdowns."

☐ Are we using our abilities to make our company a better company?

Ability is a crazy thing, said a major league baseball manager. It's fun to talk about it and beautiful to see in action, but hardly anybody really understands it. People think it's something a player keeps in his equipment bag and puts on as he does his uniform. But a true professional knows this isn't true. He knows his ability isn't real unless he's actually on the field demonstrating it.

☐ And it's the same for everybody, whether a ditchdigger or the president of General Motors. Ability must be used to be useful.

☐ Sometimes it's how we use our abilities, not what they are.

President Ronald Reagan once said that the continued existence of the world depends on the continuing ability of the United States and the Soviet Union to destroy each other, yet we must make sure that terrible ability is never proven. Nuclear war is an unthinkable concept, but I know of no more graphic illustration of the crucial difference between having the ability to do something, and actually getting it done.

ABSENTEEISM

How do you know when to miss work? If you really look like your work ID picture, you're too sick to come in.

There is an unconfirmed story that a worker who·had used up all her sick leave called in dead the other morning.

☐ Absenteeism can be cut with the proper incentive.

At Compton, a textile plant in Alabama, the mill employees were put on a three-day, twelve-hour-a-day week. In addition, they got off a full week every eight weeks. If employees worked thirty-six hours without absenteeism, they got paid for forty.

☐ There are any number of excuses for missing work.

Employee: "Hello, boss, I just called in to say that I won't be able to come to work for a few days. My wife broke an arm."
Employer: "That's too bad, but that doesn't seem like it's serious enough to keep you away from work."
Employee: "Well, it's my arm she broke."

☐ A man took off from work because of sickness.

Boss: "You sure didn't look sick when I saw you at the race track yesterday."
Man: "You should have seen me after the fourth race."

Here's a way to get your employees to work on time: provide forty-five parking spaces for fifty employees.

The boss called an absent employee.

Boss: "Why haven't you shown up for work today?"
Employee: "I lost my American Express card, and I can't leave home without it."

☐ Proper incentives will decrease absenteeism and increase productivity.

When James A. Todd took over Birmingham Bolt Company, a maker of bolts used in coal mines, the company lay in ruins. To turn the company around, he offered a radical incentive program for his workers. He insisted they agree to base a chunk of their weekly salary on the extent to which they exceeded minimum quotas. Workers who showed up more than thirty minutes late lost their incentives for the day; missing a day's work without an excuse forfeited the extra pay for a week.

Productivity shot up. In three years, revenues quadrupled to $345 million, and profits zoomed to $25 million.

█ ACCOUNTANTS

"Without personality, a public accountant my be likened to a nourishing food without flavor."

A. C. Ernst, founder, *Ernst & Whinney*

Audits are like icebergs. What is visible—the auditor's report—is a minor portion of the total bulk.

A funny accountant is an oxymoron, a contradiction in terms, like "business ethics."

Accountants are so boring that if they were drowning and their whole life flashed before them, they'd probably fall asleep.

Accountants invented actuaries so that they could laugh at someone else.

An accountant went to see an eye doctor who told the accountant to "cover one eye and read the bottom line." The accountant asked, "Before or after taxes?"

Comedian Jackie Mason said that every family's greatest dream is to have a son become a doctor. But if he's a little retarded, a lawyer. And if his mind doesn't work at all, an accountant.

Pad the expense account too much and it might turn into severance pay.
If you must pad your expense account, at least do it creatively. The accounting department can always use a good laugh.

Audit is the Matt Dillon of business, always ready to head off trouble.

This story about George Eastman tells how accountants think. He was having a theater built in Rochester, New York, where Eastman Kodak is headquartered. He was going over the blueprints for the 6,000-seat theater. He told the architect that he thought they could squeeze in two more seats into the orchestra. The architect was surprised at this attention to detail. Eastman went on to explain that each seat would bring in 30 cents per performance or 60 cents for the two. With six performances a week, that would be an extra revenue of $3.60 a week. In a year, that would be an extra $187.20, which is the interest on $3,120 for a year.

☐ Every company needs an accountant who thinks of ways to maximize profits.

Andrew Carnegie liked accountants.

When he was ten years old, he attended Sunday school in Scotland. The teacher asked him what scripture he could quote from the Bible. He quoted the famous Scottish proverb: "Take care of your pennies and the pounds will take care of themselves."

The preacher quickly admonished him and said, "That's not in the Bible."

Carnegie replied, "It ought to be."

☐ Every successful business needs someone to watch the pennies.

ACHIEVEMENT

☐ Achievement comes after hard work, not before.

"If people knew how hard I worked to get my mastery, it wouldn't seem so wonderful after all."

Michelangelo

☐ Extraordinary people achieve extraordinary things.

"One machine can do the work of fifty ordinary men. No machine can do the work of one extraordinary man."

Elbert Hubbard

☐ You must know your strengths and weaknesses before you can be a real achiever.

The old Greek philosophers were right. To "know thyself" is the starting point of all achievement.

"Achievers are not only persistent, they are also hard workers who believe in themselves."

Timothy L. Griffith

☐ A company must first value achievement.

"The basic philosophy of an organization has far more to do with its achievements than do technological or economic resources, organizational structure, innovation and timing."

Thomas J. Watson, Jr., IBM

☐ People need a chance to achieve.

"Men and women want to do a good job, and if they are provided the proper environment, they will do so."

Bill Hewlett, founder, Hewlett-Packard

☐ Great achievements are often initially misunderstood.

"To be great is to be misunderstood."

Ralph Waldo Emerson

☐ To achieve, we must be obsessed by it.

When Truman Capote was asked why he wrote, he responded, "The serious artist is obsessed by his material."

☐ We are more likely to achieve if we want more than others.

"I have no respect for the passion for equality, which seems to me merely idealizing envy."

Oliver Wendell Holmes, Jr.

"Achievement in general appears to be a middle-class prerogative. The rich do not appear motivated by particular ambition, other than to rule. They are brought up to feel that they have already somehow made the grade. The poor or near-poor, having all they can do to keep their heads economically above water, cannot aspire even in fantasy to do much in the way of achievement except possibly in sports or entertainment."

William H. Vanderbilt

"The greatest achievements are those that benefit others."

Lillian Gilcrest, author

"Today's achievement is only tomorrow's confusion."

William Dean Howells

"All achievers experience their goals in vivid detail."

Joe L. Whitley, management consultant

☐ We were made to achieve.

"The guiding power in the world would not have made us with the yearning for infinite achievement without giving us the ability and the opportunity for realizing it, any more than it would have made the wild birds with an instinct to fly south in the winter without giving them a sunny South to match the instinct."

Robert Searfoss

☐ We achieve to the degree that we believe in ourselves.

The night before Douglas MacArthur took his entrance exam for West Point, he was all nerves. His mother said to him, "Doug, you'll win if you don't lose your nerve. You must believe in yourself, my son, or no one else will believe in you. Be self-confident, self-reliant, and even if you don't make it, you will know you have done your best."

When the test scores were announced, Douglas MacArthur was number one on the list.

☐ We can achieve remarkable results if we don't lose our nerve.

☐ Achievement is like a three-legged stool.

"The three great essentials to achieve anything worthwhile are first, hard work; second, stick-to-itiveness; third, common sense."

Thomas Edison

☐ There is a difference between achievement and success.

Helen Hayes, the great actress, said her mother drew a distinction between achievement and success. Her mother advised her that "achievement is the knowledge that you have studied and worked hard and done the best that is in you. Success is being praised by others, and that's nice, too, but not as important or satisfying."

☐ Aim for achievement and success will follow.

☐ Long-term achievement needs constant motivation.

After Mickey Spillane, the writer of detective stories, achieved his first big success, he decided to work less and play more. He took up residence at a popular seaside resort and started having a great time. In the little time he found to work, the ideas wouldn't come. Being financially secure he wasn't concerned. All the while, his bank account was steadily shrinking. Once, some unexpected bills came up and overnight Mickey's financial situation went from comfortable to desperate. Almost immediately, good salable ideas began to percolate in his mind, and out of necessity he wrote one of his best stories and went on to enjoy a long and outstanding career.

☐ We can continue to achieve if we don't get too comfortable.

◼ ACTION

☐ Seek steady progress.

"Be not afraid of going slowly; be only afraid of standing still."

Chinese proverb

☐ Hoping won't make something happen.

"Man who waits for roast duck to fly into mouth must wait very, very long time."

Chinese proverb

☐ Action speaks louder than words.

"If you do not wish a man to do a thing, you had better get him to talk about it; for the more men talk, the more likely they are to do nothing else."

Thomas Carlyle

☐ Don't make excuses.

"If you wait until the wind and the weather are just right, you will never plant anything and never harvest anything."

Ecclesiastes 11:4

☐ Thinking about it won't make it happen. You've got to do something.

"Even if you're on the right track, you'll get run over if you just sit there."

Will Rogers

☐ Action begets action.

"A man grows most tired while standing still."

Gregory L. Griffith, Attorney

☐ Don't depend on others.

"I wondered why somebody didn't do something; then I realized that I was somebody."

Anonymous

☐ Action speaks louder than words.

"As I grow older, I pay less attention to what men say. I just watch what they do."

Andrew Carnegie

"Science may have found a cure for most evils; but it has found no remedy for the worst of them all—the apathy of human beings."

Helen Keller

☐ Getting started is the hardest part.

"It seems to me that the most difficult part of building a bridge would be the start.

Robert Benchley

"Above all, try something."

Franklin D. Roosevelt

"Chaotic action is preferable to orderly inaction. Don't just stand there, do something."

Karl Weick, Cornell University

☐ More people would take action if they knew why they were doing something.

"The first step toward writing a novel is to write a one-page statement of purpose."

John Steinbeck

"It is common sense to take a method and try it. If it fails, admit it frankly and try another. But above all, try something."
Franklin D. Roosevelt

"You can't build a reputation on what you are going to do."
Henry Ford

"Everything comes to him who hustles while he waits."
Thomas Edison

Electricians put wires in a new house, but the lights won't go on until we flip the switch.

☐ Don't sit idly by.

"The only thing necessary for the triumph of evil is for good men to do nothing."
Edmund Burke

☐ Do something now.

Opportunities do not come to those who wait. They are captured by those who attack.

The old American expression, "If it ain't broke, don't fix it," can be costly if it keeps us from taking action before it's too late.

"A good plan violently executed right now is far better than a perfect plan executed next week."
George S. Patton

As long as he coached, Paul "Bear" Bryant had this sign hanging in his locker room: Cause something to happen.

☐ Having a new idea isn't new.

"Everyone who's ever taken a shower has an idea. It's the person who gets out of the shower, dries off and does something about it who makes a difference."
Nolan Bushnell, founder, Atari

Wayne Gretzky, the hockey player, reported the comment of an early coach who was frustrated with his lack of scoring in an important game. The coach made his point privately when he said. "You miss 100 percent of the shots you never take."

"Thinking is easy, acting is difficult, and to put one's thoughts into action is the most difficult thing in the world."
Johann Wolfgang von Goethe

☐ Often success means just taking something one step further than others.

George Westinghouse, founder of the company that bears his name, said that others in his day knew as much about railroads, electricity, and natural gas. But he took the next step. He invented the air brakes to make trains safer, and other devices to transmit gas and alternating current at a low cost.

Colonel Sanders was broke at age sixty-five and used a small Social Security check to start what became Kentucky Fried Chicken.

"The time for action is now. It's never too late to do something."
Carl Sandburg

"Chaotic action is preferable to orderly inaction."
Karl Weick, Cornell University

"Success is turning knowledge into positive action."
Dorothy Leeds, author

Our rural bus was chugging along a gravel road in Louisiana when we came upon a countrywoman loaded with packages standing beside the road. The driver, thinking her a would-be passenger, came to a stop and opened the door. She stepped up on the step and looked all around. The driver asked where she was going. She said, "Well, I ain't going anywhere. Just wanted to see who was."

Husband, lounging on the sofa, to wife: "I'll think about spading the garden in a little while. Right now I'm thinking about painting the screens."

☐ Keep moving.

"There is a condition or circumstance that has a greater bearing upon the happiness of life than any other. It is to keep moving. If it stops, it stagnates."

John Burroughs

A wise man once said that God gave man two ends: one to sit on and one to think with. It has been evident ever since that the success or failure of any individual has been dependent on the one he used most.

☐ To have a successful company, go where the action is.

When Robert Townsend took over as head of Avis Corporation, he created the now famous "We Try Harder" slogan. He decided that every vice president should spend time behind the counter doing face-to-face duty with the customer.

He wanted every key employee to have the knowledge of the customers who rented cars.

☐ Talk is cheap.

A fisherman walked past a game warden with a line of fish over his back. The game warden said, "Great looking fish. Where'd you get them?"

The fisherman said, "Come with me, and I'll show you."

He took the game warden out in his boat, took out a stick of dynamite, lit it, and threw it in the water. After a big shuttering blast, hundreds of fish came to the surface.

The game warden said, "That's the most illegal way I ever saw of catching fish, and you're coming in with me."

The fisherman took out another stick of dynamite, lit it, handed it to the game warden and said, "Ya gonna talk or you gonna fish?"

Irving Shapiro, a highly successful attorney, said that proving your point through actions is much more effective than argument. He said, "You don't get ahead by confrontation, but by demonstrating that someone misjudged you."

☐ Forget your mistakes and keep swinging.

Babe Ruth is in the Hall of Fame and rightly so. He once held the major league record for home runs in a season. But Ruth also once held the record for strikeouts.

You can't hit a home run every time at bat, and a lot of times you're going to strike out. But keep swinging because you won't get a home run by waiting.

"People say to me: 'You are a roaring success. How did you do it?' I go back to what my parents taught me. Apply yourself. Get all the education you can, but then, by God, do something. Don't just stand there, make something happen."

Lee Iacocca

"One who gains strength by overcoming obstacles possesses the only strength which can overcome adversity."

Albert Schweitzer

◼ ADVERSITY

☐ Be thankful for adversity.

"No man is more unhappy than the one who is never in adversity; the greatest affliction of life is never to be afflicted."

Anonymous

"There is no education like adversity."

Benjamin Disraeli

"A man sometimes finds profit in adversity."

Ecclesiasticus 20:9

"The very difficulty of a problem evokes abilities or talents which would otherwise, in happy times, never emerge to shine."

Horace

"We learn as much from sorrow as from joy, as much from illness as from health, from handicap as from advantage—and indeed perhaps more."

Pearl Buck

☐ Adversity shows us our potential.

"The man of character finds a special attractiveness in difficulty, since it is only by coming to grips with difficulty that he can realize his potentialities."

Charles de Gaulle

"What a testing of character adversity is!"

Harry Emerson Fosdick

"Every adversity carries with it the seeds of a greater benefit."

Lillian Gilcrest, author

William M. Batten, former chief executive of J. C. Penney, said, "When I hear my friends say they hope their children don't have to experience the hardships they went through—I don't agree. Those hardships made us what we are. You can be disadvantaged in many ways, and one way may be not having had to struggle."

☐ Opportunity comes from adversity.

Before the Civil War, Edmund McIlhenny operated a sugar plantation and a saltworks on Avery Island, Louisiana. Yankee troops invaded the area in 1863, and McIlhenny had to flee. When he returned in 1865, his sugar fields and saltworks were ruined.

One of the few things left were some hot Mexican peppers that had reseeded themselves in the kitchen garden. McIlhenny, who was living hand to mouth, started experimenting with the ground peppers to make a sauce that would liven up his dull diet. His newfound sauce is known today as Tabasco sauce. To this day, over a hundred years later, the McIlhenny Company and its Tabasco business is still run by the McIlhenny family.

☐ Adversity can lead to cooperation.

In 1973, the Kaiser Steel Company decided to permanently close their mill in Fortuna, California. The decision was based on the idea that they couldn't compete with foreign competition. The workers, faced with losing their jobs, quickly agreed to change their behavior. Their attitude became one of cooperation, not confrontation. Also, management began to listen to workers on how to improve the maintenance of machines that led to increased productivity. In a short time, the plant was once again profitable.

To understand adversity, think about the following story:
Take two acorns from the same tree, as nearly alike as possible; plant one on a hill by itself, and the other in the dense forest, and watch them grow. The oak standing alone is exposed to every storm. Its roots reach out in every direction, clutching the rocks and piercing deep into the earth. Every rootlet lends itself to steady the growing giant, as if in anticipation of fierce conflict with the elements. Sometimes its upward growth seems checked for years, but all the while it has been expending its energy in pushing a root across a large rock to gain a firmer anchorage. Then it shoots proudly aloft again, prepared to defy the hurricane. The gales that sport so rudely with its wide branches find more than their match, and only serve still further to toughen every minutest fiber from pitch to bark.
The acorn planted in the deep forest shoots up a weak, slender sapling. Shielded by its neighbors, it feels no need to spread its roots far and wide for support.

☐ We grow from adversity.

☐ Be thankful for adversity.

Ask the majority of men and women who have done great things in the world to what they owe their strength, their breadth of mind, and the diversity of experience that has enriched their lives. They will tell you that these are the fruits of struggle; that they acquired their finest discipline, their best character drill, in the effort to escape from an uncongenial environment; to break the bonds that enslaved them; to obtain an education; to get away from poverty; to carry out some cherished plan; to reach their ideal, whatever it was.

☐ Greatness springs from adversity. The problems we are experiencing now are setting the foundation for our success.

The Continental Army failed in many campaigns before it succeeded in Cornwallis's defeat at Yorktown. The Union Army suffered many defeats before General Grant was able to victoriously receive General Lee's surrender at Appomattox. Every blessing that we enjoy—personal security, individual liberty, our free enterprise system, and our constitutional freedom—has been obtained through long apprenticeships of adversity. The right of existing as a nation has been accomplished only through ages of wars and horrors. It required four centuries of martyrdom to establish Christianity as one of the world's great religions.

There is a great quote: "Life doesn't do anything to you, it only reveals your spirit."

The pages of history are filled with stories of undaunted men and women who triumphed over disabilities and adversities to demonstrate victorious spirits.

Bury him in the snows of Valley Forge, and you have a George Washington.

Raise him in abject poverty, and you have an Abraham Lincoln.

Deafen a genius composer, and you have a Ludwig van Beethoven.

Have him born of parents who survived a Nazi concentration camp, paralyze him from the waist down when he is four, and you have an incomparable concert violinist, Itzhak Perlman.

Raise him in a ghetto; because of malnutrition, afflict him with rickets so that his legs are permanently bowed, and you have Heisman trophy winner O. J. Simpson.

Call him a slow learner, retarded, and write him off as uneducable, and you have an Albert Einstein.

Each one of these great men have experienced first the lash and then the laurel; first the trial and then the triumph.

☐ There are opportunities in every adversity.

When IBM invented the self-correcting typewriter, everybody told Vic Barouh, president of the company that made Ko-Rec-Type, a product that corrected typing errors, that his company was doomed. Instead of believing the naysayers, Barouh went to an IBM showroom and had the salesperson demonstrate the new self-correcting typewriter. Barouh went back to his plant, gathered his employees around him, and told them, "Here is what we have to do. We have to make this ribbon, and we have no idea what this ribbon is. We have to make the cartridge, because the cartridge isn't available. And we have to go into the injection-molding business to make the spools that hold that tape. So first we've got to come up with the ink, then we've got to come up with a machine that puts ink on film . . . and with a machine that would split the rolls and with the cartridges that these things go into."

Within six months, the company produced the first ribbon. Within six months, it went from a problem to the only company in the world that made a product everybody was going to need.

ADVERTISING

"There is no more important word that 'test.' The most important word in the vocabulary of advertising is TEST."

David Ogilvy, founder, Ogilvy & Mather

Advertising is the fine art of convincing people that debt is better than frustration.

"If you think advertising doesn't work, consider the millions of Americans who now think that yogurt tastes good."

Joe L. Whitley, management consultant

"You can fool all the people all the time if the advertising is right and the budget is big enough."

Joseph E. Levine

"No one ever went broke underestimating the taste of the American people."

H. L. Mencken

Thomas Jefferson observed with a tone of irony: "Advertisements contain the only truths to be relied on in a newspaper."

☐ You can't advertise too much.

"Advertising is like learning—a little is a dangerous thing."

P. T. Barnum

☐ If the business is worth having, it is worth going after, so you must advertise.

"How can people know what a bank will do for them unless they're told?"

A. P. Giannini, founder, Bank of America

☐ To be successful, advertising needs to know what the product does for the consumer.

In 1979, McCann-Erickson had handled Coca-Cola's advertising for almost twenty-four years. When asked to come up with a presentation for a new ad campaign, McCann discovered that all Coke ads as far back as 1900 showed Coke drinkers smiling. Their new ads continued the old successful theme of "have a Coke and a smile."

☐ Advertising is only one part of product success.

A department store advertised a holiday sale. Full-page newspaper ads featured price reductions and invited readers to phone in their orders. When they called, the telephone operator knew nothing about the sale because no one had informed her. Results: customers irritated and sales lost because one store executive failed to tell a telephone operator about his plans.

"Ninety percent of the battle is what you say and ten percent is what medium you say it in."

Bill Bernbach

☐ Can you spend too much on advertising?

Two companies—Miles Laboratories and General Foods—spend more than twice as much on their ads as they make in after-tax profits.

☐ Advertising is not always the answer to a product's success.

"Too many people advertise a mediocre product and fail. Eighty percent of all newly advertised products fail. The manufacturer decides the consumer is a fool. That's why the product fails. People think advertising is a cure-all."

Frank Perdue, Perdue Farms

Remember the old Malayan proverb, "The turtle lays thousands of eggs without anyone knowing, but when the hen lays an egg, the whole country is informed."

☐ Advertising is a way to let people know that eggs are available.

A salesman for a nationwide chain of medium-priced steak houses confides, "Our advertising doesn't try to sell steak, we sell the sizzle."

☐ Advertising does seem to work.

Lewis Kornfeld, vice chairman of Tandy Corporation, cites in his 1927 book a study by Robert Vaile on advertising during the depression of 1920–24. It concluded that when times got tough and corporations were hard-pressed to find cash, those firms that increased their advertising expenditures generated 14–20 percent more relative sales than those who decreased their advertising.

☐ Advertisers sometime stretch the truth.

A young man applied for a job at an ad agency. He was told, "Your resume is full of distortions, half-truths, and bald lies. Welcome aboard!"

☐ Sometimes advertising can be *too* successful.

A reporter asked a businessman if advertising paid: "Yes, why only the other day, we advertised for a night watchman, and that night the safe was robbed."

☐ There are lots of ways to advertise.

A restaurant customer summoned his waiter and said, "Look at this small piece of meat. Last evening, I was served with a portion more than twice the size of this."

"Where did you sit?" asked the waiter.

"I sat by the window," replied the customer.

The waiter said, "The explanation is simple. We always serve customers by the window large portions."

☐ Keep it simple.

A subordinate reported to his boss with posters that said, "We're people people," "People count with us," "People are where it's at," and the like.

His boss said, "I'm sick of the whole approach. Just tell the public we're cold and aloof, and we make a damned good carburetor."

R. J. Wrigley commented on advertising: "Tell them quick and tell them often. You must have a good product in the first place and something that people want, for it is easier to row downstream than up. Explain to folks plainly and sincerely what you have to sell, do it in as few words as possible, and keep everlastingly coming at them."

☐ Put ads in the right place.

If advertising agents were smart, they'd schedule deodorant commercials to follow political ads.

☐ Never stop reminding people you are around.

Store owner: "I've been in business for fifty years and never once needed to advertise.

Ad salesman: "Excuse me, sir. But what is that building on the hill?"

Store owner: "It's the village church."

Ad salesman: "Been there long?"

Store owner: "Over a hundred years."

Ad salesman: "Well, they still ring the bells."

☐ Make sure your ad is understood.

Spinster: "Last week I advertised in the paper for a husband, and I got a lot of replies. They all said, 'You can have mine.' "

There are three things in the world that every man can do better than anyone else. One is coach a football team. The second is judge a beauty contest. The third is write advertising.

☐ Advertising is good when the product is remembered.

For its first forty-seven years, Merle Norman Cosmetics relied on word-of-mouth advertising. When it decided to launch an advertising campaign, it studied the ads from other major cosmetic firms. When it blocked out the name of the advertiser, no one could identify the maker with the ad. It is because of this that Merle Norman came up with a woman shown "before" and "after" using Merle Norman cosmetics. Sales tripled in the next five years.

On a plane trip to Chicago, a friend of multimillionaire R. J. Wrigley asked why he continued to advertise all the time when his was already the most successful chewing gum company in the world.

Wrigley said, "The same reason the pilot of this airplane keeps the engines running when we are already in the air."

☐ What is advertising?

Albert Lasker, one of the pioneers in advertising, wanted to know what the word *advertising* meant. He asked everybody for a definition.

One man said, "Advertising is keeping everlastingly at it."
Another said, "What is right is advertising."
Still another said, "Keeping your name before the public."
None of these definitions satisfied him. Finally he came to the conclusion that "advertising is news." This definition satisfied him until one day he was told that this was not the right definition. He was told "Advertising is salesmanship in print."

☐ Sell benefits and solutions, not features.

A few years ago, Federal Express had a very expensive commercial running on television. It showed a beautiful fleet of airplanes sitting on an airport ramp. The commercial was taken off the air when it was realized that the viewer couldn't put a benefit to the ad. They were beautiful planes, but what did they do for the viewer?

The replacement ads explained how Federal Express benefited the consumer by getting your packages to their destination overnight.

☐ No matter how true advertising is, it must be believable.

A few years ago, Minolta came out with their advertising that asked, "Who is the largest manufacturer of photocopiers in the world?" The response was Minolta. Even though it was the truth, nobody believed it. How often is somebody asked to go down to the photocopier to get a Minolta? Not often; they are asked to get a "Xerox" copy. Xerox has a name identification that kept Minolta from believability.

☐ ADVICE

"Ask people's advice, but decide for yourself."

Ukrainian proverb

"Accepting good advice increases one's own ability."

Johann Wolfgang von Goethe

"Advice is seldom welcome. Those who need it most, like it least."

Samuel Johnson

"If someone gives you so-called good advice, do the opposite; you can be sure it will be the right thing nine out of ten times."

Anselm Feuerbach

"There are exceptions to all rules, but it seldom answers to follow the advice of an opponent."

Benjamin Disraeli

"I have found it advisable not to give too much heed to what people say when I am trying to accomplish something of consequence. Invariably they proclaim, 'It can't be done.' I deem that the very best time to make the effort."

Calvin Coolidge

" 'Be yourself!' is about the worst advice you can give to some people."
Tom Masson

☐ Don't offer advice too quickly.

Socrates was a Greek philosopher who went around giving people good advice. They poisoned him.

☐ Advice after the fact isn't very helpful.

"If you really want to give me advice, do it on Saturday afternoon between one and four o'clock, when you've got twenty-five seconds to do it, between plays. Don't give me advice on Monday. I know the right thing to do on Monday."
Alex Agase, football coach

☐ There are times to follow your instincts instead of taking well-meaning advice.

"Many receive advice, few profit by it."
Publilius Syrus

☐ Sometimes it pays not to follow advice.

In 1963, Mary Kay Ash and her husband invested their life's savings in Mary Kay Cosmetics. A month later, her husband died, and she was told by her attorney and other advisors to liquidate the company in hopes of salvaging some of her investment. Instead of quitting, she pressed on.

Later, her accountant told her that she paid too much commission and that she couldn't succeed without reducing her pay scale. Again she failed to heed the advice and eventually built one of America's largest cosmetics companies.

☐ Good advice doesn't come cheap.

A business type who was trying to arrange a personnel seminar said that he kept reading reports by psychologists who maintain that people seek other rewards besides money. He said, "That may be true, but I haven't been able to get those same psychologists to talk about those theories at my management conference for less than $1,000 plus expenses."

"Too much advice is based on limited knowledge."
"Here is a true example. I was privileged to hear a conversation several years ago between Mr. Smith and Mr. Jones. They were in different segments of the same industry. Both were using the franchising method of marketing. Mr. Smith had been in business for many years and had a large, successful company. Mr. Jones had been in business for only about five years but had made substantial progress. Since their businesses were closely allied in the same industry, Mr. Smith assumed he knew all about Mr. Jones's concept. He told Mr. Jones he had better give up his methods or one day he would wake

up and find out he was broke. He said, 'One cannot make money in our business, the way you are trying to.'

"I stood by and listened because I knew Mr. Jones had refined his concept uniquely and was prospering. He was considered a pioneer in his specialized field. Now, six years later, he is more successful than ever . . . in the same business. Mr. Smith's limited knowledge of his friend's concept resulted in dangerous advice."

Lloyd T. Tarbutton, Franchising—The How-To Book

AMBITION

☐ Don't become too ambitious.

"The man who wants to build and make a contribution in the business world must not neglect his family or his church, but he can't lead a 'vacation' life."

Bill Marriott, Sr.

☐ Without ambition, we will always come up short.

"He who shoots at the midday sun, though sure he shall never hit the mark, yet sure is he that he shall shoot higher than he who aims but at a bush."

Philip Sidney

☐ Some people just think they are ambitious.

Judge: "You've committed six burglaries in a week."
Defendant: "That's right—if everyone worked as hard as I do, we'd be on the road to prosperity."

☐ Lack of ambition shows.

Boss: "Mike, how long does it take you to get to work in the morning?"
Mike: "About an hour after I reach the factory."

☐ Overambition can backfire.

Harry Levinson says that "workaholics" who are thwarted in their ambitions "become increasingly irritable and abusive with their spouses, children and fellow employees. Some suffer chronic depression, others die early from heart attacks."

☐ Men of achievement often are men whose ambition has no end.

When author Peter Evans was invited to write a book about Aristotle Onassis, he asked the shipping magnate why he would want another book written about him.

Onassis replied, "For the same reason I wasn't satisfied with one ship."

AMERICA

☐ Free men do not know the value of things.

"If a nation values anything more than freedom, it will lose its freedom; and the irony of it is that if it is comfort or money that it values more, it will lose that, too."

Somerset Maugham

"It is your responsibility to pick up the torch and preserve these liberties for your children and their children."

James Bishop

"Freedom did not come to America on a silver platter. Our ancestors, praying for divine guidance, shed their blood to win it."

Robert Kerns

"America is like a gigantic boiler. Once the fuse is lighted under it, there is no limit to the power it can generate."

Winston Churchill

George Romney, in a speech made as candidate for governor of Michigan, said: "The strength of America is not in a few strong industrial giants. It is not in a few strong union giants. It is not in a few strong political giants. Our strength is the strength of the people. More people must exercise their rights as citizens. The important words are 'as citizens,' not as businessmen or union members or as members of any other special-interest group."

"America is a land where a citizen will cross the ocean to fight for democracy—and won't cross the street to vote in a national election."

Robert Kerns

When I get to thinking about the need for Americans to participate in politics, I recall what an Italian immigrant once told me: "Ah, these Americans, they don't appreciate democracy because they don't know what it ain't!"

"If history tells us anything, it tells us that the United States, like all other nations, will be measured in the eyes of posterity not by its economic power nor by its military might . . . but by its character and achievement as a civilization."

Arthur Schlesinger, Jr., historian

We must show faith in ourselves and in our role as the world's last best hope for freedom. We must use our strength as President Dwight D. Eisenhower instructed: "Resolutely, to hearten our friends; wisely, to confound our enemies; constantly, to give hope to the hearts of the enslaved;

prudently, to guard the trust of the free; and courageously, to be worthy of the high commission history has conferred on us."

☐ America is more than a spot on a map.

Adlai Stevenson put it this way: "When an American says he loves his country, he means not only that he loves the hills, the prairies glistening in the sun, the wide and rising plains, the great mountains, and the sea. He means he loves an inner air in which freedom lives and in which a man can draw a breath of self-respect."

"Freedom cannot be separated from responsibility."
Henry Grady Weaver

"A nation stays healthy as long as it deals with its real problems, and starts to decline when it takes on peripheral issues."
Arnold Toynbee

Alexis de Tocqueville had this to say about America: "America is great because its people are good. And if the American people ever lose their goodness, America will cease to be great."

☐ What is an American?

"An American is not delineated by a particular skin color, or way of life. He is a person from many places, with many shades of skin; of different sizes and varied energies. He has a Master's Degree, or he may never have finished high school. He may drive an expensive automobile, or perhaps he relies on two mules to carve his living out of the earth. But regardless of what he is, lacing the different physical features together is a bond of strength in tradition which exemplifies the American way; a way which opens the doors of opportunity to all peoples who may knock upon them. An American has a spirit which was born when the bells tolled of independence, and which has released the adrenalin of his nation time and time again when its existence was threatened by an aggressor.

"An American does not view armed conflict as a means of getting what he wants, but rather as a means of protecting what he has. He is one who loves the very concept of Peace for all nations, but will not hesitate to fight on the shores of others if required to protect his own. An American sees the knowledge of experience in his past, feels pride in the accomplishments of the present, and has hope for the future of the world, even when others would view the days to come with dismay. But a realistic American finds no guarantee of freedom or security in the future solely because he has always had it in the past.

"An American recognizes the faults of his system and seeks to correct them through a process unknown to many nations. A process which does not promise absolute perfection, but one which allows for peaceful change, if change is needed. That process is democracy, and an American holds that word so dear, that he stands ready at a moment's notice to lay down his life for its perpetuation.

"An American finds nothing at all unusual about getting cold chills when his flag passes in review, for his flag has always been a source of inspiration; when the smoke cleared over Fort McHenry, when its sheen was reflected on the sands of Iwo Jima, and when the colors glistened on the side of the craft which took the first man to the moon. An American sees nothing strange about getting a lump in his throat when the National Anthem is played, or weeping unashamed when taps is played for one who paid the ultimate price for his freedom. He realizes that the only thing that exceeds that price is the freedom itself. An American never forgets the indebtedness he has because of that sacrifice, for without it, his freedom would only be an unreachable concept in some philosopher's mind.

"A true American is the essence of pride in a way of life. What is an American, you say? He is fortunate."

Michael Brown

"In the United States, people can join voluntary organizations known as associations. Those who join these associations are individuals who have a common interest in anything from stamp collecting to medicine to firearms to exotic goldfish to bird watching. The book known as the *Directory of Associations in the United States* runs to several hundred pages, with thousands of entries. As a citizen of this free country, you might ask yourself, 'How many voluntary associations do you suppose exist for a person who lives behind the Iron Curtain? How many people in Russia, for example, have the option to join an association with those who are interested in the ownership and use of firearms?' When you consider the great number of choices that are possible for Americans, you begin to realize the tremendous blessing we have."

Lin Bothwell, The Art of Leadership

"You may go to France, but you will never become a Frenchman. You may go to Greece, but you will never become a Greek. You may go to China, but you will never become a Chinese, to Japan and never become a Japanese, but anyone can come to America and become an American. This is the greatness of this country we call the United States of America."

Angie Papadakis

☐ America isn't perfect.

"Americans are wasting a truly frightening amount of time either putting down others or living in a state of inner panic that others will put them down because they've used the wrong word, ordered the wrong wine, praised the wrong book, suggested the wrong restaurant, or visited the wrong Greek island. The time wasted is time taken away from real communication with others, whether about individual human problems or vital issues facing the nation and the world. Snobbery may be at its most dangerous when it counsels that one of those vital issues is chic and encourages us to ignore others that are in fact of equal or greater importance."

Charles Peters

☐ Freedom is something Americans take for granted.

There is a joke in which an American and a Russian argue about who has more freedom. The American says, "I can come up to the White House and yell, 'Down with the president of the United States!' "

The Russian says, "Well, I can come up to the Kremlin and yell, 'Down with the president of the United States!' too."

☐ ATTITUDE

"Your attitude, not your aptitude, will determine your altitude."

Zig Ziglar

"Human beings can alter their lives by altering their attitudes."

William James

"A man is not hurt so much by what happens, as by his opinion of what happens."

Michel de Montaigne

☐ Our performance can depend on our attitude.

"When people are not happy doing what they do, they don't do it as well as when they are happy."

Tom Landry, football coach

☐ With a good attitude, we can turn negative experiences into positive lessons.

"You either emulate the faults or virtues of parents or you turn them around—reverse them."

Charles F. Luce, former CEO, Consolidated Edison

☐ A positive mental attitude is the right attitude in a given environment.

Patrick O'Malley, who started as a truck driver and ended his career as chairman of Canteen Company, says, "I think it is absolutely essential that you have PMA in every aspect of life and that you start early."

"The habit of looking on the best side of every event is worth more than a thousand pounds a year."

Samuel Johnson

□ We get what we think about.

"What we sow or plant in the soil will come back to us in exact kind. It's impossible to sow corn and get a crop of wheat, but we entirely disregard this law when it comes to mental sowing."

Orison Swett Marden

The optimist sees a glass that is half full. The pessimist sees one that is half empty. The comedian George Carlin said that he sees a glass that is twice the size it needs to be.

□ Our attitudes are a reflection of how we look at things, whether it be a water glass or our job.

□ Positive attitudes can work miracles.

"Of one incident when she operated on a patient for gallstones and discovered an inoperable case of cancer. The patient was diagnosed as having only two months to live, but her family decided not to tell her the news. Eight months later, the patient had no signs of cancer. Several years later, she revealed to the doctor that before her surgery for gallstones, she had been convinced that she had had cancer. But when she heard after the operation that it was just gallstones, she promised herself never to be sick another day in her life.

Deepak Chopra, Creating Health: Beyond Prevention, Toward Perfection

There is an old Hindu legend that at one time all men on earth were gods, but the men so sinned and abused the Divine that Brahma, the god of all gods, decided that the godhead should be taken away from man and hid someplace where he would never find it again to abuse it.

One god said, "Let's bury it deep in the earth."

Brahma said, "No, man will dig down in the earth and find it."

Another god said, "Then let's put it in the deepest ocean."

Brahma said, "No, man will learn to dive and find it there someday."

A third god suggested, "Why don't we hide it on the highest mountain."

Brahma said, "No, man can climb the highest mountain. I have a better place. Let's hide it down in man himself. He will never think to look there."

□ Deep down inside all of us is the power to accomplish what we want to if we'll just stop looking elsewhere.

□ It's not what happens but what you think is happening that matters.

A little parable entitled "The Man Who Sold Hot Dogs" evidently dates back to the 1930s but it bears repeating today.

There was a man who lived by the side of the road and sold hot dogs. He was hard of hearing, so he had no radio. He had trouble with his eyes, so he read no newspapers. But he sold good hot dogs.

He stood at the side of the road and cried: "Buy a hot dog, mister?" and people bought. He increased his meat and bun orders. He bought a bigger stove to take care of his trade. He finally got his son home from college to help him out. Then something happened.

His son said, "Father, haven't you been listening to the radio? Haven't you been reading the newspapers? The European situation is terrible. The domestic situation is worse." Whereupon the father thought, "Well, my son's been to college, he reads the papers and he listens to the radio, and he ought to know." So the father cut down his meat and bun orders, took down his signs, and no longer bothered to stand out on the highway to sell his hot dogs. And his hot dog sales fell almost overnight.

The father said to the boy, "You're right, son, we certainly are in the middle of a great depression."

Attitude is how you look at things. Take this poem written by an anonymous Civil War soldier:

I asked God for strength that I might achieve;
I was made weak that I might learn humbly to obey.
I asked for help that I might do greater things;
I was given infirmity that I might do better things;
I asked for riches that I might be happy;
I was given poverty that I might be wise.
I asked for power that I might have the praise of men;
I was given weakness that I might feel the need of God.
I asked for all things that I might enjoy life;
I was given life that I might enjoy all things.
I got nothing that I asked for, but everything I hoped for.
Almost despite myself my unspoken prayers were answered.
I among all men am most richly blessed.

BANKING

Banking is so competitive it is now possible to borrow money to put in a savings account.

Comedian Joey Adams used this definition of a banker: A pawnbroker with a manicure.

We all need a good banker. As someone said, "He's a self-made man— with a big assist from a bank loan officer."

What this country really needs is a bank where you deposit a toaster and they give you $250.

A banker is a guy who charges you high interest to borrow somebody else's money.

☐ Banks are marketing-oriented today.

Banks are really pushing savings accounts. A bandit robbed a bank of $2,000 the other day, and the teller tried to talk him into opening an IRA.

I went golfing with my banker, but never again. Every time I yelled *"Fore!"*—he yelled *"Closure!"*

Bank accounts give a person a good feeling until he realizes that banks are insured by an agency of a federal government that's over $2 trillion in debt.

"Bankers are just like anybody else, except richer."

Ogden Nash, poet

"Banks will lend you money if you can prove you don't need it."
Mark Twain

A banker, Abe, and his customer, Sol, were fishing off Miami Beach when their boat capsized and pitched them into the sea.

Sol cried, "Abe! Can you float alone?"

Abe gasped, "Sol, this is not time to talk business! I'm drowning."
Myron Cohen, comedian

☐ Bankers are known to pass out titles.

The city banker was visiting a customer's farm.

He said, nodding to a figure in the farmyard, "I suppose that's the hired man."

The farmer replied, "No, that's the first vice president in charge of cows."

Sign on a bank loan officer's desk: "In this office, the word *no* is a complete sentence."

"I hear the bank is looking for a cashier."

"Thought they just hired one a week ago."

"They did. He's the one they're looking for."

☐ Banks are becoming more service-conscious.

A bank executive told me that, since there were so many bank heists in his city this year, his bank was establishing an express line—for those who wish to rob $1,000 or less.

There are three stages to the failure of a bank: concern, panic, and desperation. Concern is when they put a limit on withdrawals. Panic is when they put a moratorium on withdrawals. Desperation is when they call you up and ask for their toaster back.

Banks are having their troubles. A lot of banks have failed recently. I haven't been worried until recently. I told the manager, "I'd like to see someone about a loan."

He said, "Great, how much can you let us have?"

BANKRUPTCY

Statistics show that fewer and fewer people are trying to keep up with the Joneses these days. After all, most people don't want to take bankruptcy.

In a conversation with three successful entrepreneurs over cocktails, the conversation shifted to bankruptcies. All had gone through at least one. The oldest said confidently, "I've had three, but it was the second one I learned the most from."

"Sir, why are you filing for bankruptcy?"
"Because I sent two kids through a free state college."

☐ Sometimes layoffs can prevent bankruptcy.

In 1969, Boeing lost $14 million. In 1979, instead of losing money, it made $875 million. In 1969, Boeing had 25,000 workers producing seven 747 jumbo jets a month. In 1979, it produced the same seven 747s with only 11,000 workers.

In 1979, when Carlo de Benedetti took over Olivetti, the company was heavily in debt, and the year before had lost about $100 million. In 1977, the company's annual production per employee was $25,000, about half of other competitors. The first year, de Benedetti terminated 6,000 workers. These cuts, along with other streamlining, turned Olivetti around. A few years later, Olivetti had doubled sales to $2.2 billion and had a profit of $65 million. De Bendetti said that overmanning doesn't defend jobs, it destroys them. "Had we not cut 6,000 jobs, we would have lost 22,000 jobs."

☐ Too much inventory can ruin you.

A grocer had gone broke. The receivers were taking an inventory. They found the stored filled to the brim with bread. There was bread in the front and bread in the back. They found white bread, whole wheat bread, French bread, rye bread, potato bread, cracked wheat bread, Roman meal bread, and other kinds of bread.

They asked the grocer, "You sure sold a lot of bread, didn't you?"
The grocer answered, "Oh, no, but the fellow who calls on me from the baker sure sells a lot of it."

☐ Sometimes bankruptcy can be a stepping-stone to success.

H. J. Heinz's creditors forced him into bankruptcy.
Walt Disney suffered bankruptcy along with a nervous breakdown.
Milton Hershey went bankrupt before he dominated the chocolate industry.

▊ BOSS

"One person has to be in charge. You can't divide authority and have any left."

Randall Price

☐ The boss is the morale leader.

"Morale comes down from the sky like rain. If you're the boss and you're feeling lousy, watch out—you're like the plague going around. If I wake up in a terrible mood, I don't go near the store—I work at home. I don't want to bring any of my people down."

Stew Leonard, Sr., owner, Stew Leonard's

☐ A good boss is a good role model.

"Of course, it's what we do that counts, not what we say. Therefore, I set an example through my actions, and I believe it is critically important to be consistent, predictable, and dependable.

Donald E. Petersen, past chairman and CEO, Ford

"If he has the qualities of a boss, he will thrive; if he doesn't, no matter what he does or says, he is not going to thrive."

Milton Glass, Gillette

"It never occurred to me that I was going to be a boss. I never said, 'I want to be boss.' You grow into it. Maybe you are bossy by nature. I was a stage manager first, and that means that you gave a lot of orders. 'Go over there, and move this over here.' You have to learn how to be a boss without being a bully. Yet you must be authoritative. You learn how."

George Cukor, film director

☐ A good boss is a good delegator.

An admiral and a commander were having a heated discussion about lovemaking. The admiral claimed it was 80 percent work and 20 percent pleasure. The commander said the admiral was nuts; it was 10 percent work and 90 percent pleasure. They were at loggerheads on the issue and wanted an impartial opinion. They saw the chief petty officer and called him in on it. They explained the dispute and asked his opinion.

The chief said, "Sirs, with all respect, you're both wrong."

They wanted to know how an admiral and a commander could be wrong about anything.

He said, "Well, if there's any work to it, you would have me doing it for you."

☐ Good bosses aren't always popular.

A collection was being taken for a going-away present for the domineering boss.

Contributor: "Is he going away?"
Collector: "No, but it's worth a try."

☐ Bosses can feel more important than they are.

A fellow asked his boss for a raise. The boss asked how much he wanted a raise.

Employee: "I've been praying in church for one."
Boss: "Don't you know you can't go over my head?"

□ Being a successful boss requires flexibility.

Fred Bucy, past president of Texas Instruments, said, "It doesn't take much talent to issue orders. It does take continued discipline to study the variety of people you are leading in order to understand what it takes to motivate them and to inspire them to do their very best to make the company and themselves a success. Also, it is a never-ending task to be an effective leader, because time changes all things. What might work at one point in time will not work at another point in time; for example, what would work in the sixties would not work in the seventies. What was effective in the seventies is not effective in the eighties. Therefore, you must discipline yourself to keep up with changing values.

"It takes one set of leadership skills to motivate a manager with many years of experience and another to motivate young people just arriving from universities. Also, what is effective is motivating a person at one point in his career will not be effective in motivating him later; an individual's values change depending upon what is happening in his personal life as well as his success with his career. Therefore, one of the most important things that a boss or leader must do is to continue to study how to be effective. This does take discipline. It is much easier to assume that what worked yesterday will work today, and this is simply not true."

□ What is the profile of a good boss?

"The boss must first of all be a dedicated man. He is usually happily married to an understanding woman, but he has an equally strong love for his job. It is not merely a way of making money; it is a fascinating chess game, combined with a table stakes poker game, with a touch of pure poetry thrown in for good measure. The poetry that I speak of is the fitting together of the diverse pieces made up of ideas, things, and people which the boss daily rearranges and develops into a finished lyric of coordination."

Ed McElroy, US Air

◼ BUDGETS

"A weekly budget is just something to help you explain why the money ran out about Tuesday."

Ervin L. Glaspy

□ Budgets don't make everybody happy.

Good budgeting is the uniform distribution of dissatisfaction.

□ Budgets require making tough choices.

Husband to wife in a restaurant: "Would you prefer sirloin steak, lobster tails, or electricity the rest of the month?"

"The trouble with the average family budget is that at the end of the money there's too much month left."

A. James Grant

Customer: "I want to return my computer."
Salesman: "What's wrong with it?"
Customer: "I programmed it to fix my budget, and it told me that I could not afford a computer."

☐ We have to live within our budget.

A research organization was polling a small town to find out how families spent their money. One old man told the young researcher that he spent 30 percent for shelter, 30 percent for clothing, 40 percent for food, and 20 percent for everything else.

Researcher: "But that adds up to 120 percent."
Old man: "I know. And it gets worse every year."

Here's a piece of advice
That's worth a king's crown:
To hold your head up,
Hold your overhead down.

Ruth Boostin

☐ A budget can make a big difference.

A few years ago, Paramount Studios became notorious for being hard on filmmakers. If a producer wanted to make a movie at Paramount, he had to play by their rules, which resembled a dictatorship. Budgets were usually half what was asked for. If you wanted a $10 million budget, you got $5 million. An auditor was assigned to monitor every penny spent. The supervision didn't stop with cost. It spilled over into everything from casting to costuming to music. Sometimes Paramount would even ask that the ending be changed.

All of this supervision went totally against the norm in the film industry awash with waste and overspending. But Paramount's success with this watchful approach had other filmmakers following suit.

■ BUREAUCRACY

"If you want to know how to do a job right, ask the people who are doing it; don't have some corporate bureaucracy tell them how to do it."

Jack Reichert, chairman, Brunswick

☐ Bureaucracy leads to inefficiency.

Before the divestiture of AT&T, they had over one thousand managers to help create a no-fault decision-making environment.

☐ Bureaucracy can stifle creativity.

Gene Amdahl was once one of IBM's most brilliant designers. Since IBM was slow to exploit his ideas, he left and started his own company. Some people believe that had Amdahl been with a Japanese company, he wouldn't have had to leave IBM to fulfill his dreams.

☐ Bureaucracy reduces leadership.

"Most hierarchies are nowadays so cumbered with rules and traditions, and so bound in by public laws, that even high employees do not have to lead anyone anywhere, in the sense of pointing out the direction and setting the pace. They simply follow precedents, obey regulations, and move at the head of the crowd. Such employees lead only in the sense that the carved wooden figurehead leads the ship."
Laurence J. Peter and Raymond Hull, The Peter Principle

German sociologist Max Weber described a perfect bureaucracy as a system in which everything is decided by inflexible written rules of operation. Important decisions are made at the top, then orders flow down a chain of command. Members of the command are chosen for their technical competence. Everything works according to a rigid set of rules. Weber believed that this made people more, not less, productive.

☐ Bureaucracy can stifle creative thinking.

The American Business Conference, made up of fast-growing companies, concluded, "One of the great problems associated with success and the achievement of great size is the risk that executives will behave as bureaucrats, not as creative thinkers."

☐ Bureaucracy can get so entangled that the customers get forgotten.

Paine Webber, the nationally recognized investment house, once had a back office so entangled in its own bureaucracy that the customers were all but forgotten. Stock certificates were lost; customers couldn't get a correct confirmation of a buy or sell. Finally, in 1980, Paine Webber was fined $300,000 by the New York Stock Exchange, the largest fine ever. All the problems were caused by the bureaucracy.

"Bureaucracy is the layer, or layers, of management that lie between the person who has decision-making authority on a project and the highest-level person who is working on it full-time."
Herbert Rees, Eastman Technology

President Harry S. Truman once said of Dwight D. Eisenhower's future as president: "He'll sit there and he'll say, 'Do this! Do that!' And nothing will happen. Poor Ike."

☐ Here is what a bureaucracy looks like.

The number of farmers in the nation may be dropping dramatically, but the number of employees in the Department of Agriculture stays steady. An apocryphal story is told of a tour group in Washington visiting the Department of Agriculture and inquiring about why one of the department's employees, seated at an empty desk, was crying. The answer: "His farmer died."

The consequences of anonymity in responsibility once prompted an aggrieved President Lyndon B. Johnson, who answered why he had not fired a man who had scuttled one of the president's favorite programs. "Fire him? Hell, I can't even find him."

Czar Alexander of Russia once said, "I do not rule Russia; ten thousand clerks rule Russia."

☐ Cutting bureaucracy can increase product development and decrease the time it takes to get to market.

Jack Reichert, CEO of Brunswick, the $3-billion-a-year sporting goods company, decided in the mid-1980s that developing new products—outboard motors, automatic bowling scorecards, fishing reels—took too long. Reichert said, "Product development was like elephant intercourse. It was accompanied by much hooting, hollering, and throwing of dirt, and then nothing would happen for a year." To solve the problem, Reichert cut the layers of management between him and the shop worker from ten to five.

BUSINESS

☐ What makes your business succeed?

"Almost everybody agrees, people are our most important asset. Yet almost no one really lives it."

Rene McPherson, former chairman, Dana

☐ There is a secret to a successful business.

"In the best institutions, promises are kept no matter what the cost in agony and overtime."

David Ogilvy, founder, Ogilvy & Mather

"Business is like roller skating—either you keep moving or you fall down."

Doc Blakely, humorist

Al Williams, a former president of IBM, offered this definition of a business: "A business is an organization that has customers."

☐ A good business has a good reputation.

King Solomon, the richest man who ever lived, said, "A good name is rather to be chosen than great riches, and living favorably rather than silver and gold."

"A business is customer driven. A company thrives when their customers thrive."

Mark D. Griffith, attorney

"What is a corporation? Plants? Product lines? Assembly lines? Bottom lines? Distribution lines? Not really. A corporation is people. People organized and working and producing to serve people. That's what it's all about in the end."

Donald E. Petersen, past chairman and CEO, Ford

☐ Why are we in business?

The purpose of a business is to create and keep a customer. To do that, you want to do those things that will make people want to do business with you.

"In any business, there is always one person who knows what is going on. This person must be fired."

Doug Gamble, humor writer

Running a business is about 95 percent people and 5 percent economics.

The genius of American industry is in building things to last twenty years and making them obsolete in two.

☐ What does it take for a business to be successful?

"The secret of any business success is to understand the customer's problems and to provide solutions so as to help them be profitable and feel good about the transaction."

Francis G. "Buck" Rodgers, IBM

☐ Here is a secret to business success.

"People spend money when and where they feel good."

Walt Disney

☐ For a business to grow, it needs some structure.

Napoleon's command structure, which served him well during his early victories, led in the end to his downfall.

His army became so large that, without a well-organized staff, even a genius couldn't manage it.

His marshals were trained to obey orders, not command men. So in battle they were ineffective leaders.

Both shortcomings made him vulnerable in a big battle, so his enemies organized to fight him en masse.

☐ Make sure your organization structure is not counterproductive or you will lose the battle.

☐ What business are you in?

The Cadillac Division of General Motors makes Cadillacs. Do people spend $25,000 to $30,000 on a Cadillac to buy transportation? In other words, does the Cadillac compete with less expensive cars like Ford or Chrysler? Or does it compete with other luxury items like Rolex watches and mink coats?

☐ Your business is more important than you realize.

Charles "Mike" Harper attended ConAgra's 1974 annual meeting wearing a name tag identifying himself as a corporate officer, although he had yet to receive his first paycheck from the company.

"I should have come incognito," recalled Harper. ConAgra had announced publicly that it had lost a lot of money and that it had cut out the dividend." Your instinct is to mingle with the crowd so I mingled with the crowd. I tried to make a friend someplace.

"I remember there were two ladies who must have been in their sixties or seventies sitting four or five rows back. I stopped at the row in front of them, leaned over, and introduced myself. One of the ladies said, 'I have a question for you. We drove 150 miles from Grand Island to make this meeting.' I didn't know where Grand Island was at that time—whether it was in Hawaii or what.

"She had one question, she said. 'When is the dividend going to be reinstated?' She had a good reason for that question. That dividend was her livelihood.

"I was hardly even an employee of the company yet. I suspect I gave one of those answers where you try to reassure them yet at the same time don't promise anything. But, you know, you think of stockholders as big fat guys in blue suits, sitting on Wall Street, big gold chains thumping on their rich old tummies. And here are two elderly ladies who will starve to death unless we get that dividend going."

☐ What does it take for a business to become effective?

C. L. Ferguson said that good organization is one of the four factors in a well-managed company:

Four basic elements are present in an exceptionally well-run company. First, it has direction. It knows where it is going. Second, it has a well-designed structure that can perform effectively and withstand the battering of competition. Third, it has a fine set of controls so that it handles well. And finally, it has the power or energy to move itself.

☐ Every business needs a sense of order.

In 1913, Thorlief Schieldorup-Ebbe, a Danish zoologist, discovered that the lowly barnyard chicken lived within a strict organizational structure. Inevitably there was a top chicken who could peck any other chicken in the yard to express its dominance, a second layer of chickens that could peck a third group of still lower-ranked chickens but could not peck the boss chicken, and so on down the hierarchy. He called the phenomenon "the pecking order," a phrase that has become a part of our modern vocabulary.

☐ Point out to your customers the positive side of doing business with you.

Once a man was eating in an Italian restaurant in New York City. He told the owner, "Your veal parmigiana is better than the one I had in Italy last week."

The owner replied, "Of course it is. You see, they use domestic cheese and ours is imported."

BUSINESS CYCLES

"The trouble with the business cycle is that there just aren't enough people pedaling."

Sharyn Katalinich

Variety store cashier: "Perhaps business isn't so bad after all. Things are selling so fast that even shoplifters have to wait in line."

☐ Down cycles can cause drastic action to be taken.

In the early 1980s, RCA was plagued by mounting debt and poor earnings. To solve their problems, they started selling off divisions that didn't fit in its core business and that they didn't have the expertise to manage.

☐ Per-item fixed cost can be lowered when a company levels out seasonal fluctuations.

Sun-Diamond produces Diamond walnuts and Sun-Maid raisins. Along with other products, they reduced their fixed-cost per item by promoting year-round baking uses for its products.

All markets have a life cycle all their own. They begin with a period of slow growth, then suddenly take off and grow fast until they reach a plateau of little or no growth. This market maturity has happened in every industry from zippers to automobiles.

☐ Companies, like the industries of which they are a part, have their ups and downs. They go through periods of prosperity and opposite periods of difficulty. The key is to survive.

Once there was a man who ran a sawmill in a small south Georgia town. Through fat times and lean, he went on dealing for timberland, logging it and milling the logs. He ran an efficient, careful operation. He always bought timber as low as he could and sold his finished wood for whatever the market allowed, even if he sometimes had to take a loss. He often said, "Somebody's going to be cutting timber even in the middle of a depression, and it might as well be me."

☐ The key to survival in tough times is a good attitude.

☐ Cyclical downturns don't have to be accepted. There are opportunities in them.

The Cliff Lodge, a ski lodge in Snowbird, Utah, is an example. During the winter, you couldn't get into the place. But at other times, The Cliff Lodge couldn't give away rooms. So management decided to lure the local philharmonic, and built the first artificial climbing wall for international tournaments. The following year, five thousand off-season tourists bought weekend packages of $45 to $125.

◻ BUSINESSWOMEN

"The only real drawback to being a woman in the business world is you have to deal with men."

Alex Thien

Joyce Rogers (past president of the National School Boards Association) said, "Sure God created man before woman—but you always make a rough draft before the final masterpiece."

"Bonnie Predd, vice president for marketing of Waldenbooks said, 'I don't think women have to become macho in order to make it into top management. You have to have confidence, an awareness of yourself, a real tough skin, and a sense of humor. You've got to prove yourself as a woman manager, and when you've done it—to your own satisfaction—you will know you've made it.' "

Paula Bern, How to Work for a Woman Boss

☐ Women encounter the same problems that men do.

When Mary Kay Ash, founder of Mary Kay Cosmetics, wanted to borrow $12 from a friend to attend a sales convention, the friend told her she'd be better off using the money to buy her children shoes instead of wasting it on some dream.

☐ What makes achievement possible in business?

"Being willing to learn new things, being able to assimilate new information quickly, and being able to get along with and work with other people."

Sally Ride, astronaut

"I don't mind living in a man's world as long as I can be a woman in it."

Susan Barkley

Judith Bogart, past president of the Public Relations Society of America, said that you should always do more than is expected of you and you will be a success.

"A woman has to be twice as good as a man to go half as far."
                                                              Fannie Hurst

G. K. Chesterton, British author and essayist, asked a poignant question, made more so by the reality of life late in the twentieth century. He wondered why any woman would choose to leave the home in order to do the same thing over and over when she had the opportunity to stay at home and teach everything in the world to one person.

☐ It is dreams that make women successful.

It is dreams of someone like Golda Meir, a common woman who became the prime minister of a major country. And Margaret Thatcher, living over her father's grocery store until she was twenty-one, who became prime minister of England. Or Grandma Moses, who started painting when she was in her seventies and painted over five hundred works of art that are celebrated around the world.

☐ Equality doesn't mean that men and women should do the same jobs.

Auctioneer:	"At any rate, mine is a business that a woman can't take up."
Liberated woman:	"Nonsense. A woman would make as good an auctioneer as any man."
Auctioneer:	"Would she? You try and imagine an unmarried woman standing up before a crowd and saying, 'Now, gentlemen, all I want is an offer.' "

☐ To be successful, businesswomen need the same qualities that have made men successful.

"Katharine Graham, publisher of the *Washington Post*, said, 'Power has no sex. Ambition and aggression are not masculine characteristics. Sensitivity and consensus-building are not female traits. Women must be willing to embrace all of these qualities—and use them to gain power.' "
                                   Paul Bern, How to Work for a Woman Boss

In a commencement address at Radcliffe College, Adlai Stevenson said:

"In previous appearances at women's colleges, my solemn remarks were addressed to women specifically—about the place of educated women in our society; about bringing up children in a neurotic world; about the conflict between the office desk and the kitchen sink.

"After listening to my highly instructive address, I came to the enlightened conclusion that women would not be truly emancipated until commencement speakers ignored the fact that they were women."

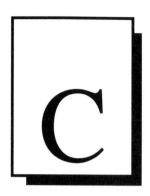

CAPITAL

☐ Money makes things happen.

"It is discretionary capital that finances most of what is original and idiosyncratic in our culture and economy."

Malcolm S. Forbes

☐ Use your capital wisely and you won't need much.

In the early 1970s, Atari was started with $500 of capital. They bought their supplies on credit and demanded immediate payment from customers. Three years later, Atari was sold to Warner Communications for $28 million.

☐ How important is working capital?

To demonstrate the importance of working capital to a business, one executive suggested that salespeople be paid the same way they sell. If a sales manager hired a new salesperson in January and agreed to pay the person $100,000 a year, he should hold back the person's paychecks during the first eleven months and pay him his entire salary in December. This would be a great way to demonstrate how difficult it is to run a company with no cash.

☐ You don't need as much capital if you get paid up front.

Companies like airlines and investment houses improve their cash flow by not extending credit.

☐ You can fail because you have too much initial capital.

When the De Lorean Auto Company started up, they spent money as if they had already achieved success. Soon afterwards, the company failed.

☐ The need for capital can cause you to lose control.

Because of capital needs, Henry Ford was forced to take a minority share of the Ford Motor Company.

☐ Money rules.

"The men who manage men manage the men who manage things, but the men who manage money manage the men who manage men."

J. Paul Getty

"The most valuable of all capital is that invested in human beings."

Alfred Marshall

☐ Collecting past-due accounts can improve cash flow and reduce capital requirements.

Linda Miles of Virginia Beach found that instead of sending out a second statement for an overdue account, they call the overdue account and suggest in a friendly and firm manner that they can settle the account by placing it on their credit card. She has found this seven to ten times more effective than sending out additional bills.

☐ Lack of working capital can be a benefit to a company.

Harvey Firestone, founder of Firestone Tire & Rubber, said, "I lacked capital. Because of this, I was forced to keep down overhead and watch every expenditure.

"In fact, I feel that if I had had all the money I wanted when I founded my present business, it never would have become so big as it is. I never would have found it necessary to make such a close study of details to promote the efficiency of the organization. I would have accomplished less because I would have lacked the prod of necessity for surefooted, painstaking accomplishment and the elimination of waste."

CAPITALISM

Capitalism has been presented as a transitory and conditional compromise: the worst possible system, as Winston Churchill once said of democracy, except for all the others.

"Not taking and consuming, but giving, risking, and creating are the characteristic roles of the capitalist."

Malcolm S. Forbes

One thing that Karl Marx and Andrew Carnegie agreed on was that capitalism means competition, and competition means change and uncertainty, and that is what makes our system successful.

"Capitalism is seeking the highest rate of return on your investments."

Mark Camp

You can understand capitalism when you realize that Thomas Edison improved the world more than Karl Marx.

"Capitalism without bankruptcy is like Christianity without hell."
Frank Borman, past chairman, Eastern Airlines

☐ CAREER

"A successful career requires falling in love many times with your work."
Frank Watson

☐ Find a career that fits you.

"I don't take new jobs as much for the challenge as for the opportunity. There are some jobs so challenging that there is no opportunity to succeed in them."

Tommy Prothro, football coach

An experienced mountain climber once explained that a mountain climber should always be assured of three good holds before moving up. They have two feet and two hands to climb with. Three of these should be firmly anchored before moving upward.

☐ In building a career, get good solid footholds along the way.

☐ Choose a career for the right reasons.

Guidance counselors in schools often advise students to train for certain vocations because the salary and benefits are good, or because there are plenty of vacancies, or because there is less danger of unemployment, rather than because a particular career might bring intellectual or emotional stimulation and satisfaction.

Talking about careers reminds me of the mail clerk who was studying to become an accountant. He was very thorough, and he planned where he wanted to be at each step in his life. He worked very hard to get there. But one day he refused to empty a wastebasket because it didn't fit his career plan. Well, you can imagine what happened.

Some of us, like the mail clerk, confuse our careers with our jobs when the truth is, if we get the jobs done, our careers will take care of themselves.

Albuquerque businessman Jeff Stone gave this definition of a career: People think a career is important and that young men and women often spend a lot of time planning and preparing for one, but actually a career is what happens next, and that includes a lot of hard work and luck.

So go ahead and make your plans, but don't forget that the planning is just the beginning. It's the hard work that makes a career.

☐ To have a championship career, make sure you always come to play.

☐ We are all led to our chosen careers for different reasons.

"After three years of delivering over 400 copies of *The Portland Oregonian*, beginning at 3:30 a.m., seven days a week, rain or shine, was a powerful incentive to find a job that started later, paid better, and offered working conditions indoors. After wearing out several bicycles, maybe that's when I truly began my life's interest in cars."

Donald E. Petersen, past chairman and CEO, Ford

The best career decision is to choose something you really like to do. Take the example of the late Art Rooney, owner of the Pittsburgh Steelers' NFL franchise. Because of his love for sports, he bought the Steelers in 1933 for $2,500. The Rooney family still owns the Steelers, but based on the price of the Dallas Cowboys' sale price of $145 million in 1989, the value increase was about sixty thousand times the original investment—all because he loved the game.

CHALLENGE

☐ Our challenge in business is to endure problems.

"Life asks not merely what can you do; it asks how much can you endure and not be spoiled."

Harry Emerson Fosdick

Life is a grindstone. Whether it grinds you down or polishes you up depends on what you are made of.

"Success is measured not so much by the position that one has reached in life as by the obstacles which he has overcome while trying to succeed."

Booker T. Washington

☐ We are our biggest challenge.

"It is not the mountain we conquer, but ourselves."

Edmund Hillary

☐ Don't avoid challenges.

"One person sees a mountain as a mountain. Another takes it personally, as a thing to be climbed, or else. Awful as the climbing might be, the or-else is worse."

Amy Gross, writer

☐ Accepting challenges is a positive experience.

"Striving is perhaps the one and only true elixir, for while we converse with what is above us, we do not grow old, but grow young."

Ralph Waldo Emerson

☐ An industry leader can be challenged if you find its vulnerability.

Nike deposed Adidas in athletic shoes. Stouffer's overcame Banquet and Swanson in frozen dinners.

☐ Industry leaders can be challenged by marketing differently.

In the 1950s, Timex opened up drugstores as a distribution channel. They overtook Bulova and the Swiss watchmakers who had used the traditional jewelry store channel.

☐ Industry leaders can be challenged when they are complacent.

Harley Davidson missed the consumer need for small motorcycles and watched Honda capture the market. Zenith clung too long to the handcrafted TV set despite the new streamline models available.

After Linus Pauling won the Nobel Prize, he was asked how he rechallenges himself. He replied, "You change fields."

"Somebody once asked President Eisenhower why he ever bought that farm of his in Gettysburg, Pa. He told them that all his life he wanted to take a piece of ground that really hadn't been cared for—cultivated or fertilized or watered—and work with everything he had and leave it in better condition that he found it. It's a simple statement, but I think maybe many men in life, regardless of their profession, have that inner urge to make a winner of a loser. That's our way of life. There's no challenge too big for anyone."

Hayden Fry, football coach

Jim Treybig, founder of Tandem Computers, said that the real challenge in business is not to worry about other people, but to worry about yourself.

☐ Chase the challenge, not the reward.

A television talk show had a panel of millionaires. Each of them was asked, "What is your goal?" Not one answered, "To make money." For each, the goal was the challenge of making it to the top.

"I'd like to win every game, but I'm not sure winning would mean much if I always won. I think that's why Vince Lombardi quit. He'd won too much. He came back because he missed it, but by then he had a new challenge—making a comeback, succeeding in a new place as he had in an old place."

Tommy Prothro

☐ Challenges in business are building blocks to success.

"Seek out the struggle that will toughen you up. Negativeness is a sin; so is self-indulgence. Bad times, such as depression or a state of war, should be a challenging test. Real men tighten their belts, throw full weight into the harness of their daily activities, and pull with all their might and main."

J. C. Penney

The legendary samurai swordsman Miyamoto Musashi once wrote to his students, "You cannot profit from small techniques, particularly when full armor is worn." Today a very great challenge approaches us dressed in full armor. [Mention the challenge.]

Meeting that challenge successfully together will require a very great effort from each of us. We cannot profit from small techniques. This is a time for bold action.

█ CHANGE

"When you're through changing, you're through."

Bruce Barton

☐ Change is easier with the right incentive.

"Remember the guy who wouldn't dream of his wife working? He's the same guy who now wakes her up in the middle of the night to suggest that she ask her boss for a raise."

Leonard Bookings

"Change is the only thing that offers new opportunity."

Ross Shafer

☐ Change gives us new opportunities.

With the invention of the magnetic compass, Columbus was able to sail across the Atlantic. Until the compass, ships stayed close to land.

As Heraclitus said five hundred years before the birth of Christ: "The only permanent thing is change."

☐ Don't wait too long to change.

One of the biggest reasons why a once successful business fails is that it rides a horse until it drops before it shifts horses.

☐ Don't wait to change.

A frog can sit in a pot of hot water and not notice the temperature rise. Many managers are this way. They ignore changes occurring in their environment, and by the time they wake up, they're boiled.

☐ Change helps us refocus.

IBM recently started changing the way it did things. The old IBM had too many layers of bureaucrats planning budgets, too many people double-checking products, but the loudest revisionist of all was Chairman John Akers, who bluntly said, "The old IBM was so flush with success, it lost track of its customers."

☐ To survive, we must change our products and the way we make them.

In 1950, Britain made 80 percent of the world's motorcycles. Today it makes less than one percent. Triumph, a leader in motorcycle manufacturing, kept using inefficient and old-fashioned production methods, outdated marketing and product development while the Japanese modernized the motorcycle and produced it cheaper and to a higher standard.

☐ You can get rich by changing things.

You can never make much by simply "assuring" or "controlling." Police officers try to keep things under control. Lawyers often work at prevention. You have never seen a rich policeman. There are a lot of rich lawyers.

"Progress is impossible without change, and those who cannot change their minds cannot change anything."

George Bernard Shaw

"There is nothing wrong in change if it is in the right direction. To improve is to change, so to be perfect is to have changed often."

Winston Churchill

"The art of progress is to preserve order amid change and to preserve change amid order."

Alfred North Whitehead

"If you want to make enemies, try to change something."

Woodrow Wilson

"Of the top 25 industrial corporations in the United States in 1900, only two remain in that select company today. One has its original identity; the other is a merger of seven corporations on that original list. Two of those 25 failed. Three others merged and dropped behind. The remaining 12 have continued in business, but each has fallen substantially in its standing."

Thomas J. Watson, Jr., IBM

In 1968, *Forbes* magazine selected the ten then most profitable U.S. companies in terms of equity, growth, and five-year performance. By 1985, three of them no longer even existed as independent companies. Four others had returns on equity that barely rivaled bank certificates. In fact, one of the above-mentioned three had a return on equity below that achievable by hiding one's money under the mattress: It was involved, following a takeover, in bankruptcy proceedings.

The grim reaper of businesses is, unfortunately, still alive and well today.

☐ Small changes can alter our destination.

Sea captains know that there are many forces that control the movement of a giant ship in the open seas, especially in bad weather. They have to contend with the weight of the ship, the movement and mass of water, along with the forces of the wind. But they also know that turning the relatively small rudder only a degree or two can alter the destination of the ship by as much as a thousand miles.

Tex Schramm, past president of the Dallas Cowboys, explaining why they had losing seasons after almost twenty-five years of success, said, "We didn't react quickly enough to our failures. I think it's too easy to get caught up in your own success. You've got to know when to change. We didn't know when to change."

☐ A great talent is to recognize change.

What special talent does Bob Hope have that enables him to have success in the toughest business for an unheard-of fifty years? He started out in vaudeville, moved on to Broadway, then movies, radio, and finally to television, mastering each medium along the way. He was able to recognize the changes taking place around him. He saw the industry changing and tailored his style of performing accordingly.

That's what we have to do. Change to fit the way our customers want our product and to introduce new products.

☐ The biggest change we can make is within ourselves.

"Everybody talks about wanting to change things and help and fix, but ultimately all you can do is fix yourself. And that's a lot. Because if you can fix yourself, it has a ripple effect."

Rob Reiner, actor and director

☐ Some things never change.

A daughter rushed home to her father.

"Dad, Bill asked me to marry him."

Father: "How much money does he have?"

Daughter: "You men are all alike. He asked the same thing about you."

☐ Before you can get people to change, you have to find out why they are doing what they're doing.

A husband and his wife were having a heart-to-heart talk. The wife asked, "Will you give up drinking for me?"

The husband answered: "What makes you think I'm drinking for you?"

Here are some examples of what can happen if you don't change:

Royal and Underwood typewriters don't exist today because they refused to recognize that electricity was coming into typewriters.

Stetson is out of business because they didn't recognize the changing needs of their customers.

Singer Sewing Machine Company, which became Singer, no longer manufactures sewing machines.

☐ We can't sit around and say we have a hot product; we must constantly change to meet the customers' new wants.

Today's fad may be tomorrow's antique. A profitable business can easily fade into obscurity if times change and customer needs change.

The original Fortune 500 was published fifty years ago. Today, only a few of the original companies are still on the list, and those that are still counted are in different businesses.

☐ Sometimes it's easier to ask others to change than to change ourselves.

One night at sea, a ship's captain saw what he thought were the lights of another ship heading toward him. He had his signalman blink to the other ship, "Change your course 10 degrees south."

The reply came back, "Change your course 10 degrees north."

The ship's captain answered, "I am a captain. Change your course south."

Another reply came back, "Well, I'm a seaman first class. Change your course north."

The captain was mad now. "Damnit, I said change your course south. I'm on a battleship!"

To which the reply came back, "And I say change your course north. I'm in a lighthouse."

Motorola's Robert W. Galvin had this to say about change: "A lot of companies that used to be competitors to Motorola aren't around anymore, because they haven't adapted to the environments—companies that used to be household names, like Admiral and Philco."

The markets that Motorola thrived in weren't radios but semiconductors, communications, and computers, products high on every corporate buying list.

☐ Changing corporate culture can be difficult for employees.

Johnson & Johnson, the maker of products such as Band-Aids and baby shampoo, once decided to start selling medical technologies. To move into these new areas, J & J had to change from a corporate bureaucracy to a decentralized management structure. This new structure would ensure the flexibility needed in the health care field. The change caused many J & J executives to leave because they couldn't adjust to the loss of autonomy.

☐ It's easier to make drastic changes when things are drastic.

In the 1970s, Sears Roebuck began to suffer financially. They were losing market share. From 1967 to 1970, Sears' market share dropped from 9.3 to 8.2 percent.

In 1978, Chairman Edward Telling changed Sears' course and began to turn things around. All the old stores were updated to compete with their competitors' newer stores. They added new products such as personal computers and auto insurance. Sears' earnings began to climb, getting higher every year until 1984, when Sears reported sales of $36 billion, more than companies like IBM or General Electric.

Shopping malls have replaced downtowns, television has replaced radio, now cable is diluting the major networks, jet airplanes have replaced ocean liners and railroads, stereos have replaced phonographs, tapes have replaced records, and tapes are being replaced by compact disks, and computers have replaced people. Photocopying has replaced mimeographing.

☐ Most people like change to be gradual.

David Mahoney wrote in his book, *Confessions of a Street-Smart Manager*, of a story one of his professors, Mike Dorizas, told him in college:

If you drop a frog into a pan of hot water, the frog will immediately react to the heat by jumping out of the pan. But, if you carefully place the same frog in a pan of comfortably cold water, then slowly raise the temperature of the water a degree at a time, the frog will accept this change, perhaps without noticing it, and stay in the water until the heat kills it.

We all run the risk of getting cooked when we fail to notice the small, slow changes taking place around us. The small changes, like a sunrise, often bring about changes as dramatic as night and day.

COMMENCEMENT SPEECH

☐ Success is a never-ending process.

"The toughest thing about being a success is that you have to keep on being a success."

Irving Berlin, songwriter

☐ You have to be willing to pay the price for your success.

"Our success doesn't come out of a computer. It comes out of the sweat glands of our coaches and players."

Tom Landry, football coach

☐ Success doesn't come. You go after it.

"Whatever you do, do it with all your might. Work at it, early and late, in season and out of season, not leaving a stone unturned, and never deferring for a single hour that which can be done just as well now."

P. T. Barnum

I can think of the president of the university who opened his remarks about college saying, "This college is an institution that prepares students for the real world."

Before he could continue, a student hollered out, "It sure does. Right off the bat, I'm in debt $50,000."

"The fullness or emptiness of life will be measured by the extent to which a man feels that he has an impact on the lives of others. To be a man is to matter to someone outside yourself, or to some calling or cause bigger than yourself."

Kingman Brewster, former president, Yale University

"The purpose of life is not to be happy. The purpose of life is to matter, to be productive, to have it make a difference that you lived at all. Happiness means self-fulfillment and is given to those who use to the fullest whatever talents God or luck or fate bestows upon them."

Leo Rosten, author

"The only place success comes before work is in the dictionary."

Donald Kendall, chairman, PepsiCo

View your professional success as something larger, as something worthwhile. Take the words of Fred Smith, founder of Federal Express, who said, "Achieving success, being rich—that doesn't do anything for you. Mostly what it does is bring you a lot of problems. The people who handle that well are people like Ross Perot, and I could name you five or ten others—people who believe that what they are doing is important, is making a contribution. They are inner directed, not outer directed. They are not living off the publicity and the accolades of the public."

☐ Use as a close to a commencement speech.

Kierkegaard said, "Life must be lived forwards but can only be understood backwards."

Let me close with the words of Theodore Roosevelt: "We see across the dangers of the great future, and we rejoice as a giant refreshed, the great victories are yet to be won, the greatest deeds yet to be done."

As Sugar Ray Leonard, the prizefighter, told a group of students at Harvard, "I consider myself blessed. I consider you blessed. We've all been blessed with God-given talents. Mine just happens to be beatin' people up."

No matter what your talent is, use it.

☐ Develop your special talents.

Neal Austin has had a long and distinguished career as a librarian and a leader in the library field. Also a widely acclaimed author, he has written several biographies of literary figures. Yet Neal was born with seriously deformed hands.

His father told him at an early age, "Son, because you will never be able to make a living with your hands, you'd better develop your brain."

"I studied the lives of great men and famous women, and I found that the men and women who got to the top were those who did the jobs they had in hand, with everything they had of energy and enthusiasm and hard work."

Harry S. Truman

☐ Never stop reaching for more.

Do more than exist—live.
Do more than touch—feel.
Do more than look—observe.
Do more than read—absorb.
Do more than hear—listen.
Do more than listen—understand.

John H. Rhoades

When Charles Wilson was president of General Electric, he was asked by the president of a small midwestern company how his experience as president of a major company could apply to the president of a very small company.

Wilson answered by detailing a job he had had when he was a kid. He worked for a dairy, and his job was to fill milk bottles. The bottles were different sizes. Some were pint, some half-gallon, and others gallon bottles. They all had different size necks. On his way home from a ten-hour workday, he asked himself what he was learning. The answer was that no matter what size the bottle, the cream always came to the top.

Improve yourself to become the cream.

☐ Short-term compensation can cause you to miss long-term opportunity.

Frank Woolworth, founder of Woolworth's, hated farming so much that he offered to work in a dry goods store for free just for the opportunity to have a future other than farming. This experience gave him the knowledge that led to his eventually owning over one thousand stores before he died.

☐ Never lose your enthusiasm for what you are doing.

J. C. Penney started his business career as a lowly clerk in a general store. One day, an older employee invited Penney to lunch. As soon as Penney finished eating, he rushed back to the store. The veteran employee told him not to be a fool by rushing back. Two months later, Penney was made manager of the store. Other promotions quickly followed, and he soon started his own chain that still exists today.

Even though this is an old story, it is a principle that still applies today: the principle of loving what you do and doing what you love.

☐ Success is hard work.

I can give you the same advice as Kemmons Wilson, Sr., founder of Holiday Inns, who was asked to give a commencement speech at the high school he once attended. Wilson, who didn't graduate from high school, told the graduating students: "I really don't know why I'm here, I never got a degree, and I've only worked half days my entire life. I guess my advice to you is to do the same. Work half days every day. And it doesn't matter which half. The first twelve hours or the second twelve hours."

☐ What is success?

Let me paraphrase the words of Thomas Watson, Jr., founder of IBM.
There is no such thing as standing still.
You must never feel satisfied.
Time lost is time gone forever.
Teaching is valueless unless someone learns what is taught.
Forgive your thoughtful mistakes.

Do more than is expected.

☐ We all have different talents, but it's how we use them that matters.

When Henry Ford finished giving a visitor a tour of his automobile factory, the visitor said: "It seems almost impossible that a man, starting out with practically nothing, could accomplish all this."

Ford replied: "You say I started out with practically nothing, but that isn't correct. We all start with all there is. It's how we use it that makes things possible."

☐ Enjoy what you do.

"You can be born with $100 million, but unless you find something you really enjoy, the money is of no consequence. I believe that you're OK if you do something you like. I always did something I would do for nothing."
David Brown, film producer

Seventeen Secrets to Success

1. Keep your temper to yourself.
2. Give your enthusiasm to everybody.
3. Be yourself, forget yourself, become genuinely interested in the other person.
4. Be fair, honest, friendly—and you'll be admired and liked.
5. Make other people feel important.
6. Count your assets and stamp out self-pity.
7. Meet people at their own level.
8. Put your smile power to work.
9. Keep moving.

10. Keep trying.
11. Give the gift of heart.
12. Get off to a good start in anything you do.
13. Forgive yourself if you fail.
14. Be lavish with kindness.
15. Overwhelm people with your charm, not your power.
16. Keep your promises.
17. Be an optimist.

Listen to the advice of J. Peter Grace, chairman and CEO of W. R. Grace & Company:

"Here is an apple. My generation has already taken a bite out of it. But, like Adam, you have to make the best of an imperfect garden. What can you do? Two things: continue to learn and be sure to vote.

"First, learn. Inform yourselves. Read and think. Don't swallow what others say. Reflect continually about your government and who's running it because they'll be doing it with your money.

"Second, vote. How can you correct the follies of my generation unless you vote against them?"

The singer John Denver giving a commencement speech to his old high school offered encouragement to his audience to be themselves in all things.

He said: "The best thing you have to offer the world is yourself. You don't have to copy anyone else. If you do, you're second best. To achieve success is to be first, and that's being yourself."

He recalled how after high school he went on to Texas Tech with the intention of becoming an architect.

He said: "But I quit to become a singer. Not one person said I was doing the right thing. Everyone said I was making a big mistake. They even turned me down for the shows at Six Flags, and I wound up handling the little cars the kids drive.

"But I knew deep down inside I was born to sing for people. And singing is the most joyful thing in the world for me. It's what's inside you that counts. And if it's not what you want to do, don't do it. Listen to yourself. You'll always know what's right. Listen to that voice. That's how you find success as a human being. Don't be afraid to be who you are. It's not that tough."

Many people have written creeds, those principles by which they live and in which they believe. One of the finest is this one by John D. Rockefeller, Jr. It is familiar to many people, but is so good that it should be reread at least once a year.

I *believe* in the supreme worth of the individual and in his right to life, liberty, and the pursuit of happiness.

I *believe* that every right implies a responsibility; every opportunity, an obligation; every possession, a duty.

I *believe* that the law was made for man and not man for the law; that government is the servant of the people and not their master.

I *believe* in the dignity of labor, whether with head or hand; that the world owes no man a living, but that it owes every man an opportunity to make a living.

I *believe* that thrift is essential to well-ordered living and the economy is a prime requisite of a sound financial structure, whether in government, business, or personal affairs.

I *believe* that truth and justice are fundamental to an enduring social order.

I *believe* in the sacredness of a promise, that a man's word should be as good as his bond; that character—not wealth or power or position—is of supreme worth.

I *believe* that the rendering of useful service is the common duty of mankind and that only in the purifying fire of sacrifice is the dross of selfishness consumed and the greatness of the human soul set free.

I *believe* in an all-wise and all-loving God, named by whatever name, and that the individual's highest fulfillment, greatest happiness, and widest usefulness are to be found in living in harmony with His will.

I *believe* that love is the greatest thing in the world; that it alone can overcome hate; that right can and will triumph over might.

Alistair Cooke said in a commencement address:

"You may think that the pursuit of happiness is a very frivolous task to recommend to you in the cloudy world of today. But I suggest we look for the symptoms of our world disorder in the individual. If you consider the personalities of the great tyrants of this century, it will be plain, I think, that they were unhappy people, above all embittered and envious; and in their supposed dedication to the vague mass of mankind they revealed an apathy or contempt toward the worth of any one man. It will, I think, become irritatingly plain to you as the years go by that people unhappy in their private lives are a great liability as citizens, for they have little energy or benevolence left over from their enmities and anxieties to begrudge to other people around them.

"As you go into your future, find time to become a happy person."

COMMITMENT

☐ A commitment means doing your best.

"Whatever I have tried to do in life, I have tried with my heart to do well."

Charles Dickens

"Commitment gives us new power. No matter what comes to us— sickness, poverty, or disaster, we never turn our eye from the goal."

Ed McElroy, USAir

"I can't imagine a person becoming a success who doesn't give this game of life everything he's got."

Walter Cronkite

"People must believe that a task is inherently worthwhile if they are to be committed to it."

Edward Deci, University of Rochester

"Whatever I have tried to do in life, I have tried with all my heart to do it well; whatever I have devoted myself to, I have devoted myself to completely; in great aims and in small I have always thoroughly been in earnest."

Charles Dickens

☐ Commitment means knowing what you are committed to.

Former All-Pro wide receiver Paul Warfield said this about catching passes: "I would block out everything else that was occurring. It was just the football, and I had an obsession with catching it."

☐ For employees to be committed, the company must be committed.

The Minneapolis-based department store chain Dayton Hudson has a company mission: "Purchasing agent for its customers." This statement boldly reminds all eighty thousand plus employees that the company exists to serve the customer.

☐ Commitment is what transforms a promise into a reality.

"Commitment unlocks the doors of imagination, allows vision and gives us the 'right stuff' to turn our dreams into reality."

James Womack

☐ Commitment guarantees victory.

You cannot keep a committed person from success. Place stumbling blocks in his way, and he takes them for stepping-stones, and on them he will climb to greatness. Take away his money, and he makes spurs of his poverty to urge him on. The person who succeeds has a program; he fixes his course and adheres to it; he lays his plans and executes them; he goes straight to his goal. He is not pushed this side and that every time a difficulty is thrust in his way. If he can't go over it, he goes through it.

"Commitment can create its own confirmation. To the man who dares not love, the entire world seems barren and dull, the future pregnant with doom. It is love and faith that infuse ideas with life and fire."

George Gilder, Wealth and Poverty

☐ Be committed to be your best under all conditions.

Katharine Hepburn once accepted a certain script, but she became dissatisfied once production began. The easy decision was to withdraw. But she continued to give it the best of her talents. This was her attitude toward her business. What's yours?

☐ Your commitment is where your thoughts are.

"Are you a fanatic? A manager must care intensely about running a first-class operation; if his golf game is what he thinks about while shaving, the business will show it."

Warren Buffett

☐ Employees will become committed once they know their employers are committed.

Stew Leonard, Sr., owner of "the world's largest dairy store" in Norwalk, Connecticut, carved his policy on a 6,000-pound rock right at the entrance of the store.
"Rule 1—The customer is always right.
Rule 2—If the customer is ever wrong, re-read rule 1."

Leonard said it's chiseled in stone because it's never going to change. He believes his policy is responsible for the store's growth from a 1,000-square-foot mom-and-pop store into a 100,000-square-foot shopper's festival with annual sales approaching $100 million.

☐ The way to succeed is to be committed enough to give your very best all the time.

"There is only one way to succeed in anything and that is to give everything. I do and I demand that my players do. Any man's finest hour is when he has worked his heart out in a good cause and lies exhausted on the field of battle . . . victorious."

Vince Lombardi, football coach

☐ To succeed, total commitment is needed.

Sometimes we think we are committed and we aren't. A chicken and a pig were talking about commitment. The chicken said, "I'm committed to giving eggs every morning." The pig said, "Giving eggs isn't commitment, it's participation. Giving ham is total commitment!"

◼ COMMITTEES

"A committee is a group of people who keep minutes and waste hours."
Anonymous

"A committee is a collection of the unfit chosen from the unwilling by the incompetent to do the necessary."
Anonymous

"A committee can't succeed if everybody's on board, but nobody's at the wheel."

Kathy Griffith, writer

"A committee is a thing which takes a week to do what one good man can do in an hour."

Elbert Hubbard

Lee Iacocca said that most important decisions in corporate life are made by individuals, not by committees.

Ross Perot said that after Electronic Data Systems was bought out by General Motors, he discovered a difference in management style. "At EDS when we saw a snake, we'd kill it. At GM when they saw a snake, they'd form a committee."

☐ The point is that action, not committees, gets results.

"I believe committees should be made up of three people: one who is always out of the country; one who is sick at home; and the chairman, who makes a decision and moves things forward quickly."

Mike Doyle

A story is told of the former president of General Motors, Charles Kettering. When the radio broke the news of Charles Lindbergh's crossing the Atlantic, someone rushed into Kettering's office and said, "Charlie Lindbergh just flew the Atlantic alone." He looked up and said, "Heck, that's nothing, let him try it with a committee."

C. Northcote Parkinson, of Parkinson's Law fame, said:
Committees of twenty deliberate plenty.
Committees of ten act now and then.
But most jobs are done by committees of one.

◼ COMMUNICATION

Peter Drucker claimed that 60 percent of all management problems result from faulty communications.

"I'll pay more for a man's ability to express himself than for any other quality he might possess."

Charles Schwab

☐ Poor communication causes problems.

"Nine-tenths of the serious controversies which arise in life result from misunderstanding."

Louis D. Brandeis

"If an organization is to work effectively, the communication should be through the most effective channel regardless of the organization chart."

David Packard, founder, Hewlett-Packard

"Half the world is composed of people who have something to say and can't, and the other half who have nothing to say and keep on saying it."

Robert Frost

"By definition, communication means two-way communication. Insecure individuals don't like it. Bosses don't like it, but leaders and innovators do like it."

Mark Shepherd, past chairman, Texas Instruments

"The communicator is the person who can make himself clear to himself first."

Paul D. Griffith

☐ How important is communication?

"You can have brilliant ideas, but if you can't get them across, your ideas won't get you anywhere."

Lee Iacocca

At Ford Motor Company, communication with employees is a priority. Communication lets them know both good news and bad. And by knowing, they become part of it, for better or worse.

☐ To get your message across, make it a positive one.

"It takes an average person almost twice as long to understand a sentence that uses a negative approach than it does to understand a positive sentence."

John H. Reitmann, psychiatrist

"No act in all of management—save that of thinking itself—is given as much time as the spoken word. Yet no other act in all of management is as grossly underutilized as this one in which one executive speaks to another."

Allan Cox, The Making of the Achiever

☐ Communication is very important.

"An executive can't ignore his communications any more than a driver can forget to oil his engine. The car will run briefly without outward signs of damage until suddenly overheated parts burn out the engine. So it is with an executive's communications. Neglect them, and damaging consequences will quickly appear."

Chester Burger, Survival in the Executive Jungle

Communication skills are more than talking well. L. A. McQueen, a General Tire & Rubber executive, said, "People judge you by what you say and write. I don't know a successful man in business who is not a good letter writer."

Russian scientist Pavlov said, "Men are apt to be much more influenced by words than by the actual facts of the surrounding reality."

"If people around you will not hear you, fall down before them and beg their forgiveness, for in truth you are to blame."

Fyodor Dostoyevsky

☐ How important is good communication to business success?

John Brogan, in his book *Clear Technical Writing*, wrote that an engineer can earn substantially more in his lifetime if he is an effective writer.

A leading marriage counselor says that at least half of the divorces in this country can be traced to faulty communication between spouses.

☐ How many problems in business are caused by the same problem?

☐ It's important to communicate exactly what you want.

An artist was asked to do some drawing for an advertising layout. One of the requests was for him to draw a beautiful woman. He turned in the first drawing, and it was rejected because the woman wasn't pretty enough. The second attempt was also unsatisfactory. Finally, the advertising agency got another artist to draw the beautiful woman.

When the advertising campaign was ready, all the participants were brought together for the kickoff of the campaign. To everyone's surprise, the original artist showed up with his wife, who was the woman he had been drawing.

A student pilot was on his first solo flight. When he called in for instructions, the control tower said, "Would you please give us your altitude and position?"

The pilot said: "I'm 5 feet 10 inches, and I'm sitting up front."

Are our words being understood, or do we react like the pilot?

☐ The bigger a corporation gets, the more important communication becomes to maintaining high productivity and enthusiasm in the workplace.

A few years ago, Rolls-Royce audited communications among the fifty thousand employees in its plant. It discovered that machinists had been working on components for years without even knowing what they were for. Nobody ever looked at the company bulletin boards, and few people even knew how much their engines sold for. Most of the employees didn't know the name of the chairman of the company or even the name of the local manager.

☐ The cost of poor communications can be demonstrated by this perhaps apocryphal story.

A young FBI man was put in charge of the FBI's supply department. In an effort to cut cost, he reduced the size of memo paper.

One of the new memo sheets ended up on J. Edgar Hoover's desk. He disliked it immediately and wrote on the narrow margin, "Watch the borders."

His message was misinterpreted. For the next six weeks, it was extremely difficult to enter the United States by road from either Mexico or Canada.

Communication can break down when we use words that have different meanings to different people.

For example, to a European, a "Yankee" is an American; to a member of the Boston Red Sox, a "Yankee" is a member of a rival baseball team; and to the Southerner, a "Yankee" is a Northerner.

☐ How important is communication?

Every Monday morning, Westinghouse chairman John C. Marous brings fourteen executives—from Pittsburgh, Baltimore, and New York City—for a no-agenda hour and a half in which ideas are shared and problems talked out. If there's especially good news—a big contract won, an acquisition—Marous will uncork a bottle and pour everybody a little glass of champagne. The first time he did it, it shook people up. But they're getting used to it.

A farmer in West Texas came home after listening to a politician talking at a political rally.

Wife: "Who spoke?"
Farmer: "The mayor."
Wife: "What did he talk about?"
Farmer: "Well, he didn't say."

Some of us have the same experience. We hear others talk forever and they never get to the point.

■ COMPENSATION

"Folks who never do more than they get paid to do, never get paid for any more than they do."

Elbert Hubbard

☐ You get what you deserve.

"What you have put into the kettle comes afterwards into your spoon."
Turkestan proverb

We get what we send. Our ships come homeward bound, laden with the same kind of merchandise as on their outward voyage.

"Every man shall receive his own reward according to his own labor."
I Corinthians

"The busy worker is the happy worker—until he finds out the lazy worker is being paid the same or more."
Bob Talbert

☐ We will get paid what we are worth once we prove our worth.

"Every act rewards itself."
Ralph Waldo Emerson

☐ Financial rewards aren't always necessary.

Clinical psychologist Jim Johnson said that you can motivate employees by giving them noticeable rewards. He said that you should offer rewards each day to the salesperson who has sold the most by the end of it. He said that you should give rewards so that others will notice. For example, to get a pair of Gucci shoes, you have to work forty-five hours a week. If 90 percent of the employees are walking around in Gucci shoes, the other 10 percent are going to feel embarrassed.

☐ Out-of-line compensation can cause long-term problems.

In 1985, Chrysler chairman Lee Iacocca paid himself a large multimillion-dollar bonus and at the same time cut blue-collar workers' wages by 30 percent. Soon after this, the union stood fast on demanding a new contract that called for higher than normal compensation.

Is your pay competitive? The president of a college board of trustees, addressing fellow board members said, "Perhaps the salaries we pay are lower than we thought, gentlemen. We're not only losing professors to industry— we're losing them to government!"

☐ To get paid more, you have to do more.

Erick Jonsson, founder of Texas Instruments, said that he always told his employees; "Look, we want to pay you better than our competition pays their employees. But to afford that, we have to ask you to produce something of more quality, perhaps, or do it more quickly; in all, to do the best you know how."

☐ Listen to these words about overcompensation.

"These compensation packages are getting out of control. For some entrepreneurs—well, that's different. But for a professional manager to put himself in that category just isn't right."

Donald Kendall, chairman, PepsiCo

The definition of a living wage depends on whether you are getting it or giving it.

☐ When managers think about giving themselves a raise, they should think of the impact on the other employees.

Once David Sarnoff, an Avis director, wanted to give Robert Townsend, the company's chairman, a raise. When Townsend turned down the gesture, he explained himself saying that if he got a raise, it would decrease the company profits and lower the amount of profit-sharing contribution that the employees would get. If I were an employee, I wouldn't stand for my getting a raise.

☐ Executive compensation like everybody else's should be tied to performance, not to position.

Archie R. McCardell was chairman of International Harvester during 1980 and 1981, when they were losing nearly $400 million a year, and he still got paid $1.4 million.

Golden parachutes are not offered by all corporations. Companies like H. J. Heinz offer merit pay instead. Executive compensation is linked with shareholders' gain. Because of their pay-as-you-perform method, sometimes managers can earn 30 to 50 percent over their annual salaries.

☐ Compensation should be tied to productivity.

Parker Pen Company offers hourly employees bonuses if they reach certain productivity targets. Workers regularly get monthly bonuses. During one economic slump, they didn't get the bonuses. One company executive said, "Workers are disappointed when the bonuses aren't there, but they know why they aren't there."

☐ What goes around comes around.

"The universe pays every man in his own coin; if you smile, it smiles on you in return; if you frown, you will be frowned at; if you sing, you will be invited into cheerful company; if you think, you will be entertained by thinkers; if you love the world, and earnestly seek for the good therein, you will be surrounded by loving friends, and nature will pour into your lap the treasures of the earth."

Mike Lea

☐ Offer rewards with specific goals in mind.

Despite the state's economic woes, there are still some rich Texans. One of them became friendly with a New Yorker.

Rich Texan: "I'd like to send my jet up for you, and we'll go hunting on my son's ranch west of Austin. It's 80,000 acres stocked with purebred cattle and exotic game. I'm real proud of the boy. He's just fourteen years old and earned it all himself."
New Yorker: "How on earth did he do that?"
Rich Texan: "He got four A's and a B."

The self-made tycoon was bragging to a reporter about the secret of his success.

Tycoon: "I've always had the theory that salary is the least important part of the job. Doing things wholeheartedly to the peak of your ability brings you greater satisfaction than money."
Reporter: "And you became rich after you convinced yourself that this was true?"
Tycoon: "No. After I convinced the people who worked for me."

General Electric's John F. Welch said, "If you pick the right people and give them opportunity to spread their wings—and put compensation as a carrier behind them—you almost don't have to manage them."

☐ Giving bonuses can cause problems.

After winning his first Super Bowl, Vince Lombardi surprised the Green Bay players' wives with mink coats. Next year, the Packers won again, and this time Lombardi gave the wives diamond brooches. And some new wives openly complained because it wasn't fur coats again.

☐ Some people not only look a gift horse in the mouth, but they will jerk out its teeth if it isn't careful.

☐ Salary—especially early in a career—isn't nearly as important as the opportunity to demonstrate your talents.

Victor Kiam said in his book *Going for It!* that he started as a management trainee at Lever Brothers in the 1950's for about $3,000. At the same time, a Harvard Business School classmate began as a market researcher at nearly twice the salary. But Kiam said it never bothered him.

Three years later, the friend was making $7,500, and Kiam was making $17,000. The friend's job was a dead-end position.

☐ Sharing the profits creates more profits.

Andrew Carnegie understood the importance of commitment and knew the surest way to get it. If we expect our employees to act like entrepreneurs, then it is logical that they should share in the rewards of entrepreneurship.

Carnegie went on to say, "A man, to be in business, must be at least owner of the enterprise which he manages and to which he gives his attention, and is chiefly dependent on for his revenues not upon salary but upon its profits."

☐ People become more productive with a good incentive.

When Donald Kendall, chairman of PepsiCo, was growing up, he had a job working on commission in a shoe store. They made him a deal where he got paid extra if someone asked for him when they came into the store. He began to pass out his business card to residents in the area.

As a result of this incentive, he was able to buy a new car and have money in the bank.

As managers, we should remember the connection between the amount of work we ask our employees to do and the amount of money we pay them.

Lee Iacocca once said, "When you give a guy a raise, then it's time to increase his responsibility. If you don't do that, you aren't getting the most performance for your dollar and you aren't making the most of your people."

☐ When you pay more, you get more in return.

☐ The more profit you share, the more profit you'll make. Offering employees good compensation can help your company grow.

Dave Liniger, founder of RE/MAX real estate, watched his company grow to a billion dollars in sales by using the "100 percent solution" which lets his sales people keep 100 percent of their commission while charging them a monthly fee to office with RE/MAX.

His employees were making so much money that they never left him.

One day a few years later, he went into his regular three-chair barbershop. The owner was lamenting how hard it was to hang onto good barbers—they'd leave and go into business for themselves. He explained how his company held onto talent using the "100 percent solution." The barber nodded politely.

A few months later, Dave was back. When he reached for his wallet to pay, the barber waved him off. He said, "This one is on me. I took your advice, and we're a 100 percent barbershop now."

☐ Workers need to be compensated by more than just money.

"Getting people to chase money produces nothing except people chasing money. Using money as a motivator leads to a progressive degradation in the quality of everything produced."

Philip Slater, sociologist

☐ Make sure you are compensating your people to do the correct thing.

One furniture company was actually paying its salespeople to fail. A study was done of their falling sales trend. It was discovered that the average sales made in the home was $2,200 compared with $568 in the store. But the salespeople paid their own mileage, and a commission wasn't paid until the furniture was actually delivered.

The company started paying mileage and paid a portion of the commission when the order was taken. The result was that sales shot up nearly 50 percent.

COMPETITION

"People most strenuously seek to evaluate performance by comparing themselves to others, not by using absolute standards."

Leon Festinger

☐ Make workers compete.

"Bicyclists race faster against each other than against a clock."

Norman Triplett

☐ Competition gives us a reason to live.

"I wouldn't give one iota to make a trip from the cradle to the grave unless I could live in a competitive world."

Adolph Rupp, basketball coach

"Those who will only compete when they can dominate are not actually competing at all."

Thomas Paulman

Advice from a caddie to a PGA tour player: "There're plenty of guys out here who are perfectly willing to beat you. You don't have to beat yourself."

☐ Victory is usually a thin margin.

"The difference between the top money winners on the PGA golf tour and the bottom money winners can be as little as one stroke a day."

Steve Miller, former PGA tour player

"Everyone likes to know what he could do against competition with no unfair advantage."

J. Peter Grace

☐ Learn to fear the competition.

Jack Lambert, the great Pittsburgh Steelers linebacker, once said that he played with such intensity because of the way he felt about the opposing team. "If we lose, they could affect my livelihood. It's not just a game to me."

☐ Competition improves quality.

When Eastman Kodak entered the copier market, it made Xerox improve its quality. With Kodak being a quality and well-financed competitor, Xerox was forced to compete on quality, not price cutting.

☐ A well-positioned product can prevent competition.

General Foods has the muscle to protect itself from competition. For example, their Maxwell House Coffee brand enjoys such a high brand recognition that the cost of a new coffee trying to compete against a well-financed company like General Foods prevents many competitors from taking on the challenge.

☐ Be positive when dealing with the competition.

Ray Kroc, McDonald's founder, said, "My way of fighting the competition is the positive approach. Stress your own strengths, emphasize quality, service, cleanliness, and value, and the competition will wear itself out trying to keep up."

☐ Competition protects the consumer.

Clarence Randall, former head of Inland Steel, put it succinctly when he said: "In the management of a business the sharp bite of honest aggressive competition is the automatic corrective measure to safeguard the public from extortion. A man cannot be making too much profit if others are trying to beat him at his own game."
Mortimer R. Feinberg, Effective Psychology for Managers

☐ You can beat the competition if you offer something unique.

Cyrus McCormick's reaper was not the first ever patented, but McCormick offered an installment plan and a money-back guarantee, which swept aside the competition.

"The purpose of competition is not to beat someone down, but to bring out the best in every player."
Amos Alonzo Stagg, football coach

"I have no friends and no enemies—only competitors."
Aristotle Onassis

☐ One way to protect yourself from the competition is to diversify.

"We've set out to diversify geographically in a way that would make us hard to be squashed. As the World War II pilots said, there's a difference between being shot up and shot down. We can be shot up a little bit, but I don't think we can be shot down."
Herbert Kelleher, chairman, Southwest Airlines

Competitiveness in sports and business have certain common elements: The essential building blocks are basic health and well-being (the social and economic situation), conditioning (worker-corporate relations), special training (product competitiveness), and fine tuning (government-business cooperation).

☐ Make the competition fight your fight.

One thing that made Muhammad Ali practically unbeatable during his prime was that he always made his opponent "fight his fight." He would "float like a butterfly and sting like a bee." Beneath the poetry and self-adoration lay a great fighter who knew what he could do best and stuck to it. No wonder he made many far more powerful fighters believe he was "the greatest."

☐ To beat your competition, don't depart from your area of superiority.

How can you beat Bobby Fischer, the greatest chess player of all time? Get him to play you any game except chess.

☐ Competition is good for the consumer.

In the early 1950s, many American children could name every car on the highway. General Motors controlled 60 percent of the car market and, within that 60 percent, it controlled the price, quality, and appeal of every brand: Chevrolet, Pontiac, Buick, Oldsmobile, and Cadillac.

Choices were limited and real options were few. Then the Volkswagen Bug arrived in America, quickly followed by the Honda. When the smoke cleared, limited competition was out of the bottle, never to return.

☐ Hit the competition head on.

Competition is illustrated by the two merchants who set up shop across the street from each other. One had moved to his newly expanded location from an older and smaller site. And he proudly hung the sign that read, "Murphy and Sons, Established 1875."

His competitor across the street—seeing a good opportunity— responded with a sign of his own, "Johnson and Company, No Old Merchandise."

Many inventors were very close to inventing the airplane before the Wright brothers. The Wright brothers were using the same principles that were being used by the others, but they added something more. They attached movable flaps, the forerunner of the modern aileron.

To beat our competition, we need movable flaps.

☐ Compete with yourself first.

Ed Rensi, president of McDonald's USA, said, "We don't spend a lot of time looking at our competition." Instead, McDonald's focuses on corporate introspection. Rensi himself spends three days a week inspecting restaurants and running down a mind-boggling checklist—from the painted stripes in the parking lots to the temperature of the refrigerators and whether the brooms are clean. He talks to employees about their aspirations and their training, then wanders among the customers, handing out free fries and sundaes in exchange for frank opinions.

Look for the weak spots in the positions of your competition, and then launch attacks against those weak points.

For example, while other computer companies were showing losses, Digital Equipment Corporation was making big profits by taking advantage of IBM's weakness in small computers.

The way to beat the competition is to become the industry standard. Coca Cola is an example of this. In fact, Coca Cola had a law passed that said that if you went into a soda fountain or a restaurant and you ordered a Coke, and they didn't have it, they had to tell you they didn't have it and would Pepsi be okay.

☐ Product name can give you advantage over the competition.

IBM named their personal computer system after the name of the industry. They named it "the personal computer."

Now, by law, if you go into a computer store and say, "I'd like to see a personal computer," they legally have to show you the IBM personal computer. If they don't carry the IBM PC, they have to say so and ask if you'd like to see another brand.

Years ago, a Massachusetts company that made an industrial cleaner branded it as a heavy-duty consumer product called Lestoil. Their mission was simple. They wanted to take an industrial cleaner and make it known as a consumer cleaner. They created new value. But they failed to protect themselves against the muscle of Procter & Gamble. So instead of Lestoil, we know about Mr. Clean instead.

☐ To maintain a competitive advantage, you must compete with and beat the big boys.

☐ Competition makes us find ways to respond to the market faster.

Based on a survey of fifty major U.S. companies, Kaiser Associates, a Vienna, Virginia, consulting firm, found that General Electric used to take three weeks after an order to deliver a custom-made industrial circuit-breaker box. Now it takes three days. AT&T used to need two years to design a new phone. Now it can do the job in one. Motorola used to turn out electronic pagers three weeks after the factory got the order. Now it takes two hours.

☐ Competition is good within reason.

"We compete as a society. And you can't have a good society with everyone stabbing everyone else in the back, with everyone trying to steal from everyone else, with everything requiring notarized confirmation in writing because you can't trust the other fellow, with every little squabble ending in litigation, and with Congress writing more and more pages of regulatory legislation to tie American business hand and foot to keep it honest. That's a recipe not only for headaches in running one's company; it's a recipe for a wasteful, inefficient, noncompetitive society."

M. John Akers, chairman, IBM

☐ A love of combat is essential to success.

Leonard H. Golderson, who rescued American Broadcasting Company from ruin, recalls that in the dark days, "Everybody at ABC kept saying to me, 'It can't be done, you can't compete.' "

Golderson commented, "I don't understand that language."

COMPUTERS

"The real danger is not that computers will begin to think like men, but that men will begin to think like computers."

Sydney Harris

☐ A computer can't do everything.

Computers will never replace man entirely until they learn to laugh at the boss's jokes.

We seem to be approaching an advanced state in human progress where people are perfect and anything that's wrong is the fault of computers.

A computer can do more work faster than a human because it doesn't have to answer the phone.

☐ Computers offer a bright future.

Experts are telling us that eventually every home will have a computer. "This means that our personal lives will be just as screwed up a things are at the office."

The computer has really revolutionized small business and farming. Without it, it would be months before they'd know they were broke!

To err is human, but to really screw up requires a computer.

There is a new computer out that won't tell the Internal Revenue Service you cheated on your income tax if you promise to buy it.

Go ahead and put it on the computer; or least you'll know where it is even though you can't find it again.

☐ Computers can be excuses.

A firm we know is having so many errors it's thinking of buying a computer to blame them on.

Stenographer showing a huge electronic machine to a coworker: "The darned thing won the office football pool!"

"In a few minutes, a computer can make a mistake so great that it would take many men many months to equal it."

Merle L. Meacham

☐ Blaming the computer works both ways.

Howard Mayer, the public relations tycoon, for years maintained a small account at the main Hollywood branch of the Bank of America in Los Angeles. One month, he received a statement advising him that his account was overdrawn by $2,999,450. He called the bank and was told the machines probably confused him with a movie producer.

☐ Computers can make life impersonal.

A teacher made an inquiry to the Internal Revenue Service and received a reply that did not answer her question.

After several follow-up inquiries with the same futile response, she wrote a letter addressed: "Dear Computer: Please have your mother call me."

Within a week, she received a handwritten note telling her exactly what she wanted to know.

☐ Some people think computers have all the answers.

When the computer arrived at a large business concern, the movers found it too big for the elevator.

Deliveryman: "How are we going to get this thing to the third floor?"
Manager: "Plug it in and let it figure it out for itself."

☐ Computers don't always give us what we want.

In a computer dating office, an employee said to a client, "You wanted a date who is warm, soft, sweet, and quiet. The computer matched you up with a loaf of zucchini bread."

☐ Computers won't change bad habits.

A young woman who worked for one of the banks was telling her parents about what her boyfriend, a computer expert, had been telling her.

Young woman: "He says it won't be long before all financial transactions are handled by computers. Checks will be a thing of the past. It will be totally a cashless society."
Father: "Well, I'm ahead of the times. I'm cashless right now."

☐ Computers are helpful.

Computers are definitely smarter than people. When have you ever heard of six computers getting together to form a committee?

A speaker gave a brief rundown on computers—past, present, and future.

Speaker: "The World War II computer covered thousands of cubic feet and could do only fairly simple functions.

"A decade ago, a computer smaller than the podium from which I speak could perform may more functions. A decade from now, a computer the size of a man's thumbnail will have more capabilities than today's."

Student: "There's hope for the next century. Perhaps they'll either disappear or we'll lose them."

CONSULTANTS

A consultant is someone whose approval is sought after the decision has been made.

"A consultant is an ordinary man away from home giving advice."
Oscar Wilde

□ The person performing the job is often the best consultant.

"Until we believe that the expert in any particular job is most often the person performing it, we shall forever limit the potential of that person, in terms of both his own contributions to the organization and his own personal development."
Rene McPherson, former chairman, Dana

"It used to be that a guy went into the Army when everything else failed; now he goes into the consulting business."
Blackie Sherrod, sportswriter

"After the ship has sunk, a consultant knows how it might have been saved."
Newt Hielscher, humorist

"A consultant is someone who knows more and more about everything until he knows nothing about anything and then charges for it."
Robert H. Henry, humorist

"Consultants are people who come down from the hill to shoot the wounded after the battle is over."
Doc Blakely, humorist

"Someone who borrows your watch and charges to tell you the time."
Jeanne Robertson, humorist

Henry Ford distrusted outside experts. He said: "The moment one gets into the expert state of mind, a great number of things become impossible."

"A consultant is someone who saves his client almost enough to pay his fee."

Arnold Glasow

Advice one businessperson offered about consultants: "Some of these guys are good—but expensive. Some of them are just expensive."

A lot of consultants are hired to be scapegoats for poor managers. U.S. business spends over $3 billion annually on consultants.

A consultant is a man who knows 146 ways to make love but doesn't know any women.

A plumber was called to fix a leak. He looked at the pipe, gripped the hammer with both hands, struck the pipe as hard as he could, and the leak stopped.

He presented the customer with a bill for $250.35. The owner was furious. "This is outrageous; you were here only two minutes and all you did was hit the pipe."

The plumber itemized his bill. Wear and tear on the hammer—35 cents. Knowing where to hit—$250.00.

☐ Sometimes consultants get paid to know what to do more than for doing it.

One way to deal with consultants is to make sure you don't pay for the same information twice.

Listen to the advice of Robert E. Kelly, a CPA and management consultant: "A good example is the experience of a CEO I know who owns a meat company in New England. He wanted to explore the possibilities and benefits of an addition to his main building, so he brought in an industrial engineer. The consulting engineer made a complete product flow study at various volume levels and proposed several expansion plans to handle the work. Throughout the project, the CEO had paid close attention to what the engineer was doing. When he didn't understand a particular scheme, he asked questions. Or if the engineering jargon got in his way, he kept after the consultant until he understood the concepts. He saved copies of layout diagrams, product flow charts, and other instructive materials.

"In the end, none of the consultant's plans felt right to the CEO, so he didn't accept them. But over a period of time, he designed an additional series of layouts, using techniques he'd learned from the consulting engineer. Eventually, he came upon the right combination of dollars and space. In the process, he'd saved himself thousands of dollars in consulting fees and had considered many more options than a consultant might normally suggest.

And he now is his own layout man for modest projects. Even for ambitious projects, he needs less help from professionals than most of his peers."

CONVICTION

☐ Have the courage of your convictions.

"I have found that the greatest help in meeting any problem with decency and self-respect and whatever courage is demanded is to know where you yourself stand. That is, to have in words what you believe and are acting from."

William Faulkner

☐ There's a fine line between too much and too little conviction.

"There are those who believe something, and therefore will tolerate nothing; and on the other hand, those who tolerate everything, because they believe nothing."

Robert Browning

"The man who doesn't stand for something will fall for anything."
Peter Marshall

"Be sure you put your feet in the right place, then stand firm."
Abraham Lincoln

☐ We must have the conviction of our actions to get the best results.

A minister confessed that the reason most people's prayers aren't answered is that when they pray, they don't really believe they will be answered.

"Conviction is a flame that must burn itself out—in trying an idea or fighting for a chance to try it. If bottled up inside, it will eat a man's heart away."

Robert Townsend, Avis

☐ To achieve success, you need firm beliefs.

"I firmly believe that any organization, in order to survive and achieve success, must have a sound set of beliefs on which it premises all its policies and actions. Next, I believe that the most important single factor in corporate success is faithful adherence to those beliefs. And, finally, I believe if an organization is to meet the challenge of a changing world, it must be prepared to change everything about itself except those beliefs as it moves through corporate life."

Thomas J. Watson, Jr., IBM

☐ We won't survive if we don't first believe we will.

Historian David E. Lilienthal pointed out back in 1949, "Legislation alone would never have ensured the right of free criticism if the people hadn't believed it in their hearts."

☐ Only when you have personal conviction can you overcome the nay-sayers.

When artist Charles Kennedy realized that Americans were on a cultural kick, he wanted to open an art store to capitalize on this trend.

His attorney said that his idea about reproducing oil paintings from photographs couldn't possibly be a money-maker. His banker wouldn't lend him money on this risky venture.

Kennedy sold his car, borrowed on his insurance policies, cashed in his government bonds, and set up his art gallery. Within three years, he was making a net profit beyond what his nay-sayers predicted.

CRITICISM

"A critic is a legless man who teaches running."

Channing Pollock

"Watch what people are cynical about, and one can often discover what they lack, and subconsciously, beneath their touchy condescension, deeply wish they had."

Harry Emerson Fosdick

☐ Learn from your critics.

"A successful man is one who can lay a firm foundation with the bricks that others throw at him."

David Brinkley

"One of the problems in American corporations is the reluctance of the CEO to listen to criticism."

Ed Carlson, United Airlines

"The person who has been punished is not thereby simply less inclined to behave in a given way; at best, he learns how to avoid punishment."

B. F. Skinner

"Remember, anything you say about someone may get back to them. There are few secrets."

Bill Marriott, Sr.

☐ Jealousy breeds criticism.

Nobody casts stones at a fruitless tree.

Never point a finger of scorn at another, for in so doing you are pointing three fingers of scorn at your own self.

☐ Criticism comes from those that can't do.

The person who can't dance says the band can't play.

"It is much easier to be critical than to be correct."
Benjamin Disraeli

☐ Criticism comes with the territory.

"To avoid criticism, do nothing, say nothing, be nothing."
Elbert Hubbard

☐ Criticism is like a gnat.

"A gnat can't do you any real harm; the worst he can do is irritate you flying around in your ear."
Jimmy W. Marsh

"I am always ready to learn, although I do not always like being taught."
Winston Churchill

☐ Don't let possible criticism stop you from moving forward.

"A man would do nothing if he waited until he could do it so well that no one could find fault."
John Henry Newman

Allen H. Neuharth, founder of *USA Today* said, "Nothing kills hope faster than cynicism."

"Criticism should be like a sandwich. If you want to motivate people, slip the criticism in between layers of praise."
Henry C. Rogers

"It's one thing to be critical and another to supply instant answers. If you say, 'That's lousy; here's what you ought to do,' the next time the guy's going to ask you first, 'What do you think I ought to do?' It's something else to say, 'That doesn't do anything for me; what else do you think you can do?' "
Donald Seibert, chairman, J. C. Penney

"Managers should never review past bad performance with their employees. Criticism just doesn't work."
Edward J. Feeney, consultant

☐ Criticism affects all of us.

Ted Williams, one of baseball's greatest hitters, said, "When somebody says nice things about me, it goes in one ear and out the other. But I remember the criticism longer. I hate criticism—and the sportswriters who write the way they feel instead of what they've actually seen."

"I do not resent criticism even when for the sake of emphasis it parts for the time with reality."
Winston Churchill

☐ Some people look for bad things to say.

A supervisor at a plant had called one of the workers on the carpet for talking back to his foreman.

Supervisor: "He says you called him a liar. Is that right?
Worker: "I suppose it is."
Supervisor: "And he says you called him stupid."
Worker: "He is and I did."
Supervisor: "And a slave driver."
Worker: "Yes."
Supervisor: "And a genuine, gold-plated, twenty-four-hour, open-all-night, neon-lighted revolving SOB."
Worker: "No—but let me write that one down so I can remember it."

In the midst of the Civil War, Abraham Lincoln was beseiged by irate citizens, advisers, politicians, crackpots, and military leaders, all telling him what he should do in equally loud voices to win the war. He is said to have remarked that he felt like "the man lost in a dense forest during a severe thunderstorm who prayed, 'Oh, Lord, if it's all the same to you, please give me more light and a little less noise.' "

Our industry is being beseiged by [name the outside forces that are complicating your situation]. And we are like Lincoln—we need more light and less noise. We need to move forward.

☐ Critics criticize because they don't really know.

A noted bullfighter wrote a poem, a few lines of which seem appropriate.

The bullfight critics ranked in rows
Fill the enormous plaza full.
But only one is there who really knows,
And he's the one who fights the bull.

Jean Paul Lyet, CEO of Sperry Corporation, once said that probably no amount of money could ever be quite enough for someone who grew up poor. It is always important, when we are puzzled by the actions of others, to try to understand their motivations.

Welcome to the club. When business gets bad, managers have to take the heat. Will Rogers joked that during the Depression a woman bit into a rotten apple and exclaimed: "Damn Hoover."

This statement credited to Theodore Roosevelt is perhaps the most eloquent defense of the man or woman living where the rubber meets the road that has yet been offered:

"It is not the critic who counts, not the man who points out how the strong man stumbled, or where the doer of deeds could have done them better. The credit belongs to the man who is actually in the arena; whose face is marred by dust and sweat and blood; who strives valiantly; who errs and comes short again and again; who knows the great enthusiasms, the great devotions, and spends himself in a worthy cause; who, at best, knows in the end the triumph of high achievement; and who, at the worst, if he fails, at least fails while daring greatly, so that his place shall never be with those cold and timid souls who know neither victory nor defeat."

CUSTOMER SERVICE

☐ We would all be better off if we copied IBM.

"IBM always acts as if it were on the verge of losing every customer."
Jacques Maison-Rouge, IBM World Trade

"One airline gives such lousy service they canceled one flight while it was in midair."

Joe L. Griffith

☐ Make your customer number one, then they'll make you number one.

Companies with a tradition of success have always put the customer first. Domino's Pizza started home delivery in the fast-food business because they wanted to make life easier for the customer. Disneyworld and Disneyland call their customers "guests." Microage calls their customers "clients."

☐ The customer is our employer.

"There is only one boss. The customer. And he can fire everybody in the company from the chairman on down, simply by spending his money somewhere else."

Sam Walton, founder, Wal-Mart

Over the useful life of a product, the cost of service may be greater than the original purchase price of the product. As a result, customers are not only more sensitive to the cost of service, they expect more from it.

TRW manager

☐ Sometimes we forget the power of the customer.

Historically the service on Eastern airlines was so bad that "I hate Eastern" clubs were formed by angry passengers. They were popular for over twenty-five years.

☐ Never stop trying to satisfy the customer.

Customers are like Oscar Wilde, who said, "I have the simplest of taste. I'm easily satisfied with the best."

Treating customers as if they were one in a million pays big dividends.

Remember the IBM commercial that said, "If your failure rate is one in a million, what do you tell that one customer?" The ad closed with the line, "At IBM, we treat every customer as if he or she is one in a million."

Treating customers as if they were one in a million has been the key to success in other companies, like McDonald's, Disney, and Domino's Pizza.

"When a customer enters my store, forget me. He is king."

John Wanamaker

☐ Sell service.

IBM credits its success to service—IBM's contracts have always offered, *not* machines for rent, *but* machine services.

☐ The best way to give good customer service is to hire people who are service-conscious.

A grocery store clerk, tired of his job, quit to become a traffic policeman. After a few days, a friend asked him how he liked his new job.

He said, "The pay and hours aren't too good, but at least the customer is always wrong."

☐ It takes a long time to build customer confidence but once you do, it lasts.

Thomas Horton, CEO of the American Management Association, told this story:

He went to visit his ninety-year-old mother in Florida. She asked if he would like an electric blanket she had purchased at Sears. He told his mother he would take it for his daughter. She told him that it was a funny color, avocado green, but if she didn't like it she could always exchange it at Sears.

When he looked at the blanket, he discovered that his mother had purchased it from Sears in 1949 for $8.89. He couldn't convince his mother that Sears wouldn't take it back. She said, "They'll take it back, just you see."

His mother remembered her long-ago dealings with Sears and had faith in its reputation for customer service.

☐ The Ten Commandments of Good Business

Clients are:

1. The most important people in any business.
2. Not dependent on us—we are dependent on them.
3. Not interruptions of our work—they are the purpose of it.
4. Doing us favors when they call—we are not doing them favors by serving them.
5. Part of our businesses—not outsiders.
6. Not cold statistics—they are flesh-and-blood human beings with feelings and emotions like our own.

7. Not someone with whom to match wits.
8. People who bring us their wants—it is our job to fill those wants.
9. Deserving of the most courteous and attentive treatment we can give them.
10. The lifeblood of this and every other business.

☐ When you offer the customer a service, make sure it's what they want.

"We believe many hotels get too distracted by advertising, promotions, and giveaways and lose sight of the basics. The only real way to differentiate yourself from the competition is through service.

"For instance, we believe in guest recognition rather than guest rewards. What's more, we've found that our guests prefer it that way. They prefer to be upgraded to a suite, to be remembered by name, and to receive their favorite amenity, rather than pay a higher room rate so that we can afford to send them on a free trip to Europe."

Jonathan Tisch, president, Loews Hotels

☐ Everybody is in customer service.

Back in the early days of gas being used commercially, gas meter readers pounded on doors hard enough to knock them down. They were rude to customers. Before the gas companies learned how their meter readers were creating a large group of disgruntled customers, the polite salesmen of oil burners came along and quietly did a booming business.

Always be courteous because if we don't have competition now, we will one day, and we may never recapture lost customers.

☐ How do you satisfy the customer?

Chrysler once ran a full-page ad in the *Wall Street Journal* with a big picture of Lee Iacocca. On top of the ad were these words: "There's no great mystery to satisfying your customer. Build them a quality product and treat them with respect. It's that simple."

Statistics prove that employees treat customers the way their employer treats them.

Remember, you can't give something you don't have any more than you can come back from someplace you haven't been. Treat employees with respect and they're more likely to treat the customer the same way.

☐ Make your organization chart customer-oriented.

Jan Carlzon made a name for himself in 1981. He became president of Scandanavian Airlines Systems and in one year led the airline from a loss of $17 million to a profit of $54 million.

How did he do it? By turning the organization chart upside down. He put the people who dealt with the customers in charge of the company. And the rest of the employees on the upside-down organization chart worked for those who dealt with the customers.

General Electric has used a commercial that promises: "We don't desert you after we deliver it." This commercial says you can count on GE.

Customers want to know that they can count on the people they buy from to give "fix it" service.

☐ The customer wants everything done quickly.

Telephone books are filled with business names that employ the words, "quick," "quik," "jiffy," "instant," and "one-hour."

Pizza makers now offer thirty-minute delivery. Domino's Pizza, for example, subtracts $3 from the bill if the carrier is late.

Jiffy Lube International, which offers a ten-minute oil change, has grown from nine outlets to over one thousand.

Americans resist the relative snail's pace of the U.S. Postal Service. Now, even overnight services such as Federal Express don't get it there fast enough. Overtaking express mail is the facsimile machine which, when paired with a telephone and a second "fax," transmits documents across the country in seconds.

People will take two to three months to shoot a roll of film, but when they take that last shot, they want their pictures back right away.

☐ The more you know about your customers, the better you can serve and sell them.

Mystery writer John D. MacDonald produced one best-selling novel after another in paperback. His books never appeared in hardback first. When one finally did, he told an interviewer how concerned he was. He said, "My audience is $3.95 readers."

He was successful because he knew whom he was writing to. He knew his customers.

No matter how fast we grow or how big we become, we will only continue our success if we keep the customer first. Take this story from the *Wall Street Journal*:

"Joe Bildner founded an upscale grocery store chain called J. Bildner & Sons. In September 1986, he went public, raising $15 million. A year later the once successful company was in serious trouble. Stores that were at one time being opened at a rapid rate were closing with the same speed. The problem was that they forgot the customer along the way. Rapid expansion caused the company to adopt more formal policies for its store managers. However, those new rules caused the stores to lose some of their personalized service. Mr. Bildner says: "I can think of tons of examples of people who followed company policy but made the wrong customer decision."

"For example: A New York customer dropped into one store to find out the cost of buying a roasted turkey, plus a fee for cooking it. The manager went by the book: he multiplied the price of the store's sliced turkey by the number of slices in a whole turkey. It was a ridiculously high price—and it drove the customer away."

☐ Sometimes public perception of service becomes expectation.

For decades, everyone poked fun at AT&T. Was it deserved? Considering the system's awesome complexity, not to mention the dismal phone service in many other nations around the world, AT&T put out a top-notch performance. A similar contention can be made for U.S. airlines, which routinely dispatch eighteen thousand flights a day, the vast majority without a hitch, but the public expects perfection.

☐ Don't argue with customers.

Years ago when Marshall Field was walking through his original store in Chicago, he heard a clerk arguing with a customer. He stopped and asked: "What are you doing?"

The clerk answered: "I'm settling a complaint."

Field said: "No, you're not. Give the lady what she wants."

☐ Service after the sale is important to the sale.

Two friends were talking about buying a VCR. One said that he was going to buy Brand X and the other said that he was thinking about buying Brand Y.

"I'm buying Brand X because when it breaks down, I know the manufacturer will fix it quick."

The other said: "But if you buy Brand Y, it won't break down."

The first man replied: "Yeah, but it might, and I don't want to have to worry about it."

USA Today ran a story about John Barrier, who didn't like the way a bank manager in Spokane, Washington, looked at him. John was wearing construction clothes and got a look as if he had crawled out from under a rock.

The problem began when Barrier went to Old National Bank to cash a $100 check. When he tried to get his parking slip validated to save 60 cents, a receptionist refused, saying he hadn't conducted a transaction. "You have to make a deposit," she told him.

When told he was a substantial depositor, she looked at him as if . . . well.

He asked to see the manager, who also refused to stamp the ticket. Barrier went to the bank headquarters vowing to withdraw his $2 million-plus unless the manager apologized. No one called. So the next day, he withdrew over $1 million.

☐ Treat every customer as if they have a million dollars because they may.

☐ Treat your customers right—customers are important if you view them for their lifetime purchasing power.

Stanley Marcus's father, the founder of Neiman-Marcus, gave Stanley some valuable advice early in his career. It was advice that later helped build Neiman-Marcus into a first-class store. A woman ruined a dress she had worn just once and wanted her money back. His father told him to give the woman her money back, and Stanley argued that they shouldn't do it since the woman had obviously abused the dress. Stanley continued to press his point since the manufacturer wasn't going to help pay for it. His father reminded him that the woman wasn't doing business with the manufacturer, she was doing business with Neiman's. His father told him that it didn't matter if it cost $200 to get a customer, and he didn't want to lose her over a $175 dress. He also told Stanley to refund the money with a smile. During the years, the woman spent over $500,000 at Neiman-Marcus.

D

DEBT

A bar owner said, "I opened this place fifteen years ago with $78 in my pocket. We've been tremendously successful. Today I'm $298,000 in debt."

"An acquaintance is a person we know well enough to borrow from but not well enough to lend to."

Ambrose Bierce

"He spends money as if he can't stand to keep anything that has anybody else's picture on it."

Jeanne Robertson, humorist

The nation's economy started to go to hell when it became possible for people to charge more than they could carry.

"People usually borrow because they want to get rich soon; the journey should be as much fun as the destination, so why take chances?"

Warren Buffett

"Paying alimony is like having the TV on after you have fallen asleep."

Doc Blakely, humorist

☐ It takes money to make money.

"Show me a millionaire, and I will show you almost invariably a heavy borrower."

William Nickerson

Some debt is good. Like the farmer's attitude toward natural fertilizer. Using it may be an unpleasant experience, but it sure can do a lot for productivity.

"Live within your income even if you have to borrow to do it."
Josh Billings

Prospective borrower at a loan company: "Just enough to tide me over until I can get a credit card."

☐ Some people go into debt for the wrong reasons.
This conversation was about what parents do for their kids these days:

First Parent: "I'm proud to say that I've worked for thirty years, saved, scrimped, budgeted, and invested, just so I could give my kids what I never had."
Second Parent: "And what's that?"
First Parent: "A father up to his armpits in debt."

A man said he had arrived at that point in life where he was "just about even" financially.
He said, "I figure I owe about the same number of people that I don't owe."

Sometimes we view debt like the federal government. Their long-range goal is to have both massive defense spending and a balanced budget. That way, if World War III does start, at least we'll know it's paid for.

President [name the current president] is ready to help Mexico with its debt crisis. That's like Liz Taylor offering to help Zsa Zsa Gabor with her marriage problems.

☐ There are lots of uses for credit cards.
In his book *Minding the Store*, Stanley Marcus wrote that one of Neiman-Marcus's customers landed in jail after a drunken brawl during a Texas-Oklahoma football game. The judge set bail for $250, but the man was away from home and didn't know anyone in Dallas who could help him with the bail money. Eventually the man pulled out his Neiman-Marcus credit card and the judge gave him permission to call the store. A Neiman vice president arranged for the bail and charged it to his Neiman's account.

My friend's aunt, in her seventies and traveling alone in Italy, became ill and was advised to fly home. Two hours after her plane took off from Rome, one engine conked out and another caught fire, so they had to turn back. After they landed safely, the flight attendant told the woman that she was the calmest of all the passengers during the crisis.
The old woman answered briskly, "Well, at my age, I'm living on borrowed time, and I'm taking this trip on borrowed money. So I figured I didn't have much to lose!"

DECISIONS

A frustrated executive has replaced the "In" and "Out" trays on his desk with one labeled "Stalled."

"Men grow making decisions and assuming responsibilities for them."
Bill Marriott, Sr.

"There is no more miserable human being than the one in whom nothing is habitual but indecision."
William James

There is a Texas saying about making a bad decision: "He flew all over the pasture and landed in the cow patty.

☐ Not all decisions are going to be right.
"Whenever I make a bum decision, I just go out and make another."
Harry S. Truman

☐ Don't let previous decisions cloud future decisions.
Fletcher Byrom, retired president of Koppers Company, said, "I don't know what a hard decision is. Whenever I make a decision, I start out by recognizing that there's a strong likelihood that I'm going to be wrong. All I can do is the best I can. To worry about it puts obstacles in the way of clear thinking."

☐ I don't mind telling you exactly what I think. I'm undecided.
"When somebody says they need to refer to a committee before making a decision, you have the wrong person."
Jeanne Robertson, humorist

"Decisions put us in charge of our own lives. Every time we make real decisions, we find out who we really are, because we make use of our own priorities and values. On the other hand, difficulty with decisions complicates all aspects of our lives."
Theodore Isaac Rubin, Overcoming Indecisiveness

David Mahoney said that the worst mistakes he ever made were because of the decisions he failed to make.
In 1966, he was the head of Canada Dry. The stock was selling at a low price of $11, and with about two and a half million shares outstanding, he could have bought the entire company for $30 million. About twenty years later, it would have been worth about $700 million.

"One reason executives have trouble making decisions is that they have less decision-making authority than they wish to admit."
Mike Doyle

"To be great, to be a person of stature, a man must have character, judgment, high intelligence, a special aptitude for seeing his problems whole and true—for seeing things as they are, without exaggeration or emotion—and above all the ability of decision, the right decision, of course."

Bernard Law

Robert Townsend said in his best-seller *Up the Organization* that "all decisions should be made as low as possible in the organization. The Charge of the Light Brigade was ordered by an officer who wasn't there looking at the territory."

☐ Our problem in making decisions is we have too many.

It's harder to make decisions today than it ever has been. When I was a kid, there was a soda fountain in a drugstore near my house. They only had three flavors—vanilla, chocolate, or strawberry. It was easy to decide. Today when I go into an ice cream store, they have ten times more choices, and I have trouble deciding.

"Decisions rise to the management level where the person making them is least qualified to do so."

Laurence J. Peters and Raymond Hull, The Peter Principle

"If you want to make decisions, then eliminate all the alternatives with the power of factual data. If you do not want to make decisions, then do us all a favor by staying out of the way."

John Mott, president, AMR Travel Services

Edmund C. Lynch, the founding partner of Merrill, Lynch & Company, said: "If I made a decision fast, I was right 60% of the time. If I made a decision carefully, I'd be right 70%, but it was always worth it."

☐ Indecision will stop your progress.

Before mechanical sorters were invented, the manager of an apple orchard needed a sorter to separate the apples into three sizes. Logically, he selected the best picker he had and promoted him to the position. Before the picker were placed three baskets, each for a different size. The pickers would bring their apples and pile them on a large table beside him, and he was to sort them into the baskets.

Knowing the man to be a good worker, the manager left him at work and went to town. Upon his return, he was shocked to see a mountain of apples completely covering the table and falling off on all sides. There, before the empty baskets, sat his new sorter—with an apple in each hand and a puzzled look on his face. He was a great picker, but he simply couldn't make a decision as to whether an apple was big, little, or middle-sized.

☐ Making decisions is a criterion for success.

It has been my experience that a man who cannot reach a decision promptly once he has all the necessary facts for the decision at hand, cannot be depended upon to carry through any decision he may make. I have also discovered that men who reach decisions promptly usually have the capacity to move with definiteness of purpose in other circumstances."

Andrew Carnegie

☐ No decision can be a bad decision.

Storage Technology developed a disk drive costing $1,500 more than it sold for. Jessie Aweida, president of Storage Technology, raised the price 50 percent, and when that didn't work, killed off the product, after investing $7 million in it. He said, "I believe that making a decision, even a bad decision, is better than making no decision at all."

☐ Make decisions based on information.

Some decisions are not scientific. Some come from the gut. Once Thomas J. Watson, Jr., then chairman of IBM, was being told by an assistant that he had made a decision.

Watson asked, "On just what basis did you reach that decision?

The assistant replied, "In the final analysis, I guess it was a visceral decision."

Watson replied, "Well, if there are going to be any visceral decisions around here, I'd like to use my own viscera."

☐ You don't get paid to make easy decisions.

Marion Folson, the architect of our nation's social security system, said, "You are going to find that 95 percent of all decisions you'll ever make in your career could be made as well by a reasonably intelligent high school sophomore. But they'll pay for the other 5 percent."

Dwight D. Eisenhower nearly blew D-Day because he could not make up his mind on the best moment for the attack. Finally, he said, "No matter what the weather looks like, we have to go ahead now. Waiting any longer could be even more dangerous. So let's move it."

There is a point at which we have to make a leap of faith, the point after which the right decision becomes wrong because it has been made too late.

☐ We can't be like the little boy with the big dog waiting to see where the big dog wants to go so that he can take him there. We must make decisions and learn to live with them.

"The qualities that make a good manager is decisiveness."

Lee Iacocca

☐ Decision-making is a lonely endeavor.

John Connor believed a person must be independent in his approach to all activities and not depend on someone else to make decisions for him. His father encouraged him to get the facts on both sides and come up with a view that reflected his own thinking.

☐ The importance of the decision is in relation to the position of the person making it.

A decision by the president or chairman of the board may change the entire future of the company. Years ago at the Old Martin Company, now Martin-Marietta Corporation, a decision was made by the president to transform the airplane manufacturer into a missile manufacturer; the decision required many years, thousands of men, and millions of dollars to implement.

A similar situation occurred at General Mills after World War II. The decision was made to broaden the food processing company into the research field, to experiment with high altitude weather balloons at the same time it was making Wheaties.

Sigmund Freud and his niece once discussed how difficult it was for some people to make a decision. He said, "I'll tell you what I tell them. I ask them to toss a coin."

His niece said, "I can't believe it. You, a man of science, guided by senseless chance!"

He answered, "I did not say you should follow blindly what the coin tells you. What I want you to do is to note what the coin indicates. Then look into your own reactions. Ask yourself: Am I pleased? Am I disappointed? That will help you to recognize how you really feel about the matter, deep down inside. With that as a basis, you'll then be ready to make up your mind and come to the right decision."

◻ DELEGATION

☐ Good managers delegate.

"Don't do anything someone else can do for you."

Bill Marriott, Sr.

☐ Good managers delegate.

Overburdening yourself means you aren't delegating properly. If you try to do too many jobs at once, it's like spinning china plates on sticks: the longer you keep it up, the greater the odds of a crash.

☐ Not being able to delegate can have a negative effect on a company.

Henry Ford once took over all the decision making at Ford Motor Company. He even set spies about to try to catch his managers actually making decisions on their own. Eventually his company crashed, and it was fifteen years before Ford showed a profit again.

☐ Fear of the loss of power is the reason why some managers don't delegate.

The Roman Emperor Augustus was afraid to delegate and often took personal command of his most troubled provinces. He thought that if others handled the responsibility for the toughest job in his empire, he might be creating an even greater problem than he was solving.

☐ Learn to delegate with freedom.

Paul Meyer, president of the Success Motivation Institute, was quoted on this subject in *Business Management* magazine: "Give your man a project and the freedom to do with it as he wants. Make sure he can either break it or make it on his own. Meanwhile, protect yourself by making sure the project is in an area of his interest. Chances are, the man will work like the devil to make the project 'go.' "

"When you do for a man what he can and should do for himself, you do him a great disservice."

Benjamin Franklin

Homer, in about 700 B.C. had this to say about delegation: "You will certainly not be able to take the lead in all things yourself, for to one man a god has given deeds of war, and to another the dance, to another the lyre and song, and in another widesounding Zeus puts a good mind."

G. Kingsley Ward, Mark My Words

"We are all not capable of everything."

Virgil

If you don't learn to delegate, you will become what Harry S. Truman called "a four-ulcer man in a five-ulcer job."

"Proper delegation is an indication of a manager's trust and faith in his people."

James F. Evered

"We give our managers a lot of responsibility, and we expect them to be fair. A manager should be able to fire somebody he really likes and promote a guy who picks his nose."

Gary Hoover, founder, Bookstop

☐ Pick the right person for the job.

Henry Ford often said that when he had a time-consuming and unpleasant task to do, he would assign the "laziest man I can find" to do the job. He observed, "Within a day or two, he will come up with a quick and easy way to do it."

☐ When delegating, make sure you are understood.

A utility company superintendent took two crews into the field to install poles. He gave each foreman his assignment and left to do other duties, saying he'd be back later to check on their work progress. Upon his return, he asked one foreman how many poles his crew had installed.

First foreman: "Twelve."
Second foreman: "Two."
Superintendent: "Just two? The other crew installed twelve."
Second foreman: "I know. But look how much they left sticking out of the ground."

John Connor said that it is important for managers to resist the temptation to handle every problem personally. "Professionals take pride in doing things for themselves; for example, writing briefs if you're a lawyer. If you're gonna be a generalist, you have to let others do things, and accept their conclusions."

☐ Delegate what someone else can do better.

Trammell Crow, the real estate developer whose buildings make architectural statements around the world, is a great delegator of authority, so much so that he often leaves crucial decisions to others. Actually, Crow just has his own method of delegation.

A colleague once said, "If I wanted to buy a new boiler, Trammell couldn't have cared less. But if I wanted to repave a sidewalk, he was down there making sure the right texture was used."

Crow is an idea man, a dreamer, and he knows it. His greatest value is in design, and he lets others deal with construction deadlines and cost per square foot, items that are the primary concern of most developers.

☐ Successful leaders know how to delegate.

"Ross Perot, CEO of the Perot Group, said, 'I surround myself with smart people, and I tell them what the goal is but I never give them any kind of checklist.' I say, "Next year, we're going to the moon. You're in charge." That's how John F. Kennedy approached the lunar launch. He said, "Within ten years, we're going to put someone on the moon." He never told anyone how to do it, but it happened anyway."
Wess Roberts, Ph.D., Leadership Secrets of Attila the Hun

"The benefits of delegation include:
• Saving time for other pressing work;
• Increasing effectiveness; and
• Providing on-the-job growth for workers.

☐ In any business, the more we can multiply our hands, the more successful we can be.

My father was a cotton farmer. I remember asking him why he had so many farms. He replied, "Son, the more pickers I can find, the more farms I can plant and harvest."

A problem with entrepreneurs is they don't learn to let go of some of their responsibilities so that they can grow.

An example is a successful entrepreneur who almost single-handedly got his company sales to $100,000 a year. When he sought venture capital to expand, the potential investors asked him:

"Who is your president?"

"Me."

"Who is your chief financial officer?"

"Me."

"Who is in charge of sales?"

"Again the answer was "Me."

One of the panelists asked, "How much time do you spend on sales?"

His answer was "About 10 percent."

He was told, "You don't need money to expand. If you spend 100 percent of your time on sales, you should quickly get to the million mark."

☐ Evaluate how you are spending your time.

Bob Fosse, on being replaced as director-choreographer on the short-lived Broadway musical *The Conquering Hero* said: "I conceived this show. I outlined it. I cast it. I choreographed it. I drew the first sketches for the design. I directed it. And the first thing that goes wrong, they blame me!"

■ DEMOCRACY

"Democracy is the worst type of government except for all the other types that have been tried before."

Winston Churchill

"Absolute freedom is not freedom at all, but license."

Erwin D. Canham

"We do not learn the full value of liberty until we are imprisoned."

Heinrich Heine

"The death of democracy is not likely to be an assassination by ambush. It will be a slow extinction from apathy, indifference, and undernourishment."

Robert M. Hutchins

"The only standard of performance that can sustain a free society is excellence."

John R. Silber

"Democracy is based on an educated citizenry."

David T. Kerns, chairman, Xerox

☐ Democracy lasts when it's protected.

Charles Malik, physicist, philosopher, and diplomat, cited the reason throughout history for the failure of nations and that it could have been avoided. "If only they rose to the occasion; if only they were not overwhelmed by their softness and apathy; if only they overcame their greed; if only they knew what was at stake; if only they had trampled underfoot the wide and easy way."

☐ Democracy may be accompanied by the destruction of freedom.

Alexis de Tocqueville visited the United States in the 1830s and wrote: "I think that democratic communities have a natural taste for freedom; left to themselves, they will seek it, cherish it, and view any deprivation of it with regret. But for equality, their passion is ardent, insatiable, incessant, invincible, they call for equality in freedom, and if they cannot obtain that, they still call for equality in slavery. They will endure poverty, servitude, barbariansim, but they will not endure aristocracy."

◼ DETERMINATION

"If a person desires to develop himself along any line whatsoever, the secret of his ultimate success will be found in this, that he has the determination and persistency to live constantly in the presence of his supreme ambition."

John Herman Randall

"The power of your ambition depends wholly on the vigor of the determination behind it. What you accomplish will depend on the amount of live energy, of enthusiasm, and willpower you put into your efforts to achieve."

Randy D. Marsh

"Few things are impossible to diligence."

Samuel Johnson

☐ Don't give up.

"A determined person is one who, when they get to the end of their rope, ties a knot and hangs on."

Joe L. Griffith

"Be like a postage stamp. Stick to something until you get there."

Josh Billings

"If anything is worth trying at all, it's worth trying at least ten times."
Art Linkletter, Yes, You Can

"Great people are just ordinary people with an extraordinary amount of determination."
Garner Dunkerley, Sr., founder, Ennis Business Forms

"It's not whether you get knocked down. It's whether you get up again."
Vince Lombardi, football coach

"The battle of life in most cases is fought uphill, and to win it without a struggle is almost like winning without honor. If there were no difficulties, there would be no success; if there were nothing to struggle for, there would be nothing to be achieved. Difficulties may intimidate the weak, but they act only as a wholesome stimulus to men of resolution and valor. All experience of life, indeed, serves to prove that the impediments thrown in the way of human advancement may, for the most part, be overcome by steady good conduct, honest zeal, activity, perseverance, and by a determination to overcome difficulties."
Edmund Burke

When General Grant was at Shiloh, he thought he was going to fail, but he kept right on. It was just this keeping right on which made him one of the greatest military figures of his age. After his defeat at Shiloh, nearly every newspaper in the United States demanded his removal. Lincoln's friends pleaded with him to give the command to someone else; but to all appeals, Lincoln replied, "I can't spare this man. He fights. He's got the grip of a bulldog, and when he gets his teeth in, nothing can shake him off."

We need to be like Grant—so determined that we are indispensable.

☐ Determination comes from a vision.

Our Apollo and other space programs were not without many temporary defeats. The entire nation wept at the deaths of Virgil Grissom, Edward White, and Roger Chaffee, in a ground test of an Apollo spacecraft. What most people would consider failures were not recognized as such by the mastermind group of our National Aeronautics and Space Administration team. They refused to let anything keep them from achieving their goal.

You have to be single-minded,
Drive only for one thing on which you have decided.
And if it looks as if you might be getting there,
All kinds of people, including some you thought were your loyal friends,
Will suddenly show up . . .
to trip you, blacken you,
And break your spirit.
George S. Patton

☐ Determination of purpose is important.

When astronaut Scott Carpenter was a small boy, he was in lots of trouble. His misconduct led to a near fatal automobile accident. While recuperating, he made a personal determination to settle down. Sticking to that decision made him the second American to orbit the earth.

▊ DISCIPLINE

> "Some people regard discipline as a chore. For me, it is a kind of order that sets me free to fly."
>
> *Julie Andrews*

☐ It takes discipline to get better.

McDonald's Ray Kroc had the discipline to automate every step of the preparation process for his fries and burgers.

A young sentry, on guard duty for the first time, had orders not to admit any car unless it had a special identification seal. The first unmarked car the sentry stopped contained a general. When the officer told his driver to go right on through, the sentry politely said, "I'm new at this, sir. Who do I shoot first, you or the driver?"

It's not enough as a manager to teach your employees how to do the work. You've also got to make sure they do it.

Coach Vince Lombardi put it this way: "A player's got to know the basics of the game and how to play his position. Next, you've got to keep him in line."

That's discipline, and that's what a good manager has got to have.

☐ Discipline helps ensure continued success.

In a business like advertising, where agencies experience rapid growth and then fade from sight, how has Doyal Dane Bernbach maintained their lofty heights for so many years? The secret is the discipline and focus of the leaders, Ned Doyle and Bill Bernback.

ECONOMICS

Economists not only can't agree on the answer, they can't agree on the problem.

An economist is a man who talks about things you don't understand and makes you believe it's your own fault.

I think I've finally pinpointed when we lost control of our economy. It was when we discovered that fifty weeks of work couldn't pay for a two-week vacation.

The economy has improved so much you now have to wait in line at the "cash only" registers when Christmas shopping.

The purpose of learning economics is to avoid being deceived by economists.

An economist is a fortuneteller with a job.

Economic forecasting is the occupation that gives astrology respectability.

Economists are the only people who can make an abundant living without ever being right.

"An economist is a guy with a Phi Beta Kappa key on one end of his watch chain and no watch on the other end."
Alben Barkley

The paradox of economics: At a time when none of the economic theories are working, all the economists are.

The groundhog is like most other economists; it delivers its prediction and then disappears.

President Harry S. Truman used to quip that he was looking for a one-armed economist, one who never could say, "On the one hand this, but on the other hand that."

An economics professor went to some out-of-state city. He liked the hotel so much that, when checking out, he made a reservation for an upcoming visit.

He said, "I want that same room."

When he went in a month later, he reminded the desk clerk of his request.

The clerk said, "Yes, sir, we have the same room set aside for you, but I'm afraid we can't let you have it at the same price. This is a big football weekend, you know, when the demand for rooms exceeds the supply, so . . ."

He said, "You needn't explain. I teach the course."

Henry Ford rarely talked to reporters. But when he did, he seemed to have a ball.

The retired Ford Motor Company chairman toyed with the press once when he appeared before a group of Detroit executives.

Reporter: "Mr. Ford, what is your sense of the direction of the economy next year?"

Ford: "I don't have any sense; I'm retired."

The main qualification for an economist is the ability to forecast what is going to happen tomorrow, next week, next month, and next year—and to have the ability afterward to explain why it didn't happen.

Talking about economics is sometimes difficult. Take this letter to Dear Abby:

"I'm a twenty year old girl, and I've been dating the same boy for seven months. We have been intimate, and I used the pill but now I'm pregnant. I believe he should share the cost of having the baby, but I don't know him well enough to discuss economic matters."

▮ EDUCATION

"The object of education is to prepare the young to educate themselves throughout their lives."

Robert M. Hutchins

"Your education has been a failure no matter how much it has done for your mind, if it has failed to open your heart."

J. A. Rosenkranz

"Education should prepare people not just to earn a living but to live a life—a creative, humane, and sensitive life."

Charles Silberman

"I believe the true road to preeminent success in any line is to make yourself master in that line."

Andrew Carnegie

Father to son: "These days, education is all-important. Either you have to go to college, or start your own business so that you can hire people who did."

"Education will not simply be a prelude to a career, but a lifelong endeavor."

Maud Barkley

"Education is an investment—and never an expense."
Nick Goble, Pennsylvania School Boards Association

☐ Education is the light that shines in the darkness, the lighthouse in a storm.

"There are few earthly things more splendid than a University. In these days of broken frontiers and collapsing values—when every future looks somewhat grim, and every ancient foothold has become something of a quagmire—wherever a University stands, it stands and shines; wherever it exists, the free minds of men, urged on to full and fair inquiry, may still bring wisdom into human affairs."

John Masefield

"What one knows is, in youth, of little moment; they know enough who know how to learn."

Henry Adams

"Fortunately for us, Japan is opening its first business school in the near future. This is likely to produce a measurable drop in Japanese productivity."
Felix Rohatyn, investment banker

Over a hundred years ago, Herbert Spencer, the great philosopher, wrote, "Education has for its object the formation of character."

President Theodore Roosevelt said, "To educate a man in mind and not in morals is to educate a menace to society."

Steven Muller, president of Johns Hopkins University, said: "Universities are turning out highly skilled barbarians because we don't provide a framework of values to young people who more and more are searching for it."

"Education is the transmission of civilization. Civilization is not inherited, it has to be learned again by each new generation."
David T. Kerns, chairman, Xerox

"Education is the ability to listen to almost anything without losing your temper or your self-confidence."
Robert Frost

"When you are educated, you'll believe only half of what you hear. When you're intelligent, you know which half."
Jerome Perryman

"An educated man is one who can entertain a new idea, entertain another person, and entertain himself."
Anonymous

"Whom, then, do I call educated? First, those who control circumstances instead of being mastered by them; those who meet all occasions manfully and act in accordance with intelligent thinking; those who are honorable in all dealings, who treat good-naturedly persons and things that are disagreeable; and furthermore, those who hold their pleasure under control and are not overcome by misfortune; finally, those who are not spoiled by success."
Socrates

▢ EFFICIENCY

"There can be no economy where there is no efficiency."
Benjamin Disraeli

"It is more than probable that the average man could, with no injury to his health, increase his efficiency fifty per cent."
Walter Dill Scott

☐ It is better to be effective than efficient.
"Effectiveness is doing the right thing, whereas efficiency is doing things right."
Daniel Stamp, founder, Priority Management Systems

The late-nineteenth-century industrial engineer Frederick J. W. Taylor observed that the workers under his supervision at Midvale Steel Company in

Philadelphia brought their own shovels to work, regardless of what size coal lumps they would have to shovel. He suggested to management that the company furnish shovels corresponding to the size and weight of the individual load, thus increasing the total amount of coal each worker could shovel in a day.

To become more efficient, we need to evaluate our shovels. Are we performing every task in the most efficient manner?

☐ Planning saves time and makes you more efficient.

"Marilyn Powers, a veteran executive secretary, found that increasing responsibilities were overwhelming her. It became almost impossible to keep up with all of the details connected with managing the work flow of an expanding sales office. When convinced that she could profit from laying out her work by the day, week, and month, she found that having the *total picture in focus* increased her efficiency tremendously. By spending thirty minutes a week in planning, Marilyn found that all of the important details relating to various jobs were remembered, pressure decreased, and the work got out on time."

Genevieve Smith, Genevieve Smith's Deluxe Handbook for the Executive Secretary

◨EMPLOYEE BENEFITS

☐ Benefits can signal the type of company you work for.

Overheard: "You get five days sick pay the first year and ten days a year after that. They must figure the longer you work here, the sicker you get."

☐ Some benefits will never be seen.

Personnel director to job applicant: "Retirement plan? I wouldn't worry about that. You'd be out of your mind to work here that long."

☐ Employee benefits can be counterproductive.

I asked my neighbor's wife, "When will your husband's leg be well so he can return to work?"
She said, "Not for a long time."
I said, "Why I thought it was almost well."
She explained, "It was—but then compensation set in."

☐ Too many employee benefits aren't good.

Job applicant: "The last company I worked for paid for my Blue Cross, Blue Shield, life insurance, vacations, profit sharing, year-end bonuses, and pension plan."

Personnel director: "Why did you leave?"
Job applicant: "They went broke."

☐ You don't always have to compensate employees with money.

One company had such a positive and profitable relationship with all its clients that it decided, after extensive review, not to give an incentive program to its salespeople. The company was afraid the salespeople, being on salary, would start thinking about their short-term profit instead of taking care of the client. So instead of offering a new incentive program that would cost the company $40,000 annually and only benefit salespeople, they offered a new, all-inclusive dental plan that only cost the company $10,000 per year. Immediately many employees were able to provide for their children orthodontic care that they couldn't afford previously.

☐ By encouraging incentives for good health, companies are realizing more and more that healthy employees boost profits far beyond the cost. For example:

Hospital Corporation of America pays participants 24 cents for each mile run or walked, each ¼ mile swum, or 4 miles biked.

Johnson & Johnson's "Live for Life" program awards health-oriented prizes for adhering to good health practices (seat belts, workshops, smoke detectors, and so on).

The Scherer Lumber Company is proud to say, "We have no sick pay, we have well pay." For each month workers are not ill or late, they are given two extra hours of pay. At the end of the year, if they have missed no more than three days, they collect a $300 bonus.

SpeedCall Corporation gives $7 a week for not smoking at work. It's interesting to note that at the end of four years, smoking had declined by 65 percent, and the number of insurance claims filed by former smokers dropped 50 percent.

The U.S. Health Care Systems gives out three hundred apples a day to employees in their smoke-free facilities.

Control Data Corporation reports that nonexercises cost the company an extra $115 a year in health care costs.

Lockheed Missiles and Space Company estimates that in five years it saved $1 million in life insurance costs through its wellness programs. Absenteeism is 60 percent lower and turnover rate 13 percent lower among regular exercisers.

Dallas schoolteachers who enrolled in a fitness program took an average of three fewer sick days per year, a saving of almost a half million dollars a year in substitute pay alone.

Marriott Hotel housekeepers do an early morning poolside aerobics class; the result has been fewer pulled muscles on the job.

Atco Properties pays $100 per pound lost during a five-month period of time, $500 to stop smoking, and $500 for regularly climbing stairs.

◨ EMPLOYEE RELATIONS

☐ Human relations pays off in quality and increased productivity.

"Employees make the best product when they like where they work."
Gary Hollister, Merle Norman

The name employees are called says how you feel about them. For example, at NCR, employees are called NCR people. Domino's Pizza has team members, team leaders, and the coaching staff. Du Pont is steering away from "employee" in favor of "people" and "team members."

☐ Never underestimate the value of your employees.

"You can take my factories, burn up my building, but give me my people and I'll build the businesses right back again."
Henry Ford

Companies that spend time on work-force relations get better results than those that don't. For example, Black & Decker treats the highest and lowest employees as equally as possible. They do this by having the same restaurant for every employee, and everyone gets the same percentage raise, paid on the same day.

"I believe people will do their best, provided that they are getting proper support."
Debbie Fields, found, Mrs. Fields Cookies

☐ Good customer relations starts with good employee relations.

"Motivate employees, train them, care about them, and make winners of them. At Marriott we know that if we treat our employees correctly, they'll treat the customers right. And if the customers are treated right, they'll come back."
Bill Marriott, Jr., chairman, Marriott

☐ Show employees that they are important.

A. G. Edwards & Son operates with a small-town family feeling. Howard R. Posner left E. F. Hutton's New York office to head the syndication department of Edwards. He recalled that five months after he joined the firm, he lunched with Ben Edwards for forty minutes. He said, "Business never came up once."

☐ Good human relations is showing people they are not just employees but human beings you are interested in.

☐ Employee relations is realizing that it's the frontline employees that build an organization.

People like Tammy Senkbeil. Tammy worked as a cashier for Giant Foods store. One Saturday night at 10:30 when she was closing out her register, she found a discrepancy, and after forty-five minutes of auditing her checks, she found the problem and called the family with the news. Giant owed the couple $9. Interestingly, the couple didn't have an address or telephone number printed on the check. But Tammy tracked the couple down on her own time. It's employees like Tammy that made the multibillion-dollar, Washington, D.C.–based Giant Foods a first-class organization.

☐ The right personal philosophy can make you successful.

Arthur Imperatore, president of A-P-A Transport, said, "My whole philosophy is that we build men. Incidentally, we move freight."

A-P-A is at the top of a tough industry.

ENCOURAGEMENT

☐ If you aren't encouraged where you work, find someplace to work where you will be.

My humorist friend, Joe Larson, once told me, "My friends didn't believe that I can become a successful speaker. So I did something about it. I went out and found me some new friends!"

Think of how much more people could accomplish if they were encouraged.

When Nathaniel Hawthorne, a heartbroken man, went home to tell his wife that he had been fired from his job in a customhouse and confessed that he was a failure, she surprised him with a exclamation of joy.

She said triumphantly, "Now, you can write your book!"

He replied with sagging confidence, "Yes, and what shall we live on while I am writing it?"

To his amazement, she opened a drawer and pulled out a substantial amount of money.

He exclaimed, "Where on earth did you get that?"

She answered, "I have always known that you were a man of genius. I knew that someday you would write a masterpiece. So every week out of the money you have given me for housekeeping, I have saved something; here is enough to last us for one whole year."

From her trust and confidence came one of the greatest novels of American literature—*The Scarlet Letter*.

☐ Encourage employees to take risks that will move your company forward.

H. J. Heinz's highly successful frozen foods subsidiary, Ore-Ida, was trying an intriguing variation on positive reinforcement to encourage more learning and risk-taking in its research activities. It had carefully defined what it calls the "perfect failure," and had arranged to shoot off a cannon in simple recognition that all research and development is inherently risky, that the only way to succeed at all is through lots of tries, that management's primary objective should be to induce lots of tries, and that a good try that results in some learning is to be celebrated even when it fails.

John Powell told the story about the time a friend of his was in the Bahamas and saw a crowd gathered on a pier. He went over to the pier and saw a young man getting ready to make a solo journey around the world in a homemade boat. Everyone on the pier was offering pessimistic warnings, telling the sailor of all the things that could go wrong. "There will be storms, the sun is too hot, you'll run out of food." Hearing all these discouraging words, Powell's friend shouted to the sailor, "Bon voyage! Good luck! You are really something!"

□ Offer encouragement to your coworkers so that they can achieve the seemingly impossible feat.

ENTHUSIASM

"Nothing great was ever achieved without enthusiasm."
Ralph Waldo Emerson

"Every production of genius must be the product of enthusiasm."
Benjamin Disraeli

"The very first step toward success in any job is to become interested in it."
William Osler

"When people are bored, it is primarily with their own selves that they are bored."
Eric Hoffer

"The real secret of success is enthusiasm. Yes, more than enthusiasm I would say excitement. I like to see men get excited. When they get excited, they make a success of their lives."
Walter Chrysler

"Nothing is so contagious as enthusiasm."
Samuel Taylor Coleridge

"Without enthusiasm there is no progress in the world."
Woodrow Wilson

"Apathy can be overcome by enthusiasm, and enthusiasm can be aroused by two things: first, an idea which takes the imagination by storm; and second, a definite, intelligible plan for carrying that idea into action."
Arnold Toynbee

"I have found enthusiasm for work to be the most priceless ingredient in any recipe for success."

Samuel Goldwyn

"If you don't have enthusiasm, you don't have anything."
Kemmons Wilson, Sr., founder, Holiday Inns

"The great accomplishments of man have resulted from the transmission of ideas and enthusiasm."

Thomas J. Watson, Jr., IBM

"Nobody can be successful if he doesn't love his work, love his job.
David Sarnoff, RCA

"No person who is enthusiastic about his work has anything to fear from life."

Samuel Goldwyn, Metro-Goldwyn-Mayer

J. Paul Getty ranked enthusiasm ahead of imagination, business acumen, and ambition.

Donald Kendall, PepsiCo's chairman, said that he favors people who are enthusiastic and "on fire" with the work they are doing.

☐ Enthusiasm can turn losers into winners.

When Vince Lombardi took over the Green Bay Packers, they were at the bottom. In 1958, they lost 10 out of their 12 games, tied 1 and won 1. When they came to camp in June of 1959, the players were greeted by a new coach, Vince Lombardi.

According to an article in *Guideposts* magazine, the new coach said, "Gentlemen, we are going to have a football team. We are going to win some games. Get that!"

Now how were they going to do that?

He said, "You are going to learn to block, run and tackle. You are going to outplay all the teams that come up against you."

Then he threw the clincher!

He ordered, "You are to have confidence in me and enthusiasm for my system. Hereafter, I want you to think of only three things: your home, your religion, and the Green Bay Packers! Let enthusiasm take ahold of you!"

☐ It is the irresistible power of enthusiasm—

that enabled Noah Webster to spend thirty-six years on his dictionary,
that kept George Stephenson working for fifteen years to perfect his locomotive,
that saw Thomas Edison endure ten thousand defeats before he perfected the incandescent lamp,

and that was the driving force that enabled Cyrus W. Field to endure nearly thirteen years of anxious watching and ceaseless toil and over thirty voyages across the Atlantic Ocean, before he successfully laid the Atlantic cable.

☐ We are all born excited, and if we've lost it, we can get it back.

Mark Twain was once asked the reason for his success.
He said, "I was born excited."

Pete Rose was asked which goes first on a baseball player—his eyes, his legs, or his arm. He said, "None of these things. It's when his enthusiasm goes that he's through as a player."

☐ Enthusiasm for something is worth more than money.

When Charlotte Ford, wealthy daughter of Henry Ford, was asked why she started her own highly regarded line of women's fashions, she said, "Because getting up in the morning and having something to do is terrific."

Enthusiasm is a commodity more important than all other commodities: It will find solutions where there appear to be none, and it will achieve success when success was thought impossible.

☐ ENTREPRENEURS

"In industry, it is never the industry leader who makes the big leap. On the contrary, it is the inventor or small guy who makes the big leap."
Burton Klein

☐ Entrepreneurs lead the pack.

"When the Mayflower hit the beach, somebody had to jump off first."
Karl H. Vesper

Entrepreneurs understand that you can't examine every option, limit every threat, analyze and eliminate every risk. They don't wait until every thing is perfect.

Alan Zakon, CEO of the Boston Consulting Group, defined an entrepreneur as someone who can look at the products and services, even commonplace ones, and see what others fail to see: "opportunities to create new value."

☐ Not all entrepreneurs come from bleak beginnings.

Fred W. Smith, founder of Federal Express, was a graduate of Yale University, and his father built Greyhound's bus system in the South. He also used $4 million of his family's money to get started.

It's small entrepreneurs who make America prosperous. Take Edwin Land who started Polaroid Corporation. He was still in college when he started tinkering in his barn. About twenty years later, Land gave the world the first instant camera and created thousands of jobs.

Most of the great corporations today were started by one person who followed through on an idea.

Here are a few familiar names: IBM, Electronic Data Systems, General Motors, Xerox, Control Data, Polaroid, and Texas Instruments.

☐ Entrepreneurs show themselves early.

When John D. Rockefeller was seven years old, he was raising turkeys for profit.

☐ Entrepreneurs want to work for themselves.

David Packard, founder of Hewlett-Packard, said that he didn't start his company to make a lot of money. He wanted to be his own boss, and working for General Electric, he didn't think he'd ever be his own boss.

"Entrepreneurs have an action orientation, but it is more than that. They want to build something, to make something. The pride is in taking a product and making it commercial."

Allan A. Kennedy, Corporate Cultures

To be an entrepreneur takes more than just a good idea. As the founder of Atari said, "The critical ingredient is getting off your butt and doing something. It's as simple as that. A lot of people have ideas, but here are few who decide to do something about them now. Not tomorrow. Not next week. But today. The true entrepreneur is a doer, not a dreamer."

"Entrepreneurs have an action orientation, but it is more than that. They want to build something, to make something. The pride is in taking a product and making it commercial."

Allan A. Kennedy

☐ Entrepreneurs have a special talent.

"Say a man is walking down the road barefoot. It's a hot day, his feet are sore, and he sees a piece of leather in the road. He imagines he could make a pair of shoes. That's an entrepreneurial act: to see something over there that fits in this niche here. You can't program that, you can't plan it."

James Buchanan, Nobel laureate

☐ Entrepreneurs create because of fulfillment more than money.

We've heard the old saying, "Like what you do and do what you like." Mike Whitaker took action on this idea. He took his love for bass fishing,

$5,000 life savings, and founded Operation Bass. In less than ten years, he had $3.5 million in revenues and profits of $250,000, making it the country's largest organizer of fishing tournaments.

☐ Entrepreneurs believe in making things happen. They don't wait for someone to tell them that it's okay.

People like William Paley, Walt Disney, or Edwin Land never waited for a printout to see if they should launch a network, a fantasy world, or a technological wonder.

☐ Entrepreneurs succeed by finding solutions to problems.

An entrepreneur is like a fireman running into a situation everyone else is trying to leave. But successful entrepreneurs know what they're doing. They have a mission and a plan just like the firemen. They know what caused the fire and how to put it out.

☐ Entrepreneurs must have faith.

The habit of looking on the dark side of any situation is fatal to a businessperson. Optimism is the heart and soul of the entrepreneur. If he didn't believe in the future, he couldn't invest in it.

New companies are always needed. Look at the Fortune 500 of twenty-five years ago, or ten years, or even five. Many of those companies, including some former "highfliers," are gone as if vaporized.

☐ Entrepreneurs keep the economy energized.

☐ Entrepreneurship is finding a new way to do something.

Jack Miller sells office supplies via direct mail, but he thinks the key to increased sales is in luring new customers with the personal computer. Miller, president of Quill Corporation in Chicago, hooked up all of his 650,000 customers to a personal computer ordering system. For $14.95 they are able to use specially designed software to order items in just thirty seconds.

☐ Entrepreneurs are never content with their success. They are always looking for new territory.

Julia Walsh, a frequent panelist on the popular PBS TV series "*Wall Street Journal*," is an outstanding example of seeking new horizons. She was the first woman graduate of the Harvard Business School's Advanced Management Program, the first woman member of the American Stock Exchange, and the first to represent the securities industry on the Amex Board of Governors. In 1977, President Jimmy Carter offered her the commissionership of the Securities Exchange Commission, but she chose instead to form her own investment firm, Julia M. Walsh & Sons.

☐ People will always make mistakes, and that's good news for entrepreneurs.

Joseph Tilkin started Woopps Enterprises in Paterson, New Jersey to repair damaged garments. His idea was to repair large shipments of damaged clothes for retailers so that the salvaged goods didn't have to be scrapped.

The concept is that Woopps not only saves retailers the time it takes to send items back to the manufacturer, but it also saves money. For example, Woopps once repaired 144,000 pairs of shoes that were sewn incorrectly. By hiring Woopps, the loss was reduced to just 20 percent.

☐ An entrepreneur needs the agility of a juggler.

There is a famous circus act where the juggler starts one plate spinning on a stick, then he puts the stick on a slot on a table and starts another plate spinning on another stick, and then he gets a third one started. By this time, the first plate needs some help to keep going. Now he starts a fourth plate spinning and gives some needed attention to plates two and three. The juggler has to keep moving around, keeping all the plates spinning.

An entrepreneur is like that. He needs to keep moving to keep all the plates spinning.

☐ Entrepreneurship can be just taking an old idea to market.

If you are fishing at 40 degrees below zero and you pull a fish up through the ice, an obvious thing happens. The fish freezes, fast and hard. But Clarence Birdseye, grinding out a living as a fur trader in Labrador in the years before World War I, noted something not so obvious about these quick-frozen fish.

When thawed, the fish were tender, flaky, and moist—almost as good as fresh caught. The same was true for the frozen caribou, geese, and heads of cabbage that he stored outside his cabin during the long Canadian winter.

That observation, recalled a decade later, made Clarence Birdseye a wealthy man. The quick-freezing process pioneered by Birdseye produced frozen foods that were palatable to consumers. It created a multibillion-dollar industry, and gave farmers the incentive to grow crops for a year-round market. In the case of frozen orange juice, it created a product where none existed before.

"There was nothing remarkable about what I had done." Birdseye wrote years later, noting that northern aboriginal people had practiced quick-freezing for centuries. "What I accomplished . . . was merely to make quick-frozen goods available to the general public."

Most entrepreneurs are seldom qualified to stay with their "baby" all the way to maturation.

People like Steven Jobs were eventually forced out at Apple Computer, the company he founded. A noted exception was Kenneth Olsen, founder of Digital Equipment Corporation. He was one of the founding partners in the 1950s, and almost forty years later he still heads the company.

◻ ETHICS

"Some people are like dirty clothes. They only come clean when they're in hot water."

J. W. Sullivan

☐ Maintaining business ethics isn't always easy.

"Ever notice how much less immoral something seems after we discover how much fun it is?"

George E. Scherer

Some companies are going beyond the usual degree of ethics. For example, Raytheon Company has a director of ethics compliance. All wrong-doings, difficult personnel issues, and ethical quandaries are reported to the same person.

☐ It's always better in the long term to be ethical.

Robert A. Cialdini used the example of a trusted mechanic who told him the repairs necessary on his car would be $45. The previous mechanic had estimated $500. Cialdini said the mechanic was ethical and he has him as a customer for life.

Marvin Bower, former managing partner of McKinsey & Company, said, "There is no such thing as business ethics. There's only one kind—you have to adhere to the highest standards."

"There's only one standard. Once you're stuck on the flypaper, you're stuck. If you don't set a high standard, you can't expect your people to act right."

Donald Kendall, chairman, PepsiCo

"I don't believe unethical people get ahead in business. If ethics are poor at the top, that behavior is copied down through the organization."
Robert Noyce, inventor of the silicon chip

Donald T. Regan, former chairman of Merrill Lynch, secretary of the treasury, and White House, chief of staff, advises executives who suspect malfeasance "to dig it out, and then call it to the attention of the authorities."

☐ We usually accept ethical standards in others that we accept in ourselves.

Salomon Rothschild was walking down a street in Vienna. A pickpocket tried to lift a silk handkerchief from the banker's pocket. A friend tried to warn Rothschild: "That man is trying to steal your handkerchief."

Rothschild said, "So what? We all started small."

Honeywell and many other defense contractors have extensive education programs that drill employees in doing something from deciding whether to take a $10 meal to properly filling out a time card. The company tries to make it easier for employees to detect black and white and not put everything in a gray area. Paul Towne, corporate director of ethics at Honeywell said, "We can't mandate morals. We ask employees to bring their ethics to work with them."

EXCELLENCE

"Set and demand standards of excellence. Anybody who accepts mediocrity—in school, in job, in life—is a guy who compromises. And when the leader compromises, the whole damn organization compromises."
Charles Knight Emerson

"Nobody gets to run the mill by doing run-of-the-mill work.'
Thomas J. Frye

"The road to business success is paved by those who continually strive to produce better products or services. It does not have to be a great technological product like television. Ray Kroc of McDonald's fame did it with a simple hamburger."
G. Kingsley Ward, Mark My Words

☐ Everything starts with a commitment to excellence.
"Caterpillar's operating principles seem to be an individual version of the Boy Scout law: the main principles are excellence of quality, reliability of performance, and loyalty in dealer relationships."
Article in Fortune

☐ Do anything for excellence.
For over thirty years, Al Boyajian has been operating Sears Restaurant in San Francisco. His longtime patrons wait up to forty-five minutes to eat. Al said that the reason was because he treated every customer as if they were guests in his home. He constantly asked them how he could improve the "little" things.
☐ Striving for excellence is what keeps customers coming back.

☐ You get more if you expect more.
Former Secretary of State Henry Kissinger asked an assistant to prepare an analysis. The assistant worked day and night. An hour after he gave it to Kissinger, he got it back. There was a note attached that said redo it.
The assistant stayed up all night redoing the report. Again Kissinger asked him to redo it.
After redoing the report three times, the assistant asked to see Kissinger. He told him, "I've done the best I can do."
Kissinger: "In that case, I'll read it now."

☐ Striving for excellence is what it's all about.

☐ Excellence comes from practice.

A lady told a concert pianist after a recital, "I'd give half of my life to be able to play the piano that well."
The pianist's response: "Madam, that's exactly what I gave."

EXCUSES

"It takes less time to do a thing right than to explain why you did it wrong."

Henry Wadsworth Longfellow

Business office receptionist to salesman: "I'm sorry, but he isn't seeing anyone until his biorhythm goes back up."

Justifying a fault doubles it.

"Unwillingness easily finds an excuse."

Benjamin Franklin

"He is foolish to blame the sea who is shipwrecked twice."

Publilius Syrus

"He who is good at making excuses is seldom good for anything else."

Benjamin Franklin

"Excuses interest no one except the competition."

Overheard by a NFL football coach

"Ninety percent of the work done in this country is done by people who don't feel well."

Theodore Roosevelt

"An important task of a manager is to reduce his people's excuses for failure."

Robert Townsend

☐ No one got successful making problems into excuses:
Colonel Sanders was "too old" to start a business.
The Wright brothers knew that no one had ever flown.
Florence Chadwick knew that others had died trying to cross the English Channel.
Henry Ford faced a "lack of demand" for his automobiles.
David was too young, too unskilled, and too poorly equipped to face Goliath.

After Fred Astaire's first screen test, the memo from the testing director of MGM, dated 1933, said, "Can't act! Slightly bald! Can dance a little!" Astaire kept that memo over the fireplace in his Beverly Hills home.

An "expert" said of Vince Lombardi, "He possesses minimal football knowledge. Lacks motivation."

Someone said of Albert Einstein, "He doesn't wear socks and forgets to cut his hair. Could be mentally retarded."

Socrates was called "an immoral corruptor of youth."

☐ Sometimes there isn't a good excuse.

Samuel Johnson spent years compiling the first significant English dictionary. Along the way, he made a few goofs, like identifying the "pastern" as the knee of a horse, when any person of learning knew it was part of the hoof.

A critic assailed, "How could you make such a mistake?"

Johnson said, "Ignorance, madam! Pure ignorance!"

☐ Ambitious people don't make excuses.

"People are always blaming their circumstances for what they are. I don't believe in circumstances. The people who get on in this world are the people who get up and look for the circumstances they want, and if they can't find them, make them."

George Bernard Shaw

☐ Losers blame their circumstances, winners rise above them.

Norman Vincent Peale was told by a young man that he wanted to start his own business but that he didn't have any money.

Peale told him, "Empty pockets never held anyone back. Only empty heads and empty hearts can do that."

Aristotle Onassis, at one time one of the world's richest men, had a plaque on the wall behind his desk so that the employees who came into his office could easily read it. It read, "Find a way, or make one."

Onassis didn't tolerate excuses, and we should not either.

The time had come for a retiring chairman to turn over his company to his successor. After the standard speeches and banquets, the old chairman handed over two envelopes to his replacement. One envelope was marked number 1 and the other number 2.

His replacement asked, "What are these for?"

The old chairman answered, "When a management crisis arises and you want to know what to do, open envelope number 1."

Sure enough, a few years later a crisis faced the new chairman. He went into the privacy of his executive office and opened envelope number 1. It read, "Blame your predecessor."

Relieved, he followed the advice. Then a few years later another crisis developed and he found the second envelope. Looking for a solution to the problem, he opened the faded envelope, and the contents said, "Prepare two envelopes."

☐ Blaming someone else is a favorite excuse.

One way to reduce or eliminate excuses is to make each department compete with outside vendors.

After the AT&T divestiture, Bell Atlantic set up a structure where each department must bill other departments for their services. Before this idea was started, various departments made lots of excuses. For example, the information systems area used to respond to the needs of other departments with, "We can't do that, we don't have the time, or we don't have the money." Now that information systems must show a profit, they are much more responsive because they can't survive making excuses.

☐ EXECUTIVES

Born executive: the one whose father owns the place.

"An executive knows how to be wrapped up in his work without being tied down."

Ann H. Griffith

An executive is one who never puts off until tomorrow what he can get someone else to do today.

"The single most important factor in determining the climate of an organization is the top executive."

Charles Galloway

"Executive ability consists in getting the right men in the right place and keeping them willingly at the top notch."

Herbert G. Stockwell

"The best executive is the one who has sense enough to pick good men to do what he wants done, and self-restraint enough to keep from meddling with them while they do it."

Theodore Roosevelt

☐ The same principles of management hold true whether it's a controller's section or a paper bag company.

"Executives have the same qualifications everywhere—getting along with people, monitoring them, and managing them."

Alan Haemer, U.S. Air Force

"There is a tendency for the person in the most powerful hierarchical position to spend all his or her time performing trivial tasks."
Laurence J. Peter

☐ Too many CEOs lose touch with their customers.

Lewis H. Young, one-time editor in chief of *Business Week*, said "I don't meet many CEOs who are concerned about their customers; in fact, I don't run across many who ever see any customers."

"The single most important function of a chief executive officer is to surround himself with individuals who are more astute and knowledgeable in their positions than he is."
Edward L. Flom, chairman, Florida Steel

☐ Executives need to stay in touch.

Philip K. Wrigley, chairman of the world's biggest chewing-gum company, still works in his shirtsleeves from 8:30 to 5:00 every day, answers his own telephone. He warns, "One can't get too uppity. I went into our New York office one day, and they asked who was calling. I told them it didn't make a bit of difference. It might be a guy wanting to buy some gum—and that's all that mattered."

☐ EXPERIENCE

"Experience has taught me this, that we undo ourselves by impatience."
Michel de Montaigne

Experience teaches you to recognize a mistake when you've made it again.

"Experience is the name everyone gives to his mistakes."
Woodrow Wilson

☐ Our experience makes us what we are.

An optimist is a father who will let his son take the new car on a date. A pessimist is one who won't. A cynic is one who did.

"Experience is not what happens to a man. It's what a man does with what happens to him."
Aldous Huxley

☐ Sometimes the lack of experience is good.

When you are young, you are not experienced enough to know you cannot possibly do the things you are doing.

☐ Experience can be more important than education.

"MBA's know everything but understand nothing."

Lee Iacocca

"Every experience is worth having."

Henry Ford

☐ It's not experience but what kind that matters.

A man asked his boss why three other people were promoted past him. He said, "Boss, I have twenty years of experience in this job."

The boss replied, "No, you don't have twenty years of experience. You have one year of experience twenty times. You've been making the same mistake since you first started."

☐ Experience is a great teacher.

Reportedly IBM's Tom Watson was asked if he was going to fire an employee who made a mistake that cost IBM $600,000.

He said, "No, I just spent $600,000 training him. Why would I want somebody else to hire his experience?"

FAILURE

"My great concern is not whether you have failed, but whether you are content with your failure."

Abraham Lincoln

"Little minds are tamed and subdued by misfortunes, but great minds rise above them."

Washington Irving

Failure either crushes a life, or solidifies it. The wounded oyster mends his shell with pearl.

"Failures either do not know what they want, or jibe at the price."

W. H. Auden

"Show me a thoroughly satisfied man, and I will show you a failure."

Thomas Edison

"The only failure which lacks dignity is the failure to try."

Malcolm F. MacNeil

"There is no failure except in no longer trying. There is no defeat except from within, no really insurmountable barrier save our own inherent weakness of purpose."

Elbert Hubbard

"Setbacks lead to innovation and renewed achievement."

John Condry, educator

"Failure is the path of least persistence."

Anonymous

"Failure is the opportunity to begin again, more intelligently."

Henry Ford

"Failure is a man who has blundered, but is not able to cash in on the experience."

Elbert Hubbard

☐ Don't worry about your failures.
Even a horse, though he has four feet, occasionally stumbles.

"The danger is not in a fall, but in failing to rise."

Anonymous

☐ Failure is the stepladder to success.

Thomas J. Watson, Jr., past president of IBM, said that the formula for success is to double your failure rate.

"Failure is a harsh teacher, but the best."

Ervin L. Glaspy

"People are known as much by the quality of their failures as by the quality of their successes."

Mark McCormack

"If at first you don't succeed, destroy all evidence that you tried."

Newt Hielscher, humorist

Robert Schuller in his book *Tough Times Never Last, But Tough People Do,* said, "Failure is never final and success is never-ending. Success is a journey, not a destination."

☐ Be determined to give your best and you will win.

Famed attorney Edward Bennett Williams said: "When I come out of a courtroom, I never feel like I've lost, because I always give my client my best. If you give your best, you don't lose. The case may be lost, but I don't lose."

Henry Ford, who was very successful at making cars, failed at almost every enterprise outside of cars.

Bill Cosby gave this advice to comic Arsenio Hall early in his career: "I don't know the key to success, but the key to failure is trying to please everybody."

"People fail in direct proportion to their willingness to accept socially acceptable excuses for failure."

W. Steven Brown, president, Fortune Group

"If you think education is expensive, try failure."

John Condry, educator

"I have had a lot of success with failure."

Thomas Edison

☐ We all make mistakes, but it's overcoming them that determines our eventual success.

"There is the greatest practical benefit in making a few failures early in life."

Thomas Henry Huxley

"No failure in life is as final as the failure to find out what you do best."
Bernie Weiner, U.S. Shoe

Frederick Forsyth's best-selling book, *The Day of the Jackal,* was once turned down with the comment of "no reader interest." It has since sold eight million copies.

"People fail forward to success."

Charles McElroy

"Failure is a disappointment but not a defeat."
Jeanne Robertson, humorist

"Failure is inevitable and provides valuable feedback that can move you in the right direction. You have to risk failure to succeed. The important thing is to not make one single mistake that will jeopardize the future."
An Wang

"Success covers a multitude of blunders."
George Bernard Shaw

"You may have a fresh start any moment you choose, for this thing that we call 'failure' is not the falling down, but the staying down."
Mary Pickford

Eighty percent of all newly advertised products fail. The manufacturer decides the consumer is a fool. That's why the product fails. Period.

In addition, 58 percent of all innovations ultimately fail. Except, that is, for those originated by top management—these fail at a rate of 74 percent.

R. H. Macy failed seven times before his store in New York caught on. Novelist John Creasey got 753 rejections slips before he published 564 books.

☐ The biggest failure is the one we regret.

☐ Failure is in the eyes of the beholder.

Christopher Columbus set out to discover a new trade route to India. He missed by half a globe. Yet few of us would call him a failure.

In perfecting the incandescent lamp, Thomas Edison experienced ten thousand failures before he finally succeeded. A friend of Edison's chanced to remark that ten thousand failures were a lot of failures, to which Edison replied: "I didn't fail ten thousand times. I successfully eliminated, ten thousand times, materials and combinations which wouldn't work."

"It is defeat that turns bone to flint, and gristle to muscle, and makes people invincible, and formed those heroic natures that are now in ascendancy in the world. Do not, then, be afraid of defeat. You are never so near to victory as when defeated in a good cause."

Henry Ward Beecher

☐ When you fail, you are in good company.

Thomas Edison was thrown out of school in the early grades when the teachers decided he could not do the work.

Harry S. Truman failed as a haberdasher.

When Bob Dylan performed at a high school talent show, his classmates failed to realize he was a kid bound for glory and booed him off the stage.

W. Clement Stone, successful insurance company executive and founder of *Success* magazine, was a high school dropout.

☐ Failure is the instructive side of experience.

Everybody encounters failure in life and in business. But what so many of us don't understand is that failure can actually be a step forward. A legendary Chinese emperor attacked an enemy castle ninety nine times and failed to conquer. But on the ninety ninth try, he discovered the weakness that made his one hundredth attack successful.

Aristotle Onassis, one of the world's richest men, once said, "You don't fail until you give up."

In other words, giving up is not just quitting, it is actually choosing to fail.

Failure could be called "the Wallenda factor." You remember tightrope walker, Karl Wallenda. He was killed years ago in a tragic fall.

His widow was quoted as saying: "All Karl thought about for three straight months prior to the accident was falling. It seemed to me that he put all his energy into not falling—not into walking the tightrope."

Don't put your energy into not making a mistake but into doing something terrific!

■ FIRING

"It isn't the people you fire who will make your life miserable, it's the people you don't fire."

Harvey Mackay

"Firing someone is healthy. It gets rid of a poor performer and gets the attention of everyone that wasn't fired."

Doc Blakely, humorist

☐ Being fired isn't the end of the road.

Thomas Edison was fired from the Grand Truck Railway for accidentally setting the baggage car on fire with one of his chemical experiments. The conductor threw him off the train.

When firing someone, pick the right time and place. Remember back in the early 1950s when Arthur Godfrey fired Julius LaRosa on national television. The incident forever tarnished Godfrey's image.

"Managers often avoid firing because it's unpleasant. But getting rid of the bad performers is as good a tonic for the company as a reward that can be given to a star performer."

Arthur Boldger

☐ Look at the positives of getting fired.

"I was fired from my first three jobs, which in a funny way gave me the courage to go into business for myself."

Alfred C. Fuller, founder, Fuller Brush

☐ As Bum Phillips, former NFL coach, said, "There's only two kinds of coaches, them that's been fired and them that's about to be fired."

"Why did the foreman fire you?"
"Well, you know, the foreman is the person who stands around and watches other people work."
"But why did he fire you?"
"He was jealous. A lot of other people thought that I was the foreman."

Jack Kent Cooke, owner of the Washington Redskins, said, "Hiring and firing people is the most unpleasant part of being an employer, but it is a major part of the responsibility a proprietor has to himself, his organization, the persons who are dependent on that organization for their living, and those who support it."

When Winston Churchill was defeated in his reelection bid as Great Britain's prime minister, his wife told him it was a blessing in disguise. Churchill responded: "If it is, then it is very effectively disguised."

Keep in mind that Lee Iacocca got fired by Henry Ford and that Ronald Reagan's contract was terminated by Warner Brothers.

"A man was applying for a job as a prison guard. The warden said, 'Now these are real tough guys in here. Do you think you can handle it?' "

"The applicant replied, 'No problem. If they don't behave, out they go!' "

Joey Adams

FORECASTING

"I've been studying all the economic forecasts and have come to the conclusion that the best time to buy anything is when I don't have any money."

David N. Griffith

"Forecasters are dangerous, particularly those about the future."

Samuel Goldwyn

John Naisbitt, author of *Megatrends*, said that the most reliable way to anticipate the future is to try to understand the present.

"Predicting the future is, intellectually, the most disreputable form of public utterance."

Kenneth Clark

"Prophecy, however honest, is generally a poor substitute for experience."

Benjamin N. Cardozo

"Forecasting is very difficult—expecially if it is about the future. He who lives by the crystal ball soon learns to eat ground glass."

Edgar Fiedler

"Man prefers to believe that which he prefers to be true."

Francis Bacon

☐ The future is never what it seems.

Take Coca Cola. Coke's planners, aided and abetted by their colleagues in marketing, decided to replace Old Coke with New Coke. In the ring of consumer products, however, New Coke couldn't win the decision, and Old Coke refused to stay down for the count. Both New Coke and New Old Coke had to be kept on the market, and Old Coke's demise never happened.

"It seems to me that no soothsayer should be able to look at another soothsayer without laughing."

Cicero

Samuel Goldwyn reputedly said, "Never make predictions—especially about the future."

☐ If you are a forecaster, it's important not to be too specific.

"The rule on staying alive as a financial forecaster is to give them a number or give them a date, but never give them both at once."

Here is a list of some major blunders in forecasting:

1. In 1926, Lee de Forest, the man who invented the cathode ray tube, said: "While theoretically television may be feasible, commercially and financially I consider it an impossibility, a development of which we need waste little time dreaming."
2. In 1943, Thomas J. Watson, chairman of the board of IBM said: "I think there is a world market for about five computers."
3. In 1945, Admiral Leahy said this about the atomic bomb: "This is the biggest fool thing we've ever done—the bomb will never go off—and I speak as an expert on explosives."
4. Said a recording company executive, turning down the Beatles in 1962: "We don't think they will do anything in this market. Guitar groups are on the way out."
5. Wrote *Business Week* in 1968: "With over fifteen types of foreign cars already on sale here, the Japanese auto industry isn't likely to carve out a big share of the market for itself."

☐ Consider the following potpourri from history, which serves as a warning to all who listen to forecasters:

"Rail travel at high speeds is not possible because passengers, unable to breathe, would die of asphyxia."

Dionysius Lardner

"Fooling around with alternating currents is just a waste of time. Nobody will use it, ever. It's too dangerous . . . it could kill a man as quick as a bolt of lightning. Direct current is safe."

Thomas Edison

"X-rays are a hoax."

Lord Kelvin

"What, sir, would you make a ship sail against the wind and currents by lighting a bonfire under her deck? I pray you excuse me. I have no time to listen to such nonsense."

Napoleon to Robert Fulton

(On the occasion of the dedication of a physics laboratory in Chicago, noting that the more important physical laws had all been discovered): "Our future discoveries must be looked for in the sixth decimal place."

A. A. Michelson

"The [flying] machines will eventually be fast; they will be used in sport but they should not be thought of as commercial carriers."

Octave Chanute

"We hope the professor from Clark College [Robert H. Goddard] is only professing to be ignorant of elementary physics if he thinks that a rocket can work in a vacuum."

Editorial, The New York Times

"I have not the smallest molecule of faith in aerial navigation other than ballooning."

Lee DeForest, Physicist

"The energy produced by the breaking down of the atom is a very poor kind of thing. Anyone who expects a source of power from the transformation of these atoms is talking moonshine."

Ernest Rutherford, Physicist

"We must not be misled to our own detriment to assume that the untried machine can displace the proved and tried horse."

John K. Herr

"As far as sinking a ship with a bomb is concerned, it just can't be done."

Clark Woodward

"That is the biggest fool thing we have ever done . . . . The [atomic] bomb will never go off, and I speak as an expert in explosives."

William Leahy to President Truman

"Space travel is utter bilge."

Richard van der Riet Wooley, astronomer royal

█ FRANCHISING

Franchising as we know it today started around 1863 with the Singer Sewing Machine Company. Coca-Cola sold its first franchise in 1899. Next came the automobile and petroleum dealers, who decided to use the distributorship method of franchising in about 1910. They were soon joined by the soft-drink bottlers.

The word *franchise* originally came from the French, meaning to be "free from servitude."

☐ Anything can be franchised.

Kenton Granger, A Kansas attorney, told the following story:
"A group of us are considering investing in a large cat ranch near Hermosillo, Mexico. It is our purpose to start rather small, with about one

million cats. Each cat averages about twelve kittens each year; skins can be sold for about $0.20 for the white ones and up to $0.40 for the black. This will give us twelve million cat skins per year to sell, at an average price of around $0.32, making our revenues about $3 million a year. This really averages out to $10,000 a day—excluding Sundays and holidays.

"A good Mexican cat man can skin about 50 cats per day at a wage of $3.15 a day. It will take only 663 men to operate the ranch, so the net profit would be over $3,200 per day.

"Now, the cats would be fed exclusively on rats. Rats multiply four times as fast as cats. We would start a rat ranch adjacent to our cat ranch. If we start with a million rats, we will have four rats per cat each day. The rats will be fed on the carcasses of the cats that we skin. This will give each rat a quarter of a cat. You can see that this business is a clean operation—self-supporting and really automatic throughout. The cats will eat the rats and the rats will eat the cats and we will get the skins.

"Eventually, it is my hope to cross the cats with snakes, and they will then skin themselves twice a year! This would save the labor costs of skinning, as well as giving me two skins for one cat.

"Let me know if you are interested because I want only a limited number of investors. I think once we get the pilot operation going, we could franchise this business easily."

■ FREE ENTERPRISE

"Free enterprise will work if you will."

Ray Kroc, founder, McDonald's

"Free enterprise is that political system in which the state leaves producers and consumers free to produce and consume as they choose."

Adam Smith

☐ Your business can be affected by the decisions of others.

A peach grower in California is affected by McDonald's success. McDonald's? Yes, McDonald's, because McDonald's does not serve canned peaches, and McDonald's today is the most potent factor in the food industry. And what McDonald's decides has an impact on hundreds of thousand of individuals who do not work for the company. Just ask a chicken rancher who has benefited from Chicken McNuggets.

☐ Free enterprise is what enables a society to prosper.

Where each family raises its own food, builds its own house . . . none can have more than the barest necessities. . . . This social condition, to which the protective theory would logically lead, is the lowest in which man is ever found—the condition from which he has toiled upward. He has progressed only as he has learned to satisfy his wants by exchanging with his fellows and has freed and extended trade.

"Among our socialist friends, there is a great confusion about private enterprise. Some see it as a predatory tiger to be shot. Others as a cow to be milked. Only a handful see it for what it really is—the strong and willing horse that pulls the whole cart along."

Winston Churchill

Over forty years ago, Joseph Schumpeter described the reaction of business people to attacks on the free enterprise system and commercial society.

"They talk, they plead, or hire people to do it for them. They snatch at every chance to compromise. They are ever-ready to give in. They never put up a fight under the flag of their own ideals or interest."

Winston Churchill stated eloquently in 1945 the value of free enterprise:

"I do not believe in the power of the state to plan and enforce. No matter how numerous are the committees they set up or the ever-growing hordes of officials they employ or the severity of the punishments they inflict or threaten, they can't approach the high level of internal economic production achieved under free enterprise.

"Personal initiative, competitive selection, the profit motive, corrected by failure and the infinite processes of good housekeeping and personal ingenuity, these constitute the life of a free society. It is this vital creative impulse that I deeply fear the doctrines and policies of the socialist government have destroyed.

"Nothing that they can plan and order and rush around enforcing will take its place. They have broken the mainspring, and until we get a new one, the watch will not go. Set the people free—get out of the way and let them make the best of themselves.

"I am sure that this policy of equalizing misery and organizing scarcity instead of allowing diligence, self-interest and ingenuity to produce abundance has only to be prolonged to kill this British island stone dead."

Under free enterprise, new companies can succeed in an area where the giants are if they find a different niche.

Take the example of Control Data, founded by eight engineers to make the world's largest computer for the Atomic Energy Commission. At the time, IBM was already dominating the world computer market. IBM was also in the education business as well the computer business. They sold computers and trained people to use them. On the other hand, Control Data was able to make a computer for the Atomic Energy Commission for 40 percent less than IBM because they didn't have to teach anyone to use it.

■ FUND-RAISING

"In this world it is not what we take up, but what we give up, that makes us rich."

Henry Ward Beecher

"In charity there is not excess."

Francis Bacon

"No man becomes rich unless he enriches others."

Andrew Carnegie

"Success in life has nothing to do with what you gain in life or accomplish for yourself. It's what you do for others."

Danny Thomas

☐ You will get what you want when you give others what they want.

"He who confers benefits will be amply enriched, and he who refreshes others will himself be refreshed."

Proverbs 11:25

☐ People need to be inspired to give.

Two men were leaving church in their underwear. One said to the other: "That was the best sermon I ever heard on giving."

"It is one of the most beautiful compensations of this life that no one can sincerely try to help another without helping themselves."

Ralph Waldo Emerson

☐ We need money to help others help themselves.

"Give a man a fish, and he will live for a day; give him a net, and he will live for a lifetime."

Chinese proverb

There are two seas in the Holy Land. The Sea of Galilee takes in fresh water from a brook, uses it to produce a wide variety of marine vegetation life, and then gives it to the Jordan River. The Jordan, in turn, spreads the life down throughout the desert and turns it into fertile plain. While the Sea of Galilee bustles with life, the Dead Sea is exactly that—a dead sea. Its water is so full of salt that it cannot sustain life. Why? It takes in the water from the Jordan River and hangs on to it. It has no outlet.

We need to quit hanging on to our success. By sharing, we become like the Sea of Galilee—full of life.

☐ Learn early about money.

Being a fund-raiser is like the little girl who asked to see the president of a large company. She explained that her club was raising money and asked if he would contribute?

Smiling, he laid a dime and a dollar bill on his desk.

He said: "Take whichever one you want."

               She said: "My mother taught me to take the smallest piece, but I'll take this piece of paper to wrap it in so I won't lose it."

We will take anything you have wrapped or unwrapped.

☐ There is an old saying, "To those that much is given, much is expected."

In 1988, Johnny Carson donated $650,000 to the Lutheran Community Hospital in his hometown of Norfolk, Nebraska. When asked why, he said that he felt an obligation to respond to the fund drive because, "If you're lucky enough in this life to accumulate enough funds to live better than you have any right to, then you have a moral obligation to pay back to the community or to the country or to the place that brought you up."

☐ We need your help.

There is the story of the businessman who called to complain to a florist. For the grand opening of his new business he had received a floral arrangement with a ribbon that said, "May you rest in peace."

The florist apologized profusely but reminded the businessman that out there somewhere was a funeral parlor with a wreath that bore the inscription, "Good luck in your new location."

A rich man asked his minister, "Why is it that everybody calls me stingy when everyone knows that when I die I'm leaving everything I have to this church?"

The minister said: "Let me tell you a story of the pig and the cow. The pig was unpopular and the cow was beloved. This puzzled the pig. The pig said to the cow, 'People speak warmly of your gentle nature and your soulful eyes. They think you're generous because each day you give them milk and cream. But what about me? I give them everything I have. I give bacon and ham. I provide bristles for brushes. They even pickle my feet. Yet no one likes me. Why is that?' "

The minister continued: "Do you know what the cow answered? She said, 'Perhaps it's because I give while I'm still living.' "

We have a choice today to be a pig or a cow. I hope you will give now because we need it now.

A state trooper observed a truck with a completely closed aluminum trailer moving erratically in the slow lane. The truck would go fast for about a mile, suddenly lose speed, and then come to a stop on the shoulder. The driver would get out, take a long stick, and start beating the side of the trailer. After about three minutes of frenzied pounding, the driver would jump quickly into his cab and drive off, only to repeat the performance a mile or two down the road.

When the trooper stopped him, he said, "Look, officer, this is a one-ton truck, and I'm trying to haul two tons of canaries. So I got to keep half of them in the air all the time."

We are a lot like that overloaded, underpowered truck, trying to get by on limited resources. It takes money to keep things going because we can't keep beating the side of the truck.

Recently a man's wife stood at the weight scale in an airport.

He: "Well, what's the verdict, a little overweight?"
She: "No, not really. But according to this I should be six inches taller."

Without your help, we will always be a little short for what we need to do.

☐ This can be used to close a fund-raising speech.

As Longfellow so ably expressed:

Lives of great men all remind us
We can make our lives sublime,
And, departing, leave behind us
Footprints on the sands of time.

You are asked to leave your footprints in time by donating to the cause today. I hope you step forward.

▊ FUTURE

"He who does not look ahead remains behind."

Spanish proverb

Believing in the future helps us to have hope and, as Dwight Morrow said, "Hope is greater than history."

"Wise men say, and not without reason, that whoever wished to foresee the future might consult the past."

Machiavelli

☐ Your future may be where you already are.

"Hills look green that are far away."

Harry R. Kramer

☐ Your future depends on your attitude toward it.

"The future has several names. For the weak, it is the impossible. For the fainthearted, it is the unknown. For the thoughtful and valiant, it is ideal."

Victor Hugo

"There is not future in any job. The future lies in the man who holds the job."

George W. Crane

☐ Charles Kettering, the great industrialist, inventor, and philanthropist, once said, "My interest is in the future . . . because I'm going to spend the rest of my life there."

☐ Long-term planning is what keeps us from spending too much time on the present.

John Templeton, founder of Templeton Funds, said, "You can deal with the future more clearly if you don't focus on the next week."

☐ Plan for the future, where the company will be, not where it is now.

Wayne Gretsky, possibly the greatest hockey player of all time, said, "I skate to where the puck is going to be, not where it has been."

☐ Our future is determined by what we do today.

"An election goes on every minute of the business day across the counters of hundreds of thousands of stores and shops where the customers state their preferences and determine which company and which product shall be the leader today and which shall lead tomorrow."

Bruce Barton

"We know only two things about the future: It cannot be known, and it will be different from what exists now and from what we now expect."

Peter Drucker, Managing for Results

"It is futile to try to guess what products the future will want. But it is possible to make up one's mind what idea one wants to make a reality in the future, and to build a different business on such an idea."

Peter Drucker, Managing for Results

☐ It is better to understand your business than to worry about its impact on society.

The men who built Sears Roebuck had no idea that they were developing the concept of mass marketing until they had done it.

☐ Some forward-looking corporations were forced into the future.

In the mid-1940s, IBM had an antitrust suit brought against it for monopolizing the punch card. Soon after this suit, punch cards were already becoming obsolete. But because of the antitrust suit, IBM had already started getting into computers.

☐ We can influence our future.

"The future never just happened. It was created."
Will and Ariel Durant, The Lessons of History

"The danger of the past was that men became slaves, the danger of the future is that men may become robots."
Erich Fromm

"The world of the future will be an ever more demanding struggle against the limitations of our intelligence."
Norbert Wiener

"The future isn't what it used to be."
Yogi Berra

☐ Keep an eye on the future.

A veteran employee being honored for fifty years with the same firm said, "Not a day passed all that time that I wasn't trying to get a better job."

☐ Believing in the future gives us hope.

Hope is the last life preserver on a sinking ship.
Hope is a lottery ticket bought with the last dollar.
Hope is the flirt that keeps the working stiff at his bench.
Hope is what kept William Kennedy writing ignored novels for years, before a book titled *Ironweed* caught fire and made him rich and famous.
Hope is actor Ben Johnson, who was in the background of a hundred movies until he won an Oscar for *The Last Picture Show.*

☐ Always believe that the best is yet to come.

During a 1890 sermon, Bishop Wright was expounding the fact that the second coming of Christ was near. He said that everything God had sent man to earth to do was done.

A member of the congregation jumped to his feet and said that someday man would fly.

The bishop responded with the now famous line, "If God had intended man to fly, he would have given him wings."

Thirteen years later, in 1903, Bishop Wright's sons, Orville and Wilbur, made the first powered flight by man at Kitty Hawk.

☐ We can't predict everything; the future will always offer surprises.

The space suit in the 1930s Buck Rogers cartoons turned out to be remarkably similar to what American astronauts wore when they actually landed on the moon. No one was greatly surprised by the success of the moon shot. The prediction of a moon voyage runs through history. Science fiction writer Isaac Asimov reminds us that not one of the writers had predicted the most remarkable thing about the event—that when it happened, the whole world would be watching on television.

"If you do not think about the future, you cannot have one."

John Gale

☐ One thing about the future is certain. An imbalance in one sector of the economy can affect the whole.

John Scully, chairman of Apple Computer, explained it this way:

"I like to use the analogy of the shrinking rain forests of Brazil. Eighty percent of the world's oxygen comes from the rain forest. Yet every year we lose, through the cutting of trees and the clearing of land, a land mass the size of the state of Nebraska. If we keep doing that long enough, not only will we scar the natural and social ecosystem of Brazil, but the decreasing amount of oxygen in the atmosphere will alter the entire ecosystem of our planet."

GENIUS

When asked to explain his genius, Thomas Edison replied, "It's 99 percent perspiration, and 1 percent inspiration."

"A genius? Perhaps, but before I was a genius I was a drudge."
Paderewski

"All the genius I have is the fruit of labor."
Alexander Hamilton

"A genius is a talented person who does his homework."
Thomas Edison

"Genius is the capacity for seeing relationships where lesser men see none."
William James

"The secret of genius is to carry the spirit of childhood into maturity."
Thomas H. Huxley

"When a true genius appears in the world, you may know him by this sign, that the dunces are all in confederacy against him."
Jonathan Swift

"Thousands of geniuses live and die undiscovered—either by themselves or by others."

Mark Twain

"Genius: a person who aims at something no one else can see and hits it."
Ervin L. Glaspy

◼ GOALS

"The greatest thing in this world is not so much where we are, but in what direction we are moving."

Oliver Wendell Holmes

☐ Goals should be specific and have a time limit.

"I believe this nation should commit itself to achieving the goal of putting a man on the moon before this decade is out."

John F. Kennedy

☐ A goal makes us take action.

"Goals help you overcome short-term problems.

Hannah More

"Aiming for perfection is always a goal in progress."

Thomas J. Watson Jr., IBM

"No one ever accomplishes anything of consequence without a goal. . . . Goal setting is the strongest human force for self-motivation."

Paul Myer

"Before you can score you must first have a goal."

Anonymous

"There are two tragedies in a man's life. One is not having reached one's goal, and the other is having reached it."

Friedrich Nietzche

☐ Goals make work more fun.

One of the secrets of job satisfaction is being able to see beyond the routine.

"A goal is nothing more than a dream with a time limit."

Joe L. Griffith

☐ We need goals to create excitement in our lives.

Remember George Sanders, the actor? He was a gifted man, a fine actor, a linguist, musician, painter, writer, what have you. And yet he committed suicide. He left a note explaining why. He was bored. He was bored because he didn't have anything he was trying to achieve.

☐ We need a goal to give us a sense of accomplishment.

How important are goals? Listen to what John Condry said: "Happiness, wealth, and success are by-products of goal-setting; they cannot be the goal themselves."

☐ The purpose of a goal is to lead you someplace.

"I will go anywhere as long as it's forward."

David Livingstone

☐ The quickest way to get what you want is to identify what you want.

Years ago, advertising legend David Ogilvy, set out to establish a great advertising agency within a dozen years. At the time, he was a small tobacco farmer in Pennsylvania. On his second day of business, he made a list of five clients he most wanted to get. They were Bristol-Myers, Campbell Soup, General Foods, Lever Brothers, and Shell Oil Company. Eventually he had them all.

☐ People who know where they are going know how to get there.

When Steven Jobs, founder of Apple Computer, was twelve years old, he called Bill Hewlett, founder of Hewlett-Packard, and asked if they would give him some parts.

☐ A goal makes us do more.

As a boy, John Goddard dared to visit the magic kingdom of "What If." When he was fifteen years old, John Goddard made a list of all the things he wanted to do in life. That list contained 127 goals he hoped to achieve. It included such things as: explore the Nile, climb Mt. Everest, study primitive tribes in the Sudan, run a five-minute mile, read the Bible from cover to cover, dive in a submarine, play "Claire de Lune" on the piano, write a book, read the entire *Encyclopedia Britannica*, and circumnavigate the globe.

Now middle-aged, he has become one of the most famous explorers alive today. He has reached 105 of his 127 goals and done many other exciting things. He is still looking forward to visiting all 141 countries in the world (so far he's visited only 113), exploring the entire Yangtze River in China, living to see the twenty-first century (he'll be seventy-five years old), visiting the moon, and having many other exciting adventures.

☐ Goals give you determination.

Jim Marshall has been described as the most indestructible man ever to play professional football. In a sport where thirty is considered old age, he played defensive end until he was forty-two—starting in 282 consecutive games. He is what famous quarterback Fran Tarkenton called "the most amazing athlete I've ever known in any sport."

Jim has had his share of problems. He was once caught in a blizzard in which all of his companions died. Twice he suffered from pneumonia. While cleaning a rifle, he suffered a gunshot wound. He's been in several automobile accidents and has undergone surgery.

The secret of Jim's amazing success is in his two guidelines: Find a direction and dedicate yourself to it, and remember that you can go as far as you want to go if you have a goal.

☐ Goals should stretch you.

The chances are that you will "shoot too low" when you decide your major goal in life. Douglas MacArthur did the same thing. When he entered West Point, he announced two objectives: to lead his class and to one day become chief of staff. To lead his class was the great general's short-range goal. To someday become chief of staff was his one great vision—what he thought, at this time, was to become the greatest thing possible for a West Point cadet.

MacArthur bettered his goal. In his four years at the U.S. Military Academy, he set a scholastic record still unbroken. He won fame as a front-line general in World War I. In 1930, President Herbert Hoover appointed him army chief of staff.

The question is, was this "reaching the goal" really the end result of which MacArthur was capable, or could he push on to even larger horizons? History has answered this for us. He was supreme allied commander in the Southwest Pacific in World War II. He headed the occupation government in Japan and later led our forces successfully against the Communists in Korea.

"If you don't know where you are going, you might wind up someplace else."

Yogi Berra

☐ Goals give you a vision that keeps you pressing on.

Florence Chadwick decided that she would become the first woman ever to swim the English Channel. For years she trained and disciplined herself to keep going long after her body cried out for relief. Finally, in 1952, the big day came. She set out full of hope, surrounded by new people and well-wishers in small boats. And, of course, there were the skeptics who doubted she'd make it.

As she neared the coast of England, a heavy fog settled in, and the waters became increasingly cold and choppy.

Her mother encouraged her, "Come on, Florence, you can make it! It's only a few more miles!"

Finally, exhausted, she asked to be pulled aboard the boat—just a few hundred yards from her goal. She was defeated and heartbroken, especially when she discovered how close she had been to reaching her goal.

Later, she told news reporters, "I'm not offering excuses, but I think I could have made it if I had been able to see my goal."

Florence Chadwick decided to try again. This time, she concentrated on developing a mental image of the coast of England. She memorized every feature of the distant coast and fixed it clearly in her mind. On the appointed day, she encountered all of the choppy waters and fog that she had met before, but she made it.

A rookie U.S. Navy jet pilot once said he was terrified about landing his airplane on the deck of an aircraft carrier.

He said, "Everything is in constant motion."

The ship was tossing up and down, and back and forth. Trying to get everything to move together seemed impossible until an old pro gave him some good advice.

He said, "There is a yellow line down the center of the flight deck that always stays still. I always line up the nose of the airplane toward that line and fly straight toward it."

☐ If we have a goal that we are shooting at, then all other problems fade into the background.

"I started out with three general ideas in mind. One was to render friendly service to our guests. The second was to provide quality food at a fair price. The third was to work as hard as I could, day and night, to make a profit."

Bill Marriott, Sr.

"For the persuasive power of leadership to be really effective, the organization needs this goal—a dream that the institution is living out and that the leadership is serving. It is not the I or the ultimate leader that moves an institution to greatness, but the dream. We are all subordinate to the great idea."

Mark Shepherd, past chairman, Texas Instruments

In 1970, Kenneth Cooper came out with his well-known point system for figuring out how much aerobic exercise we get for jogging, swimming, and other exercise. We could go out, run around the block, and say, "Boy! I really feel great." But Cooper changed all that. All of a sudden, there was an easy-to-understand, foolproof way to determine how much cardiovascular benefit we were really getting from those jogs around the block. He told us how many points we got for every exercise and how many points we needed each week to maintain good cardiovascular fitness. No ifs, ands, or buts.

☐ With goals, we have a foolproof way to know when we are meeting the standards of good business fitness.

☐ Goals give us a much needed sense of purpose.

Charles Lazarus, founder and chairman of **Toys 'R' Us** discount toy stores, said his one ambition when he opened his first store thirty years ago was to run the largest toy store chain in the world. He seized every opportunity, no matter what size, to push the nearly $2 billion operation a little closer to his goal. He became obsessed with sales. When particular toys didn't sell well, he'd make telephone calls to the buyers to find out why they weren't selling. Recently, he installed a computer terminal in his house to keep track of the sales in his "spare" time.

☐ To be successful, we need a mission and the dedication to make the mission become a reality.

☐ Goals give you a vision of being in a successful situation.

"Fantasizing, projecting yourself into a successful situation, is the most powerful means there is of achieving personal goals. That's what an athlete does when he comes onto the field to kick a field goal with three seconds on the clock, 80,000 people in the stands, and thirty million watching on TV. The athlete, like the businessman, automatically makes thousands of tiny adjustments necessary to achieve the mental picture he's forming of the successful situation: a winning field goal."

Leonard Lauder, president and CEO, Estée Lauder

☐ It's great to have goals, but don't let them get in the way of what has to be done today.

Henry Morton Stanley, the nineteenth-century British explorer, after fighting his way through an incredibly horrifying jungle, was asked if he'd been frightened. He said: "I didn't think about it that way. I did not raise my head to see the whole. I saw only this poisonous snake in front of me that I had to kill to take the next step. Only after I had gotten through did I look back and see what I had been through. Had I taken a look at the whole thing, I would have been so scared that I would never have attempted this."

☐ Long-term goals aren't a substitute for solving short-term problems.

☐ Goals should be progressively raised.

"Alfred J. Marrow, a company president with a Ph.D. in psychology, once set up an interesting experiment in his factory. Marrow was interested, as are most businessmen, in having new employees reach optimum performance as quickly as possible. He began to try different methods of motivating his new and unskilled employees to reach standards of skilled performance.

"With one group, Marrow set a goal that was difficult to achieve. He ordered the unskilled workers to reach their quota within 12 weeks after they were employed. Interestingly, after 14 weeks the group had reached only 66 percent of standard performance. The individuals of this group missed their goals by about one-third.

"With the second group that was equally unskilled, Marrow established weekly goals. The goals were progressive; that is, each was slightly more ambitious than the goal of the previous week. As the level of the employees' proficiency increased, the goals were advanced. At the end of 14 weeks, the average member of the second group had reached a standard of proficiency equal to that of a skilled operator!"

Mortimer R. Feinberg, Effective Psychology for Managers

■ GOVERNMENT

"One way for voters to get better government is to vote for the charisma of principle instead of the charisma of personality."

Ivan Hill

Government should not interfere with any business capable of failing by itself.

Government workers never carry picket signs very long. They aren't used to lifting anything heavier than a requisition slip.

Most people would be glad to tend their own business if the government would give it back.

"The government wants us to report our costs, performance, and reliability? Tell 'em we will if they will!"

Mike Doyle

The economy is booming . . . mainly because Americans are spending borrowed money before the U.S. government can get its hands on it.

A contradiction in terms is a government agency called the Department of Labor.

"Bureaucracy is the enemy of innovation. It breeds mediocrity."
Mark Shepherd, past chairman, Texas Instruments

William Fulbright once said of the U.S. government, "We have the power to do any damn fool thing we want to, and we seem to do it about every ten seconds."

Senator Strom Thurmond, explaining why Congress doesn't decrease deficit spending, said: "It's awfully hard to get a hog to butcher itself."

The incredible thing about the federal debt is that we actually got into this terrible shape by buying from the lowest bidder.

☐ Government can play a large role in the success of private enterprise.

During the 1930s, IBM was on the verge of bankruptcy. But two new acts passed by Congress dramatically increased IBM's sales. The Social Security Act of 1935 and the Wage-Hours Act of 1937–38. Both of these acts created a need for records of wages paid, hours worked, and overtime earned by employees. Since IBM was in the punch-card business they were poised to tackle this new problem, creating an opportunity not only for survival but for success.

☐ No matter how hard the federal government tries to manage the economy, it's still a difficult task.

"The problem of the managed economy is like the problem of the waves of the sea. We have identified the forces that cause them, we apprehend the conditions which must be met for a solution of the problem, and we can even reduce it to an equation—but its solution is hopelessly beyond our capacities."

Jacques Reuff

☐ Sometimes we act as if we never got along without the government helping us.

"We've always had a finite amount of energy. . . . We had finite supplies of wood in the early pioneer days. How did we make the transition from using wood to using coal, from using coal to using oil, from using oil to using natural gas? How in God's name did we make that transition without a federal energy agency?"

Milton Friedman

"Liberty has never come from the government. . . . The history of liberty is the history of the limitation of governmental power, not the increase of it."

Woodrow Wilson

"Government, even in its best state, is but a necessary evil; in its worst state, an intolerable one."

Thomas Paine

"You don't see me at Vegas or at the races throwing my money around. I've got a government to support."

Bob Hope

"It is hard to feel individually responsible with respect to the invisible processes of a huge and distant government."

John Gardner

"To make crime unprofitable, let the government run it."

Irene Peter

"The government is doing a whole lot of things that our Founding Fathers never meant it to do."

J. Peter Grace, chairman, W. R. Grace

"If tomorrow it was announced that all government intervention in business were ended, there would be coronaries in every boardroom."

Paul Laxalt

"Government is a reality of life. Denying it is just letting your own biases influence your business judgment."

Bill McGowan, founder, MCI

Columnist George Will once said that Washington, D.C., is a small town on the Potomac "completely surrounded by reality."

"The natural progress of things is for government to gain ground and for liberty to yield."

Thomas Jefferson

"With all these economic blessings, what more is necessary to make us a happy and prosperous people? Still one more thing, a wise and frugal government, which shall restrain men from injuring one another, which shall leave them otherwise free to regulate their own pursuit of industry and improvement, and shall not take from the mouth of labor the bread it has earned."

Thomas Jefferson

Job applicant to civil service employment interviewer: "My boss didn't exactly give me a letter of recommendation. But he did say that a guy like me should be working for the government."

California Governor Deukmejian told a high-tech industry executive on a Capitol tour about the Cray supercomputer he inspected at UCLA: "It can make a billion calculations a second, almost as fast as the legislature spends money."

Banker: "I can't loan you money to pay interest on what you already owe."
Customer: "Why not? You make those kinds of loans to the government all the time.

☐ Passing laws or spending more money isn't always the best action.

John Gardner, the founder of Common Cause, once said, "Some people seem to believe that for each problem there is a solution readily available—a solution that can be promptly achieved by passing a law or voting some money. I think of this as the vending machine concept . . . put a coin in the machine and out comes a piece of candy. If there is a social problem, pass a law and out comes a solution."

Insurance executive Peter Frame used the following analogy to help explain billions of dollars of debt:

"The next time you read about the way billions are being spent in Washington, you might think about a billion in this way. Let's assume that you have a billion dollars and decide to transport the bills to your bank by truck. How many trucks will be required? By accurately weighing a one-dollar bill, it is found that it weighs 1.02 grams; it will require 445 bills to equal one pound. By computation, it is found that the billion bills will weigh 2,247,191 pounds and require 1,123 one-ton trucks to transport them, with enough one-dollar bills left over to fill a half-ton pick-up and still leave $84,995 for pocket change."

Government waste causes lots of governments problems. In 1973, when New York City was near financial collapse, the Treasury Department made an analysis of New York's spending and compared it to other major American Cities. Among other things, the report discovered the following:

• New York City was spending three times more per capita than any other city with a population of more than one million.
• New York City employed 49 people for each 1000 residents. Other major cities ranged from 30 to 32 per 1,000.
• Salaries were far higher than other comparable cities. For example, a subway changemaker earned $60 a week more than a bank teller. A city porter earned $20 a week more than an X-ray technician.
• City bus drivers worked eight-hour shifts and were paid for fourteen.

☐ Government trying to help others often misses the mark.

In a 1976 lecture at Hillsdale College, M. Stanton Evans made this point with a shocking calculation. He said that there were twenty five million poor people in the United States. And from 1965 to 1975, the total federal expenditure on social programs increased by some $209 billion to a ballooned total of $286.5 billion. In his speech, he said:

"If we take those 25 million poor people and divide them into the $209 billion increase—not the whole thing, just the increase—we discover that if we had simply taken that money and given it to the poor people, we could have given each and every one of them a stipend of some $8,000 a year, which means an income for a family of four of approximately $32,000. That is, we could have made every poor person in America a relatively rich person. But we didn't. Those poor people are still out there.

"What happened to the money? The answer is that some of it did get into hands of the people who are supposed to get it. But a lot of it didn't. I would say the majority of it went to people who are counseling the poor people, working on their problems, examining the difficulties of the inner city, trying to rescue poor families and devise strategies for getting them out of their doldrums. It went to social workers and counselors and planners and social engineers and urban renewal experts and the assistant administrators to the administrative assistants who work for the federal government."

▌ GROWTH

☐ For a company to grow, it's got to think big.

"If you want to be a big company tomorrow, you have to start acting like one today."

Thomas J. Watson, Jr., IBM

☐ A good sales strategy is to grow your business with the customers you already have.

"We are measuring the success of our selling efforts not only in terms of volume of business but in planned growth of business with individual customers over the years."

Warren Anderson, former chairman, Union Carbide

☐ Don't grow at the expense of what you already have.

Quaker Oats, the food company, branched out into selling toys and restaurants. Once they expanded into new areas, they lost their dominance in the food business.

☐ Growth opportunities can appear in the most stagnant of industries and in the worst of times.

In the 1960s and 1970s, the railroads were dying on the vine. But in the 1980s, the American railroad made a dramatic comeback. During the depression, IBM laid its foundation for its future growth. Some of today's largest Wall Street brokerage houses were started during the Depression.

"The key to growth is quite simple: creative men with money. The cause of stagnation is similarly clear: depriving creative individuals of financial power."

George Gilder

"To grow faster than one is able to manage is flirting with disaster."
An Wang, founder, Wang Laboratories.

One quick way to rapid growth is to learn how to duplicate what you do with little variations. Examples are McDonald's and Federal Express.

☐ With growth there is no way out of risk.

"There is nothing more difficult to plan, more doubtful of success, nor more dangerous to manage than the creation of a new system."

Machiavelli

☐ One way to stunt growth is to get into areas that we don't know.

"I think a lot of American managers get fascinated with vertical integration. It's like the really great hamburger joint that adds a dining room, starts serving steak, and winds up going out of business. Doing too many things isn't always a good idea—no matter how much better you think you can do them than someone else."

Dan Ciampa, president, Rath & Strong

A wise man said: "If you want one year's prosperity, grow grain, but if you want ten year's prosperity, grow men and women."

☐ For a business to grow, customers have to like doing business with you.

"If you don't genuinely like your customers, the chances are they won't buy."

Thomas J. Watson, Jr., IBM

Growth consumes cash, and cash is what you use to meet the payroll. An example of no growth because of no cash is Braniff Airlines; they ran out of cash twice.

☐ Money to grow on can be found in inventory.

Consultant Henry Ekstein told about the time a company desperate for cash called him in for help. They had $10 million in annual sales from making refrigerators and were barely paying their bills.

After touring the factory, he told the CEO, "You don't need any money. Pick up the money from the floor of your factory." Ekstein showed how they could pay their bills and have money to expand just by reducing their inventory.

☐ A business doesn't grow making cosmetic changes.

A nurse insisted that her patients be comfortable. She made them fluff up their pillows, she changed the angle of the hospital bed and the sheets to make sure the patient was comfortable. Once she walked into a room, and the patient was pleasantly watching television when the helpful nurse told him to start getting comfortable.

He told her, "I am comfortable."

She said, "No you're not." She started fluffing up his pillow and adjusting the bed.

Finally, he said to the nurse, "Do I look comfortable enough for you?"

☐ We don't want the customer to just *look* comfortable doing business with us; we want them to *be* comfortable.

☐ Growth can accelerate if we can develop a product and get it to market quicker.

Compaq Computer Corporation (the company that took only four years to go from startup to Fortune 500 status) attributes its success to rapid new-product development—six to nine months, far ahead of the industry's typical twelve to eighteen months. Compaq was the first to introduce a transportable PC following IBM's desktop PC introduction. After staying roughly even with IBM on introductions of 286 machines, Compaq leaped ahead of IBM with a PC based on Intel's more powerful 386 microprocessor. Compaq worked closely with Intel to ensure compatibility of the 386 chip with existing PC software; once Intel finished redesigning the chip, it took Compaq only one and a half months to introduce the DeskPro 386.

Big companies usually get big doing what small companies don't want to do. A good corporate plan starts in the personnel department. For example, Nordstrom, an upscale department store, hires one out of every ten people interviewed. Each employee hired is given the freedom to "use your own best judgment at all times." That's the whole company manual, and it works.

The company's success comes from this flexibility. A salesman, without consulting a manager, once chose to issue a full-purchase credit to a customer who had ruined a new suit by accidentally putting it in the wash. Nordstrom's answer to such a story is that "we profit by making a customer for life."

Some people would say that's good, but we're a small company and we'd go broke if we tried that. The answer is, "How do you think Nordstrom got that big in the first place?"

☐ Do you need money to grow?

F. W. Woolworth, founder of the stores by the same name, said he learned how to be successful by following the example of Dutch businessmen who grew without borrowing money.

"They ran their stores on the same policy for more than half a century; they did not progress, except as a tree progresses in size. They grew wealthy slowly, but surely. They never went into debt; they always paid for what they bought, and paid with cash. They bought at the lowest price, and they bought not a cent's worth more than they actually needed. When they put money in the bank, it was put there to stay. There are no liens on anything they owned. These Dutch farmers taught me to manage my own business and never to let my business manage me."

☐ Growth can be achieved by buying existing businesses.

Liberal economist Lester Thurow, wrote in his book the *Zero-Sum Society*, "Firms should be encouraged to engage in different activities. That way they can reinvest their earnings in products and services that bring a higher rate of return. For example, if steel is stuck in one old product, managers tend to pour all corporate funds into a dying industry with low returns. But if a steel company buys into a new computer company, it has a chance to grow and be more prosperous."

☐ To stop learning is to stop growing.

"There is a theory of human behavior that says people subconsciously retard their own intellectual growth. They come to rely on clichés and habits. Once they reach the age of their own personal comfort with the world, they stop learning and their mind runs on idle for the rest of their days. They may progress organizationally, they may be ambitious and eager, and they may even work night and day. But they learn no more. The bigoted, the narrow-minded, the stubborn, and the perpetually optimistic have all stopped learn-ing."

Philip B. Crosby, Quality Is Free

☐ For an organization to grow and survive, it must change the structure as well as the people.

Prior to World War II, an American general was observing British army maneuvers and noted that mobile artillery pieces were served by seven sol-diers, one of whom did nothing but stand at attention while the other six prepared and fired the gun. He inquired what the seventh man was for. He found out that in the old days before trucks, the seventh man held the horses so that they wouldn't run off when the gun was fired. The horses were gone but the original structure, now useless and expensive, remained.

Every business needs to constantly evaluate the horses and the person who holds them.

☐ Changing a marketing approach can accelerate growth.

In a recent year, WD-40 Company, located in San Diego, earned $5 million on $34 million sales. Interesting though is the fact that the product is the same as it was when sales were only $2 million. Why the sudden growth? WD-40 decided to diversify the uses of the product, not the product itself.

So remember that new growth may mean the same old product going into new markets.

Can growth come from a name change? Take the story of Richard Hendler, owner of Saxony Ice Company in Mamaroneck, New York. He had always wondered how humdrum products like water, bananas, and chicken suddenly became big sellers after they were promoted under brand names like Perrier, Chiquita, and Perdue.

After being in business for twelve years, sales were only $485,000. In 1975, Hendler and Harold Reynolds, another ice company in New York, formed a two-man trade association under the name "Leisure Time Ice." Three years later, Leisure Time Ice association boasted fifteen members and sixty trucks with thirteen million bags of ice with the new name and logo being sold a year.

Let's compare our business to the growth cycle of a tree.

If a tree is given minimal nourishment, it will live, but it will not grow. If nourishment is given over and beyond what is needed for life, the tree will live and grow upward, downward, and outward. But if a tree is given nourishment over and beyond what is needed to support life, needed for growth, and more, it will produce fruit. Fruit is the overflow, a surplus of excess nourishment.

HIRING

☐ Hiring is the key to a manager's success.

"There are only three rules of sound administration: pick good men, tell them not to cut corners, and back them to the limit; and picking good men is the most important."

Adlai Stevenson

☐ Applications can tell you if a person reads instructions.

"After reading the line on the job application blank that said, 'Sign here,' the bright young thing pondered briefly, then wrote: 'Capricorn.' "

Red O'Donnell

☐ Hire people to do the jobs you don't want to do.

"If the rich could hire other people to die for them, the poor could make a wonderful living."

Yiddish proverb

Trammell Crow Company looks for people "we'd like to go out and have a beer with."

☐ Look for employees who can grow.

"I will have no man work for me who has not the capacity to become a partner."

J. C. Penny

☐ Hire good people.

"Good people do good work; lousy people don't."

Mike Dunkerley

"Recruiting is a lot like shaving. You miss a day and you look like a bum."

Jackie Sherrill, football coach

☐ It's people that make things happen.

Don't bet on horses. Bet on jockeys.

☐ Hire the right people for the right job.

"I'm known as a recruiter. Well, you got to have chicken to make chicken salad. But you have to know a good one when you see one, too."

Paul "Bear" Bryant

☐ Make sure you hire people who improve your organization.

There is an old East Texas saying, "If you lay down with dogs, you'll pick up fleas."

☐ It's never too expensive to hire the best.

"People are a firm's most important asset. If you have an excellent product but only mediocre people, the results will be only mediocre."

Richard S. Sloma, The Turnaround Manager's Handbook

☐ Don't hire from the resume alone.

"Everybody looks good on paper."

John Y. Brown, former governor of Kentucky

☐ If a company fails, it's not because of the people who were hired, it's because of the person who hired them.

"First-rate people hire first-rate people, second-rate people hire third-rate people."

Leo Rosten

☐ Don't make hiring rules that can't be bent.

Look at the person more than your "must" list. Pro football coaches always say they want quarterbacks who are 6 feet 4 inches and weigh 230 pounds, but they bend a little when a Doug Flutie shows up.

☐ Picking people is one of an executive's most important jobs.

Alfred P. Sloan, Jr., who ran General Motors for over forty years, chose every GM executive, including the manufacturing managers, controllers, master mechanics, and engineering managers at even the smallest plant. His long-term performance in placing people in the right jobs was flawless.

☐ Hiring is important because it's the people around you that make you successful.

Presidents Harry S. Truman and Franklin D. Roosevelt had the strongest cabinets of any other presidents in this century. Their criterion was, "Never mind personal weaknesses, tell me first what each of them can do."

☐ A goal in hiring is to find people better than yourself.

The following inscription is on Andrew Carnegie's tombstone: "Here lies a man who knew how to enlist the service of better men than himself."

Back in the early 1950s, Ralph J. Cordiner, then president of General Electric, said that within three years after a chief executive takes over a company, he should have at least three people equally capable to succeed him.

☐ Finding the right employee isn't always easy.

"It's easy enough to find a Minister of Education; all the job needs is a long white beard. But a good cook is different; that requires universal genius."

Bismarck

James A. Mather, founder and chairman of the board of the Mr. Steak chain of restaurants, once offered some good advice. "If you want the best guidance for your company, choose people who are not subordinate to your position or your personality."

☐ Hire someone hungry for opportunity.

"Many young people have never experienced need. But I have had more success in hiring people who came from modest backgrounds."
John Swearingen, former executive, Standard Oil of Indiana

Frederick R. Kappel, former chairman of A.T.&T., had this to say about hiring:

"When you hire a man of high intelligence but low grades, in effect you have to bet that a drive he hasn't yet shown will show after he goes to work. If, on the other hand, you are considering a high scholarship man, your bet is that a drive already demonstrated will be sustained.

"As we look for career managers, why should we spend a large part of our effort searching among men who have made a career of just getting by? The proper goal of a business can't be just to get by. No enterprise with that objective in life will be able to do what the times demand. But if we should content ourselves with get-by people, that is the way they would shape the business."

Chester Burger, Survival in the Executive Jungle

☐ Putting people into the right job is important to the success of any company.

Mary Kay, of Mary Kay Cosmetics, tells of the time one of the secretaries on her support staff wasn't living up to her potential, so instead of firing her, Mary Kay transferred her to the accounting department, where the woman quickly began to shine.

☐ When you find good people, put them in the right job.

"When hiring key employees, there are only two qualities to look for, judgment and taste. Almost everything else can be bought by the yard."
John W. Gardner

☐ Some executives believe in bringing in talent from the outside to add new ideas.

Donald N. Frey, chairman of Bell & Howell Company said in a *Business Week* interview, "We needed new thoughts on a financial function that had become inbred. Inbreeding causes you to talk among yourselves. And when this happens, the world may move beyond you."

Joseph Brooks, chairman of Lord & Taylor, said in *Chain Store Age* magazine; "I think it is terribly important for every company in this day and age to bring in outsiders. As the business expands, it's a healthy thing in the executive capacity to have 10 percent new blood brought in every year."

☐ Good employees have to be searched for.

Ross Perot, founder of successful Electronic Data Systems advised, "Eagles don't flock—you have to find them one at a time."

In writing up his resume for a full-time position, an applicant described his summer job as purchasing, being responsible for the accuracy of daily cash transactions, and maintaining the morale, alertness, and well-being of the entire office staff.

Actually—he went out for the coffee.

☐ It's critical to screen out losers.

Losers are more like swamps. They just spread out all over the place. They tend to try a little bit of everything and really succeed at nothing. If you find yourself standing beside a swamp someday, watch what comes from it. Throughout the swamp, you'll find bogs that mire people down, mosquitoes that are good for nothing but sucking blood and carrying diseases, alligators and all kinds of venomous snakes that can harm humans.

The more alligators and snakes we hire, the more our organization becomes a swamp, producing less and less until it serves no useful purpose.

☐ Applications tell a lot.

Janet Lowe, the *San Diego Tribune's* business editor, reviewed applications from students seeking summer internships. One question: What office machines do you operate? Her favorite reply: Coffee.

The big burly fellow entered the bar and started talking to the bartender.

Big man:	"I see by the sign in your window you're looking for a bouncer. Ya fill the job yet?"
Bartender:	"Not yet. You had any experience?"
Big man:	"No, but watch this!" He walked over to a loudmouthed drunk in the back of the tavern, lifted him off his feet, and threw him sprawling into the street.
Big man:	"How's that?"
Bartender:	"Great! But you'll have to ask the boss about the job. I just work here."
Big man:	"Okay, where is he?"
Bartender:	"Just coming back in the front door."

It's okay to feel confidence in a job interview, but don't overdo it.

☐ Learn to read between the lines.

The personnel manager, checking the references of a job applicant wrote to the man's former employer, asking if he was a steady worker.

He said, "Steady? Why, he was practically motionless."

Employment Agent:	"When you go in for the interview, don't tense up. Just be natural."
Applicant:	"Be natural! That's how I got fired from my last job."

☐ Big plans attract big people.

Could NASA have recruited the best possible astronauts for the moon shot if it had had small plans?

What would have happened if they had told a room full of recruits that we are going to first try to get a man off the ground, then see if we can get him up into the air, eventually trying to break out of the earth's atmosphere, and see how far up we can go. The room would have been emptied rather quickly.

Instead they announced a grandiose plan to put a man on the moon. They recruited the best man available by saying, "Who wants to be the first person in history to walk on the lunar surface?"

☐ The people you hire determine your company's future.

David Ogilvy, the legendary adman and founder of Ogilvy & Mather, placed a Russian doll in front of each director's chair. He told them, "That's you. Open it."

When they opened the doll, they found another one inside and another one inside of it. Inside the smallest doll was a note.

"If you always hire people who are smaller than you are, we shall become a company of dwarfs. If, on the other hand, you always hire people who are bigger than you are, we shall become a company of giants."

☐ Look for people with natural qualities.

I was once traveling alone in Japan. Trying to get from Tokyo to Sasebo, I inquired about the train schedule. The man who helped me wrote down all the information I needed to make my trip. He gave me the times, train number, track number, and how to get to the station. I was greatly impressed by this "service." Moments later, when I was a block away, the man who helped me, chased me down to tell me some additional information.

This man wasn't trained in customer service. He didn't even work for the train company. He was the kind of person who wanted to help others. To be of service.

☐ It's better to hire someone who is service-oriented instead of someone who has to be trained to be service-oriented.

A hard-nosed general was reviewing a squadron of paratroopers. He asked one soldier: "How do you like jumping?"
He answered: "I love it."
He asked another: "How do you like jumping?"
He answered: "It's the most exciting thing I've ever done."
He asked a third: "How do you like jumping."
He answered: "I hate it."
The general asked: "Then why do you jump?"
The paratrooper replied: "Because I want to be around guys who want to jump."

☐ Hire employees who want to be part of other people's enthusiasm.

☐ Hiring outside people is not always the answer.

Robert Townsend, author of *Further Up the Organization*, said, "When I went to Avis as CEO, I kept hearing that they needed a comptroller. So I called an accounting firm, and they sent me someone highly recommended who'd been with them for a long time. Well, he was an unmitigated disaster! He was power mad, and wanted my job, I guess. Eventually I found a marvelous comptroller within the company."

☐ Look for potential employees who are determined to work for you.

A young woman was being interviewed by a prestigious Fortune 500 company. She asked the personnel manager if she could get into their well-respected training program. The personnel manager, already flooded by applications, said, "Impossible now. Come back in about ten years."
The applicant said, "Would morning or afternoon be better?"

☐ Often the interview can tell you more than a resume.

A manager out of courtesy interviewed a young man for a sales position that the company had no intention of hiring. At the end of the interview, the prospective employee was told that his interviewer didn't have the authority to hire him. Instead of leaving, he asked, "Who does have the authority to hire me?"

He got the job because the boss was impressed that he didn't go down in defeat, a quality necessary for any good salesperson.

"People suffer all their life long, under the foolish superstition that they can be cheated. But it is as impossible for a person to be cheated by anyone but himself."

Ralph Waldo Emerson

HONESTY

"He is most cheated who cheats himself."

Leonard Drozd

"In business today, it's not the thief who can destroy a company. It's the honest man who doesn't know what the heck he's doing."

Don Epstein

☐ Honesty is a constant battle.

"The real problem is in the hearts and minds of men. It is easier to denature plutonium than to denature the evil spirit of man."

Albert Einstein

"Honesty is the single most important factor having a direct bearing on the final success of an individual, corporation, or product."

Ed McMahon

William F. James, founder of Boys Town, Missouri, said that there are only three things necessary to success: first, normal intelligence; second, determination; and third, absolute honesty. One cannot be a little dishonest—it's all the way or nothing.

☐ Honesty is not always easy.

"The line of least resistance makes crooked rivers and crooked men."

Bob Murphey, humorist

"Ask any woman her age, and nine times out of ten she'll guess wrong."

Bob Murphey, humorist

"Not only can a man be honest and grow rich, but it is almost impossible for a man to grow rich unless he is honest."

J. J. Corn

Jacob Schiff, who led the investment firm Kuhn, Loeb & Company to an industry leader, said: "After over thirty years on Wall Street, I have seen many firms who thirty or even twenty years ago occupied the front rank, recede to positions of comparative unimportance, and I have seen other firms, who two or three decades ago were quite unimportant, come to the front and become leaders in domestic and international finance. The reason is they had been more honest than those who were the leaders at one time."

☐ We learn honesty early on.

A schoolteacher asked a little girl where her father worked. She replied, "I don't know. But I guess he makes rolls of toilet paper and light bulbs because that's what he brings home in his lunch box."

☐ Being honest pays in the long run.

A cigar smoker bought several hundred expensive stogies and then had them insured against fire. After he'd smoked them all, he filed a claim, pointing out that the cigars had been destroyed by fire.

The company refused to pay, and the man sued. A judge ruled that because the insurance company had agreed to insure the cigars against fire, it was legally responsible. So the company paid the claim. And when the man accepted the money, the company had him arrested for arson.

☐ Honesty pays in the long run.

John J. Creedon of Metropolitan Life Insurance Company offered this story about how honesty pays:

"A salesman of ours in Pennsylvania was referred to a small businessman as a prospect. It turned out the man already had a policy. He showed it to our salesman who read it and told him it was well-written, and he shouldn't change a thing. The businessman was flabbergasted, and very impressed. Our man didn't try to sell him what he didn't need. He referred the salesman to his brother, who bought a $250,000 policy."

■ HUMAN RELATIONS

"Anyone can be polite to a king, but it takes a gentlemen to be polite to a beggar."

Jim Shea

"You can handle people more successfully by enlisting their feelings than by convincing their reason."

Paul P. Parker

"The way positive reinforcement is carried out is more important than the amount."

B. F. Skinner

"You can foul up on almost anything, and you'll get another chance. But if you screw up, even a little bit, on people management, you're gone. That's it, top performer or not."

IBM executive

"Human relations means treating people as if they were what they ought to be and you help them to become what they are capable of being."

Johann Wolfgang von Goethe

"Our early emphasis on human relations was not motivated by altruism but by the simple belief that if we respected our people and helped them respect themselves, the company would make the most profit."

Thomas J. Watson, Jr., IBM

☐ People respond to praise.

In his play *Pygmalion*, George Bernard Shaw observed, "If you treat a girl like a flower girl, that's all she will ever be. If you treat her like a princess, she may be one."

The old saying, "It's not what you know, but who you know," can be changed to, "It's not who you know, but who you know and how well you get along with them."

Joe L. Whitley

☐ Business is nothing more than working with people.

Like the former undertaker who applied for a job with a business firm. The application asked, "What did you like about your previous job?"
The applicant replied, "Working with people."

"You can make more friends in two months by becoming interested in other people than you can in two years by trying to get people interested in you."

Dale Carnegie

A Carnegie Foundation study once showed that only 15 percent of a businessperson's success could be attributed to job knowledge and technical skills. An essential element but a small overall contribution. It showed that 85 percent of one's success would be determined by what they call "ability to deal with people" and "attitude."

☐ The best way to head off human relations problems is in the hiring process.

"Some people have personality problems. If you're a tremendous introvert, you'll have a terrible time in management because it takes you so much longer to reach the people you're working with. An introvert, by nature, is not going to develop the necessary communication and relationships as quickly as an extrovert."

Victor Kiam

"No matter how busy you are, you must take time to make the other person feel important!"

Mary Kay Ash, founder, Mary Kay Cosmetics

☐ Human relations is making the other person feel important.

Douglas MacArthur is well known, but few know that he was not only a great general but was also very adept at human relations. He had an aide write a report of every visiting dignitary's background and interest. The next time the dignitary returned, MacArthur was able to make the visitor feel important and flattered by all that he remembered about him.

"Politeness is the hallmark of the gentle-man and the gentle-woman. No characteristic will so help one to advance, whether in business or society, as politeness. Competition is so keen today, there is so much standardized merchandise, there are so many places where one's wants can be supplied, that the success or failure of a business can depend on the ability to please customers or clients. Courtesy—another name for politeness—costs nothing, but can gain much both for an individual and for an organization."

B. C. Forbes

"Remember that a man's name is, to him, the sweetest and most important sound in any language."

Dale Carnegie

☐ Human relations is caring about your workers.

Charles Percy was made president of Bell & Howell before he was forty years old. A reporter, fascinated by his rapid rise, asked many people to what they attributed Percy's success. The answer always came back, "From the very beginning, he showed a knack for being able to get the most out of other people."

☐ Sensitivity to the needs and desires of other people ultimately leads to success.

☐ Forget the management books; use common sense.

"Do not summon people to your office—it frightens them. Instead go the see them in *their* offices. This makes you visible throughout the agency. A chairman who never wanders about his agency becomes a hermit, out of touch with his staff."

David Ogilvy, founder, Ogilvy & Mather

☐ Human relations is looking at the other person's viewpoint.

On a Saturday night, a young grocery store clerk locked the door of his store and began to clean up so that he could go home. Suddenly there was a knock on the door. An old woman was standing outside rapping on the door window.

The clerk shouted out, "We're closed!"

She said, "I need a head of lettuce."

The clerk reluctantly let her in and led her to the produce section. Finally, after about five minutes of the old lady inspecting one head of lettuce after another, she said, "Actually, I only need half a head of lettuce."

The clerk said, "I'll have to clear it with the store manager." He went back to the manger's office and hollered out, "You won't believe this, but some stupid, idiotic, cranky old woman wants half a head of lettuce!"

Just as he finished, he noticed the old woman standing behind him. He turned back to the manager and said, "Fortunately we have this fine woman who will take the other half."

This young man knew the importance of maintaining good human relation skills with other people in order to get positive results. By sparing her feelings, he knew she would be back again as a customer.

☐ Good human relations is to realize the value of your coworkers and to treat them as valuable people.

Driving by a house once, I saw smoke climbing out of the roof. A young couple was running in and out of the house carrying anything they could carry before the house was consumed with flames. I stopped and asked them if there was anything I could help them carry out. They both quickly said, "Grab the pictures."

All of their possessions, the most valuable ones were the least expensive—their pictures of themselves.

☐ Good human relations for managers is to stay in touch with their employees.

Forrest Ford, founder of the St. Louis-based Forrest Ford Consultants, is known by his employees as "the Candy Man." Every afternoon, he walks through the entire office passing out candy so that he can have personal contact with each employee every day.

☐ Poor human relations skills can make your life miserable.

During the air traffic controllers strike, Terry Paulson, author of *They Shoot Managers, Don't They?* watched an irate executive belittle a baggage handler that was moving as fast as he could. When Paulson tried to share his empathy from having to put up with such abuse, the baggage handler replied, "Don't worry, I've already gotten even."

After a brief pause, Paulson asked, "What do you mean?"

He said with a smile on his face, "He's going to Chicago, but his bags are going to Japan."

☐ As a boss, human relations can be just finding out what others need to be better.

John Doe, age about fifty, worked as an assistant manager of a branch bank in a large banking system. He had been an assistant manager for eleven years. His work was so ordinary that no branch manager wanted him. Usually his current manager arranged to move him out of the way by transferring him to a new branch that was just opening; so John had worked in eight branches in eleven years. When he became assistant manager at his ninth branch, his manager soon learned of his record. Although tempted to transfer John, the manager decided to try to motivate him. The manager learned that John had no economic needs, because he had a comfortable inheritance and owned several apartment houses. His wife managed the apartments. His two children were college graduates and had good incomes. John was contented.

The manager made little headway with John and twice considered trying to fire him. Occasionally John developed drive for a few weeks, but then he lapsed into his old ways again. After a careful analysis of John's situation, the manager concluded that although John's needs for tangible goods were satisfied, he might respond to more recognition; so the manager started working in that direction. On the branch's first birthday, the manager held a party for all employees before the bank opened. He had a caterer prepare a large cake and write on top an important financial ratio which was under John's jurisdiction and which happened to be favorable at the moment. John was greatly moved by the recognition and the "kidding" that his associates gave him about the ratio. His behavior gradually changed, and within two years he became a successful manager of another branch.

Human relations gets results. IBM is an example of how to treat people.

Thomas J. Peters and Robert H. Waterman describe the importance of recognition, or lack of it, in their book *In Search of Excellence:*

"We circle all the way to IBM, perhaps one of the biggest and oldest American companies practicing an intense people orientation. The only issue with IBM is how to start describing it. With the seventy-year-old open door policy? The senior Mr. Watson's $1-a-year country club, established for all employees in the 1920s? The philosophy that starts with 'respect for the individual?' Lifetime employment? Insistence upon promotion from within? IBM day-care centers, IBM hotels, IBM running tracks and tennis courts? Monthly opinion surveys by the personnel department? A very high success rate among salesmen? The intense training? IBM's total history is one of intense people orientation that is reflected in the tiniest details. Walk into IBM's New York financial branch. The first thing that greets you is a massive floor-to-ceiling bulletin board with glossy photographs of every person in the branch hung under the banner: New York Financial . . . the difference is people."

☐ Great leaders know human relations skills.

"I'm just a plowhand from Arkansas, but I have learned how to hold a team together. How to lift some men up, how to calm down others, until finally they've got one heartbeat together, a team. There's just three things I'd ever say:
If anything goes bad, I did it.
If anything goes semi-good, then we did it.
If anything goes real good, then you did it.
That's all it takes to get people to win football games for you."

Paul "Bear" Bryant

☐ One way to ruin human relations is to overpromise.

While browsing through a sporting-goods store, I heard the following discussion between a teenager and his father:
"Please, Dad—if you buy me the weight set, I'll lift them every day. I promise I'll train faithfully."
"Well, I don't know . . . "
"Please, Dad."
"Oh, all right. If you're really going to make good use of them, I'll buy you the weights."
The father paid for the equipment and started walking towards the door. Soon thereafter, his son's voice called after him, "What? You mean I gotta carry them out to the car?"

Perle Mesta, the popular Washington hostess, was asked the secret of her success in having so many famous and rich people attend her parties.
She said, "It's all in the greetings and good-byes."
When each guest arrived, she said, "At last you're here." And when they left she said, "I'm sorry you have to leave so soon."

☐ Everybody likes to be treated special.

Using good human relations can solve many problems. Take a group of people who produced a bad product, and the error cost the company $15,000. If the manager went down to the factory floor and got angry and screamed threats at the workers, he hasn't solved the problem.

On the other hand, if the manager said, "Hey, you guys made a mistake. It cost us money, and if we make too many of these mistakes, we'll lose customers, and I'm out of a job and you'll be out of a job. Now if a guy who gave me the bad product turns around and says the problem is that we got shipped bad raw materials, now I know how to solve the problem." If you scream at workers, you may not discover the real problem.

☐ Learning what interests others can be profitable.

Susan RoAne in her book *How to Work a Room* told of the time she called Jeff Waddle, who was then the editor of *Meeting Manger*, the journal of Meeting Planners International. Susan and Jeff talked about some articles she hoped to place, and Jeff asked if she had been to Chicago for the MPI convention. She said that because of prior commitments, she had been unable to attend, and it was too bad because she had a friend with seats in the bleachers at Wrigley Field.

Susan hit paydirt because Jeff was a diehard baseball fan. Eventually they struck an agreement, and he published six of her articles in *Meeting Manager* over the next three years.

☐ The six most important words in the English language are:
"I admit I made a mistake."
The five most important words: "You did a great job."
The four most important words: "What is your opinion?"
The three most important words: "If you please."
The two most important words: "Thank you."
The single most important word: "We."
The least most important word: "I."

Gary Feldmar, president and sole owner of Excello Press, a $25-million printing company in Chicago, built his company on good human relations.

Here are some examples of how he shows his people he cares about them:

When the son of his sales manager was hurt trying to break up a fight in school, Gary sent the youngster a book on body-building and self-defense.

A few weeks after his controller complimented him on a pipe he was smoking, Feldmar had one of his Sasieni Four Dots fitted with a new bit and gave it to him.

The morning after Feldmar hired a new manager, the man's wife received a bouquet of flowers to welcome her to the company.

One of his salesmen had been putting in long hours traveling to take care of out-of-town customers, and he was having marital problems. The problem was magnified one morning when the salesman's wife left her wedding ring in his jacket. When the salesman revealed his problem to Feldmar, he was given a two-week vacation, and Excello picked up the tab. Feldmar's answer was, "So it cost the company two weeks—it was what he needed, and we want to keep our people happy."

Human relations is getting things done in a positive way.

Listen to this conversation between the wind and the sun.

The wind said, "See how easily I can blow away the coat from that man below."

So the wind blew up a storm. But the stronger the wind, the more the man clutched the coat holding it tight around him.

Then it was the sun's turn. With a smile, the sun beamed its warming rays down until the man took off his coat voluntarily.

I

INFLATION

Yogi Berra's observation of the nation's economy: "A nickel ain't worth a dime anymore."

Inflation separates us from earnings without value received. The worst of all the bad things about inflation is that it won't let us buy the luxuries we could afford when we were poor.

You know inflation is out of hand when piggy banks cost more than they hold.

Bumper sticker: "Inflation is a stab in the buck."

Graffiti: "I'm 300 percent against inflation."

"Inflation is when your nest egg is no longer anything to crow about."
Jimmy W. Marsh

Inflation is when the decimal point is the dismal point.

Inflation is when you never had anything, and now even that's gone.

Inflation is when half your salary goes for food and shelter and the other half does, too.

There's one consolation about inflation. The money you don't have isn't worth what it once was.

Inflation has made it possible for only the wealthy to afford a recession.

Inflation has improved my memory. I no longer have to write down a grocery list for $30 worth of items.

Inflation is another one of those problems that can't be cured by throwing dollars at it.

As inflation makes your money worth less and less, it's no comfort to reach into your pocket and find that you have nothing to worry about.

Everything hasn't been affected by inflation. We still have some two-bit politicians around.

"Think of the inflation spiral as a gigantic corkscrew . . . and think of yourself as the cork."

Bert Lance

A man said, "I know inflation is really here. I dropped a dollar bill the other day and was arrested for littering."

When it comes to fighting inflation, nothing is as effective as the consumer who says, "I'll be dammed if I'll pay that much."

Inflation is being broke with a pocket full of money.

Inflation is when you're in the middle-income and upper-outgo bracket.

Inflation has hit everything but the amount of my take-home pay.

Inflation is when, if they made 'em like they used to, you couldn't buy 'em like you used to.

Inflation is when the waiter asks if you'd like that $5 lunch plain or toasted.

Inflation is when you pay cash for something, and they ask to see your driver's license.

Inflation may have been arrested, as the economists claim, but whenever we go shopping, it seems to be out on bail.

Jimmy W. Marsh

New car buyer to a friend: "I never thought I'd ever spend that much money for anything that didn't have a doorbell on it."

Kay Kirkpatrick

Inflation is when you order a $25 steak, put it on your American Express card, and it fits.

Mike Dunkerley

The cost of living is high, but it's worth it.

Wife pointing out clerk in supermarket to husband: "Get ahead of him! He's marking up the prices again!"

Teacher to class: "Inflation means that by the time teachers get a raise, it won't be enough."

"In spite of the cost of living, it's still popular."

Kathleen Norris

When you save for a long time to buy something, then find you can't afford it—that's inflation.

☐ High inflation can create jobs.

Boy: "Hey, Dad, I've got a steady job."
Dad: "Doing what?"
Boy: "Changing the interest-rate signs at the bank."

Lady to friend: "My husband is trying to explain the economy to our son, Joey. Yesterday, Joey asked his father to teach him the value of a dollar . . . so my husband gave him a quarter."

Food is now so expensive, one supermarket doesn't even post its prices anymore. They just have a sign saying: "COME IN. WE'LL TALK.

☐ What causes inflation?

I asked a presidential candidate how he'd stop inflation, and he said, "I don't know, but I'm willing to spend whatever it takes to find out."

Well, I don't know much about economics, I'll admit, but I wish somebody could tell me why inflation always shows up in all my bills at the end of the month but never shows up in my bank account.

There's always a way to beat inflation. But you have to promise not to go to the filling station, supermarket, doctor, restaurant, hospital, drugstore, hardware store, barber shop, lumberyard, or liquor store.

Husband to wife: "What do you want to do tonight? We have just enough money to see a movie or fly to the West Coast and back."

INFORMATION

An NFL coach, talking about gathering too much information about players about to be drafted said, "Too much information is worse than not enough."

☐ Too much overload can cause no effect.

"We are drowning in information but starved for knowledge."

John Naisbitt

We are more sensitive to change today because of the speed in which we receive information. In 1805, it took six weeks for word of Nelson's victory at Trafalgar to reach Montreal. Now, any news in some remote place in the world is flashed to the rest of the world in a matter of seconds.

"The Information Age is a revolution. It's a revolution that's global in scope, with few safe harbors for isolationists. It's a revolution in which winning organizations will be those that give individuals the chance to personally make a difference."

John Scully, chairman, Apple Computer

☐ Information doesn't ensure success.

"Grandpa, why don't you get a hearing aid?"
"Don't need it, Son. I hear more now than I can understand."

☐ Information doesn't have to always be right.

Marconi was criticized when he suggested transmitting wireless telegraph signals across the Atlantic. The experts logically noted that since wireless waves traveled in straight lines, they would be beamed into space instead of following the curvature of the earth.

Marconi persisted and finally succeeded, but his success was based on error. What made the transmission possible was the then-unknown ionosphere that bounced the waves back to earth.

By being wrong, Marconi arrived at a conclusion he could never have reached had he been rigidly logical all the time.

Marconi's mistake coupled with Alexander Graham Bell's invention of the telephone opened invisible waves linking the world together.

☐ The most powerful weapon for achievement is information.

As a boy, David Sarnoff was determined to know more about radio than anyone else in the world. He finally became chairman of the Radio Corporation of America.

When Lyndon B. Johnson was a freshman senator, he would leave his office as many as ten times a day to go to the bathroom. He never used his own private bathroom. He made these walks so that he could accidentally on purpose meet other senators. Johnson did this to make contacts and pick up information.

☐ To be successful, get out with the workers and pick up information.

Question information; don't just accept it. There's a story about two old men who met every day in front of the Waldorf-Astoria Hotel. They would sit side by side and say very little for hours at a time.

Finally, one said: "Life is like a fountain."

Another hour passed before the other one answered, "I don't understand. Why is life like a fountain?"

Two hours passed and the first man said, "Well, maybe life isn't like a fountain after all!"

☐ Knowledge is knowing where to get information when you need it.

Albert Einstein was once asked how many feet are in a mile. Einstein answered, "I don't know. Why should I fill my head with things like that when I could look them up in any reference book in two minutes."

☐ The ability to find information when you need it and then to act on it is what gets things done.

▉ INNOVATION

☐ Innovation is doing something different.

The National Bank of Detroit once offered their customers $10 each time they discovered an error in their checking account. The policy brought in fifteen thousand new accounts and $65.5 million in deposits in the first two months.

☐ Innovations occur when people feel that they are on a mission.

It has been said that what made Thomas Edison such a great inventor was that his unlimited enthusiasm conveyed the feeling that he would press on until he succeeded.

☐ People have always feared innovative ideas.

When Sears first started sending out catalogs, rural merchants, already wary of the growing influence of chain stores, fought back crudely. They organized catalog burnings. In the South, racial and anti-Semitic rumors were aimed at the company.

☐ Where innovation is encouraged, it flourishes.

At 3M, every division is expected to get 25 percent of its sales each year from products that didn't exist five years earlier. The goal forces managers to constantly use 3M's scientific skill to come up with new products.

☐ Innovation doesn't always mean spending big money.

When a cosmetics company needs a package for a new product, designing it can be very costly, but at Revlon, a new package was not designed, but innovated. A bottle was needed for "Jontue," and some innovator saw that if the "Charlie" bottle was turned around it looked like an entirely different package.

☐ An innovative idea will always be copied.

For example Estée Lauder was the first to use the idea of giving a gift with a purchase. From that idea, her company grew to a value of nearly $2 billion. Estée Lauder said, "Even the banks are copying me now."

☐ Innovation doesn't always come from expected sources.

Economist Burton Klein examined fifty major innovations developed in the American economy over the last several decades. He determined that none of the innovations came from a company that was an industry leader at the time of the innovation.

☐ Businesses doesn't innovate; people do.

"Innovation has never come through bureaucracy and hierarchy. It's always come from individuals."

John Scully, chairman, Apple Computer

☐ Managing innovation is somewhat like trying to manage a butterfly.

"Obviously, managing a butterfly is a contradiction in terms. So is creating innovation in the workplace. Neither can be done and we should not try. But what is most important—we do not need to try. If left alone, each will reach its full beauty and will fertilize the environment with new growth and creativity."

Jack W. Schuler, executive vice president, Abbott Laboratories

☐ Innovation requires insight.

"If you see in any given situation only what everybody else can see, you can be said to be so much a representative of your culture that you are a victim of it."

S. I. Hayakawa

"Significant progress doesn't come from the formal planning process of an American corporation. It comes from a couple of guys doing something that hasn't been set down on a list."

William G. McGowan, CEO, MCI Communications

☐ Innovation comes from people.

A few years ago, MCI separated a small group of innovators away from the rest of MCI's staff in Washington, D.C. They were given a mission: develop a new mail system, one that will replace manual with an electronic method. The result was MCI Mail, an electronic method for sending letters.

When told that MCI did it, CEO William G. McGowan disagreed. He said, "It came out of a bunch of hungry guys with high energy levels."

☐ Innovations aren't always capitalized on by the innovator.

The transistor was invented in Bell Laboratories in 1947. Yet Sony sold the first transistor radio in America in 1956. In the same year, 1956, Ampex, another U.S. company, introduced the first videotape recorder, but again Sony improved its design and introduced Betamax in 1975.

☐ Don't just innovate, but make the innovations marketable before the market gets taken over by others.

☐ Innovations don't always come from big companies with big budgets.

One study showed that out of sixty-one basic inventions, only sixteen were discovered in big companies. For example, the dial telephone was invented by an undertaker, the ballpoint pen by a sculptor.

☐ Properly motivated, employees can be a good source for innovations.

When IBM started making PCs, the company was concerned that the programs they bought from outside vendors weren't enough. So to spur software development, IBM made the PC's available at a discount to employees, who were told that if they created a new program the company would pay them royalties just like any other outside vendor. As one IBM vice president said, "This idea had 15,000 to 20,000 programmers innovating for us."

☐ Sometimes innovation is building on another person's idea.

Unlike Thomas Edison, who invented the light bulb, or the Wright brothers, who first flew an airplane, or Alexander Graham Bell and the telephone, Henry Ford didn't invent anything. What he did was to improve the way it was being done.

Innovation can come from the bottom of a company as well as from the top, if it is encouraged. For example, companies like Federal Express offer innovation awards as high as $25,000 to employees who come up with suggestions and innovations.

☐ Innovations can come from finding solutions to problems.

In the early 1980s, the airline industry was losing $1 million a day, and no one could afford to buy airplanes. Robert Crandall, American Airline's chairman, worked out a unique deal with McDonnell Douglas, which was unsuccessfully trying to sell its MD Super 80s. Crandall proposed and got thirty-day leases on twenty planes. American was allowed to return them if they didn't need them. The idea worked, and American purchased more, setting an example in the industry.

☐ What makes some new ideas attractive is the person behind the idea. Their enthusiasm and energy, along with other intangible features.

For example, Fred Smith of Federal Express came up with his revolutionary idea for an overnight air-freight service back in 1965 while he was still a student at Yale. He wrote a paper about his new idea for an economics class. His professor called it impractical and gave Fred a "C." It was six more years before Fred actually put the company together. But only Fred Smith, the innovator, could bring all the intangibles together that made Federal Express happen.

☐ Innovative ideas are not always well received.

An irate banker demanded that Alexander Graham Bell remove "that toy" from his office. "That toy" was the telephone.

A Hollywood producer scrawled a curt rejection note on a manuscript that become *Gone with the Wind*.

☐ All new ideas are worth hearing about.

A number of years ago, a young engineer put a box on the desk of the founder of one of America's major electronics companies. His message: "Put this on the market and everybody'll want one. They'll put one in every automobile on the road." The response: "No. It'll be too distracting to the driver. It could cause accidents."

No, the device was not the cellular telephone, which inspired the same fear. The contraption instead was the simple car radio. The inventor was Bill Lear of Lear Jet fame. The electronics entrepreneur was Paul Galvin. You know his company as Motorola, which today derives a great deal of its $7 billion or so of annual sales from mobile communications products and cellular car phones.

☐ Innovation is finding a new way to do something, and most managers don't try to innovate.

"Most managers come to a job, pick it up where it is and just keep going. They don't sit down and say to themselves, 'Here's a job. I know how my predecessor did it, but what is there about my environment, my responsibilities and the end result I am trying to achieve that suggest ways to do it better?' It is absolutely incumbent upon anyone who wants to do anything out of the ordinary to do that. Even if you're just running a maintenance crew sweeping out a building, you can do it. You can consider the procedures used to do the sweeping. Are they the most efficient? During what times of day is it best to sweep? In what areas? Which people can do what functions the best? You can see if you have a good mix of people, whether they're overpaid or underpaid. You have to sit down and write out the things you think you can and should achieve."

Roderick Hill, former chairman, Securities and Exchange Commission

☐ Where do ideas come from? Not where most people think.

• Leo Gerstenzang thought of Q-Tips when he saw his wife trying to clean their baby's ears with toothpicks and cotton.
• Ott Diffenbach came up with cellophane soda straws when he twisted the wrapper from a cigarette pack and saw he had created a tube.
• King C. Gillette had been looking for a throwaway product ever since having a conversation with the inventor of pop-bottle caps. When he found his razor dull, he thought of the safety razor with disposable blades.
• Ole Evinrude got angry when the ice cream in his rowboat melted before he got to his island picnic spot—so he invented the outboard motor.
• Ralph Schneider decided to form Diners Club one night after he lost his wallet.
• Charles Strite was fuming at the burnt toast in the factory lunchroom where he worked—and thought up the automatic toaster.

Karl Vesper, New Venture Strategies

INSURANCE

☐ Insurance is a costly part of doing business.

Cartoon in the *Wall Street Journal*: The proprietor of a lemonade stand to young friend, "Business is OK but I'm gonna have to shut down. I can't get any insurance."

Sometimes insurance companies are dealing with an uninformed public.
A woman called an insurance agent and said, "I want to insure my house. Can I do it by phone?

Insurance Agent: "I'm sorry, but I have to see it first."
Woman: "Then you'd better get over here right away—because it's on fire."

Two elderly men were talking in a doctor's office. One confided he was at that stage in life where he was uncertain about what type of insurance he needed—major medical or minor miracle.

☐ Make them decide to buy now.

Hank was working hard as an insurance salesman trying to get Frank as a client: "Don't let me frighten you into making a hasty decision, Frank. Sleep on it tonight. If you wake up tomorrow, call me."

Hospital nurse to patient: "Good news, Mr. James. Your insurance company says you can go home tomorrow."

☐ Some people don't understand insurance.

A few weeks after getting $1,000 compensation for the loss of her jewelry, an elderly woman wrote to the insurance company and told them she had found the missing jewelry in her dresser drawer.

She said, "I didn't think it would be fair to keep both the jewels and the insurance money, so I thought you would be pleased to know that I have given the $1,000 to charity."

Here's why insurance companies
Are mostly indestructible:
The cost of damages most times
Is less than the deductible.

G. Sterling Leiby

☐ Industry terms can sometimes be confusing.

Insurance salesman: "Now that amounts to premiums of $6.90 per month on a straight life. That's what you want, isn't it?"
Customer: "Well, I would like to fool around once in a while on a Saturday night."

☐ You don't sell more insurance unless you can present the proper reason.

Insurance salesman: "Now that you are married, I'm sure that you will want to take out more insurance on yourself."
Young man: "I don't think I need any more. I don't think she is that dangerous."

☐ The cost of insurance can put a business out of business.

In a speech before the American Bar Association, Chrysler chairman Lee Iacocca told the story of a small company in Virginia that made driving aids for handicapped people. The company went out of business because it couldn't afford the liability insurance. Too risky.

☐ Insurance offers a satisfying career.

Jerry Falick swore he would never sell life insurance when he graduated from the University of Florida. He said: "I thought you sold life insurance when you failed at everything else." He later became one of the nation's most successful life insurance salesman when he realized that he wanted to help people and to be successful, and by selling life insurance, he could combine the two.

INTEGRITY

"Morals come in handy. If you get caught, they're a good alibi."

Stephen Hendricks

"Integrity is not a 90 percent thing, not a 95 percent thing; either you have it or you don't."

Peter Scotese, retired CEO, Spring Industries

"A great business is seldom if ever built up, except on lines of strictest integrity."

Andrew Carnegie

☐ Integrity too often has a broad definition.

Sydney Biddle Barrows, the Mayflower Madam said, "I ran the wrong kind of business, but I did it with integrity."

"You don't turn integrity on and off. To have integrity you must be like the guy who uses a butter knife when nobody is around."

Wallace Carr

☐ You can be too honest.

The farmer was being examined by the insurance company doctor.
The examiner asked, "Ever had a serious illness?"
The farmer said, "No."
"An accident?"
"No, but last summer when I was out in the pasture, a bull threw me over the fence."
"Well, isn't that an accident?"
"No, he did it on purpose."

This is the difference between integrity and wisdom:

Boss: "Integrity and wisdom are essential to success in every business. By integrity, I mean when you promise a customer something, you must keep that promise even if you lose money."
New employee: "And what is wisdom?"
Boss: "Don't make any such fool promises."

☐ It doesn't pay to compromise your integrity.

Emmanuel Ninger was arrested for passing counterfeit $20 bills. A warrant was obtained to search Ninger's home. During the search, they found a $20 bill in the process of being printed. They also found three portraits that Emmanuel Ninger had painted. Ninger was an artist, and he was a good one. He was so good, he had hand painted those $20 bills. Meticulously, stroke by stroke, he had applied the master's touch so skillfully that he was able to fool everyone until a quirk of fate in the form of the wet hands of a grocery clerk exposed him.

After the arrest, his portraits were sold at public auction for $16,000—over $5,000 each. The irony of the story is that it took Emmanuel Ninger almost exactly the same length of time to paint a $20 bill as it took him to paint a $5,000 portrait.

This brilliant and talented man was a thief in every sense of the word. Tragically, the person he stole the most from was himself, Emmanuel Ninger.

Not only could he have been a wealthy man if he had legitimately marketed his ability, but he could have brought joy and benefit to others. He had a choice, and he compromised his integrity.

Winston Churchill once attended an official ceremony. Several rows behind him, two gentlemen began whispering. "That's Winston Churchill. They say he is getting senile. They say he should step aside and leave the running of the nation to younger, more dynamic, and capable men."

Churchill sat facing forward, but when the ceremony was over, he stopped by the row where the men were seated. He leaned forward and said, "Gentlemen, they also say he is deaf!"

Churchill could withstand this criticism because he took action based on what is right, not expedient. That's integrity.

INTERVIEWING

"The closest most people come to perfection is when they fill out a job application."

Don L. Griffith

☐ A resume is needed, but it won't get you the job.

"When I interview a job applicant, I am first interested in how he presents himself. How does he look; how is he dressed; what does he say; how does he answer my questions?"

Franklin Murphy, chairman, Times-Mirror

"Job applicants do not always act in their own best interest."

Robert Half

"I'm turned off by people who haven't done their homework."

Donald Kendall, chairman, PepsiCo.

Barbara Walters offers this advice to prospective interviewers, "My best advice for dealing with destructive anxiety is homework . . . homework helps enormously when you apply for a job."

"Most people who fail to get the job they really want fail not because they are not qualified but because they failed in the interview. And most failure occurs because they aren't prepared."

David W. Crawley, Jr.

☐ Don't say too much on an interview.

The personnel manager took an application from a job seeker, but he had to tell him that he didn't have anything for him.

Personnel manager: "Right now, we just don't have enough to keep you busy."

Applicant: "Oh, you'd be surprised at how little it takes."

☐ Don't exaggerate your past.

A very eager young man was applying for a job.

Supervisor: "We need a responsible person."

Young man: "Well sir, at all the jobs I had, whenever anything happened, they said I was responsible."

☐ To get hired, you may have to sell someone on the idea of how much they need you.

Victor Kiam told of the time a young man wanted to work for him at Remington. After looking over the applicant's resume, he told him there wasn't anything available. The young man refused to end the interview. He said, "I think there's an opening for me, but I don't know where it is yet."

He offered Kiam a plan. He would work for thirty days without compensation, wagering his free labor that he'd find a position for himself at Remington. Within the thirty days, he found some problems and outlined how he would solve them. He got the job.

☐ Persistence can lead to a good job.

▌INVESTING

"Prosperity is the fruit of labor. It begins with saving money."
Abraham Lincoln

☐ It takes money to make money.

"No boy will ever succeed as a man who does not in his youth begin to save."
Theodore Roosevelt

Referring to Wall Street, Gertrude Stein said, "The money remains the same, its is merely the pockets that change."

☐ Cut your losses.

Better lose the anchor than the whole ship.

Financial planner to client: "I've reviewed your financial picture, and if we manage your money properly, there should be plenty for both of us."

☐ Brokers are in business to make money for themselves first.

Sign on a successful stockbroker's desk: "The buck starts here."

Annual reports have a resistible quality. Once you put them down, you can't pick them up again.

☐ Timing isn't everything.

"It's a good deal easier to know what's going to happen than when it's going to happen."

Philip Fisher

"Investing is not as tough as being a top-notch bridge player. All it takes is the ability to see things as they really are."

Warren Buffett, chairman, Berkshire Hathaway

☐ Cut your losses.

"You only have to do a very few things right in your life so long as you don't do too many things wrong."

Warren Buffett

☐ Don't follow the crowd.

"If you see a bandwagon, it's too late."

James Goldsmith

☐ You can't lose money you don't have.

The late Joseph P. Kennedy once offered this advice: "Almost anybody can lose his shirt on Wall Street if he's got enough capital to start with and the proper inside information."

"Money is like manure. You have to spread it around or it smells."

J. Paul Getty

☐ Making money isn't always as hard as it seems.

Robert Heller, author of the book *The Age of the Common Millionaire* and a millionaire himself thanks to investments in the London real estate market, said, "People who think making a million is difficult haven't tried."

☐ Investing is easy.

Nebraska-based Warren Buffett is considered one of the smartest investors in the country. He said he had become one of the wealthiest men in the world by strictly following two rules. One is not to lose money. The second rule is not to forget the first rule.

"We believe that short-term forecasts of stocks and bond prices are useless. They tell you nothing about the future."

Warren Buffett, chairman, Berkshire Hathaway

"Few rich men own their own property. The property owns them."

Robert Green Ingersoll

Investing becomes speculation when you are like the two men buying and selling cans of sardines. They sold for 10 cents one day, 20 cents the next, and on up to over $1 a can. Finally, one man opened a can and told his partner how terrible the salty sardines tasted. His partner replied, "Sardines aren't for eating, they're for buying and selling."

When you invest, make sure you have more than a can of sardines.

"One should buy stock when it is cheap. Wait for it to go up and then sell. If it does not go up, don't buy it."

Randall Price

Edward Crosby Johnson II, creator of the mutual fund industry, viewed the stock market as "a beautiful woman—endlessly fascinating, endlessly complex, always changing, always mystifying . . . the market represents everything that everybody has ever hoped, feared, hated, or loved. It is all of life."

J. Paul Getty said that whenever he made an investment, he tried to apply this simple principle: "If you want to make money, really big money, do what nobody else is doing."

"Buy when everyone else is selling and hold until everyone else is buying. This is not merely a catchy slogan. It is a very essence of successful investment."

J. Paul Getty

☐ Don't overdiversify.

Peter Lynch, the successful portfolio manager of the Magellan Fund, offered this advice: "Compare managing a portfolio of 10 stocks to playing 10 hands of stud poker at once. As you turn up new cards, the relative value of each hand changes. To win, you must play every hand against the other, and consider shifting your bets to the most promising hands before all the cards are dealt."

☐ You don't get rich by following the crowd.

The popularity of reorganization might best be viewed from the perspective of the ad run in the *Wall Street Journal* by United Technologies Corporation. It noted: "When forty million people believe in a dumb idea, it's still a dumb idea."

☐ When an investment goes bad, our perspective changes.

"It's not whether you win or lose that counts, but who gets the blame." As Will Rogers once pointed out with respect to his business pursuits, "It is not the return on my investment that I am concerned about; it is the return *of* my investment."

☐ Don't sell too soon.

Henry's Ford's largest original investor sold all his stock in 1906. Roebuck sold out to Sears for $25,000 in 1895. Today, Sears may sell $25,000 worth of goods in 16 seconds.

☐ Invest, don't speculate.

"There are two times in a man's life when he should not speculate in stocks: when he can't afford it, and when he can."

Mark Twain

☐ Invest in a business that knows its niche.

An investor once asked the president of a company when the company was selling in the market for one-quarter of its replacement value why they didn't buy back their own stock at the discount price.

The executive said, "We should, but we don't. That's not what we are here to do."

☐ Buy value.

Benjamin Graham's idea of a good, safe investment was to buy a dollar for fifty cents over and over again.

Andrew Carnegie, the nineteenth-century steel tycoon, used to say, "Put all your eggs in one basket. And watch the basket. That's the way to make money."

Successful people will tell you that things are too complicated today to put all your eggs in one basket.

☐ It's okay to invest, but keep your priorities straight.

A stockbroker was hit by a car. A cop rushed over, placed his jacket over the victim, a sweater under his head, and said, "Are you comfortable?"

The stockbroker replied, "I'm doing okay; I've got some stocks, bonds, and a money-market account."

Remember—when investing, the assets should always equal liabilities plus capital and surplus. Just as a watermelon should always equal the sum of the slices cut by those who have a right to eat it.

☐ The best investment is an investment in people.

An oilman said to a missionary as they were being evacuated from Malaya with the coming of the Japanese during World War II, "My life's work has gone into oil wells, which I had to blow up; your life has gone into people, into their character and development. My life work has gone; yours will remain. I've failed, and you've succeeded."

☐ Nothing takes the place of research.

Often personal research is the best. Victor Kiam, in his book *Going for It!*, told the following story:

He knew little or nothing about electric razors. He even shaved with a blade. But he set about correcting that. He asked retailers about shavers and learned that while Norelco dominated the market, they thought Remington was the best product. Kiam actually tried the Remington in his own bathroom each morning. He tried it versus the razor. He tried it versus all the major electric brands. Then, when he was satisfied that the Remington really was the best, he went out and bought the company.

☐ Inventory may not be worth what we think it's worth.

When a book publishing company wanted to borrow some operating capital, they went to see their banker, who had been watching their business growing steadily year after year. The banker was reluctant to make a new loan, and one of the managers had an inspiration: "Why can't we borrow against our inventory? We have a half million dollars worth of books in our warehouse."

The banker asked: "Do these books have printing on them?"

The manager replied: "Of course, that's what we do. We print books."

The banker said: "I can't give you an additional loan based on your inventory. The paper would have been worth something, but not with printing on it."

☐ Invest in yourself.

"If you are a business executive in a growth company, forget about cattle, oil wells, and other tax-saving investments. Put your capital in your own company and leave it there. If you and your associates do a good job, you'll be far better off in the long run than if you had diverted time and money to a venture in which you would be an absentee owner."

Royal Little, founder, Textron

There is not much difference, really, between the squirrel laying up nuts and the man laying up money. Like the squirrel, the man—at least at the start—is trying to provide for his basic needs. I don't know much about squirrels, but I think they know when they have enough nuts. In this they are superior to men, who often don't know when they have enough, and frequently gamble away what they have in the empty hope of getting more."

Bernard M. Baruch, Baruch: The Public Years

☐ Be careful where you get your investing advice.

When asked by his church rector for some investment advice, Jay Gould, the Wall Street tycoon and multimillionaire, made the pastor swear he would keep the advice secret; the pastor agreed. Gould said, "Buy Missouri Pacific."

The clergyman did, and the stock went up for several months. Eventually the stock crumbled, and the rector was wiped out. Sadly, he went to see Gould. " I took your advice and lost all my savings."

Gould said, "I'm sorry. To restore your faith, I'm going to give you forty thousand for the thirty thousand you lost." Gould wrote out a check, and the minister reluctantly accepted it.

The minister said, "I must confess something, I didn't keep my word. I told several members of the congregation."

Came Gould's cheerful reply, "Oh, I know that. They were the ones I was after."

☐ At times, saying no is the best investment.

Take the case of the middle-aged school teacher who invested her life savings in a business enterprise that had been elaborately explained to her by a swindler.

When her investment disappeared and the wonderful dream of getting rich was shattered, she went to the local office of the Better Business Bureau.

They asked, "Why didn't you come to us first? Didn't you know about the Better Business Bureau?"

She said sadly, "Oh, yes, I've always known about you. But I didn't come because I was afraid you'd tell me not to do it."

Legendary investor Bernard Baruch said that there was only one question an investor should ask when evaluating whether or not to invest. He said that when you looked at a stock you already own, ask yourself every day, "Would I buy this stock today?"

If the answer is yes, then hold on or buy more. If the answer is no, then sell regardless of the price of the stock.

Baruch became very wealthy following this simple rule.

☐ The most successful step in investing is buying right.

Take the little girl who visited a watermelon farmer. She pointed to a large watermelon and asked the farmer how much it was.

He said, "That one is three dollars."

The little girl said, "But I've only got thirty cents."

The farmer pointed to a small watermelon in his field and said, "How about that one?"

The little girl said: "Okay, I'll take it, but leave it on the vine, and I'll be back to get it in a month."

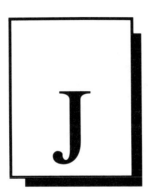

J

▯ JOB SATISFACTION

"No matter how humble your work may seem, do it in the spirit of an artist, of a master. In this way, you lift it out of commonness and rob it of what would otherwise be drudgery."

Orison Swett Marden

"It is not doing the thing which we like to do but liking to do the thing which we have to do that makes life blessed."

Johann Wolfgang von Goethe

☐ People rarely succeed at anything unless they enjoy it.

☐ You can't accomplish anything unless you are having some fun.

"When people aren't having any fun, they seldom produce good advertising."

David Ogilvy, founder, Ogilvy & Mather

☐ A little appreciation can go a long way.

"People work harder and smarter if they find their work satisfying and know that it is appreciated."

Thomas J. Frye

Peter Drucker said that every job should have a challenge for the worker and offer an opportunity to influence the speed of his work.

In an article in the *Piedmont Airlines* magazine, management psychologist James Carr wrote that we all need to feel needed—that "fulfillment lies in some combination of individual accomplishment and interaction with others . . . people who go about their daily lives trying to achieve a healthy balance between giving and receiving, between serving and being served."

"For a young engineer today, working to make the shareholders rich doesn't interest him. He is a craftsman and works for himself. He considers his company a place where he can ply his trade—rather than a company for which he works."

Tom Halliburton

☐ To have a happy work force, put your workers where they can use their skills.

An industrial psychologist stated that a number of problems in business and industry are a result of boredom. This lack of job satisfaction is not caused by repetitive jobs but rather by resentment and depression that workers feel when they are deprived of the opportunity to use their skills.

"The higher the pay in enjoyment the worker gets out of his labors, the higher shall be his pay in money also."

Mark Twain

☐ Workers can feel more satisfied in their jobs if they have an awareness of the importance of their job.

During World War II, parachutes were being made and, from the workers' point of view, the job was tedious. It was the same thing over and over every day. Then one morning, the owners started telling the workers they were making something that could save the lives of their husbands, brothers, or sons. Even though the work was still boring, it was performed with more gusto because the workers understood the importance of it.

☐ Job satisfaction can come from using our talents.

"If we have a talent and cannot use it, we have failed. If we have a talent and use only half of it, we have partly failed. If we have a talent and learn somehow to use all of it, we have gloriously succeeded, and won a satisfaction and a triumph few individuals ever know."

Thomas Wolfe, The Web and the Rock

"To love what you do and feel that it matters, how could anything be more fun?"

Katharine Graham, Washington Post

☐ You need to love and respect your work for it to be satisfying.

"My father was devoted to his family and his business; as a matter of fact, he regarded his business as a member of his family."

Stanley Marcus, Neiman-Marcus

Finding good people and paying them well isn't enough to ensure top production. As Josh Billings once said, "Money will buy a pretty good dog, but it won't buy the wag of his tail."

Somehow, we've got to get them to love this company and to love their work.

☐ We will enjoy our jobs once we realize how important the job is we are doing.

A man saw two workers breaking granite, and he stopped to talk. When he asked one worker, "What are you doing?" the man replied, "I'm trying to break this granite."

He said to the other one, "What are you doing?"

He replied: "I'm on a team of people who are building a cathedral."

☐ We are the only ones who can make our job important.

☐ Work should be fun.

One manager with a high-tech company in Chicago told me how his subordinates were always coming into his office emphasizing the high priority of one thing or another. He would listen to them and tell each one to leave their papers on the desk. Then as they were about to walk out the door, he would say, "Don't forget Rule Six."

A young man once said, "Rule Six, yes, of course."

Then he turned to walk out but stopped and asked, "What is Rule Six?"

"Rule Six is as follows: Don't take yourself too seriously."

"Thank you sir, I'll remember that. But what are the other rules?"

The reply was, "There are no other rules."

☐ When it comes to work, have fun and don't take yourselves too seriously or you'll suffer burnout.

☐ The right job for you shouldn't be hard; it should offer fun.

A producer once offered Igor Stravinsky $4,000 to score a film. He told the producer that the fee wasn't enough.

Producer: "That's what we paid the last guy."

Stravinsky: "He had talent. I don't have talent, which makes the work for me that much more difficult."

☐ Work becomes hard when it isn't what you enjoy doing because your talent lies in other areas.

☐ If you don't like your job, nothing can make it satisfying.

Tarzan came home after work and asked Jane to make him a triple scotch. He finished it off and asked for another one.

Jane: "Tarzan, I'm concerned about your drinking. Every afternoon, you come home and have two or three drinks."

Tarzan: "I can't help it, Jane. It's a jungle out there."

It doesn't matter how difficult a job is; if we like it, it won't be a jungle.

☐ JOB SECURITY

"Too many people are thinking of security instead of opportunity."
James F. Byrnes

☐ Job security can mean telling the boss what he wants to hear.

"I don't want any yes-men around me. I want everybody to tell me the truth even if it costs them their jobs."
Samuel Goldwyn

☐ There is no such thing as job security.

"Teachers are fired. Middle management is washed up on the beaches of mergers. Recessions have wiped out whole hordes of public relations, advertising, and other media personnel."
Robert Fierro, business writer

"There is no security on this earth. There is only opportunity."
Douglas MacArthur

☐ Job security is important.

"T. J. Watson didn't move in and shake up the organization. Instead, he set out to buff and polish the people who were already there and to make a success of what he had. That decision in 1914 led to the IBM policy on job security, which has meant a great deal to our employees."
Thomas Watson, Jr., IBM

☐ One way to get job security is to make yourself indispensable.

An employee who survived all sorts of personnel turnover and purges at his company was asked the secret of his survival. He said, "Oh, they don't dare fire me. I'm always too far behind in my work."

A man ran into an old pal who was worried about the employment situation at the factory where he worked.
Howard: "Is your job in jeopardy?"
Worker: "No. My job is very secure. It's me they can do without."

☐ Your job may not be as secure as you think.

Cartoon in the *Wall Street Journal*: One employee to another, after a chat with the boss, "He didn't exactly say I was doing a good job, but he did say that I'm the least of his worries."

☐ At some companies, job security is emphasized.

Nobody with more than fifteen years experience can be fired without the personal approval of the president of General Mills.

If General Mills decides to sell a subsidiary, the buyer has to agree to retain the same employee benefits package for a period of not less than five years.

At Hallmark, no one can be fired unless two corporate officers agree to the termination.

☐ Job security comes from others not knowing how to do what you do.

"My job is so secret that even I don't know what I'm doing."
William Webster, director, Central Intelligence Agency

☐ Job security can increase productivity and streamline an organization.

Digital Equipment Corporation asked its white-collar workers to suggest ways to improve office productivity.

One group of twenty eight workers had a bold idea: eliminate their own function! Obviously, these workers had to trust that management would find them other jobs in the company. Their department was eliminated, and management did find them other jobs.

JUDGMENT

"Statistics are no substitute for judgment."

Henry Clay

"Good judgment is based 80 percent on knowledge and experience and 20 percent on intuition."

Doc Blakely, humorist

☐ Sometimes good judgment is accepting obvious responsibility.

"If I catch you saying, 'It's not my fault, it was his responsibility,' with the fingers pointing around the circle, I'll fire you, because if you don't have enough interest in the company—if you're willing to stand there and watch a drunk get in a car, or let a two-year-old without a life jacket play on the end of a dock alone—well, you're not allowed to do that. You are required to run and protect that two-year-old."
Paul Charlap, chairman, Savin Business Machines

☐ Hire people with good judgment and you get good judgment.

"You want people who can be honest with themselves in analyzing a situation, making judgments and evaluating projects."
Donald Siebert, chairman, J. C. Penny

☐ People reveal their judgment level in many ways.

Gordon Crosby, chairman of US LIFE, said that he once hired a twenty-eight-year-old portfolio manager from a bank in Wisconsin. Within three weeks, the man had sold his home in Madison, purchased a new home in Summit, New Jersey, and was on the job. He had another situation, an internal transfer, where it took the man almost nine months to make the move. The second man had a tendency to get caught up in the nitty-gritty and lose sight of the big picture.

☐ People can make judgments about you by the company you keep.

When young Steve Jobs was desperately trying to get funding for Apple Computer, he was seen in a restaurant with a representative of the Rockefeller venture capital firm. The person who saw him had already turned him down but reconsidered and contributed $150,000 to Apple Computer, helping them get off and running.

☐ Good judgment comes with experience.

A young banker asked an eighty-year-old banker what the secret of success was in banking.

Old banker: "Good judgment."
Rookie: "How do you get good judgment?
Old banker: "Experience."
Rookie: "How do you get experience?"
Old banker: "Bad judgment."

☐ Nothing replaces good judgment.

"As the judge told the young lawyer, 'Young man, if you will pluck some feathers from the wings of your imagination and stick them in the tail of your judgment, you will fly better."

Newt Hielscher, humorist

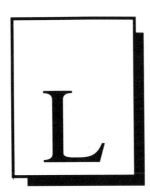

LAWYERS

"Laws are made to trouble people, and the more trouble they make, the longer they stay on the statute books."

Finley Peter Dunne

"The first thing we do, let's kill all the lawyers."

Shakespeare, Henry VI

"Lawyers are like beavers: They get in the mainstream and dam it up.

John Naisbitt, Megatrends

☐ Even the best lawyer needs evidence.

A lawyer told me that his father, also a lawyer, was once approached by a glum-looking client who asked his help in collecting a $5,000 debt.

Lawyer: "Do you have an IOU, a personal note, anything like that?"
Client: "No, I haven't got anything. I thought he was a friend. When he asked me for the money, I just gave it to him. He promised to pay it back, but so far I haven't seen a cent. And I know he has it."
Lawyer: "All right, here's what you do. You write him and tell him you've been very patient, but now you want the $10,000 he borrowed from you."
Client: "You mean $5,000."
Lawyer: "No. Say $10,000. The chances are good that he'll write back that he only borrowed $5,000, and then we'll have something in writing we can take to court."

☐ Lawyers are very expensive.

A man met a local attorney on the street one day and asked a business question. He was startled a couple of days later to get a bill for $75 in the mail

185

from the lawyer. Not long after that, he and the attorney met on the street again.

Attorney: "Good morning."
Man: "Good morning. But I'm telling you, not asking you."

☐ Some lawyers charge for time they don't put in.

A lawyer died and went to where lawyers probably go. But once there, he decided he should do a little cross-examination on his own. After all, he was only forty years old.

Lawyer: "You will agree that at my age I'm too young to be here, won't you? Consider, too, my perfect health record, not so much as a cold for years."
Admitting clerk: "It would seem so."
Lawyer: "Then what sort of explanation do you have?"
Admitting clerk: "I'll have to check my records again," [It took about ten minutes on a high-speed computer.] "I think we've found the answer."
Lawyer: "And what's that?"
Admitting clerk: "We must have calculated your age from your billing hours, and according to them, you have to be at least ninety-two years old."

☐ Suing has become an accepted behavior.

Patient to Surgeon: "I don't have any health insurance, Doc. But don't worry—I'll pay your bill out of the malpractice award.

☐ Sometimes lawyers are too quick to settle.

A man was playing in a pro-am. His first drive off the number one tee went wide right and hit a spectator in the head. The spectator shouted, "I'm a lawyer, and you hit me! I'm going to sue you for $5,000!"

The golfer asked, "Didn't you hear me holler *fore*?"

The lawyer replied, "Okay, I'll take it."

☐ Too many people will sue anybody or anything.

"[This is a true story.] For years, there was a tree in the middle of the Sahara Desert. It was a freak of nature—the only tree within hundreds of miles in any direction. During World War II, an Englishman ran into it—in a tank! If it were today—in this country—he'd sue! I don't know who, but he'd sue."

Lee Iacocca

☐ Attorneys need a good dose of public relations.

Research laboratories are beginning to replace white rats with lawyers for three reasons:

1. Lawyers are much more plentiful.
2. You don't get too attached to lawyers, and
3. There are some things not even a rat will do.

☐ A lawyer may have to do more than meets the eye to get a fair trial for a client.

A judge came out into the courtroom and said: "Gentlemen, before we start this trial, I want to make an announcement. Yesterday the defense attorney came to my office and gave me five thousand dollars. This morning, the plaintiff's attorney came to my chambers and gave me ten thousand dollars. I want the record to show that I'm giving five thousand back to the plaintiff, and we're going to try this case strictly on the merits."

☐ Not everybody cares for lawyers.

Dorothy Parker was asked to give a $25 donation toward the burial of a man she didn't know.
She asked, "Was he a writer?"
The reply was, "No, he was a lawyer."
She gave the man $50 and said, "Here. Go bury two lawyers."

▌ LEADERSHIP

☐ Leaders are needed more in difficult times.

"In calm water every ship has a good captain."

Swedish proverb

☐ To motivate people, they have to want to get better.

"You cannot push anyone up a ladder unless he is willing to climb a little."

Andrew Carnegie

☐ Leaders have direction and desire.

"In the simplest terms, a leader is one who knows where he wants to go, then gets up and goes."

John Erskine

"A good leader takes a little more than his share of blame, a little less than his share of credit."

Arnold Glasow

☐ The influences of a leader last after he's gone.

"The final test of a leader is that he leaves behind him in other men the conviction and the will to carry on."

Walter Lippmann

"Leadership is the ability to decide what is to be done and then to get others to want to do it."

Dwight D. Eisenhower

"There are no bad soldiers, only bad officers."

Napoleon

"A leader's role is to harness the social forces in the organization, to shape and guide values."

Chester Barnard, past president, New Jersey Bell

"The institutional leader is primarily an expert in the promotion and protection of values."

Philip Selznick, Leadership and Administration

☐ Leaders get followers to reach beyond themselves.

"The task of the leader is to get his people from where they are to where they have not been."

Henry Kissinger

☐ Leaders need to have foresight.

"One of the tests of leadership is the ability to recognize a problem before it becomes an emergency."

Arnold Glasow

☐ Leaders listen.

"Men pay no heed to a dog that is always barking."

Margaret L. Clement

☐ Leaders set the tone.

There is a saying in the Yukon: "The speed of the leader is the speed of the pack."

"Great leaders get extraordinary things done in organizations by inspiring and motivating others toward a common purpose."

Steve Miller, speaker

There is only one thing all great leaders have in common—their uniqueness.

"The coach is the team, and the team is the coach. You reflect each other."

Darrell Royal, football coach

☐ You learn to lead by following.

Robert Greenleaf, a noted management theorist, said that good leaders must first become good servants.

☐ Sometimes leadership is letting people do their job.

Willie Shoemaker, the best jockey ever, said that he kept the lightest touch on the horse's reins: "The horse never knows I'm there until he needs me."

"The leader's role is to create a vision, not kick somebody in the ass."
Garry Jenkin, management consultant

☐ Leadership is inspiring confidence in others.

"Now we have the finest food, equipment, the best spirit, and the best men in the world. You know, by God, I actually pity those poor people we're going up against."
George S. Patton

☐ A leader is like the captain of a ship. He must take personal command of the wheel in an emergency.

One manager told me that when his plant burned down, he was forced to shift work to other plants that weren't affected. Instead of delegating all the responsibility as he does with day-to-day activity, he personally took charge. He said that this generated a sense of urgency and enthusiasm for the changes more than if he had conducted business as usual.

"Good leaders resemble each other but each bad leader is bad in his own way, just as there is only one kind of good health but many kinds of sickness."
Anthony Jay

On the cover of their book appropriately titled *Leaders*, Warren Bennis and Burt Nanus offer the following distinction between managers and leaders: Managers do things right. Leaders do the right things.

Pat Haggerty, an early leader of Texas Instruments, was a motivator of people. A former employee said, "After you heard him talk, you would walk out through walls, ready to do it. He never told you what to do. He just showed you the possibilities."

"Leadership is also not telling people what to do but having the power to make them do it."
Mandy Marsh

"The greatest leaders throughout history have been notoriously poor followers."
Katheryn Collins

Napoleon was asked after his stunning victory in Italy how he made his army cross the Alps. He replied: "One does not make a French army cross the Alps; one leads it across."

"Leaders who win the respect of others are the ones who deliver more than they promise, not the ones who promise more than they can deliver."

Mark A. Clement

"The leader who can enlist cooperation and respect, without having to pull rank, has power of the most positive kind."

David Crawley

☐ A leader must set an example for others to follow.

"A business is a reflection of the leader. A fish doesn't stink just from the tail, and a company doesn't succeed or fail from the bottom."

Gary Feldmar

"To lead the people, walk behind them."

Lao-tzu

True leadership must be for the benefit of the followers, not for the enrichment of the leaders. In combat, officers eat last.

"A manager remains a leader only as long as he keeps proving that he is the superior man with the best method."

Kenneth "Thane" Walker

Leadership means setting an example. Take J. W. "Bill" Marriott, Marriott Corporation's chairman. Bill logs more than 200,000 miles a year visiting the various properties his company owns. When asked why he travels so much, he responded: "If I sit back and relax, a lot of other people will sit back and relax. After all, if you're going to be a star performer, you can't sit back and relax. A star performer has to work hard and make sacrifices, and at Marriott Corporation, we do both."

"A leader inspires his staff to believe in themselves and their ability to succeed long before they could recognize their own potential."

Sherman Hamilton

☐ Leadership is getting people to compromise for the good of all.

When Columbus was searching for the New World, his ship's crew became discouraged and rose in rebellion. They insisted on turning back, instead of persevering on a "fool's errand." There was no New World to be found, in their view.

But Columbus expected to find it; he had not the least doubt of it. Still, under the circumstances, he was obliged to compromise with them; and he promised that, if they would be patient and faithful three days longer, he would abandon the enterprise, unless land should be discovered.

Before the three days expired, however, the New World burst into view.

☐ A leader has lots of responsibility.

"The leader not only creates the rational and tangible aspects of organizations, such as structure and technology, but also is the creator of symbols, ideologies, language, beliefs, rituals, and myths."

Andrew Pettigrew

☐ Leadership is leading by example.

"Early in life, I decided that I would not be overcome by events. My philosophy has been that regardless of the circumstances, I shall not be vanquished, but will try to be happy. Life is not easy for any of us. But it is a continual challenge, and it is up to us to be cheerful—and to be strong, so that those who depend on us may draw strength from our example."

Rose Kennedy

☐ Leaders can't be aloof; they must show they care.

"A leader is like a battalion commander who isn't content to read the menus but insists on going into the mess hall to taste the food himself. Not only does he know more about what's being fed to his subordinates, but he's considered a better leader by his troops."

Peter Drucker

☐ A good leader keeps the entire team tuned to the fundamentals of success.

Frank Leahy, the legendary Notre Dame football coach, always stressed fundamentals. After an especially bad game, he sat his team down in the locker room, picked up an object, and said to his players. "All right men, let's return to the fundamentals. This is a football."

One of the lineman, taking notes in the back of the room said. "Wait a minute, Coach. Not so fast!"

☐ Good leaders can do the impossible.

The fundamental importance of leadership can be illustrated at Chrysler. Lee Iacocca turned this company around. Few of the environmental factors have changed significantly since Chrysler was on the brink of bankruptcy. They still faced pretty much the same competition, the same taxes, the same unions, the same regulations.

But the one thing that was different was the commitment of one man—Lee Iacocca. He turned around a $13-billion company and saved eighty-thousand jobs.

An incredible accomplishment, done through leadership.

☐ One leader can turn a loser into a winner.

In 1940, Winston Churchill took command of a nation that had drifted into near defeat. With his resolve and eloquence, he turned it into a fighting force. Britain under Churchill had no more tanks or planes at first than it had under Chamberlain. But Churchill's Britain was a far more formidable nation because of his leadership.

☐ Leaders have the ability to inspire confidence.

Joe Namath's definition of leadership: "Let's say the Baltimore Colts are losing by four points. There are three seconds left, and Baltimore has the ball on their opponent's nineteen-yard line. Baltimore needs a touchdown to win, and there is just time for one more play. In the huddle, quarterback Johnny Unitas calls a quarterback sneak, and the ten other players believe they're going to score."

☐ Leadership can be learned through apprenticeship.

Georgia-Pacific develops their branch managers by matching high-potential people with top managers as assistants until full management jobs open up.

Even the Boy Scouts know enough to have assistant patrol leaders and junior assistant scoutmasters to keep a steady flow of talent coming through their system.

☐ Leaders must learn to sacrifice for others.

Take the example of Alexander the Great, who three hundred years ago led his troops across a hot and desolate plain. After eleven days out, he and all the soldiers were near death from thirst. Alexander pressed on. At midday, two scouts brought him what little water they had been able to find. It hardly filled a cup. Alexander's troops stood back and watched as he poured the water into the hot sand.

He said. "It's of no use for one to drink when many thirst."

Being a leader, Alexander gave his followers the only thing he had: inspiration.

☐ The only real training for leadership is leadership.

When Michael Caine was a struggling actor, veteran actor Peter O'Toole gave him some advice: "If you want to play leading parts, then only play leading parts. It's better to play Hamlet in Denver than Laertes on Broadway."

☐ There are differences between leaders and bosses.

Harry Gordon Selfridge, developer of one of the largest department stores in London, achieved success by being a leader rather than a boss. He said this of the two types of executives:

The boss drives the people; the leader coaches them.
The boss depends upon authority; the leader, on goodwill.
The boss says, "I"; the leader, "We."

The boss fixes the blame for the breakdown; the leader fixes the breakdown.
The boss knows how it is done; the leader shows how.
The boss says, "Go!"; the leader, "Let's go!"

LEARNING

"The only person who behaves sensibly is my tailor. He takes new measurements every time he sees me. All the rest go on with their old measurements."

George Bernard Shaw

"One of the reasons people stop learning is that they become less and less willing to risk failure."

John W. Gardner

"Teaching should be full of ideas, not stuffed with facts."

John Condry, educator

"Anyone who stops learning is old, whether at twenty or eighty. Anyone who keeps learning stays young."

Henry Ford

☐ Everybody can teach you something.

"I have learned silence from the talkative, toleration from the intolerant, and kindness from the unkind."

Kahlil Gibran

☐ Learn from the mistakes of others.

"We ought to be able to learn some things second-hand. There is not enough time for us to make all the mistakes ourselves."

Harriet Hall

"It is what we think we know already that often prevents us from learning."

Claude Bernard

"There's only one corner of the universe you can be certain of improving, and that's your own self."

Aldous Huxley

"You are the same today that you are going to be five years from now except for two things: the people with whom you associate, and the books you read."

Charles "Tremendous" Jones

☐ Never stop learning.

Theodore Roosevelt died with a book under his pillow, consuming the ideas of others until the very last.

☐ Search for a positive lesson.

"Don't just learn something from every experience, learn something positive."

Allen H. Neuharth, founder, USA Today

"If a man will begin with certainties, he shall end in doubts; but if he will be content to begin with doubts, he shall end in certainties."

Francis Bacon, Advancement of Learning

"In the Information Age, flexibility is the critical foundation for success. Future generations will need more than just mastery of subject matter, they will need mastery of learning."

Morris Weeks

"You have got to be curious as to what makes the whole business tick and have the ambition and desire to fight to get to a place of more responsibility."

Fred Lazarus, Jr., former chairman, Federated Department Stores

"One of the best ways to learn is to fail. People who are successful often don't know why they're successful. People who have failed a couple times know where the weak links are and know exactly what are the things that must be avoided."

Maurice Kirkpatrick

"If I were to join a circle of any kind, it would be a circle that required its members to try something new at least once a month. The new thing could be very inconsequential: steak for breakfast, frog hunting, walking on stilts, memorizing a stanza of poetry. It could be staying up outdoors all night, making up a dance and dancing it, speaking to a stranger, chinning yourself, milking a goat, reading the Bible—anything not ordinarily done."

Jessamyn West, To See the Dream

◼ LISTENING

"Every man I meet is in some way my superior, and I can learn of him."

Ralph Waldo Emerson

"Big people monopolize the listening. Small people monopolize the talking."

David Schwartz, The Magic of Thinking Big

"The friends who listen to us are the ones we move toward, and we want to sit in their radius."

Karl Menninger

"A single conversation across the table with a wise man is better than ten years' study of books."

Henry Wadsworth Longfellow

☐ Co-workers will give you all the ideas you need if you'll listen.

"People will flood you with ideas if you let them."

Peter Smith, General Signal

"The way you stay fresh is you never stop traveling, you never stop listening. You never stop asking people what they think."

Rene McPherson, former chairman, Dana

"I believe I shall never be old enough to speak without embarrassment when I have nothing to talk about."

Abraham Lincoln

☐ Listening to customers can give you profitable ideas.

Stew Leonard, Sr., president of Stew Leonard's, hosts meetings with customers of his small supermarket to generate new ideas. At one, a woman requested fresh fish. When Leonard set up a fish bar on beds of ice, his fish sales doubled.

"Listen long enough and the person will generally come up with an adequate solution."

Mary Kay Ash, founder, Mary Kay Cosmetics

"To entertain some people, all you have to do is listen."

Ann Halliburton

"It is better to remain quiet and be thought a fool than to speak and remove all doubt."

Anonymous

The average employee spends about three-quarters of every working day in verbal communications. Nearly half of that is spent listening. The average employee is about 25 percent effective as a listener. This means that if a person receives a salary of $50,000 per year as a manager, over $12,500 of it is paid for being an ineffective listener.

"Filling our ears with all we have learned to say, we are deaf to what we have yet to hear."

Wendell Johnson

☐ Listening to the client always pays.

When Charles Wang's family arrived in America in 1949, they had two suitcases. Now Wang, worth over $100 million in Computer Associates International stock, said that his company grew because they listened to their clients. Wang said that most computer companies sell people what they need; Wang decided to ask them what they wanted.

☐ Listen to your customers' needs and adapt to them.

Computer giant IBM has profited by tailoring its exports to the needs of its overseas customers. Japanese industry experts credit IBM's $1.3 billion in sales to Japan in 1985 to its dedication to listening to the needs of the market and then adapting the products accordingly. Something is obviously clicking for IBM in Japan because in 1985, they transferred the Pacific region headquarters from New York to Tokyo.

Managers fear listening to the people who do the work. Instead of getting the results they want, they think it's like turning the asylum over to the inmates.

When President Lyndon B. Johnson was a junior senator from Texas, he kept a sign on his office wall that read, "You ain't learnin' nothin' when you're doin' all the talkin'."

"The key to success is to get out into the store and listen to what the associates have to say. It's terribly important for everyone to get involved. Our best ideas come from clerks and stockboys."

Sam Walton, founder, Wal-Mart

Sam Walton, founder of Wal-Mart and one of the richest men in America, still listens. Once he flew his aircraft to Mt. Pleasant, Texas, and parked the plane with instructions to the copilot to meet him one-hundred or so miles down the road. He then flagged a Wal-Mart truck and rode the rest of the way to "chat with the driver." He said, "It seemed like so much fun."

"Most of the successful people I've known are ones who do more listening than talking. If you choose your company carefully, it's worth listening to what they have to say. You don't have to blow out the other fellow's light to let your own shine."

Bernard M. Baruch

☐ Too many salespeople talk when they should listen.

Ben Feldman was the first insurance salesman to pass the goal of $25 million in one year. And then to double that figure.

He has been New York Life's leading salesman for more than two decades. He did this in East Liverpool, a small town of twenty-thousand on the Ohio River. When asked his secret, he said:

1. Work hard
2. Think big
3. Listen very well

☐ Great people are great listeners.

Anthony Eden considered Winston Churchill's outstanding leadership characteristic to be his willingness to listen; he never cut off a suggestion with a curt dismissal but encouraged elaboration.

☐ Listen to the customer.

Proctor & Gamble was one of the first companies to listen to the customer. In the 1960s, P & G publicized an 800 number to serve their customers. Trying to serve the customer, they reaped an additional benefit. The information gathered from listening to the customer told them that the average household's weekly laundry increased from 6.4 to 7.6 loads. At the same time, the average washing temperature dropped 15 degrees. This change was caused by the new fabrics introduced to the market. A new product was created to meet the demand—All-Temperature Cheer.

☐ Listening is a key to success

As Irving Shapiro, past chairman of Du Pont, said, "People who accomplish things do more listening than talking."

☐ We will be more successful if we listen more.

☐ Listening to constructive criticism can be very positive.

In 1940, *Fortune* magazine published a critical article about IBM. Thomas Watson called the magazine, wanting to talk to the author of the article. When told that the writer was not available to discuss the article, Watson explained that he wanted to hire the reporter to be his director of public relations. When asked why, Watson said, "At least he takes me seriously."

☐ To listen to your customer, you need a feedback system.

The Xerox Corporation in Rochester, New York, started systematically surveying customers. Jan Hess, manager of Xerox's Customer Satisfaction Management System, said. "We realized we were meeting internal specifications such as copy quality and speed rather than customer standards."

After finding that fewer customers were satisfied than Xerox had thought, the company redesigned its copier and also developed an ongoing system to gauge customer satisfaction.

Now Xerox sends out questionnaires to about fifty-thousand randomly selected customers monthly. Its goal is to elicit feedback from all users.

☐ Listen to your employees.

Dallas-based Chili's, one of the nations's five best-run food service chains, according to *Restaurants & Institutions* magazine, has a leader who listens to employees. Norman Brinker, Chili's chairman and the original open-door leader, held that responsive communication is the key to good relations with both employees and shareholders and that such communication pays big dividends. Almost 80 percent of Chili's current menu came from suggestions made by unit managers.

■ LOYALTY

☐ Employee loyalty usually starts with employer loyalty.

At Toshiba when a new employee is hired, management expects commitment to the company and in return treats every employee as a valuable family member.

☐ Loyalty starts at the top and works down.

An original employee who worked for Swift Packing Company for twenty-nine years had this to say about his boss G. F. Swift: "G. F. Swift was the squarest man I ever worked for. All that time, I never asked him what he was going to pay me. I never had cause to complain. If you worked well for him, he saw that you got what you deserved in money and in every other way."

☐ Loyalty does not mean you must share your superior's point of view.

An example of a situation that proves this truth is the firing of Douglas MacArthur by Harry S. Truman. When he did this, president Truman stated that he had not terminated the general's career because of their differences of opinion or because of personal insults, but because MacArthur had lost respect for the office of the president. That could not be tolerated.

☐ It's hard to build loyalty when employees move around too much.

Robert Anderson of Atlantic Richfield was troubled by what he called the "transient nature" of young managers who move when job opportunities change. "Because of this, loyalty to the corporation is no longer a value."

"Loyalty is the greatest characteristic trait needed in an executive."
Charles P. McCormick

James E. Robinson, chairman of American Express, ranks loyalty ahead of the ability to lead.

☐ We ask for loyal employees, but are we a loyal employer?

Ross Perot, founder of Electronic Data Systems, is one of the greatest corporate success stories in America. Perot's mother was his closet advisor. In

1969, when he was planning to rescue some Americans from Vietnam, his associates warned him that such a dangerous mission might make the price of EDS stock fall. Perot's mother gave him the advice to proceed, "Let them sell their shares."

Perot's loyalty got loyalty back.

☐ We need loyalty to be winners.

"We've all heard shortsighted businessmen attribute a quote to Vince Lombardi: 'Winning is not the most important thing; it's the only thing.' Well, that's a good quote for firing up a team, but as an overarching philosophy it's just baloney. I much prefer another Lombardi quote. He expected his players, he once said, to have three kinds of loyalty: to God, to their families, and to the Green Bay Packers, in that order."

M. John Akers, chairman, IBM

Jeffrey Sherman, CEO of Armor All, told this story:
"Armor All once entered negotiations for a friendly buyout of another company. The deal didn't come off, but my counterpart was so impressed with one of the executives on our acquisition team, he called me up.

"He said, 'I want to hire that guy, and I'm willing to double his pay.'

"I told him I wouldn't get in his way. The young man was making approximately $100,000. I said 'But I should warn you, not too many people leave this company.'

"They talked. Our guy had a choice between a great, high-paying job at a high-risk company—or steady, long-term advancement here with Armor All, in what we like to think is a utopian work atmosphere.

"So, what happened? He's still with us."

From the viewpoint of those who hire, John Wareham pointed out the following in his book *Secrets of a Corporate Headhunter:*
"Loyalty is the key to both getting a job and keeping it.

"The key to loyalty, whether you're recruiting an executive or making a friend, is in finding that common ideal. . . .

"We always admire loyalty, even in an enemy.

"The sort of admiration that you'd feel for the old woman who, in time of war, started out with a poker when the enemy was approaching. When asked what she could do with her rather mild weapon, she replied, 'I can show them which side I am on.' "

☐ LUCK

"Luck means the hardships and privations which you have not hesitated to endure; the long nights you have devoted to work. Luck means the appointments you have never failed to keep, the airplanes you never failed to catch."

Margaret L. Clement

"Luck seems to have a peculiar attachment to work."

Anonymous

If at first you don't succeed, you're probably lucky.

Margaret L. Clement

"I'm a great believer in luck, and the harder I work the luckier I get."

Stephen Leacock, humorist

"Luck is the residue of design."

Branch Rickey

"Luck is the sense to recognize an opportunity and the ability to take advantage of it. Everyone has bad breaks, but everyone also has opportunities. The man who can smile at his breaks and grab his chances gets on."

Samuel Goldwyn

☐ Luck plays a big part in success.

Take Dwight D. Eisenhower, who in 1940 was a soon-to-retire lieutenant colonel with a respectable but not particularly outstanding military career. But as luck had it, he turned out to be the right person in the right place at the right time. Instead of becoming a retired military officer, he became president of the United States.

☐ Luck comes from preparation.

"There are no lazy veteran lion hunters."

Randall Douglas

MANAGEMENT

"Management's principal job is to get the herd heading roughly west."
Lee Walton

"Probably the most important management fundamental that is being ignored today is staying close to the customer to satisfy his needs and anticipate his wants."
Lew Young, editor in chief, Business Week

"Management is nothing more than motivating people."
Lee Iacocca

☐ Involve those who are affected by your decisions.
"Those who *implement* the plans must *make* the plans."
Patrick Haggerty, past chairman, Texas Instruments

☐ Every company has talented employees, but successful companies are the ones where management can get them to work together.
"It's easy to get good players. Gettin' 'em to play together, that's the hard part."
Casey Stengel

"Most business failures do not stem from bad times. They come from poor management, and bad times just precipitate the crisis."
Thomas P. Murphy, journalist

"Management must guide the forces of change."
John W. Teets, chairman, Greyhound

☐ It's not good to overmanage.

"A society should be at least as good as the sum of its parts, but our society is not. Our reliance on management has produced a society that is less than it could be. We are collectively much less than we are individually. Management suppresses and limits, diminishes the quality and quantity of our human responses."

                                   Richard Cornuelle, De-Managing America

"You must manage as if you need your employees more than they need you."

                                                                     Peter Drucker

"My approach to management is to gain the information and knowledge necessary to manage my company's next stage of growth."

                                                                        An Wang

☐ The role of management is to persuade others to do better.

Harry S. Truman once said that when he was president, one of his principal activities was "to bring people in and try to persuade them to do what they ought to be doing anyway, without persuasion. That's what I spent most of my time doing."

"All management theories become conspiracies against good management and serve mainly to cover the manager's ass."

                           T. George Harris, former editor, Psychology Today

Jim Treybig, Tandem Computer's president, said, "Most companies are overmanaged. And most people need less instruction than we think."

☐ Sometimes managers should be reminded that it's people who make the difference, not the manager.

When Joe Lapchick was coaching basketball at St. John's, he collapsed on the bench, fell to the floor in a faint, and was unconscious for several minutes. The game resumed while he was being treated. When he recovered, he saw that his team had improved its lead. He said, "I just dealt strategy a helluva blow."

☐ Some things are better if they aren't managed efficiently.

An efficiency expert attended a performance of Schubert's *Unfinished Symphony* and issued the following critique:

1. For most of the performance, the four oboe players had nothing to do. They should be eliminated and their work spread out over the entire orchestra.
2. Forty violins were playing identical notes. This seemed unnecessary, and this section should be drastically cut. If more sound is required, then add more electronic amplifiers.

3. The horns repeated the passages already played by the strings. If this duplication was eliminated, the concert could be reduced by twenty minutes.

☐ Good managers understand the jobs others are doing.

Management involvement is highlighted at Disney Productions by an annual week-long program called "cross-utilization." This program entails Disney executives to leave their desks and their usual business suits. They wear a theme costume and head for the action. "For a full week, the boss sells tickets or popcorn, dishes ice cream or hot dogs, loads and unloads rides, parks cars, drives the monorail or the trains, and takes on any of the one-hundred on-stage jobs that make the entertainment parks come alive."

Randy D. Marsh

☐ Write your own rules when it comes to managing people.

Zane Tankel, president of Collier Graphic Services in New York City, said he once worked for an insurance company, and every employee lived by the bell. A bell rang starting and stopping coffee breaks, lunch, and a final bell ended the workday.

Tankel decided to make his engraving company more fun. His philosophy was simple: "A happy employee is a more productive employee, so I selfishly want my employees to be happy."

An example of how Tankel keeps his employees happy: During a transit strike, many of Collier's employees had to struggle to get to work. When the strike was over, Tankel handed out desk sets and plaques to the stalwarts who had regularly showed up. After the strike was over, he passed out gifts totaling over $3,500.

■ MANAGERS

"If you can't get people to accept ideas because they're sound, and if you are not willing to accept an idea because it's sound, then you're really not a good manager."

John Donnelly

☐ What is a manager's most important task?

"The most important thing I do is motivate people."
Mike Simmons, CIO, Fidelity Investments

"Is managing tough? What isn't if you do it right? It's not an easy life. Who wants things easy? Winners win. Losers gripe."
Ralph Houk, baseball coach

☐ Good managers should never give up customer contact.

Sometimes managers get isolated from what is really going on in the company. John Roach, president of Tandy Corporation, which owns Radio

Shack, answers his own telephone just to keep in touch with what is happening.

☐ Good managers have to understand what they are asking others to do.

"People who are going to be good managers need to have practical understanding of the crafts in their business."

Philip Oxley, president, Tenneco

☐ Good managers should help others work better together.

"Raymond T. Hickok, president of Hickok Pioneer Manufacturing Company, said, 'I will always be allergic to the subordinate who drives wedges between people. I believe that good executives should be building bridges.' "

Mortimer R. Feinberg, Effective Psychology for Managers

"The job of the manager is enabling, not a directive job . . . coaching and not direction is the first quality of leadership now. Get the barriers out of the way to let people do the things they do well."

Robert Noyce, founder, Intel

☐ Managers need to know how to sell.

"Anybody who runs a company has to have the capacity to sell, and sell well. You may be trying to sell the image of your company or selling employees on the idea of working hard, but it's all salesmanship. You can't turn your back on that part of your job."

William Kelly, chairman, Semi-Specialists of America

☐ Too many managers fail to stay close to the customer.

"The person that established the value of what you do is not some panel of blue-ribbon judges; it's the customer. And so you have to be very close to the customer as an intricate part of the way you manage your business."

Modesto Maidique, author

☐ Hire people more qualified than you are.

Several years back, Leo Durocher said that if he could find a baseball player with the five abilities of hitting to all fields, hitting with power, running bases, throwing, and fielding, then he, Durocher, would be a great coach. Along came Willie Mays.

☐ We are no better than our people.

"There are times when even the best manager is like the little boy with the big dog waiting to see where the dog wants to go so he can take him there."

Lee Iacocca, Chrysler

☐ Managers need to allow for mistakes.

Bum Phillips, former NFL coach, said, "You gotta have rules, but you also gotta allow for a fella to mess up once in a while." Like the time the

Denver Broncos' celebrated rookie quarterback, suffering a difficult first season, inadvertently lined up for the snap, in full view of seventy-thousand people, not behind the center but behind the guard. John Elway became a premier NFL quarterback.

☐ Managers must ask questions.

Isidor Isaac Rabi, one of America's outstanding physicists, became a scientist, he said, for one overpowering reason: "I couldn't help it." Brought to this country as an infant, he has never forgotten his mother's daily query when he came home from public school on Manhattan's Lower East Side: "Did you ask any good questions today?"

☐ Good managers aren't slave drivers.

There's an employer named John Smith who has the reputation of being a real slave driver. The personnel director at another company was interviewing a job applicant who had been employed by Smith's firm.

Personnel director: "How long did you work for the Smith Company?"
Job applicant: "Twenty years. From April 1976 to August 1988."
Personnel director: "That's not twenty years."
Job applicant: "Mister, you ain't never worked for John Smith."

A coach once said, "The players win, not the coach. The best thing a coach can do is get the best players in action and let them do their thing. The coach can lose for you, but he can't win for you." Managers, like coaches, are judged by the results of the people on their team.

MARKET RESEARCH

☐ Before bringing a product to market, make sure the product has a market.

"Anything that isn't good for everybody is no good at all."

Henry Ford

☐ Market research is necessary to be effective against your competition.

"In football, team members study their opponents so closely that they usually know where to position themselves advantageously on every play. Baseball players change their position in the field, depending on who is at bat."

Nido Qubein

☐ Sometimes the cheapest market research is in your own company.

At one time, Apple Computer gave each employee a computer as a way to do market research. Steve Jobs, Apple's founder, said, "One time a bunch of people came back after opening a box and said, 'There are six manuals! It's totally intimidating and we don't know which one to read first!' That comment was worth more than $100,000 of market research."

☐ You don't have to spend a lot of money to test-market a new product.

When the idea of the zoom lens for cameras was invented, a prototype was made for less than $500 and was test marketed at a dinner party.

☐ Test marketing can start slowly.

McDonald's introduction of the breakfast menu started in rural areas. A few franchisees picked it up and it then spread like wildfire. It now accounts for 35 to 40 percent of McDonald's revenues.

☐ Don't overexpand because of one successful test market.

There was a man who was making big money with the wig he invented. The wigs were complete with curlers for women to wear when they went shopping. But now he's filed for bankruptcy. Business was so great he decided to go nationwide. That's when he learned Milwaukee was his only market.

☐ It's important to understand who is buying your product.

A fisherman went into a sporting supply store. The salesman offered him a fantastic lure for bass: painted eyes, half a dozen hooks, imitation bugs—a whole junkyard.

Finally, the fisherman asked the salesman, "Do fish really like this thing?"

The salesman said, "I don't sell to fish."

☐ It doesn't matter how good a product is if you don't find the right market for it.

☐ Study the market so that you can better understand how to sell to it.

A broker in Westhampton, New York, joined a local real estate office, and the first thing he did, which no one else had done before, was to make a map of all the houses in the area, attaching a price and recent sales history to each one. This showed him where the least and most expensive sections were. It also revealed that people were constantly trading up from the homes of about $300,000 to something more expensive.

He decided to go after the market share that was trading up. Four years later, at age twenty-two, he owned the real estate agency.

☐ The more you learn about your market, the better you can sell to it.

Nordstrom's, the successful West Coast department store chain, realized that a lot of their customers had moved to Phoenix. Not wanting to lose good customers, they chartered an airplane twice a year to fly transferred customers from Phoenix to their San Diego store to shop and flew them back the same day.

☐ For a new product to be successful, make sure it's in the correct outlet.

Take the time a large manufacturer of packaged foods came out with a new line of gourmet foods. All of their other products were distributed through mass retailers such as supermarkets; they decided to sell the gourmet foods through specialty stores. The new line failed where others had succeeded that were distributed in the same old way, supermarkets. The idea behind the gourmet foods was to give people a chance to serve an unusual dinner from time to time. But for most people, going out of their way to a speciality store wasn't convenient.

◼ MARKETING

"When the product is right, you don't have to be a great marketer."
Lee Iacocca

☐ Go where the customer is and don't expect him to come to you.

"The only way to convert a heathen is to travel into the jungle."
Lane Kirkland

Harvey Mackay, author of *Swim with the Sharks Without Being Eaten Alive*, said that marketing is creating a condition that allows the buyer to convince himself to buy.

☐ One way to market is to create a demand for the product.

A successful restaurant in Los Angeles, when they first opened, told some of the people that called in for a reservation that they were full and to please call back. Actually the restaurant wasn't full, but they were making people want something they couldn't have.

Marketing can help, but it's not the answer. To quote one businessman, "I'll tell you what I do. I find out what the customers want, I give it to them, and I follow up with excellent after-sales service, and that's why I'm successful. So don't tell me that marketing is the answer."

"Marketing is an attitude, not a department."

Phil Wexler

"Marketing niche is that area of a market that offers a competitive advantage over all other competitors."

Richard Holder

☐ The success of a business doesn't depend on size. It depends on filling a void in the marketplace.

A small twenty-four-hour convenience store can't compete with Kroger, but then Kroger can't compete with the convenience store either. They serve different needs.

☐ Creating interest is a good way to prospect customers.

"Financial planner Fritz Brauner tells of the time he put a designation 'Financial Planner' on his name tag at a meeting, and no one looked twice. But when he wrote 'Money' beneath his name, he was approached by many interesting people who wanted to know more."

Susan RoAne, How to Work a Room

"Marketing has to encompass the definition of what a product is. Marketing is not just promotion, advertising, and sales; marketing also includes product planning. Any engineer who does not see himself as a marketer is not doing his job."

Modesto Maidique, author

Lazzari Fuel Company initially marketed its mesquite charcoal as a fuel. Sales weren't too good. Then Lazzari positioned the mesquites in the market as an ingredient instead of as a fuel, and sales soared.

"Sometimes marketing is just positioning your product properly in the market."

Paul Hawken, Growing a Business

☐ To succeed in any market you have to fit the market.

"If Americans want to rectify the trade imbalance, they should pause for reflection and devote their efforts to making products that really appeal to Japanese people and that they will want to buy."

Akio Morita, chairman, Sony

☐ Filling a need requires less marketing than creating a need.

Back in 1890, Johnson & Johnson put together the original first-aid kit in response to a plea from railroad workers who needed treatment on the scene as they toiled to lay tracks across America. Over ninety years later, the name Johnson & Johnson is still synonymous with first-aid care.

☐ Marketing can be creating a need.

It was the late educator Gerald Stanley Lee who almost one hundred years ago put it all in a nutshell when he said: "A man's success in business today depends upon his power of getting people to believe he has something they want."

☐ If you don't have a broad market for your product, create one.

In 1914, Henry Ford started paying his workers double what they had been making. He was creating a middle-class America—one that allowed even his workers to buy their own cars.

☐ Marketing a new product can be very expensive.

In the 1930s, Chester Carlson invented the Xerox machine. He sold it in 1946 for $6.8 million. Over $90 million was spent making his invention commercial.

Everybody markets today.

An oversupply of dentists has them embracing a variety of techniques to attract new patients.

Marvin Mansky, a New York dentist, offers wakeup calls and cleans patients' teeth for free before their wedding.

Harry Cohen of San Francisco advertises in coupon books along with the local pizza parlors and muffler shops.

In Dallas, obstetrician Walter Evans sends his new mothers and their babies home from the hospital in a white, chauffeured limousine.

Kenneth Loeffler of Lancaster, Pennsylvania, sends flowers to patients "after a particularly long or difficult procedure."

Donald Carmona, head of the East Coast District Dental Society in Miami said: "I don't do any internal marketing except to be nice to people."

The cheapest and sometimes the most appreciated marketing technique is to just be nice and considerate to your current customers.

☐ A key to success is to dominate market share.

For example, in 1982, Procter & Gamble had America's biggest advertising budget at $671 million, and they dominated the market with the following: Folger's had 24 percent of market share, Ivory 18 percent, Tide 24 percent, Secret, the deodorant, 15 percent, and the second place was Sure with 13 percent. Their diaper brands claimed 72 percent of the market share. P & G is successful because they focus on market domination. They take no prisoners. They will let a competitor get into the market, and then they will launch a retaliatory attack that will devastate the competition. The attitude at P & G is, "We'll teach you that you'd best not mess with P & G."

Let's show our competition we'll do anything to beat them.

One way to market is to find a gap in a market and fill it. This is what Tim Terry did when he founded Financial Express, a mobile bookkeeping service. Terry believed that because there was a gap between the limited services of bookkeeping firms and the often too expensive CPA firms, smaller businesses needed an alternative. Three years later, Terry had ten employees and over three-hundred clients, and was investigating the idea of expanding beyond the four franchises he already had.

☐ A good marketing strategy is to find a niche in the market that's waiting to be filled.

Mark Hulbert had thought about starting his own stock-market advisory letter, but then realized that there were hundreds of them out there. There were so many, in fact, that Hulbert could not understand how anybody could choose which advice to follow. Hulbert took a survey and found that other investors were just as confused about the conflicting market advice as he was. Instead of starting his own advice letter, he decided to create a market letter that would not promise financial advice; it would simply and accurately track the records of all the other advisers. Four years later, *Hulbert Financial Digest* was grossing $500,000 a year. Mark Hulbert was twenty-nine.

☐ Marketing is the oil that runs the machine.

Colonel Harlan Sanders founded Kentucky Fried Chicken, but the company wouldn't have gone anywhere had it not been bought out by investors who understood how to market.

Henry Ford didn't invent the automobile, but he became one of the few survivors from hundreds of manufacturers because he made it easier for people to buy his cars.

☐ It's as hard to keep market share as it is to get it.

Gillette proved that a moving target is harder to hit than a stationary one. They owned the wet-shaving market with the Blue Blade and then the Super Blue Blade. Gillette was stunned when Wilkinson Sword beat it to the market in the early 1960s with the stainless blade. In 1970, Wilkinson Sword followed with the bonded blade, a metal blade fused to plastic at the "optimum shaving angle." Shortly thereafter, Gillette counterattacked with Trac II, the world's first double-bladed razor. In 1976, Gillette introduced Atra, the first adjustable double-bladed razor. Then came the inexpensive disposable razor that was an obvious attack against Bic, which was about to introduce its own disposable razor. Introducing the Good News was good marketing strategy. It protected their market share, and, trade sources said Bic lost $25 million in its first three years in the disposable razor business.

☐ You can protect your market share by attacking yourself instead of the competition.

☐ Marketing studies don't always tell enough.

A few years ago, Sears Roebuck decided to start selling automobile insurance through their retail stores. It was a huge success. Later, Sears decided to piggyback on the automobile insurance profits by adding life insurance. It never lived up to the car insurance success. After further study, it was determined that the customer saw automobile insurance as another accessory that could be purehased for cars, like batteries and brakes. To the customer, life insurance seemed out of place, and they didn't buy.

☐ Find a gap in the market and then fill it.

In 1921, Alfred P. Sloan, Jr., took over as chief executive of General Motors. At that time, Ford, making only one model car, owned 60 percent share of the automobile market. General Motors had eight models and only 12 percent of the market. Only two of the eight models were profitable. Sloan decided to revamp GM's line of cars. He kept Cadillac and Buick, three models were dropped completely, three others were replaced by new designs. The plan was to offer the customer a complete and different choice of cars to choose. Each of the five models would be placed in different price and performance categories. One car would be for the low-income customer and would be priced just slightly higher than Ford's Model T. The customer wanting a medium-priced car could save money by buying the low-priced car with most of the features of the medium-priced car; or he could pay a little more and have a near-luxury automobile.

Five years later, General Motors was the dominant and profitable American car company.

☐ Don't try to be all things to all people.

Federal Express went after air delivery for small parcels. Their competitors, Emery and Airborne, collected freight in different sizes, shipped them by regular airlines, and then delivered them to the addressee.

Federal Express found success by limiting itself to small packages and by flying them on company-owned planes.

☐ Sometimes marketing is finding a new way to distribute your product.

Robert de Graff, a reprint publisher, decided to launch a 25-cent line of ten Pocket Books, with backing from Richard Simon and Lincoln Schuster. When he sold 1.5 million copies the first year, de Graff knew he had something, but he needed outlets. Bookstores were hardly eager for 25-cent items. But in 1941, de Graff's sales manager persuaded four major magazine distributors to take his line. Soon afterward 600 wholesalers wanted them, particularly when the wartime paper pinch cut magazine runs, and 100,000 newsstands were clamoring for wares. Pocket Books moved nine million copies in 1941 and thirty-three million in 1943. Today paperback sales now run off the charts.

☐ Marketing is giving your product a favorable position in the market.

A number of years ago, a company sold canned red salmon. It was being solidly outsold by pink salmon by a ratio of ten to one. Desperate, they called in an advertising agency and told them, "Do anything you can so long as it's legal to get our sales up."

The solution to the problem was simple. They changed the design on the label. The new label read. "Authentic Norwegian Red Salmon—guaranteed not to turn pink."

■ MARKETING STRATEGY

"Strategy is war on a map."

Henry Cannon

☐ A good marketing strategy is to attack yourself.

For example, IBM is a master of attacking itself. Frequently, IBM will introduce a new mainframe computer with a cheaper price or a better performance advantage over existing computers. This keeps the competition off guard. They are constantly trying to catch up. It's always harder to hit a moving target.

☐ Marketing strategy must change to meet changing markets.

Sears, Roebuck has always successfully adapted to a changing market need. Until the 1920s, Sears provided quality goods by mail order to the remote farmer in America. When the automobile arrived, Sears again adapted to a changing market. They shifted their emphasis from mail order to retail stores in cities.

☐ A successful marketing strategy can be to pick an area the competition is overlooking.

Control Data's spectacular success in entering the computer market against IBM is a classic example of astute segmentation. They let IBM have its area while they tackled a totally different segment of not offering IBM's extensive service.

"Marketing strategy is a lot like military strategy.
"First, in the face of the overwhelming evidence of history, no general is justified in launching his troops in a direct attack upon an enemy firmly in position. Second, that instead of seeking to upset the enemy's equilibrium by one's attack, it must be upset before a real attack is, or can be, successfully launched."

Liddell Hart, Strategy

☐ Expand your market from a solid base.

Wal-Mart decided early on that it would expand methodically by moving into another area only after they already dominated the market areas they were in.

☐ A good marketing strategy is one that keeps what you have and gets what you don't have.

In Chicago, a classical music promoter increased attendance four times in three years by offering American composers instead of the usual ones.

His success caused one promoter to call for advice after losing three hundred of his five hundred subscribers. She asked about his programming.

He replied, "Our audience likes to hear the basic traditionals such as Mozart, Beethoven, Brahms, and Schubert."

She asked, "When you say our audience, are you talking about the two hundred who stayed or the three hundred who left?"

☐ Be unique.

A few years ago, twenty-three-year-old Jeb Roth found a market niche of washing cars, and he really cleaned up. Roth's customers primarily own top-of-the-line models, and he charges $125 per car, which includes Q-tipping the vents. Today he can't fill the demand for his unique service.

☐ Your company name should reflect your market strategy.

As companies expand their market share and product line, they sometimes have to change their name to reflect their current position. For example, California Perfumes was changed to Avon Cosmetics. Allegheny Airlines changed its name to USAir, which gives a much broader market image.

One example of a corporation that didn't change its name was Eastern Airlines. It gives the impression by its name that it is a regional carrier as opposed to a full-blown trunk carrier flying coast to coast and, in many cases, abroad.

☐ Every company needs a marketing strategy.

McDonald's dominates the fast-food market. They do more in sales than second and third place combined. How did they do it? They discovered that the most vocal person when it comes to choosing where to eat as you're traveling down the highway is usually the children. McDonald's strategy was to specialize in what the decision-maker wants most, and in the case of children it's a hamburger, french fries, and soda.

McDonald's targets their advertising to children, and it works.

☐ Create a demand for your product, any way you can.

Nina Blanchard owns one of the largest modeling agencies on the West Coast. When she first started, she could only attract models who weren't big-time. She was afraid to send some of them out on jobs. So when photographers started calling to book her models, she said that they were already booked. Word quickly spread, and established models started switching to Blanchard; they wanted to be represented by the hot new agency.

☐ People want what they can't have.

☐ Good Market research can show you the best way to reach the customer in the most cost-effective manner.

Alloy Rods, the manufacturer of welding rod and wire, was selling about $85 million worth of its products through four hundred distributors to about a dozen large customers. Sixty sales representatives were servicing the large number of accounts. To reduce these costs, they changed their sales approach by switching to large distributors instead of to a big sales force. Sixty sales reps were reduced to twenty-five, creating a substantial overall savings.

☐ Limiting your marketing strategy to only your current product can eventually make you lose your position in the market.

In the 1950s, the major companies in the business were Olivetti Typewriter, Underwood Typewriter, Royal Typewriter, and International Business Machines. Their marketing strategy is revealed by their corporate names. In the last thirty or so years, the difference between the typewriter business and the business-machine business has turned out to be substantial. IBM positioned itself in the international business market and set out to capture it. Today, IBM continues to hold an edge in the office typewriter market, but typewriters are only a small part of its total business. The other companies wound up with small shares of only the typewriter market.

☐ Broaden the idea of what business you are in.

☐ Find a need and fill it.

In 1981, Scandinavian Airlines System (SAS) was flying into a headwind when Jan Carlzon took over as president and CEO. The company compiled a loss of $20 million, its second straight losing year. Morale was low. Employees were being laid off. Service was being slashed. The market for passenger and freight services was stagnant. Carlzon immediately set out to make SAS 'the best airline in the world for the frequent business traveler.' He invested $45 million to upgrade every detail of service for the business traveler, while cutting nearly as much from programs directed at tourists.

A year after Carlzon took over, SAS returned to profitability. Two years later, in 1983, SAS won *Air Transport World's* Airline of the Year award, and in 1986 it received the magazine's Passenger Service award.

☐ A poor short-term marketing strategy can cause long-term problems.

Because of their marketing strategy, Laker Airways took off fast but crash landed. Their strategy was based one feature: low fares. The weakness was that other airlines could match their prices and had a stronger balance sheet to outlast Laker.

As Laker Airways proved, if you have a marketing plan that doesn't have a significant feature to base a marketing plan on, it's doomed to failure because of forces beyond its control.

☐ A good marketing strategy is to find a gap in a market that already exists.

That's how a large supermarket across the street from a small twenty-four-hour, seven-day-a-week store can both prosper. Both are making money but in different ways. The supermarket offers variety at lower prices, and the convenience store offers day and night service at higher prices. Both are in the same area, reaching the same market but fulfilling different consumer needs.

☐ MEETINGS

Overheard in a hotel lobby: "Business meetings are important. One reason is that they demonstrate how many people the company can operate without."

Show me a person who likes to go to meetings and I'll show you a person who doesn't have enough to do.

☐ Meetings can be more effective if held outside the regular meeting room.

Campbell Soup's chairman Gordon McGovern held a board meeting in the back room of a supermarket. After the meeting, the board members roamed the aisles talking to shoppers for comments about their products.

☐ Don't let meetings take the place of action.

Sign on a wall in a conference room: "A meeting is no substitute for progress."

☐ Good meetings have priorities.

Similar to the huddle in a football game, meetings work best when specific times are set aside to meet. To be successful, each meeting must center around the idea that the number one priority is the overall health of the company.

☐ Meetings should be fun.

Sam Walton, Founder of Wal-Mart Stores and one of the richest men in America, begins every company meeting with a cheer. "Give me a W . . . give me an A . . . give me an L . . . ," he shouts, until Wall-Mart is spelled out.

☐ Where you hold meetings can be just as important as what is done in them.

Chaparral Steel in Midlothian, Texas, prospers where most steel companies are struggling. At Chaparral, the average worker produces 1,300 tons of steel, which is almost twice as high as Japan. Why? One reason is that the company believes in having informal meetings. They hold them in the hallway, parking lot, or anyplace else that makes the workers feel that they are being listened to.

☐ Don't make meetings too long.

"No more good must be attempted than the people can bear."

Thomas Jefferson

☐ Too many meetings don't accomplish anything.

"I always come to meetings with a problem. I always leave with a briefing and a problem."

Herm Staudt, Eaton

☐ Meetings can be an effective way to communicate.

"Nothing more effectively involves people, sustains creditability, or generates enthusiasm than face-to-face communication. It is critical to provide and discuss all organization performance figures with all of our people."
Dana Corporation Philosophy

Two managers were talking:
"Let's cut the staff meeting today."
"We can't. I need the sleep."

☐ Past experience with poor meetings has given them a bad rap.

There are only three things in life that are certain; death, taxes, and meetings. The corollary of this, of course, is that death always comes too soon, taxes are always too high, and meetings are always a waste of time.

A cartoon in the *New Yorker* magazine showed two secretaries preparing a conference room. One says to the other, "And don't forget the little pads. In case one of them has an idea!"
This cartoon sums up how most people feel about meetings. Instead, we should hold meetings geared more toward ideas.

☐ A meeting can reveal a person's true interest.

Joel Smilow, former executive vice president of Beatrice Companies, said, "I once hired someone with a great track record in companies somewhat different in nature from ours. His first day, we were at a meeting, and I noticed that his boss and I were taking copious notes, but the new guy wasn't taking notes or asking questions." This flagged Joel to what proved to be the case. He didn't have the interest or the drive.

☐ Meetings need showmanship.

Bill N. Newman in his book *Handbook for Successful Sales Meetings* told of the time a sales promotion manager devised a sensational way to introduce a new merchandising aid. He conducted a coroner's inquest!
Several days before the meeting, he showed the new aid to several top salesmen. In the interest of field testing, a few were permitted to use it. Then came the meeting. When the sales promotion manager was introduced, there was no mention of his subject. As he rose to speak, a recording of a funeral march was played. A mock funeral procession entered from the rear of the room! It was led by an "undertaker," complete with dark suit and stovepipe hat. Two "pallbearers" followed, carrying a "casket."
When the procession reached the front of the room, the speaker called it to a halt. The music was also stopped, and the emcee asked for an explanation. The "undertaker" explained, "We're burying an unsuccessful salesman." When asked the cause of the death, the "undertaker" replied, "I don't know,

but we're burying all of them. Something is putting an end to all the unsuccessful salesmen."

The speaker had the casket placed on a table while a coroner's inquest was conducted. Ten "witnesses" were called to the front and seated apart from the audience. They were questioned one at a time. The first expressed the opinion that unsuccessful salesmen were being eliminated by a new sales aid his department had designed. "It's a tool so powerful that no salesman will hereafter be unsuccessful." Other witnesses confirmed the opinion. Salesmen who had field tested the item told of their success in using it. By carefully selecting the "witnesses" and asking well-prepared questions, the speaker had painted a very rosy picture.

A gavel was banged and the verdict announced: "The findings are that the death was caused by the new sales aid. This new aid is bringing an end to all unsuccessful sales efforts." At that moment, the "corpse" jumped out of the "casket"! It was a real shocker since the audience had no reason to believe someone was actually in the box! He ran to the speaker's stand and grabbed the new sales aid. Then he raced out of the room yelling, "Don't bury me—I want to use it, too!"

This event lasted only twenty-two minutes. It did ten times as much good as a speech of the same duration. Try it!

☐ Someone did a study and found that managers spent up to 50 percent of their time in meetings, and implied that this was time wasted.

Peter Drucker once said that if a manager spent more than 25 percent of his time in meetings, it was a sign of poor organization.

William H. Whyte Jr., in his book *The Organization Man*, described meetings as "non-contributory labor" that managers must endure.

MERGERS

Banker, to assistant, during a robbery: "A robbery—oh, thank heavens! I thought it was an unfriendly takeover."

"Never acquire a business you don't know how to run."
Robert W. Johnson, former chairman, Johnson & Johnson

☐ Merging with another company is a way to quickly enter a market.

Procter & Gamble got into the consumer paper products industry by acquiring Charmin Paper, a regional firm. P & G invested heavily in advertising and made Charmin a highly successful product.

☐ Being merged into another company can help reposition your product in the market.

When Miller Beer was purchased by Philip Morris, it gave Miller the muscle to make an aggressive challenge of Anheuser-Busch.

☐ A successful company can be built without hostile takeovers.

Harold Geneen, who built ITT into one of the largest conglomerates in the 1960s and 1970s, purchased over one-thousand companies, and none of them were hostile takeovers. In fact, most of the companies he bought sought out ITT to buy them.

☐ Management needs help to stop a hostile takeover.

In the early 1980s, T. Boone Pickens tried a hostile takeover of Philips Petroleum in the small town of Bartlesville, Oklahoma. With the help of Phillips' employees and the community, they were able to stop Pickens' hostile takeover.

☐ Merging is a quick way to participate in the future of another business while buying their expertise.

General Motors' purchase of Electronic Data Systems broadened their earnings base and put GM into the computer business overnight.

"Takeovers are wonderful for lawyers and bankers, stock jobbers, arbitrageurs, and finders. They are keeping some of the best minds on Wall Street busy in a nonproduction pursuit. But they are just shuffling pieces of paper. Organizing and infacing new industrial productivity has taken a secondary role."

William Carey, former Securities & Exchange Commission chairman

☐ Sometimes mergers are a bad sign of the times.

Willard Thorp, in the 1931 *American Economic Review,* observed that in the wave of the 1920s, one businessman regarded it as a loss of standing if he was not approached once a week with a merger proposition.

Carl Icahn, a veteran of many raids, advised, "You learn in this business: if you want a friend, get a dog."

☐ Some mergers and buyouts just cover up problems.

A young man received a half interest in the business from his new father-in-law. But the man fouled up every job he was given.
Father-in-law: "Try the sales department. Maybe you can do well there."
    But he made a mess of things there, too.
Father-in-law: "What am I going to do with you?"
Young man: "I know. Why don't you buy me out?"

☐ Mergers shouldn't overlook long-term goals.

Felix Rohatyn, who engineered the great near-bankruptcy bailout of New York City, said, "All this frenzy about takeovers may be good for investment bankers now, but it is not good for the country or investment bankers in the long run. We seem to be living in the 1920s jazz age atmosphere."

Here is the wisdom of legendary investor Warren Buffett's thoughts on mergers and acquisitions. The following is taken from Berkshire Hathaway's 1983 annual report:

"In many of these acquisitions, managerial intellect wilted in competition with managerial adrenaline. The thrill of the chase blinded pursuers to the consequences of the catch. Pascal's observation seems apt: 'It has struck me that all men's misfortunes spring from the single cause that they are unable to stay quietly in one room.' (Your chairman left the room once too often last year and almost starred in the Acquisition Follies of 1982. . . . Had it come off, this transaction would have consumed extraordinary amounts of time and energy, all for a most uncertain payoff. If we were to introduce graphics to this report, illustrating favorable business development of the past year, two blank pages depicting this blown deal would be the appropriate centerfold.)"

As Lee Iacocca once wrote in the *Los Angeles Times:* "I don't see the raiders creating jobs. I don't see them increasing productivity, and worst of all, I don't see them doing a thing to help America compete in the world.

Again, Lee Iacocca: "The typical takeover target isn't a company in trouble, it's a company with a solid asset base, low debt, consistent profits and a few bucks in the bank to diversify or get through the next business downturn. When I went to school, we called that good management. Today that makes you fair game."

Anthony Solomon, chairman of S. G. Warburg, said, "Takeover targets tend not to be badly run companies. If they were, the raiders would have a harder time raising the money to buy them."

Andrew C. Sigler, who is president of the Business Roundtable, an organization made up of chief executives of two hundred major corporations, charged:

"It is nothing but a grubby asset play. They are acquiring the greatest accumulation of wealth of all time—greater than the Rockefellers or the Rothschilds—they are doing it by snapping it out of companies, thus damaging the capability of the economic system to perform."

In response, T. Boone Pickens, self-appointed spokesperson for aggressive corporate acquirers, observed:

"The only real stake that many managers have is their job. The two hundred members of the Business Roundtable own less than three tenths of one percent of their companies. *Fortune's* survey of May 1986 showed that 9 percent of Fortune 500 CEO's own no stock in their companies. No wonder they think like bureaucrats instead of like entrepreneurs."

 **MISTAKES**

"Stumbling is not falling."

Portuguese proverb

"He who has never made a mistake is one who never does anything."
Theodore Roosevelt

"The greatest mistake a man can make is to be afraid to make one."
Elbert Hubbard

☐ Don't repeat mistakes.

"A man who has made a mistake and doesn't correct it is making another mistake."

Confucius

"If you simply take up the attitude of defending a mistake, there will be no hope of improvement."
Winston Churchill

"If I wasn't making mistakes, I wasn't making decisions."
Robert W. Johnson, founder, Johnson & Johnson

☐ Mistakes are a byproduct of doing something right.

"A mistake only proves that someone stopped talking long enough to do something."

Michael LeBoeuf

☐ Mistakes are okay so long as you don't lose too much.

There's an old East Texas saying: "It doesn't matter how much milk you spill just so long as you don't lose your cow."

Henry Ford forgot to put a reverse gear in his first car.

Edison once spent more than $2 million on an invention that proved useless.

"By making mistakes and risking loss, a man learns things. When John Kennedy lost a bid for the Democratic vice presidential nomination in 1956 to Estes Kefauver, he didn't quit. He said. 'Okay, now we know the mistakes we made; we know what we have to do to win. In 1960 we'll go for the big job.' The rest is history."
Mortimer R. Feinberg, Effective Psychology for Managers

☐ Mistakes don't make you a failure.

Babe Ruth held the record for home runs. Everybody knows that, but how many people know he also holds the record for strikeouts. The great Ruth struck out 1,330 times.

"Don't ever be afraid to admit you were wrong. It's like saying you're wiser today than you were yesterday."
Robert H. Henry, humorist

We should look at mistakes the way world-class comedian Charlie Chaplin did: "No matter how desperate the predicament is, I am always very much in earnest about clutching my cane, straightening my derby hat and fixing my tie, even though I have just landed on my head."

"Fools you are . . . to say you learn by your experience. . . . I prefer to profit by others' mistakes and avoid the price of my own."

Bismarck

☐ What causes mistakes?

"Mistakes are costly and somebody must pay. The time to correct a mistake is before it is made. The causes of mistakes are first, 'I didn't know'; second, 'I didn't think'; third, 'I didn't care.' "

Henry H. Buckley

☐ It's not healthy to point out others' mistakes.

Here's Black Hawk announcer Pat Foley introducing hockey goalie Bannerman: "All of us make mistakes. But how would you like a job where every time you make a mistake, a red light goes on?"

☐ Some mistakes are worse than others.

A surgeon was scrubbing up after an operation and was asked by one of the interns, "How did the appendectomy go, doctor?"

The doctor answered: "Appendectomy? I thought it was an autopsy."

◼ MONEY

☐ The one with the money calls the shots.

"He who pays the fiddler, calls the tunes."

Margaret L. Clement

"Money is a very excellent servant, but a terrible master."

P.T. Barnum

If you don't know anything at all about money, you can learn all about it by going down to the bank and trying to borrow some.

"If money talks, I need a hearing aid."

Joe L. Whitley

Vacation season! That's when we find out that money won't buy happiness—but it helps you look for it in more places.

☐ Money offers freedom.

Remember, early to bed and early to rise, 'til you make enough money to do otherwise.

If you are the best at what you do, you'll eventually make a lot of money.

"I don't have a problem with guilt about money. The way I see it is that my money represents an enormous number of claim checks on society."
                                                                                    Warren Buffett

"Making money is the by-product, not the goal."
                                                                                    Randy D. Marsh

Money is like fire. You can use it wisely and become successful, or you can use it unwisely and be burned by it.

"Money is not too important. It's scorekeeping. You can't have a successful business career and not make money."
                                                                                    Charles McColough

☐ Money has a lot of pluses.
"The nicest thing about money is that it never clashes with anything I wear."
                                                                                    Myron Cohen, comedian

☐ Many of our greatest creations resulted from the desire to make money.
When George Frederick Handel was on the brink of financial ruin, he isolated himself for twenty-one days and didn't emerge until he had completed *The Messiah.*

"Money doesn't change men, it merely unmasks them. If a man is naturally selfish, or arrogant, or greedy, the money brings it out; that's all."
                                                                                    Henry Ford

"All money represents to me is pride of accomplishment."
                                                                                    Ray Kroc, founder, McDonald's

"Having money is like being a beautiful woman in a romantic novel: You are always wondering whether men are loving you for your body or your soul. You develop finely tuned antennae to detect whether somebody is being nice to you because he really likes you or because he wants you to give money to something. You distrust warm gestures and you look for their real intentions."
                                                                                    Obie Benz, filmmaker

William M. Batten, former J.C. Penney chief executive said, "There's nothing wrong with wanting to make money—except that it should not become the sole objective. The end should be to provide a service or produce a product."

"I don't like money actually, but it quiets my nerves."

Joe Louis

"A good man will work much harder for reasons other than money."
Joyce C. Hall, chairman, Hallmark

"After you reach a certain point, money becomes unimportant. What matters is success."

Aristotle Onassis

"When it is a question of money, everybody is of the same religion."
Voltaire

☐ Some people are tight with money.

Comedian W.C. Fields had great respect for the dollar and parted with one most reluctantly. A friend asked Fields for a loan, and he was told: "I'll see what my lawyer says, and if he says yes, then I'll get another lawyer."

"I have enough money to last me the rest of my life, unless I buy something."

Jackie Mason, comedian

Money can't bring happiness. The Greeks had a myth: Dionysius asked King Midas what he wanted more than anything else in the world, and Midas said. "That everything I touch turn into gold." Dionysus granted Midas his wish. Testing his new powers, he reached up and plucked a leaf from a tree—and it turned to gold in his hand. He picked up a pebble and it too turned to gold in his hand.

Midas said. "I am the richest man in the world; the happiest man in the world."

When he returned home, he ordered his servants to prepare a feast. He was thirsty so he drank some wine, and it turned to gold on his lips; the bread turned to gold before he could get his teeth into it. When he reached out to touch his daughter, she too turned to gold.

The next time you think money can buy happiness and you wish that you had that Midas touch, think again.

◼ MOTIVATION

"Keep away from people who try to belittle your ambitions. Small people always do that, but the really great make you feel that you, too, can become great."

Mark Twain

"I believe the real difference between success and failure in a corpora- tion can very often be traced to the question of how well the organization brings out the great energies and talents of its people."

Thomas J. Watson, Jr., IBM

"Motivation is when your dreams put on work clothes."

Parkes Robinson

☐ Business bulletin board message: "Warning to all personnel—firings will continue until morale improves."

☐ Make employees feel important.

Our [department, plant or other] is like the locomotive that pulls our economic train.

"The true motivator for employees is the spirit of cooperation that comes with a shared vision."

Greg Bustin, senior vice president, Tracy-Lock Public Relations

☐ To stay motivated, find the best way to motivate yourself.

Warren Lester was asked why he was such a successful salesperson. He replied: "I tell myself every night when I go to bed that I lost my job and tomorrow I must start from scratch." Lester further explained that the reason he did this was because a man in a strange job, in a new job, always gives it his best.

☐ To keep employees motivated and upbeat, many companies select an employee of the month.

Pam Reynolds, CEO of Phoenix Textiles in St. Louis, takes the idea a step further. The company also reserves a special parking slot for its employ- ee of the month, located next to the president's space near the front door.

☐ Motivation knows no age. We are motivated when we have a mission.

Apple Computer was started by two young men in their twenties. Yet IBM was founded by Thomas Watson, Sr., when he was in his fifties.

Self-motivation can be explained by the words of former heavyweight boxer, Joe Frazier. When asked why he continued to fight after he had already achieved fame and fortune, he responded, "It's what I do. I am a fighter. It's my job."

"It is well-recognized that the highly motivated person succeeds in life. All successful people are motivated people."

Henry Cannon

"You can't motivate with negatives.

"Consider for a moment the typical situation of a sales supervisor trying to read the riot act to his sales force after a particularly disappointing quarter. The more he hammers away on their inefficiency in planning, their lapses in product knowledge, their laxity in servicing accounts or any other selling weaknesses, the more he is bound to stir up resentment. The longer he dwells on their shortcomings, the more his attempt at motivation will boomerang."

Mortimer R. Feinberg, Effective Psychology for Managers

☐ Motivate people by being positive.

John Robinson, coach of the Los Angeles Rams, said that he never criticized a player until the player was convinced that he had total confidence in his talent. Robinson reminded the player that he is nearly perfect but now it was time to work on the one thing left.

"My experience with people is that they generally do what you expect them to do."

Mary Kay Ash, founder, Mary Kay Cosmetics

☐ Each employee is motivated differently.

"One company employed an independently wealthy woman as a telephone reservations agent. The company wanted to fire her for wasting time and failing to meet production standards, but its hands were tied because of a labor contract. We tried getting some clue to what might motivate her and learned she had a lot of ideas about how the company should be run. So a special incentive program was tailored for this one lady. Whenever she reached the target for making reservations, she got 15 minutes with the manager to discuss her ideas. This incentive made her an effective worker."

Edward J. Feeney, consultant

Abraham Lincoln once said that sometimes people are motivated by the lure of wealth or by the fear of being fired and that all people are probably so motivated at least some of the time.

"You cannot push anyone up the ladder unless he is willing to climb himself."

Andrew Carnegie

Nikita Khrushchev, speaking on the benefits of the incentive system, said, "Call it what you will, incentives are the only way to make people work harder."

☐ To stay motivated, we must constantly fight ourselves.

The famous tenor Enrico Caruso was waiting in the wings on opening night at the opera, and the house was packed. The great singer suddenly rasped in a loud whisper, "Get out of my way! Get out! Get out!" The stagehands were all baffled because no one was even near him. They thought he was cracking up.

The great singer later explained, "I felt within the big me that wants to sing and knows it can, but it was being stifled by the little me that gets afraid and says I can't. I was simply ordering the little me out of my body."

☐ Discover how to motivate yourself.

A great writer once confessed that the most awesome thing for him was a blank piece of paper in the typewriter. So he developed a plan to counter the problem. Each day, when he was ready to quit writing, he would leave a piece of paper in the typewriter with a sentence half finished on it. The next morning, the first thing he would do was to finish that sentence. Soon he would be thoroughly engrossed in his writing and off to a productive day.

☐ Expect more and you will get more.

"In a study of schoolteachers, it turned out that when they held high expectations of their students, that alone was enough to cause an increase of 25 points in the students' IQ scores."

Charles McElroy

☐ Fear is a great motivator.

Vince Lombardi was a genius at getting team play out of individual stars. He knew that the Green Bay Packers could not prevail over a grueling season unless each player dug deep into himself and contributed his very best . . . week after week . . . after week . . . after week. So he sent his proud gladiators into combat with this brief, inspirational message ringing in their helmets: "If you aren't fired with enthusiasm—you will be fired with enthusiasm."

☐ Appeal to selfish motives.

J. Pierpont Morgan once proved that you can motivate anybody if you find their "hot button."

His sister could never get her son who was away at college to answer her letters. Morgan wrote a letter and said, "Enclosed is a ten dollar bill," and he purposely didn't enclose the money. He immediately received a letter back saying, "The ten dollars you said was enclosed in your letter wasn't."

☐ If greed is our motivation, we can't create lasting value.

Infamous Wall Street arbitrageur Ivan Boesky was widely known to favor greed. He said, "Greed is good. Greed is natural." He wound up a criminal, of course, banned from practicing his business. But fines and expulsion and a jail term are not the only negative effects of greed. Amassing money or goods for their own sake may reward in the short term, but over the long haul it destroys those companies and individuals who give in to it.

☐ People move for their own reasons.

Ralph Waldo Emerson and his son struggled and strained trying to wrestle a female calf into the barn. Drenched with sweat, the great sage was on the brink of losing his self-control when a servant girl came by. Smiling sweetly, she thrust a finger into the animal's mouth and, lured by this maternal gesture, the calf peacefully followed the girl into the barn.

Everybody but John had signed up for a new company pension plan that required a small employee contribution. The company paid all the rest. Unfortunately, 100 percent employee participation was needed; otherwise the plan was off.

John's boss and his fellow workers pleaded with him over and over, but to no avail. John said that the plan would never pay off.

Finally, the company president called John into his inner office. The president said. "John, here's a copy of the new pension plan and here's a pen. I want you to sign the papers now, and if you don't you're fired.

John signed the papers immediately.

The president asked, "Would you mind telling me why you didn't sign earlier?"

John answered, "Nobody explained it to me so clearly before."

The loaded station wagon pulled into the only remaining campsite. Four youngsters leaped from the vehicle and began feverishly unloading gear and setting up a tent. The boys then rushed off to gather firewood, while the girls and their mother set up the camp stove and cooking utensils.

A nearby camper marveled to the youngsters' father, "That, sir, is some display of teamwork."

The father replied, "I have a system. No one goes to the bathroom until the camp is set up."

N

NEGOTIATION

> "Negotiation depends on communication."
>
> *Art Windell*

☐ Find out what the other people want before you tell them what you want.

Samuel Goldwyn was giving an inspired sales pitch to George Bernard Shaw about how he wanted to turn *Pygmalion* into an artistic film. Shaw interrupted him. "We can't make a deal, Mr. Goldwyn, because you are mainly interested in art, and I'm only concerned with money."

☐ When negotiating, you should make sure you don't give up too much too soon.

A wealthy man was lying on his death bed under an oxygen tent. One of his aides who worked for him for forty years stood by his side.

The old man told the aide: "I want you to know I appreciate your long and faithful service, and therefore I am leaving you all of my money."

The humble servant asked, "Is there anything I can do for you?"

The old man answered, "Yes, get your damn foot off the oxygen hose."

☐ Put yourself in a position to win.

J. P. Morgan once wanted to buy a large Minnesota ore track from John D. Rockefeller. Rockefeller merely sent John D. Jr. around to talk.

Morgan asked, "Well, what's your price?"

John D., Jr., said, "Mr. Morgan, I think there must be some mistake. I did not come here to sell; I understood you wished to buy."

☐ Don't win the battle and lose the war.

American Motors decided against building a new Jeep plant in Kenosha, Wisconsin. AMC blamed the United Auto Workers, who have negotiated some of the world's highest-paying former jobs.

The late Senator Henry Jackson left a warning. He said, "When the top U.S. officials give the impression that some arms control treaty or agreement is indispensable to them, they make it enormously more difficult for the American negotiating team to strike a favorable bargain in the talks."

☐ We should not negotiate any agreement just for agreement's sake.

☐ Be willing to say no.

Harvey Mackay, author of *How to Swim with the Sharks without Being Eaten Alive,* told of the time he acted as an agent for a high draft choice. Two teams were vying for his client's talent. The first team was the Toronto Argonauts of the Canadian Football League and the other was the Baltimore Colts. When face-to-face negotiations were taking place with John Bassett in Toronto, Bassett was trying to force him to make a decision before he could talk to the Colts. Feeling pressured, Mackay said no, and his client ended up playing for Baltimore, winning a Super Bowl, and he also got more money than Bassett had offered. All because he was willing to say no.

Thomas Aquinas, who knew more about education and persuasion than almost anybody who ever lived, once said that when you wanted to convert someone to your view, you went over to where he was standing, took him by the hand (mentally speaking) and guided him. You didn't stand across the room and shout at him; you didn't call him a dummy, you didn't order him to come over to where you were. You started where he was and worked from that position. That was the only way to get him to budge.

Mark McCormack explained in his book *What They Don't Teach You at Harvard Business School* how to make negotiations a win-win for both sides.
"I find it helpful to try to figure out in advance where the other person would like to end up—at what point he will do the deal and still feel like he's coming away with something. This is different from 'how far will he go?' A lot of times you can push someone to the wall, and you still reach an agreement, but his resentment will come back to haunt you in a million ways."
In other words, negotiate so that there are no bad feelings.

☐ Negotiation is to make sure you don't win the battle and lose the war.

Harvard Business School professor Elon Kohlberg told the story about a Harvard case study involving an insurance company and a lawyer for a woman who had been severely disfigured in a car accident. The class listened to Kohlberg tell the story until the woman received a settlement of $200,000.
One year, Kohlberg asked the class if they thought the $200,000 was a fair compensation for someone's face. No one responded. Finally, he said: "It's a big insurance company. Can't it afford to give more?"
He was still greeted with silence.
Frustrated, he asked, "Can't we just pass up the negotiation process and give the woman what she wants."

At this point, a student said: "If we do that, it will destroy the insurance industry."

◼ NETWORKING

"Networking is being able to help or benefit from individuals you direct-ly have a realtionship with to achieve life's ends"
Paul Drolson, division manager, American Express

"Activity is the life blood of a successful selling process. Networking is probably the most effective way of creative activity."
James F. Lewin, senior vice president, Security Pacific National Bank

☐ Networking works to the degree of your network.

"In 1984, Anne Bowe was attending the National Speakers Association's national convention in Washington, D. C. On the final banquet night, she forgot something in her room and left her tablemates to go back to get the information. She got on the elevator, and in her networking communication style, reached out and said, 'Hi, I'm Anne Bowe. I'm in career management and networking. What do you do?'

"The man in the elevator said, 'Oh, I see you are a speaker. I am not a speaker; I write about speakers.' The man on the elevator was Jeff Waddle, publisher editor of *Meeting Magazine* for Meeting Planners International. By the time they reached the tenth floor, they had exchanged business cards. He had told her that his national convention would be in Phoenix in six months and would turn her materials over to his meeting planner, Mary Hammond. Mary was the educational director of Meeting Planners International.

"Anne, six months later, did an educational session for Meeting Planners International and was asked to return the following year when the interna-tional conference was held in San Diego. She was then asked by the new educational director Karen Hodges to keynote the Miami conference and speak on networking. In her audience at the Miami conference was Karen Peterson from Tupperware Home Parties. Karen Peterson took Anne Bowe's information to her boss Fran Watkins, and Anne, in August 1988, keynoted seven Tupperware Jubilees and spoke to 18,000 people during that month. Networking has definitely paid off in Anne's career."
Anne Bowe, Is Your "NET" Working?

☐ Networking can increase profitability.

Remember the wonderful movie, *Miracle on 34th Street*, in which Macy's and Gimbels broke tradition by cooperating rather than competing? Both firms ended up having the greatest Christmas profits ever.
Theodore Levitt, Harvard University

☐ Part of networking is realizing what you can do for others.

John F. Kennedy was being patriotic when he gave his "Ask not what your country can do for you; ask what you can do for your country" speech, but the idea makes a lot of sense in many contexts, not just in a national one.

"Some of the more forward-thinking businesses might establish their own in-house networking associations. Did you ever see the movie *Desk Set* with Katharine Hepburn and Spencer Tracy? Ms. Hepburn worked in an in-house reference department for a large firm. Workers would call her with information they needed for their project; in a few moments she would find the answers.

"The same could be true with networking. One worker could supply names and information about a variety of topics."

Anne Bowe, Is Your "NET" Working

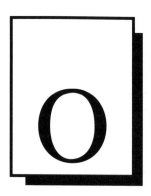

OBJECTIVES

"The way to achieve success is first to have a definite, clear, practical ideal—a goal, an objective. Second, have the necessary means to achieve your ends—wisdom, money, materials, and methods. Third, adjust all your means to that end."

Aristotle

☐ Determining objectives isn't always easy, but it's important.

When Robert Townsend took over Avis, it took him six months to define the company's objective. The objective: "We want to become the fastest-growing company with the highest profit margins in the business of renting and leasing vehicles without drivers."

"An objective is a desired state of affairs."

Anthony J. Alessandra

Operating a company without a formal set of rules and regulations is similar to sailing across the ocean without navigational charts. Objectives can seldom be achieved without a how-to approach.

☐ We need to be aware of what our objective is when we deal with customers.

Consultant Dan Bellus reminded us that the objective in selling is not to defeat the prospect but to convince him that if he buys, he's going to be happier and better off as a result.

☐ A company's main objective should be to exceed the customers' expectations.

Take the advice of Richard Thalheimer, president of The Sharper Image, who said, "People expect a certain reaction from a business, and when you pleasantly exceed those expectations, you've somehow passed an important psychological threshold."

☐ Every business enterprise needs objectives to guide its future.

"Objectives are the 'instrument panel' necessary to pilot the business enterprise. Without them management flies by the 'seat of its pants'—without landmarks to steer by, without maps and without having flown the route before.

"However, an instrument panel is no better than the pilot's ability to read and interpret it. In the case of management, this means ability to anticipate the future. Objectives that are based on completely wrong anticipations may actually be worse than no objectives at all. The pilot that flies by the 'seat of his pants' at least knows that he may not be where he thinks he is."

Peter Drucker, The Practice of Management

☐ Managers are no better than their objectives.

Joe developed a reputation as a "turnaround" manager, one who could take a sick division of any large company and within a couple of years turn it from a loser to a profit maker. He repeated his magic not once but many times. When Joe moved up to tackle bigger divisions, his old ones slowly dropped back into unprofitability again. Every new manager who succeeded Joe's success asked for major new investments in order to make the divisions profitable over the long term.

Joe wasn't concerned about what he had left behind. He had gone on to being in charge of one of the company's largest divisions, which for years had failed to reach its potential. To make the division profitable, Joe tightened budgets, cut overhead, and looked for every penny he could save. Nothing worked, and the operation continued to slip slowly downward. It wasn't too long before Joe, once a bright star, was fired.

Up and coming managers were baffled by Joe's demise. They sought out the advice of a retired old-timer wise enough to clear up their confusion.

He told them, "Business is not simple. The company set Joe's goals in terms of short-term profits, not long-term results. To meet their objectives, he cut back on advertising, product development, maintenance, training, and every other function that didn't directly reflect a positive figure on the next profit and loss statement. Joe's failure was because his company didn't have a strategy; they just wanted short-term profits without thinking of the long-term effect."

A requiem for Joe: His company wanted the impossible and expected Joe to get it. Joe gave his company what they asked for but not what they expected.

Poor Joe, he did the right thing for the wrong reason and was fired for the wrong thing for the wrong reason.

"Setting objectives accomplishes at least four purposes:

"First, it provides a clear, documented statement of what the employee intends to accomplish.

"Second, it establishes a basis for the measurement of performance.

"Third, knowing what is expected gives positive motivation to the employee.

"Fourth, knowing where you are going is much more likely to allow you to get there instead of spinning your wheels without any direction."
Lin Bothwell, The Art of Managing People

Objectives are a great guideline but must be altered to meet current demands. An example of changed objectives is the American Tobacco Company that for a long time had as its objective the manufacturing and marketing of tobacco products When the cigarette industry began to be criticized by the government and various health organizations, American Tobacco changed its objectives to include not just tobacco but other consumer goods as well. To reflect this new objective, the company changed its name to American Products company.

☐ OPPORTUNITY

"When the sun rises, it rises for everyone."

Cuban proverb

☐ Never pass up a good opportunity.
"The dawn does not come twice to awaken a man."

Arabic proverb

"When one door of opportunity closes, another opens; but often we look so long at the closed door that we do not see the one which has been opened for us."

Helen Keller

☐ Don't let others talk you out of your opportunities.
"Most of the things worth doing in the world had been declared impossible before they were done."

Louis D. Brandeis

"A wise man will make more opportunities than he finds."

Francis Bacon

"Small opportunities are often the beginning of great enterprises."

Demosthenes

☐ Your current customers offer the opportunity to sell more.
The phrase, "It can't be done" takes on a different attitude at Society Expeditions in Seattle. They are a travel agency that specializes in taking people to places they thought were impossible to get to—places like the North Pole. The company found a void in their familiar market and turned it into a

travel agency that grosses over $30 million a year selling high-adventure vacations.

An old proverb says, "Opportunity is where you find it." It doesn't say "where it finds you."

☐ At first sighting, opportunities sometimes appear as a threat.

In the 1950s, the railroads refused to accept the idea that cars, airplanes, and trucks were here to stay. They viewed the new transportation as a threat not only to the railroads but to the nation. but a decade later, the railroads began to see the threat as an opportunity. The public would accept railroads dropping unprofitable lines and merging with railroads and thus allowing them to do what they do best, making long-haul deliveries.

☐ Some old products can offer new opportunities to generate profits.

Arm & Hammer baking soda is used in over 50 percent of American refrigerators for odor control, a use that has far surpassed the original use of baking soda.

"Opportunity only knocks on the door of those that deserve it."
Win Halliburton

"The largest opportunity for any average man is right in the line where he is already established. When he is already in a business, no matter how far down the scale, he can go ahead faster in that business than he can in any other. The average man who, like myself, has no special gifts, does better to stick to the line he knows."
Charles Walgreen

☐ The more skills we have, the more opportunities we have.

"A wealth of skills doesn't ensure freedom any more than any other wealth, but it surely can expand choice, which may lead out of some corners."
Steward Brand, publisher

"Anyone who says the days of opportunity are over is copping out."
Ann Landers

"Great opportunity is usually disguised as unsolvable problems."
Gretchen G. Clement

"One cannot afford to neglect opportunity."

Sun-tzu

☐ When you see a ready opportunity, don't wait.
"Opportunity is a bird that never perches."

Claude McDonald

"You can observe a lot just by watching."

Yogi Berra

☐ Some people see opportunity, others don't.

There is also the long-enduring, probably apocryphal, story of the two market researchers who were independently dispatched some years ago to one of the world's less-developed countries by one of the world's larger shoe manufacturers. When the first telegram-reports got to the corporate headquarters, one message read, "No market here. Nobody wears shoes."; but the other one promised, "Great market here. Nobody has any."

☐ Opportunity is found by those looking for it.

An ambitious young man ventured to approach a wealthy industrialist.

Young man: "Would you mind telling me your secret of personal success?"
Rich man;   "There is no secret. You just have to jump at your opportunities."
Young man: "But how will I know when these opportunities come?"
Rich man: "You can't—you just have to keep jumping."

☐ Opportunity is everywhere.

"As bees extract honey from thyme, the strongest and driest of herbs, so sensible men often get advantage and profit from the most awkward circumstances."

Plutarch

☐ Opportunity is everywhere if you have an open mind.

A bright young man entered the employment office of a large business concern to apply for a job he had seen advertised.

Manager: "But, young man, you're much too late. We've already received a thousand applications."
Young man: "Well, how about hiring me to classify the applications?"

☐ Others will show you the way to opportunity.

During the late 1930s, an Eastern Air Transport flight crew member entered the Marriott Hot Shoppe near Hoover Airport and asked for a quart of coffee to go.

The waitress asked, "Driving to New York?"

The young man in uniform said. "No, flying to Atlanta. We'll drink this on the way."

Soon, passengers boarding planes at Hoover, began buying sandwiches, milk, coffee, fruit, and candy bars to take with them on their flights. The manager described this new business to Bill Marriott. The next day, he called the people at Eastern Air Transport, and airlines have been serving in-flight meals ever since.

☐ Look for new opportunities in old places.

This unnamed businessman took the average Laundromat, crossed it with a beer bar—"Enjoy our suds while you wash your duds" was the motto—and it was a runaway success.

☐ Opportunity is waiting for you, but you have to make it happen.

Alexander Graham Bell, inventor of the telephone, is said to have beat another inventor to the patent office by less than ten minutes.

Frank Whittle and Hans Von Oldhiam invented the jet engine at the same time without the one knowing about the other.

Opportunity should be taken advantage of. Astronaut John Glenn realized that the first astronaut would be the one the world would remember. He dreamed up a scheme to improve his chances of being the first one.

While a major in the U.S. Marines, Glenn decided to make a coast-to-coast flight at an average speed greater than Mach 1. Everybody knew it could be done, but nobody bothered to do it until Glenn did.

Jean Paul Lyet, former CEO of Sperry Corporation, once said, "Nothing is more critical to a businessman than the ability to recognize and exploit opportunities."

We must develop and encourage viewing every situation as an opportunity that we might best use it to our advantage.

☐ Opportunity occurs when you can apply a success from one business to another one.

Federal Express used the bank's method of clearing checks overnight to the movement of packages. Fred Smith, the founder, developed the hub-and-spoke concept, where every single package goes to Memphis, Tennessee, and then is flown to its final destination.

☐ Even in hard times, there are still opportunities. You just have to work harder to find them.

Tri-Tech, maker of the Stairmaster 6000, which sells to health clubs for about $4,000, has revenues of about $20 million a year. The company was founded in Tulsa by three men out of work because of the declining petroleum industry.

■ OPTIMISM

"All that is necessary to break the spell of inertia and frustration is this: Act as if it were impossible to fail."

Dorothea Brande

"The habit of looking on the best side of every event is worth more than a thousand pounds a year."

Samuel Johnson

"I am an optimist. It does not seem too much use being anything else."

Michel de Montaigne

"I've never seen a monument erected to a pessimist."

Paul Harvey

John Gardner offered this distinction between naive optimism and tough-minded optimism: "We need to believe in ourselves," he said, "but not to believe that life is easy."

"Cheer up. The worst is yet to come."

Philaster Chase Johnson

The only reason for optimism with respect to old age is offered by George Burns, who noted, "Once you get to be one hundred, you have made it. You almost never hear of anyone dying who is over one hundred."

An optimist goes to the window every morning and says, "Good morning, God." The pessimist goes to the window and says, "Good God, morning!"

My uncle is an optimist. He just asked the IRS to take him off their mailing list.

☐ Hire optimistic people.

Martin Seligman, a psychologist at the University of Pennsylvania, has proven that optimists are more successful than equally talented pessimists—in business, education, sports, and politics.

Metropolitan Life developed a test called the Seligman Attributional Style Questionnaire to sort the optimists from the pessimists when hiring sales personnel. In that experiment, he found that optimists outsold pessimists by 20 percent the first year, and by 50 percent the following year.

"There are times when I felt as if I had gone my limit. Some of my setbacks were stunners. It seemed as if I couldn't get the stamina to start over again. But every time, when I had studied things over a little, I would find a way out. No matter how hopeless things look, there is always a way out, if you look for it hard enough."

Lee De Forest, inventor

Optimism is a great thing. We need more of it today than ever before. But this doesn't mean that we should blind ourselves to reality. We need to maintain an optimistic outlook while at the same time constantly examining it to make sure we're not wearing blinders.

It's like the story of the prominent executive who had asserted that he was very optimistic about the future of his business.

He was asked, "Why, then, do you have such a worried look on your face?"

The businessman replied, "When you are optimistic, it always pays to worry about your optimism."

"One of the things I learned the hard way was that it doesn't pay to get discouraged. Keeping busy and making optimism a way of life can restore your faith in yourself."

Lucille Ball

PAPERWORK

☐ Paperwork doesn't have to be long to be effective. Sometimes less is best.

"A brief written presentation that winnows fact from opinion is the basis for decision making around here."

Ed Harness, retired chairman, Proctor & Gamble

☐ You don't need paper shuffling to be successful.

At Proctor & Gamble, one-page memos are the rule. At 3M, new product ideas must be proposed in fewer than five pages.

☐ One way to cut down on paperwork is to learn to say things in fewer words.

"Never use a long word when a short one will do."

George Orwell

☐ How expensive is paperwork?

A few years ago when Eli Lilly & Company asked the Food and Drug Administration to approve a new drug for arthritis, their application was a bulging 120,000 pages. It took two small trucks to transport the load to Washington. Lilly spent over $15 million on government paperwork, which adds about 50 cents to every prescription.

☐ A lot of paperwork is brought about because of poor listening.

Studies show that an untrained listener is likely to understand and retain only about 50 percent of a conversation, and this drops to 25 percent after forty-eight hours.

Tandem Corporation has tried to eliminate paperwork. They favor personal contact to written memos.

Too many people are like Samuel Goldwyn, who said, "I read part of it all the way through."

☐ Don't let paperwork cover up the real problem.

IBM once had a meeting of their sales managers, and Tom Watson, S., was to attend the meeting. The purpose of the meeting was to assess some customer problems.

On the table were stacks of paper identifying and explaining the source of the problem. After listening to various managers discussing the problem from their perspective, he walked to the front of the room and swept the table clean, sending the stacks of paper all over the floor.

He said: "There is only one problem here. We aren't paying enough attention to our customers." Then he walked out leaving the room stunned.

Remember that taking care of the customer is the main reason why we are in business and that anything less is avoiding the real problem.

☐ Paperwork has a purpose.

There are said to be twice as many people engaged in clerical work today than were thirty years ago. It is reassuring, therefore, to know that mixed up as we are these days, somebody is getting it all down on paper.

A woman asked Winston Churchill how much he charged to make a speech. He replied, "$2,000."

She said, "That's a lot. We only wanted you to talk for ten minutes."

Churchill said, "In that case, it will cost $4,000."

☐ A concise report is harder to prepare, but it's often much more effective and gets better results.

☐ Too much paperwork is frustrating.

An executive received a form of multi-pages asking for a list of employees broken down by sex. He put it aside because he had so many other duties to perform. A month later he received a nasty letter from the government reminding him that he hadn't returned the form.

Disgusted, he wrote across it: "We have no employees broken down by sex—alcohol is our problem."

☐ Are we the reason there is too much paperwork?

Sam Goldwyn's secretary was cleaning out file cabinets. She asked Goldwyn if she could destroy files that had been inactive for more than ten years.

He said, "Go ahead, but make sure you keep copies."

☐ The problem of paperwork can be solved with the proper incentive.

Michael Barrist, founder of NCO Financial Systems, a collection agency in Philadelphia, initiated a bonus system for his data-entry clerks that has brought the paperwork problem under control. Productivity has increased an average of 25%, which Barrist said saved him from hiring, training, and managing an additional clerk. And there has been no drop in quality.

How does he do it? Every day that NCO's seven clerks finish without a backlog, they get a point; at month's end, $250, $200, and $150 prizes are awarded to the top three performers. To keep the rest of the staff's spirits up, NCO also has a random drawing for a $100 prize.

☐ Paperwork can take away from the bottom line.

The $600 screwdrivers that the media happily attributed to contractor dishonesty probably cost more to make than the $600 being charged. The contractors may be too embarrassed about charging the real amount. The hammer probably cost under $10 to make, but the paperwork ran up the cost.

☐ "Eliminating duplication reduces paperwork.

"Joan Lamberth of Plastiline, Inc., had heard an employee, Bill Akers, complain often about not being able to get the weekly payroll completed in a shorter time. After studying the problem, Joan found that part of the work was duplicated. Identical records were kept in Payroll and Accounting. She approached Mr. Akers with, 'I have been thinking about why it takes so long to get the payroll completed every week. Yesterday I had some free time and talked to those in Accounting and Payroll. I discovered that part of Joe's work could be eliminated because Mary already had that information. By letting Joe and Mary work as a team, duplication would be eliminated and the job completed faster. I think it would be worth changing the procedures.'

"Bill Akers appreciated Joan's idea. The payroll procedure was revised. From then on, half a day's work was saved by using the new system."
Genevieve Smith, Genevieve Smith's Deluxe Handbook for the Executive Secretary

☐ There is a reason why some paperwork is required.

An executive usually got most of his staff input verbally. Then one day, he suddenly discovered a major crisis in his department. He called his staff into his office and asked why he hadn't been warned before the situation became so serious.

The accountant said: "But I did warn you. I mentioned it a week ago Friday when we were discussing the June budget."

Yes, he had been warned, but it was so obscure that he missed the significance. From that moment on, he requested that all reports be submitted in writing so that he could study them properly.

◼ PARTNERSHIPS

"If money talks, then how come it's the 'silent partners' in a business deal who do the financing?"

Scott Thomson

"Never have a partner unless it's absolutely necessary."

Victor Kiam

Andrew Carnegie's boyhood friend, Henry Phipps, became one of his lifetime trusted aides. Carnegie was an outgoing type and Phipps was the economizer, the one who kept an eye out for a way to cut unnecessary expenditures, and Carnegie used him to keep the bankers complaisant.

☐ Partners should complement each other.

☐ Opposites attract, or they'd better if a partnership is going to be stronger.

For example, David Packard and his talented partner, Bill Hewlett started Hewlett-Packard. Packard was Mr. Outside and Hewlett was Mr. Inside. Together they formed a strong team, one complementing the other.

☐ Lots of successful enterprises were started by partnerships.

Rolls and Royce founded the prestigious British motor car company. And there were Procter and Gamble; Packard and Hewlett, to name just a few.

"I'm not the smartest fellow in the world, but I can sure pick smart colleagues. Because I'm not so smart, I have to surround myself with real talent."

Franklin D. Roosevelt

"You seldom accomplish very much by yourself. You must get the assistance of others."

Henry J. Kaiser

☐ Partners need a high level of trust.

Roger was dying, and his longtime business partner stood by his bedside. Roger wanted to clear his conscience before he died.

He said, "Ed, I need to tell you that I stole $50,000 a few years ago when you were out of the country."

Ed said, "Now, Roger, this is no time to get into things like that."

Roger said, "And I also had an affair with your wife for over ten years."

Ed said, "Roger, I don't want to get into this, I've known about all these things for a long time. Why do you think I poisoned you?"

☐ A partnership is no better than the people in it.

An eighty-year-old man was about to give up golf because of poor eyesight. He could hit the ball well, but he couldn't see where it went. So the doctor teamed him up with a ninety-year-old partner who had perfect eyesight.

The first day they played, the eighty-year old man hit his first drive and asked his partner if he saw where it landed. He answered, "Yep."

He asked, "Where did it go?"

He said, "I don't remember."

☐ In a good partnership, each partner brings something to the relationship the other partner doesn't have.

There is a joke about two workmen in Moscow. One stops every 20 feet to dig a hole beside the street. As soon as he is finished, his companion fills it and they move on.

Someone asked, "What are you doing? You dig a hole and fill it up. You're accomplishing nothing."

One of the workers said, "You don't understand. Usually there are three of us, but Mikhail is home drunk today. I dig the hole, Mikhail sticks in a tree, and Dimitri here puts the dirt back in the hole. Just because Mikhail is drunk doesn't mean that Dimitri and I have to stop working."

☐ How valuable are you to a partnership? Ask what would happen if you weren't there.

☐ Two losers don't make a good partnership.

After a long day on the course, the dejected golfer turned to his caddie and said, "You must be the absolute worst caddie in the world."

Caddie: "No, I don't think so. That would be too much of a coincidence."

☐ When you form a partnership, each partner needs strengths the other partner doesn't have.

☐ Get partners who complement you.

Henry Ford was called "ignorant" by a newspaper editorial. He sued the paper for libeling him. The defense attorney put Ford on the stand with the purpose of proving to the jury that he was ignorant. After a litany of questions, Ford stopped the lawyer and said, "I may not know the answer to your questions, but I want to remind you that my pushing a button on my desk I can summon to my side someone who can tell me what I want to know. Now, tell me why I should clutter my mind with general information when I have men around me who can supply any knowledge I need?"

☐ When you pick a partner, make sure that you are both going in the same direction.

Daniel Webster told a story from his childhood about the day he and his older brother, Ezekiel, were sitting in the shade.

His father asked: "Ezekiel, what are you doing?"

Ezekiel said, "Nothing."

The father said, "Well, Daniel, what are you doing?"

Daniel replied, "Helping Zeke!"

It's obvious that Daniel Webster didn't spend the reminder of his life helping his brother do nothing. He spent more than a half century in great demand as an orator, lawyer, and statesman.

PEFORMANCE

☐ Whenever diverse people are brought together to interact in a positive way, it can produce exciting results.

Athletes reach their peak level by harnessing a perfect balance of physical capacity, mental conditioning, and inner energy. It's the same with a team brought together by the integration of the different resources and capacities of its members.

☐ People always perform better if their performance is recognized. I once spoke to a company in California that has a parking space labeled, "Salesperson of the Month" located next to the front door of the main building. The saleperson's name was put on the label. I've seen this type of recognition at other places. Ft. Worth's famous Colonial Country Club has a similar parking space for it's club president.

☐ Too many companies accept low standards of performance.

Francis G. "Buck" Rodgers, former IBM marketing vice president, said, "It's a shame that, in so many companies, whenever you get good service, it's an exception."

☐ Top performers in any field are developed, not born.

Zig Ziglar said that he had read a lot of birth announcements. They always indicated that the newborn was either a boy or a girl. He had never read of the arrival of a doctor, salesperson, accountant, or member of any other profession.

☐ Role performance depends on where you are on the corporate ladder.

"The president of an organization should be concerned with the big picture, with the vision, with planning and policy making. Those at the middle-management level should be concerned with translating those policies into plans and setting up programs that can be accomplished. The first-line supervisor is concerned with nuts-and-bolts details that have to be accomplished in order to make the programs successful."

Lin Bothwell, The Art of Leadership

☐ Past performance can be a forerunner to future performance.

At one time, AT&T studied the careers of seventeen thousand of its executives, comparing their performance to their college records. The study revealed that scholastic achievement is the single most important indicator for predicting success.

☐ Don't overpromise.

"He who is the most slow in making a promise is the most faithful in the performance of it."

Jean-Jacques Rousseau

☐ The success of any business depends on its performance.

Reginald H. Jones, chairman emeritus, General Electric Company, said that a corporation will exist only as long as the public is satisfied with its performance.

☐ Some businesses are famous for their poor performance.

A man found an old shoe ticket in a desk drawer he was cleaning out. He couldn't remember the pair of shoes it represented. He concluded that because the ticket was faded, it must be several years old. Out of curiosity, he stuck the shoe ticket into his pocket, and on his way home that night, he stopped by the shoe shop. Without saying a word, he handed the ticket to the old cobbler. The old man studied the ticket for a minute, shuffled into the back room, and soon returned.

He said, "They'll be ready next Wednesday."

Race care drivers will tell you that to become a successful high-performance driver, you must be sensitive to the signals that are picked up by the tires and transferred to the wheels and controls. Regular cars are built so that the driver can't feel the road, while race cars are built so that the driver can feel the road.

☐ Regular cars are like "comfort zones"; they isolate us from the potential of personal high-performance.

There are lots of ways to recognize employees who are peak performers.

Monsanto's recognition and motivation program was in a rut. Something new was needed, so they came up with a book called *The Master Salesman* that contained the wit and wisdom of their top salespeople.

The book idea has been taken by other companies and is often used as part of their training programs.

☐ People are more interested in what you can do than in what you have done.

Robert Chalmers, president of a small, successful communications firm, once told this story:

"When I was a kid just starting out, I would sell people on my ability. I had graduated from an Ivy League school. I was Phi Beta Kappa. I had held a succession of increasingly important positions in my chosen field. I would tell my prospective bosses (and they usually bought it), 'I've got proven ability.' I was pretty pleased with myself until the day an aging executive listened to my spiel and laughed. he said, 'Son, let me tell you something. Ability, even proven ability, is what you did yesterday. It doesn't say a thing about what you'll do tomorrow. If I hire you, it won't be for your proven ability. It'll be because I think you'll work hard for me.' "

☐ To get better performance, make people feel important.

Original Copy Centers Inc. in Cleveland decided its three-shift, 110-

person staff could use a morale booster. They published a company yearbook. The execution was simple—everybody fills out questionnaires asking about their favorite music, ideal weekend, biggest challenges, and best childhood memory. Other fill-in-the-blanks: 'What I really like about my job' and 'My role at Original.' The book devotes a full page to each person's quotes, which run alongside a large photo.

While the yearbook is for employees, marketing manager Michael Setta says that customers also browse through the books, which are displayed in the lobby of the company's headquarters.

☐ It is management that can improve employee performance.

In a large company, a department head approached his vice president and said, "Joe, I want to make some major personnel changes in my department. There are several employees I want to fire, others that should be transferred because they can't do the job, and a few that I don't know what to do with. My people are giving me strictly second-rate performance."

The vice president looked at him thoughtfully and said, "Charlie, how long have you been on this job?"

"Seven years."

"Who has been in charge of these employees all that time?"

He said, "I have."

"Well, Charlie, whose performance is second-rate?"

☐ Employees need performance standards to perform better. The following example comes from W. Steven Brown, president of the Fortune Group:

"A friend's son, Kelly, told me that he planned to resign from one insurance company and go to work for another. I knew from talking with Kelly's father that the young man had not been making his quota. Assuming that Kelly had opted for resignation instead of being fired, I asked, 'Well, do you think this new company's products are so far superior that they will be easier to sell?'

"Kelly said, "Not at all, it's a matter of performance standards. I knew that if I didn't make my quota at the old company, it didn't really matter, because they just keep on giving you another chance. With this new company, it's a different story. You produce, or you go, and I need that sort of discipline. At my age, I've got to be surrounded by winners. I find it too easy to listen to the losers.'

"Apparently that was exactly what Kelly needed, because the next year he almost made the Million Dollar Roundtable. He had a clearer understanding of the importance of this firm's quality standards than his first employer did. Kelly drew pride from the higher standards and the personal test they gave him.

"Standards have the desired effect only when management practices what it preaches. We cannot say one thing and do another. As in the firm Kelly was associated with, announced standards not adhered to become pride destroyers rather than builders."

Performance standards should be set down early. Imagine that you're the manager of a firm of CPAs. Your firm has established a minimum standard that each junior accountant bill not less than 2,000 hours per year, or 450 hours per quarter. Once you have properly communicated this standard, it provides the basis for counseling the employee without personally becoming involved. The employee who fails to achieve knows that he has not kept pace.

☐ We will improve our performance with attention to the small things.

Legendary Alabama football coach, Paul "Bear" Bryant, when asked why he had such a successful record, said, "It's the itsy-bitsy teeny-weeny things that beat you."

◻ PERSEVERANCE

"Once worthwhile task carried to a successful conclusion is better than half-a-hundred half-finished tasks."

B. C. Forbes

"Success seems to be largely a matter of hanging on after others have let go."

William Feather

"Nothing in the world can take the place of persistence."
Calvin Coolidge

"If people think they have even modest personal control over their destinies, they will persist at tasks."

Jack Reitmann

"With a little luck and a hell of a lot of persistence, one might actually get two things done in a year."

Ed McElroy, USAir

☐ Never give up hope.

"The most tragic of all, in the long run, is the ultimate attitude, 'It doesn't matter.' "

Rollo May

"Mistakes are easy, mistakes are inevitable, but there is no mistake so great as the mistake of not going on."

William Blake

Paul Harvey said that if there is one common denominator of men whom the world calls successful it is this: They get up when they fall down.

☐ We will succeed because we don't have enough sense to quit.

"There are people in show business who became major stars simply because they didn't have sense enough to quit when they should have."
Bertrand Russell

☐ Salespeople need perseverance.

When Harry Collins was asked how many calls he will make on a prospect before giving up, he said: "It depends on which one of us dies first."

Harry once made 130 calls on a prospect in one year before finally receiving an order.

3M's Post-it Notes, so familiar in offices all over America today, weren't well received initially. When the idea was presented to office-supply distributors, they thought the idea was a bad one. They took market surveys that were negative. Eventually the little note pads became successful after samples were mailed to the secretaries of the CEOs of the Fortune 500.

☐ Products we can't live without today succeeded through persistence.

"If at first you don't succeed, try, try again. Then quit. No use being a damn fool about it."
W. C. Fields

To be successful in business you've got to be like a quail dog. You know something is out there; you've just got to keep hunting and looking until you find it.

Referring to his well-known work habits, Herschel Walker, NFL running back said, "My God-given talent is my ability to stick with something longer than anyone else."

John Deere was not the first person to think about adding steel to plows, but he was the one to persist with the idea, to take the product to the farmer, to preach its virtues, and to price it right.

"Success is getting up just one more time than you fall down."
Doc Blakely, humorist

"If you only knock long enough and load enough at the gate, you are sure to wake up somebody."
Henry Wadsworth Longfellow

"Never give up, for that is just the place and time that the tide will turn."
Harriet Beecher Stowe

"Obstacles cannot crush me; every obstacle yields to stern resolve."

Leonardo da Vinci

☐ Success is failure overcome by persistence.

- Henry Ford failed and went broke five times before he finally succeeded.
- Eighteen publishers turned down Richard Bach's 10,000-word story about a "soaring" seagull, Jonathan Livingston Seagull, before Macmillan finally published it in 1970. By 1975, it had sold more than 7 million copies in the United States alone.
- Richard Hooker worked for seven years on his humorous war novel, *M*A*S*H*, only to have it rejected by 21 publishers before Morrow decided to publish it. It became a runaway best-seller, spawning a blockbusting movie and a highly successful television series.
- Babe Ruth, considered by sports historians to be the greatest athlete of all time and famous for setting the home-run record, also holds the record for strikeouts.
- Winston Churchill did not become prime minister of England until he was 62, and then only after a lifetime of defeats and setbacks. His greatest contributions came when he was a senior citizen.

☐ The will to persist creates victory.

It has been said that Wellington was considered a dunce by his mother. At Eton, he was called dull, idle, slow, and was about the last boy in school of whom anything was expected. He showed no talent, and had no desire to enter the army. His industry and perseverance were his only redeeming characteristics in the eyes of his parents and teachers. But through perseverance at age forty-six, he had defeated Napoleon, the greatest general living, except himself.

☐ Persistence is the seed of success.

Charles Goodyear purchased an India-rubber life-preserver as a curiosity. He was told that rubber would be of great value for a thousand things, if cold weather did not make it hard as stone, or reduce it to liquid. He said. "I can remedy that."

Experiment after experiment failed. The money he put into the research was sunk. His last dollar was spent. His family suffered for the necessities of life. Even his best friends hurried away from him because they thought he was going insane. Once when a man inquired where he might find Goodyear, he was told, "If you see a man with an India rubber cap, an India rubber coat, India rubber shoes, and an India rubber purse in his pocket, with not a cent in it—that is Charles Goodyear."

But Goodyear was not as insane as most people thought. For five years, he battled with obstacles and adversities that would have disheartened men of less determination. Finally, his efforts were crowned with success.

Out of humiliation, hardships, and defeat after defeat, Charles Goodyear won. He turned failure into success, defeat into victory. All because of persistence.

On the "David Susskind Show" a few years ago, he had three guests who were self-made millionaires. These men, in their mid-thirties, had averaged being in eighteen different businesses before they hit it big.

Winston Churchill personified the attitude of perseverance. Here was a man who suffered through political defeats to become Great Britain's prime minister in their hour of greatest need. Beset by superior German forces in World War II, he rallied the spirit and the action of a nation and achieved the stature of a recognized world leader.

In his later years, he was invited to address the graduating class at Oxford University. Following his introduction, he rose, walked to the lectern, and simply said, "Never, never, never give up." Then he sat down.

☐ The next time somebody tells you that you don't have what it takes, that you can't make it, push ahead with persistence.

When the debts are high and the income is low and you want to throw in the towel, think of these words from Ralph Waldo Emerson's *Self-Reliance*:

"Trust thyself; every heart vibrates to that iron string. Accept the place that divine providence has found for you. . . . Nothing at last is sacred but the integrity of your own mind. What I must do is all that concerns me, not what people think. This rule, equally arduous in actual and in intellectual life, may serve for the whole distinction between greatness and meanness."

Over and over again, we see that it's important to not give up. Take the young jockey who lost his first race, his second, his third, his first 10, his first 20. But he kept trying. In fact, he lost his first 200 races. But he kept plugging away, eventually losing 250 straight races. Then Eddie Arcaro won his first race. He went on to become one of the all-time great jockeys, winning the most money in 1948, 1950, 1952, and 1955.

☐ When we think we have failed and want to give up, we should remind ourselves of the life story of this man:

Age 22, failed in business.
Age 23, ran for legislature and was defeated.
Age 24, failed again in business.
Age 25, elected to legislature.
Age 26, sweetheart died.
Age 27, had a nervous breakdown.
Age 29, defeated for speaker.
Age 31, defeated for elector.
Age 34, defeated for Congress.

Age 37, elected to Congress.
Age 39, defeated for Congress.
Age 46, defeated for Senate.
Age 47, defeated for vice president.
Age 49, defeated for Senate.
Age 51, elected president of the United States.

This is the record of Abraham Lincoln. Throughout his life, he suffered many more defeats than victories, but because he never gave up, he won the highest office in the land.

☐ Persistence pays off in the long run. Let me give you two examples.

In 1970, the Dutch electronics firm N. V. Philips discovered how to use a lazer to play sound and pictures recorded on a plastic disk. U.S. companies like RCA and Zenith spent millions in research aimed at putting the Philips discovery to practical use. So did a Japanese company called Sony. Well, in the late 70s, the American companies dropped out of the race because their research up to that point had proven inconclusive. As John Nevin, then chairman of Zenith, put it, staying in the hunt would have been a "bet-the-company" type of decision. Apparently Sony was willing to wager, because it persisted and now dominates the growing market for this new technology.

My second example is from closer to home.

In 1957, Toyota first came to the United States with an unfortunate little car called the Toyopet. It was so far off the mark that Toyota virtually withdrew from the U.S. car market, keeping its name alive by selling small numbers of an off-road vehicle called the Land Cruiser. Toyota then intensely studied the market for several years, not returning in full force until 1965, when it introduced the Corona. The 5,400 cars sold that year were just the beginning. In 1989, Toyota sold 620,000 cars and 330,000 trucks in the United States and was the leading import nameplate in car, truck, and combined sales for the eighth consecutive year.

PESSIMISM

"To believe a thing impossible is to make it so."

French proverb

☐ Pessimism is the easy way out.

"It is inherently easier to develop a negative argument than to advance a constructive one."

John Steinbruner

"Pessimism is the triumph of worry over matter."

Anonymous

"A pessimist is one who makes difficulties of his opportunities."

Anonymous

"Pessimism is a sickness you treat like any other sickness. The object is to get well of it as soon as possible, and get back to business."

Aristotle Onassis

☐ Sometimes being pessimistic can lead to positive results.

Famed attorney Edward Bennett Williams worked off the principle of pessimism. He believed that any successful person should expect the worst. Williams approached each witness in a trial as if that witness was there to ruin his case. He was often victorious because he was prepared for the worse.

☐ Don't be a nay-sayer

"Man who says it cannot be done should not interrupt man doing it."

Chinese proverb

A pessimist is someone who can look at the land of milk and honey and see only calories and cholesterol.

A pessimist is a person who looks both ways before crossing a one-way street.

"No matter how cynical you become, it's never enough to keep up."

Lily Tomlin

When people don't like your idea, think of Walt Disney when he asked ten people what they thought of a new idea he had, Mickey Mouse, and they unanimously rejected it. Today, long after his death, his rejected idea is displayed in amusement parks in Florida, California, and Japan.

You remember the story of Chicken Little. She ran around the barnyard proclaiming that the sky was falling, and for a while she had all the other animals in a state of alarm.

Today, we have the Chicken Little theory of economics. Instead of the sky falling, we have people talking about how bad the economy is. [Substitute problems that are being talked about now.]

☐ Don't be a nay-sayer.

When Henry Ford wanted to get unbreakable glass for his cars, he wouldn't see any of the experts. They knew too many reasons why it couldn't be done. He said, "Bring me the eager young person who doesn't know the reasons why unbreakable glass cannot be made." He got unbreakable glass.

Maybe you recall the old comic routine: "With all my troubles, I went to see my priest. He said, 'Cheer up, my son, things could be worse.' So I cheered up and sure enough, things get worse."

■ PLANNING

☐ Every long-term plan should have short-term steps.

"Yard by yard, life is hard; but inch by inch, it's a cinch."

Robert Schuller

☐ Plan every day.

"He who every morning plans the transactions of the day, and follows out that plan, carries a thread that will guide him through the labyrinth of the most busy life."

Victor Hugo

"For everything you must have a plan."

Napoleon

"It is better to have a bad plan than to have no plan at all."

Charles de Gaulle

☐ Planning is a guide for today.

"Long-range planning does not deal with future decisions, but with the future of present decisions."

Peter Drucker

"If you don't know where you're going, you could wind up someplace else."

Yogi Berra

☐ No plan is worse than a bad plan.

"People who fail to plan, have planned to fail."

George Hewell

☐ A plan keeps your effort going in the right direction.

"What's the use of running if you're not on the right road."

German proverb

☐ Before we can have a plan, we have to know what we are planning for.

"I arise in the morning torn between a desire to improve the world and a desire to enjoy it. This makes it hard to plan the day."

E. B. White

"Planning is damn scary if you do it right, because what you're really talking about is change. It's much easier to just say, 'Next year's going to be better,' and leave it at that."

Graham Briggs, vice president, Charles River Data Systems

"People think planning turns a company into a bunch of gray men marching in lockstep. But planning makes things possible. It can drive you through those ignorance barriers and force you to come to terms with what you don't know."

Richmond J. Hoch, CEO, Sigma Research

☐ Don't use planning as an excuse

"A lot of companies overdo planning. They find planning more interesting than getting out a saleable product . . . planning is a welcome respite from operating problems. It is intellectually more rewarding, and does not carry the pressures that operations entail . . . formal long-range planning almost always leads to overemphasis of technique."

Ed Wrapp

Lady to friend: "Harold has all the ingredients for success but has never been able to find a suitable recipe."

A plan is a suitable recipe.

☐ Make no small plans.

Wilson Wyatt, Sr., was Harry S. Truman's administrator of the National Housing Agency in 1945. His job was to correct the housing shortage brought about by World War II. The president told him to "make no small plans."

When he announced a program to start 1.2 million houses during 1946, five times the number built the previous year, the experts attacked his plan as being an impossible goal. They gave him all the excuses why it wouldn't work.

By the end of the year, they had built one million houses. The achievement was short of their goal but higher than anybody thought was possible.

☐ A plan gives you a picture of where you are and where you are going.

In a Little League baseball game, a boy got a hit, ran to first base, on to second, then hesitated and yelled, "Where is third base?" During his confusion, the shortstop put him out.

We have to have a plan to take us all the way to home plate or we will get lost along the way.

☐ A plan keeps you going in the right direction.

There is the story about the man who pulled his car over to ask a youth on the side of the road how far it was to a certain destination, and he received this answer, "If you keep going the way you are headed it will be about 25,000 miles. But if you turn around, it will be about three miles."

☐ Knowing where we are going helps determine the best way to get there.

☐ Don't try to build a business without a plan.

If you told a contractor that you wanted to build a house, the first thing he'd ask for would be the plans. The lumber and the concrete are no good unless you have a plan to put them together into a finished product.

Suppose you were on a nonstop flight to the Orient and heard this announcement:

"Ladies and Gentlemen, this is your captain speaking. We're traveling west across the Pacific Ocean. In a few hours, you will be able to look down and see land. When that happens, we're going to start looking for a big city with an airport. If we find one before our fuel runs out, we'll land. Then we'll figure out where we are and decide where we want to go next. In the meantime, folks, just sit back and relax and enjoy your trip."

Would you have a relaxed flight? Would you wish somebody had planned ahead?

☐ When the stakes are high, there is no substitute for advanced planning.

☐ We can lose all we have by changing the plans that made us a success.

In the first century B.C., the gladiator Spartacus led a rebellion in the city of Capua to gain freedom for himself and for other slaves from the dominion of Rome. His rag-tag army was invincible whenever Spartacus was in the field, and they defeated increasingly impressive forces sent against them. His plan was to fight their way northward into the Alps and escape, each man to his homeland, for the slaves had been stolen from all over the known world. The plan would have worked, but the slaves, overconfident from their successes, refused to continue their retreat and insisted that Spartacus lead them against the full might of the Roman Empire. Spartacus could not dissuade them and was destroyed, his followers killed or returned to captivity.

☐ A plan gives you a reason for doing what you do.

President Lyndon B. Johnson is said to have often related the story of a man who had applied for a job as a flagman at a railroad crossing and was told he would be given the job if he could pass a test consisting of but a single question. Agreeing, the applicant was told to imagine he was a flagman at a crossing having but a single track when he suddenly observed the Continental Express approaching from the east at 95 mph and, looking in the other direction, saw the *Century Limited* bearing down from the west at 100 mph. Having further been told that the two trains were at the time 100 yards apart, the job-seeker was then asked what he would do under such a circumstance. Without hesitation, the would-be flagman responded that he would go and get his brother-in-law. Puzzled, the railroad's examiner inquired what good that would do, to which the job-seeker promptly replied, "He ain't never seen a train wreck?"

◾ POLITICS

☐ Politicians make too many promises.

"There are some politicians who, if their constituents were cannibals, would promise them missionaries for dinner."

H. L. Mencken

☐ Politics is big business.

Maybe money won't buy happiness, but it'll buy you a seat in the U.S. Senate.

I love the way the Democrats are acting upset over big deficits. That's like Hugh Hefner coming out against skinny-dipping.

☐ Politics is tough.

I've always wanted to go into politics, but I get too nervous in court.

We've always been suspicious of public works programs. The politicians always seem to get the money—and the public the works.

Successful politician: a person who can stand on a fence and make people believe it's a platform.

☐ Politicians play both sides.

"Politics is the gentle art of getting votes from the poor and campaign funds from the rich, by promising to protect each from the other."
Peter Frame

He's like the politician who robbed the bank. Not for the money—all he wanted was the publicity.

"Politics is almost as exciting as war, and quite as dangerous. In war, you can only be killed once, but in politics, many times."
Winston Churchill

George Lansbury, a leader in the British government, once said, "I have not been unsuccessful in politics, but if I had to do it over again, I would invest my life in people, in personally changing people, rather than investing in programs."

A survey shows that wrestling on TV is taken seriously by 93 percent of the viewers. That's disturbing when you consider that some of them may be registered voters.

"No man's property is safe while Congress is in session."
Mark Twain

A Republican is a Democrat who knows he's crazy.

"If there were no poor, the liberals would have to invent them."
Lawrence Chickering, Jr.

The difference between Uncertainty and Awakening is somewhat like what President Dwight D. Eisenhower used to say was the difference between a true conservative and a liberal conservative. The conservative didn't want to do it. The liberal conservative definitely wanted to do it, but not at this time.

We may not imagine how our lives could be more frustrating and complex—but Congress can.

"The farther you get away from Washington, D.C., the more you think that things are under control here."

Art Buchwald

"Nothing is easier than spending public money. It does not appear to belong to anybody. The temptation is overwhelming to bestow it on somebody."

Calvin Coolidge

"Politics is a field where the choice lies constantly between two blunders."
John Morley

"No man is good enough to be President, but someone has to be."
Abraham Lincoln

☐ Most politicians can't say no.

Congresswoman Pat Schroeder, once expressed her exasperation at the inability of government officials to make difficult choices and thereby eliminate costs in the following terms: "If those guys were women, they'd all be pregnant—they can't say no to anything!"

A successful politician is one who can get in the public eye without irritating it.

It could be worse. Asked what he thought of the two candidates in the election, an enlightened voter replied, "Well, when I look at them, I'm thankful only one of them can get elected."

☐ Politicians are often judged by a different standard.

When Ted Kennedy was campaigning for the Senate in 1962, he approached a factory worker, who said, "I understand you never worked a day in your life."

Kennedy was braced for the man's resentment to come flowing out. Instead, the worker grabbed Kennedy's hand and said, "Let me tell you something, you haven't missed a thing."

Discussing a certain legislator, someone said, "He acts like a fool." Someone else said, "Believe me, he's not acting."

☐ Politicians don't always get a fair shake.

When President Ronald Reagan visited China, he made several broadcasts on Chinese television. Some parts of his message were deleted before it was shown. Chris Wallace, one of the network reporters who accompanied the president, asked him how he liked having his material censored.

Reagan replied, "It didn't bother me a bit; you people do it all the time."

☐ It's not easy to be a politician in America today.

An English politician was interviewed by reporters on his arrival in Washington, D.C. He remembered that he had been warned before leaving London that American journalists would probably try to make a fool of him.

The first question asked was; "Are you going to visit any nightclubs during your visit in Washington?"

The politician replied, "Are there any nightclubs in Washington?"

The following day, the headlines of the newspaper said that the first question he asked was, "Are there any nightclubs in Washington?"

☐ Politicians sometimes expect special treatment.

A governor running for reelection once attended a barbecue. As he moved through the serving line, the woman serving chicken put one piece on his plate.

Governor: "Excuse me. I'd like to have another piece."
Woman: "I'm only supposed to give one piece of chicken to each person."
Governor: "I'm starved."
Woman: "Sorry, only one piece per person."
Governor: "Do you know who I am? I'm the governor of this state."
Woman: "Do you know who I am? I'm the person in charge of the chicken."

☐ No matter who you are, there is always somebody who isn't impressed.

Sam Levinson told about a youngster whose teacher asked him to explain the difference between a king and a president.

The boy said thoughtfully, "Well, a king has to be the son of his father, but a president doesn't have to be."

I. E. Solberg, member of the North Dakota state senate may have had his tongue in his cheek when he said: "What we ought to do now, obviously, is suspend all activity until we can hold a plebiscite to select a panel that will appoint a commission authorized to hire a new team of experts to restudy the feasibility of compiling an index of all the committees that have in the past inventoried and catalogued the various studies aimed at finding out what happened to all the policies that were scrapped when new policies were decided on by somebody else. Once that's out of the way, I think we could go full steam ahead with some preliminary plans for a new study with federal funds of why nothing can be done right now."

Winston Churchill was asked what he considered to be the most important qualification for a politician. He said, "It's the ability to foretell what will happen tomorrow, next month, and next year—and to explain afterward why it did not happen."

◻ POTENTIAL

The reason we do not accomplish *MORE* in life is because we do not expect *MORE* of ourselves.

◻ We have more potential than we think.

"There is no man living who isn't capable of doing more than he thinks he can do."

Henry Ford

"If you don't expect the unexpected, you will never find it."

Jurgen Moltmann

◻ Try to reach your potential, but some things will never happen.

"Remember, you can't put a quart in a pint jar."

Joe L. Griffith

◻ Success is reaching for your potential.

H. G. Wells said that wealth, notoriety, place, and power are no measures of success whatever. The only true measure of success is the ratio between what we might have been and what we have become.

"Wealth comes to the man who can see the potential for wealth."

Peter Frame

◻ Life is one step after another leading toward our full potential.

"A man's reach should exceed his grasp, or what's a heaven for?"

Robert Browning

"Anything is possible if you do not know what you are talking about."

Parkes Robinson

◻ Success is living up to your potential.

"What small potatoes we all are, compared with what we might be!"

Charles Dudley Warner

◻ Our potential comes from necessity.

"Thank God—every morning when you get up—that you have something to do which must be done, whether you like it or not. Being forced to work, and forced to do your best, will breed in you a hundred virtues which the idle never know."

Charles Kingsley

☐ Potential can be increased when a market is defined.

Leslie Bernard Kilgore had a dream about building a newspaper across the United States. To increase his potential for success, he broadened his editorial content of a financial trade sheet to make it appeal to everyone who earned a living. His dream is known today as the *Wall Street Journal.*

☐ So much potential is left unreached because of the nay-sayers who tell us something can't be done.

This was the case with Chuck Yeager, the famed pilot. In the 1940s, aeronautical engineers and physicists believed that no one could break the sound barrier. But Chuck Yeager, believing it could be done, flew right through it.

"Do what you can, with what you have, where you are."
Theodore Roosevelt

"The biggest waste is the untapped potential of people in a corporation. We haven't found the way to tap their motivation."
Jude Rich

☐ Potential can show itself early.

When Henry Ford was still a young boy, he set up a watchmaker's bench in his bedroom and repaired watches. This proclivity to tinker eventually led to his famous name.

Yogi Berra said this about Don Mattingly, "He has exceeded my expectations and done even better."

☐ We can become great by trying to fulfill our own potential.

A reporter asked George Bernard Shaw to play the "What If " game shortly before he died. He said, "Mr. Shaw, you have visited with some of the most famous people in the world. You've known royalty, world-renowned authors, artists, teachers, and dignitaries from every part of the world. If you could live your life over and be anybody you've known, or any person from history, who would you choose to be?"

Shaw replied, "I would choose to be the man George Bernard Shaw could have been, but never was."

Nearly five hundred years ago, as Balboa stood on the Pacific shores of Panama looking out at that expanse of water he had just discovered, he didn't have the faintest idea of how large the Pacific Ocean really was.

☐ Most of us are like Balboa. We don't have any idea of how large our potential is.

In 1492, Christopher Columbus discovered the fringes of a new world. Instead of dropping anchor in the San Salvador harbor of the Bahamas,

Columbus sailed westward just a little longer and reached the mainland of North America.

☐ Most people explore only the outer fringes of their possibilities instead of searching out their full potential.

☐ We determine our own potential.

"The horizon is not where the sky comes down. We set our own boundaries. We have the making of our own horizons. We do not have to live in walled-in spaces."

Grove Patterson

A minister was washing his new car when a little boy saw him and asked, "Where did you get the car?"

The preacher replied, "My brother gave it to me."

What response do you think the little boy gave? "I wish I had a car like that"? No.

He said, "I wish I was a brother like that."

To reach our full potential, we have to become a better brother.

☐ Our attitudes can control how close we come to reaching our potential.

Henry Ford once observed, "Whether you believe you can do a thing or believe you can't, you are right." You must learn to develop a "Yes, I can" response to negative thinkers.

If someone says, "It won't work," immediately think of reasons why it will work and ways you will try to make it work.

"The late Henry Fonda once said that a thoroughbred horse never looks at the other racehorses. It just concentrates on running the fastest race it can.

"We have to fight the tendency to look at others and see how far they've come. The only thing that counts is how we use the potential we possess and that we run our race to the best of our abilities."

Dennis Waitley and Reni L. Witt, The Joy of Working

☐ We can't reach our potential if we get complacent.

Penn State football coach Joe Paterno hasn't had a losing season in twenty years. He felt that part of his success was getting off to a bad start.

He said, "We lost five and won five my first year. Then we lost our opening game the following year. Everybody was placing bets on who would succeed me. Had we been moderately successful, I never would have questioned the way I coached. Now I question everything."

☐ A business can fulfill its potential by defining its purpose.

Back in 1968, John Bunting took over as president of First Pennsylvania Bank & Trust Company, which at the time was Philadelphia's biggest and oldest bank. He quickly realized that he'd never be able to compete with the big banks like Bank of America, Chase Manhattan, or other giants in the industry. So instead of setting out to be the biggest, he wanted to become one of the four or five most influential institutions in the country.

After amendments to the Bank Holding Company Act, he quickly created the First Pennsylvania Corporation, a holding company. Soon thereafter, First Pennsylvania Corporation was a major player in the banking industry.

▌POWER

"Power does not corrupt men; fools, however, if they get into a position of power, corrupt power."

George Bernard Shaw

"The measure of man is what he does with power."

Pittacus

"I'm caught in a power struggle. My boss has the power, and I have the struggle."

Bill Halliburton

☐ Who has the power to make or break our company?

Charles Kettering, one of the world's greatest inventors, said: "In business the one fellow you never think much about, whom you don't know, sits back and controls the whole thing, and that fellow is your customer."

Sam Walton, founder of Wal-Mart, said that he may be the wealthiest man in America, but it will end tomorrow if he quits satisfying the customer.

"When power is in the hands of men it will be sometimes abused."

Samuel Johnson

"I had a power breakfast this morning; it took me three tries to get the lid off the peanut-butter jar."

John H. Dromey

"Power tends to corrupt and absolute power corrupts absolutely."

Lord Acton

"Most powerful is he who has himself in his own power."

Seneca

"There are but two powers in the world: the sword and the mind. In the long run, the sword is always beaten by the mind."

Napoleon

"You have to usurp power. It doesn't come to you except by usurping it. But it's easy to do because the lazy ones sit back and let you."
Paul Charlap, chairman, Savin Business Machines

☐ At times the thirst for power can be destructive.

The late Sewell L. Avery, during his reign at Montgomery Ward fired or forced the resignation of more than sixty-five vice presidents. They questioned his infallibility.

☐ In the 1960s, a popular slogan was, "Power to the People."

"The power of the public to determine what will succeed in the marketplace is astounding. Take the Edsel, the Vietnamese war, mandatory seat belts, antismoking ordinances, and the Sony Walkman as examples of how the public determines what will stay on the market.
Joe L. Griffith

"The very essence of all power to influence lies in getting the other person to participate."
Harry A. Overstreet

"Leadership is power, and how one perceives power is likely to influence how one behaves as a leader."
Michael Maccoby, social psychologist

Philosopher Friedrich Nietzsche said the pursuit of power explains most human behavior.

☐ Knowledge is power.

Read on one statue at the United States Air Force Academy: "Man's flight through life is sustained by the power of his knowledge."

"Power is usually recognized as an excellent short-term antidepressant."
Charles McElroy

"Power is the ability to make changes."
Hugh Cullman

☐ Power is whom you know.

Two guys were arguing after a car wreck: "I had the right of way when he ran into me, yet you say I was to blame."

"You certainly were."

"Why?"

"Because his father is mayor, his brother is chief of police, and I'm engaged to his sister."

The person with power is like the old ruler who ran a benevolent dictatorship. To impress his guest, the ruler paraded the guest past a glass cage in which a lion and lamb lay together.

The guest marveled at the sight. "How could a lion and lamb coexist?" he asked.

The ruler said, "I am a little like the lion."

When asked how so, he said, "Because this proves that natural enemies can find peace."

The guest said, "My, how do you do it?"

The ruler said, "Simple. Every day I add a new lamb."

☐ Some one is always in control, no matter how things appear.

Success comes with the power to control ourselves under pressure. For example, take the 1980 U.S. hockey team. They entered the Olympics ranked seventh in an eight-team field. Yet they won the gold medal against a superior Russian team. Why? Coach Herb Brooks selected adaptable individuals who could not only work together but respond effectively to pressure.

☐ Few people ever experience real power.

Real power can be explained by the legendary movie director John Huston, who said that when he made a movie he was like God. "I have the world in my hands. I can make it come out any way I want, decide who lives and who dies, who gets punished, who gets to live happily ever after. In between pictures is my seventh day, I rest."

▌PRAISE

"If you want employees to improve, let them overhear the nice things you say about them to others."

Haim Ginott

"I can live for two months on a good compliment."

Mark Twain

"A man doesn't live by bread alone. He needs buttering up once in a while."

Robert H. Henry, humorist

☐ Spread the credit around.

Walter Payton, who holds the National Football League rushing title, always acknowledged his offensive line.

☐ Praise should be given on a regular basis.

Donald E. Peterson, past chairman of Ford Motor Company, said that feedback and coaching for employees is best accomplished as an ongoing performance with suggestions that are constructive.

Woman golfer, teeing off, to husband: "Now tell me if you notice anything I'm doing right."

"In experiment after experiment, the workers who thought they were doing better did better.

"In one experiment, ten people were given puzzles to solve. They were all given fictitious results. Half were told they had done well, the other half were told they had done poorly. They were then given a second test and this time they all did as well or as poorly as they were told they did on the first test."

Warren Bennis

☐ Encourage people, they don't like to hear about failure.

"Psychologists find that we typically treat any success as our own and any failure as the system's. People tune out if they feel they are failing, because 'the system' is to blame. They tune in when the system leads them to believe they are successful."*Lee Ross, Stanford University*

How important is it to praise the performance of subordinates? Consider the words of Charles Schwab, who was paid $1 million (back when a million was really worth a million) to run Andrew Carnegie's steel empire: "I consider my ability to arouse enthusiasm among people the greatest asset that I possess, and the way to develop the best that is in people is by appreciation and encouragement. There is nothing else that so kills the ambitions of a person as criticism from his or her superiors. I never criticize anyone. I believe in giving people incentive to work. So I am anxious to praise but loath to find fault. If I like anything, I am hearty in my appreciation and lavish in my praise."

When, with pleasure, you are viewing
Any work that one is doing
And you like him or you love him tell him now.
Don't withhold your approbations
'til the parson makes orations and he lies with snowy lilies on his
    brow....
If *you* think that praise is due him,
Now's the time to show it to him.
'Cause a man can't read his tombstone when he's dead.

Author unknown

▊ PREPARATION

"Before everything else, getting ready is the secret of success."

Henry Ford

☐ Prepare for the future.

"We can't cross a bridge until we come to it; but I always like to lay down a pontoon ahead of time."

Barnard Baruch

"The future belongs to those who prepare for it."

Ralph Waldo Emerson

"Thinking is more interesting than knowing, but less interesting than looking."

Goethe

"If you don't do your homework, you won't make your free throws."

Larry Bird

☐ Don't overprepare.

"Some people are making such thorough preparation for rainy days that they aren't enjoying today's sunshine."

William Feather

"Good fortune is what happens when opportunity meets with preparation."

Thomas Edison

Mark Twain claimed that it took him two weeks to prepare an impromptu speech.

"The secret of success is to be ready for opportunity when it comes."

Benjamin Disraeli

"When Arthur Goldberg was Secretary of Labor under John Kennedy, it was said that he never went within 100 feet of the President without having all his documents in order, fully prepared to answer any reasonable question Kennedy might ask."

Mortimer R. Feinberg, Effective Psychology for Managers

For all your days, prepare;
And meet them ever alike;
When you are the anvil, bear;
When you are the hammer, strike.

Edward Markham

☐ One way to prepare is to visualize success.

It is said that the Duke of Wellington, on the eve of his great struggle with Napoleon, really fought the battle of Waterloo by pins and strings and matches on the map of Europe that was stretched before him.

Most vacations are well planned. If the trip involves air travel, reservations have been made in advance. If the trip is by automobile, the car has been serviced and made ready. Maps have been obtained, and the vacationer knows which roads will take him to this destination.

☐ We can enjoy our work like our vacations if we make the same preparation.

☐ A man that is prepared has won half the battle.

A young man named Demosthenes, by asking to speak to the leaders of ancient Athens, stepped into a spot that some of the greatest orators of history had occupied. His voice was weak and faltering, his manner timid, and his thoughts muddled. Also, he spoke with a stammer. When he had finished, the crowd booed and hissed him off the platform.

But Demosthenes was not to be held down.

He promised himself, "Never again will I speak unprepared!" And prepare he did! He cultivated his voice by shouting at the top of his lungs into the Aegean Sea. He practiced his speeches under a dangling sword to bolster his courage. He practiced for hours on end with pebbles in his mouth to eliminate his stammer. He prepared his speeches so well that he was accused of overpreparing them.

The next time he addressed the assembly, he was a different man. With eloquent words, powerful voice, and stately manner, he drew uproarious cheers from his audience. When he had finished, the crowd arose as one person and shouted, "Let us go and fight Philip!"

Bobby Knight, Indiana's basketball coach, was once asked if he was successful because his team had the will to win.

He said, "The will to succeed is important, but what's more important is the will to prepare."

☐ Preparation means working smart, not hard.

"I don't care to work around the clock. I'm not particularly fond of hard work. I believe in preparing my own team to play its best and not worrying too much about the other team. I believe too much information can confuse you. I want to win, but if I can get the job done without killing myself, I'll be just as happy."

Tommy Prothro, football Coach

☐ You should never go before a prospect before you have rehearsed your presentation.

In his book *Iacocca*, Lee Iacocca tells of when Ford came up with padded dashes on their 1956 models. Lee wanted to show how padded the dash was by dropping an egg on it without the egg breaking.

Over one-thousand people were attending the meeting where he would demonstrate the beauty of the padded dash. He climbed up on a ladder with his eggs.

The first egg he dropped missed the padding and broke. Just as he was dropping the second egg, the man holding the ladder moved and it broke on his shoulder. The third and fourth eggs landed on the dash, but both of them broke. The fifth egg finally proved his point that you could drop an egg on the dash without breaking it.

In George Gallup's book *The American Success Story*, he told the story of newscaster Morton Dean.

When Dean was on his high school football team, he did a lot of bench time. During one crucial game, he was suddenly called off the bench with his team a yard and a half from the goal line. Before his coach sent him in, he said, "Throw a jump pass."

Dean ran onto the field knowing that all he had to do was step back, jump up, and pop the ball to the end. Good execution would mean a certain touchdown on his first play.

Dean's big moment became a nightmare. He fumbled and claimed to have suffered nightmares about the experience ever since. But his father's advice after the game almost made the experience worthwhile.

He said, "Morton, you've got to be prepared to come off the bench."

That's the way it is in business. You must be prepared when your time comes.

■ PRICES

"You win customers by quality rather than price."
Jean Ridley, retail consultant

☐ Price can often determine a product's value in the marketplace.

In 1975, Hunt-Wesson spent $6-million to advertise Orville Redenbacher's Gourmet Popping Corn. Four years later, Orville Redenbacher was the nation's number one brand of popcorn in spite of the fact that it was priced 2½ times higher than other leading brands.

Many firms have succeeded in gaining a cost advantage by eliminating frills to a price-sensitive buyer. For example, Federal Express concentrated on small packages and fast delivery. La Quinta offered only guest rooms and lowered its cost by eliminating restaurants, meeting rooms, and other services not desired by its target market, the mid-manager who makes repeated trips to the same area.

☐ Low prices can help beat off the competition

Gallo's strength in the wine industry, brought about by a low-cost advantage, was the reason Coca-Cola decided to quit the wine business.

☐ People will pay a higher price for quality.

"Swiss watchmakers don't rely on cheaper prices to gain a big trading advantage over their competitors. Nor do they rely on lower labor costs. Instead, the Swiss turn out a *somewhat* better product so they can charge a much, much better price."
Mortimer R. Feinberg, Effective Psychology for Managers

Stanley Marcus's father taught him early in his career that every time a manufacturer cuts his price, he cuts quality.

☐ If you can convince people you have something they want, they will pay your price.

Henry R. Luce launched his magazine *Fortune* in 1930 at the astoundingly high price of $1 a copy.

☐ Lowering costs help lower prices, which is important to fighting off competition.

The price of Henry Ford's Model T was raised the first year it was produced, but thereafter the price went down dramatically. In 1908, it cost $825; by 1916, it was down to $345. Henry Ford prided himself on being able to reduce the price and increase his profits at the same time.

Henry Ford said that every time you reduce the price of a product without reducing the quality, you increase the possible number of purchasers.

☐ Prices can be cut if you cut cost.

Southwest Airlines offered a fare that averaged almost 30 percent lower than the competition. For example, Southwest saved $25 million a year by making travel agents call to book flights instead of using their computers.

☐ Prices are controlled by what it costs to make a product. And this changes regularly.

The Ford Motor Company once raised its own sheep to provide wool for the car's upholstery. Today, it buys elsewhere half the components that go into the car, if not the entire car itself.

"Large increases in cost with questionable increases in performance can be tolerated only for race horses and fancy women."
Lord Kelvin

"The American car buyer wants economy so badly he'll pay almost anything to get it!"
Lee Iacocca

□ Don't buy on price alone. If it breaks, can you get it serviced?

Customer to computer salesman: "If you're selling these machines way un-
                                 der cost as you say, how can you make a
                                 living?"

Computer salesman: "Simple. We make our money fixing
                                 them."

□ Don't just sell price.

Bill Gove is a motivational speaker who told the following story about a
businessman named Harry, the owner of a small general-appliance store in
Phoenix, Arizona:

Harry was accustomed to being price-shopped by young couples looking
for their first new refrigerator or washer-dryer or air conditioner. When a
young couple came into the store, pen and paper in hand, asking detailed
questions about prices, features and model numbers, Harry was pretty sure
that their next move would be to trot off to a nearby discount appliance dealer
to compare tags. When, after spending half an hour with such a couple and
patiently answering all their questions, Harry suggested an order, he usually
got a firm, "We want to look around some other places."

His rebuttal was to nod, smile, move up close, and deliver this little
speech:

"I understand that you are looking for the best deal you can find. I
appreciate that because I do the same thing myself. And I know you'll
probably head down to Discount Dan's and compare prices. I know I would.

"But after you've done that, I want you to think of one thing. When you
buy from Discount Dan's, you get an appliance. A good one. I know because
he sells the same appliances we do. But when you buy the same appliance
here, you get one thing you can't get at Dan's: you get me. I come with the
deal. I stand behind what I sell. I want you to be happy with what you buy. I've
been here thirty years. I learned the business from my Dad, and I hope to be
able to give the business over to my daughter and son-in-law in a few years. So
you know one thing for sure: when you buy an appliance from me, you get me
with the deal, and that means I do everything I can to be sure you never
regret doing business with me. That's a guarantee."

With that, Harry wished the couple well and gave them a quart of ice
cream in appreciation for their interest.

Gove asked his audience, "Now, how far away do you think that young
couple is going to get, with Harry's speech ringing in their ears and a quart of
vanilla ice cream on their hands, in Phoenix, in August, when it's 125 degrees
in the shade?"

□ Don't price a product too low.

Pathmark's Premium All-Purpose Cleaner seemed to have all the elements of the perfect store brand. Its packaging plainly mimicked that of

Fantastic, the top seller in the category. Its chemical composition precisely duplicated the national brand's, too. Best of all, Premium cost shoppers only 89 cents, compared with $1.79 for Fantastik.

But from its introduction in 1980, Premium gathered dust. In 1986, Pathmark decided consumers simply didn't understand the product. Store clerks stamped **Day-Glo** stickers on every bottle that read: "If you like Fantastic, try me."

Consumers declined the invitation, and Pathmark finally yanked Premium off the shelf in early 1988. Partmark believed that even though the product was clinically outstanding, the price was so low that it discredited the intrinsic value of the product.

☐ Cheap can sometimes be too cheap.

☐ How do you get your price higher than the competition? By offering a higher "perceived value."

Marketing guru Philip Kotler used Caterpillar as an example of exploiting how customers view a product by using a "perceived value" to set a higher price for a tractor. Caterpillar's goal is to outsell the competition even though the competitor's similar tractor may be priced at say $20,000 instead of Caterpillar's $24,000. When a prospective customer asks a Caterpillar dealer why he should pay $4,000 more, the dealer says:

$20,000 is the tractor's price if it were equivalent to the competitor's tractor
$ 3,000 is the price premium for superior durability
$ 2,000 is the price premium for superior reliability
$ 2,000 is the price premium for superior service
$ 2,000 is the price premium for the longer parts warranty
$28,000 is the price to cover the value package
$\underline{-\$ \; 4,000}$ discount
$24,000 final price

Even though the customer is asked to pay $4,000 more up front, they are convinced that the lifetime operating cost will be smaller than if they buy the other tractor.

☐ Pricing a new product as if it is already successful can help make it that way.

When Texas Instruments, an early player in the semiconductor industry, wanted to dominate the market, they used pricing. Instead of charging what it actually cost, they priced it as if they were already selling millions of them. Texas Instruments not only accelerated their profit curve by taking early losses but gained market share on possible competitors.

Zig Ziglar revealed in his best-selling book, *Zig Ziglar's Secrets of Closing the Sale*, how to overcome the objection of "It costs too much." Ziglar's reply: "The price is high. I don't think there's any question about the price being high, Mr. Prospect, but when you add the benefits of quality, subtract the disappointments of cheapness, multiply the pleasure of buying something good, and divide the cost over a period of time, the arithmetic comes out in your favor. . . . If it costs you a hundred dollars but does you a thousand dollars worth of good, then by any yardstick you've bought a bargain, haven't you?"

Once a man drove into my friend's service station. He said that he was penniless, almost out of gas, and needed to get across town.

My generous friend offered to put a couple of gallons in his car. The man hesitated and then asked, "Could you give me the money instead? The station across the street is cheaper."

A friend of ours recently stopped at a motel bearing the sign: "Free TV." When he asked about rates, the manager told him, "We have $6 and $8 rooms."

My friend asked, "What's the difference?"

The manager replied, "Well, the $8 rooms have the free TV."

▊ PRIORITY

☐ Set your priorities.

"Our main business is not to see what lies dimly at a distance, but to do what lies clearly at hand."

Thomas Carlyle

"Read the best books first, or you may not have a chance to read them at all."

Henry David Thoreau

☐ A vital ingredient to leadership is getting people to prioritize their work.

"Some people go through the day just doing their jobs, never realizing there are only two or three things that are important to this department, and they should do those first, and the very best they can. Getting them to realize that—that's running a department."

John Bryan, chairman, Consolidated Foods

☐ Priorities tell us a lot about management's desires.

Four of six Japanese air-conditioner manufacturers surveyed said that quality was most important to management. Their counterparts at nine of eleven U.S. companies surveyed said that meeting the production schedule was the highest priority.

☐ Setting priorities makes things happen.

Charles M. Schwab, the famous past-president of Bethlehem Steel Company, made it a practice to invest five minutes analyzing the various problems he should tackle the next day. He would write down those tasks in the order of their priority. When he arrived at the office the next morning, he would start with task number 1 as soon as he got in. When he had completed that task, he would move on to tasks 2, 3, 4, and 5 in order.

The multimillionaire said, "This is the most practical lesson I've ever learned." He gave this example to prove his point: "I had put off a phone call for nine months, so I decided to list it as my number one task on my next day's agenda. That call netted us a $2 million order."

☐ Priority breeds dedication.

Samuel Goldwyn, the famous Hollywood producer, confessed, "For as long as I can remember, whatever I was doing at the time was the most important thing in the world for me."

PROBLEM SOLVING

☐ Don't repeat problems.

"The measure of success is not whether you have a tough problem to deal with, but whether it's the same problem you had last year."
John Foster Dulles

☐ To solve a problem, ask the person who performs the task for the solution.
"Who knows the job better than the man close to it?"
Kimsey Mann, chairman, Blue Bell

☐ Don't be bashful. Take hold of a problem.

"All problems become smaller if, instead of indulging them, you confront them. Touch a thistle timidly and it pricks you; grasp it boldly, and its spine crumbles."
William S. Halsey

"A problem well stated is a problem half solved."
Charles F. Kettering

☐ Break down problems

"Nothing is particularly hard if you divide it into small jobs."
Ray Kroc, founder, McDonald's

☐ The best place to solve a problem is at the point of complaint.

American Airlines has always had a commitment to the customer being satisfied. Years ago, American realized that a large percentage of their passengers who had complaints had them around the ticket counter and boarding gate. To head off complaints before they got started, American created a position of special-passenger service agent to deal with the problems as they arose so that the customers' problems could be solved before they could criticize the airline.

☐ Treat the problem, not the symptom.

Suppose your boss comes to you one morning and says, "We have a problem, your tardiness rate is 10 percent and that's unacceptable. You've got to do something about it."

The problem still hasn't been identified. Tardiness is a symptom, not the cause of the problem. If you treat a fever by packing the patient in ice, the patient will die. If you eliminate the cause of the fever, the fever will subside. In this example, the fever is tardiness.

☐ Before you think about how many problems you wish you didn't have, stop to remember that you get paid to solve problems.

☐ Understanding the other person can solve problems.

"So many of our problems could probably be solved if the rich man could find out how badly the poor man lives and if the poor man could find out how hard and long the rich man has to work."

Bob Talbert

☐ Every problem has within itself its own solution.

A pilot was asked what the worst difficulty was in flying through the Caribbean. Was it cyclones?

He replied, "No, we can even use cyclones. They move slowly at the center, so we get on the edge and get a hundred-mile-an-hour tail wind, and then coming back we get on the other side."

A ten-year-old child was riding his bicycle when he saw traffic backed up for miles. There was a truck stuck under an overpass. The little boy asked, "What happened to the truck?"

The policeman patiently told him that the truck got stuck, and the firemen were trying to get the truck unstuck.

The little boy looked at the firemen working with their crowbars trying to free the truck. The little boy said, "Why don't they let the air out of the tires?" And that is exactly what they did.

☐ A solution is sometimes so simple that it gets overlooked.

☐ No matter what your problem is, remember it could be worse.

The day after a doctor amputated a patient's leg, he made a bedside call.

Doctor: "I'm afraid I have bad news and I have good news. Which do you
           want first?"
Patient: "Give me the bad news first."

Doctor: "We cut off the wrong leg."
Patient: "Well, what's the good news?"
Doctor: "I think we can save the other leg."

The worst thing to do is to act as if there isn't a problem. It's like the battered fighter hearing his trainer say between rounds, "Champ, you're going great! He ain't laid a glove on you!"

The champ says, "Well, you better keep an eye on the referee then, because somebody in this ring is beating the hell outta me."

☐ There is more than one way to solve a problem.

W. Clement Stone, founder of Combined Insurance, was a poor boy who started peddling newspapers on the streets of Chicago when he was six. The bigger boys tried to keep him out of their territories, so he tried selling his papers inside Hoelle's Restaurant. Stone's persistence taught him a valuable lesson.

Stone said, "I learned that if I couldn't solve a problem one way, I could another."

☐ A lot of problems can be solved by going back to the basics.

Witness what happened to Ford Motor Company back in the late 1970s when oil shocks, regulatory excess, economic recession, and escalating import competition all converged on the U.S. auto industry—and changed forever the environment in which Ford did business. The cumulative effect of these changes was like the Big Bang. At the worst of it, Ford recorded the most severe financial losses in its history, to say nothing of the losses to their corporate self-esteem and public reputation.

To solve the problem, Ford went back to the basics. Quality, first and foremost. Product. Cost competitiveness. And the one that really was the key to everything else: People.

▌PROBLEMS

☐ We can learn from problems.
    "After all, a smooth sea never made a successful sailor."
                                                                    Herman Melville

    "A problem is an opportunity in work clothes."
                                                                    Henry J. Kaiser

☐ Problems have their own reward.
    "The greater the difficulty, the greater the glory."
                                                                    Cicero

"Work only on problems that are manifestly important and seem to be nearly impossible to solve. That way, you will have a natural market for your product and no competition."

Edwin Land, founder, Polaroid

"Problems are not stop signs, they are guidelines."

Robert Schuller

"To overcome difficulties is to experience the full delight of gexistence."

Arthur Schopenhauer

☐ Everyone overcomes problems to get where they are.

Lord Nelson, England's famous naval hero, suffered from seasickness throughout his entire life. The man who destroyed Napoleon's fleet did not let his seasickness stop him from having a brilliant naval career.

"Problems should be utilized. If you've never been unhappy, how would you know what happy is?"

Malcolm S. Forbes

"I am grateful for all my problems. After each one was overcome, I became stronger and more able to meet those that were still to come. I grew in all my difficulties."

J. C. Penney

Remember the time Linus from the "Peanuts" comic strip said to Charlie Brown, "There's no problem too big we can't run away from."

☐ Problems sometimes don't seem to stop coming.

When former President Richard Nixon was autographing his book *Six Crises* at a bookstore, he asked the buyer whom to autograph his book to. The man smiled and said, "You just met your seventh crisis; my name is Stanislaus Wojechzleschki!"

☐ There's always someone with more problems.

An automobile dealer, asked how business was, said, "I'll tell you how business is. Yesterday I got three calls from Prime Minister [current prime minister] in England and two calls from President [current president] in Washington. You know why they called me?"

Friend: "No, why did they call you?"

Dealer: "Because they wanted to talk to somebody who's got more problems than they have."

"I learned during my year out of coaching that, regardless of what business you're in, you're going to have problems. How you deal with them is what counts. You don't turn your back on them."

Dan Reeves, football coach

☐ Some people aren't ready to solve a problem until later.

The psychiatrist was awakened in the dead of night by his patient, a kleptomaniac who hollered into the phone, "Doctor, I've got this urge to steal read bad!"

Psychiatrist: "For heaven's sake. It's two in the morning. Just take two ashtrays and call me in the morning."

☐ Keep your problems in perspective. Someone always has it worse than you.

Two expectant fathers were nervously pacing the floor of the maternity ward waiting room. One said, "What tough luck. This is happening during my vacation."

The other said, "What are you complaining about? I'm on my honeymoon."

☐ Keep problems in perspective.

Dear Mom and Dad:

I'm writing on this school paper because my stationary got lost in the fire. Just the other day, I got out of the hospital and moved in with Bill my boyfriend. Your new grandbaby is due next fall. Signed, your loving daughter, Peggy.

P.S. The above didn't happen, but I made a "C" in French and a "D" in History.

PRODUCTIVITY

☐ Productivity would go up if people would just think.

"The brain is a wonderful organ; it starts working the moment you get up in the morning and does not stop until you get into the office."

Robert Frost

☐ Challenging your work force can add to productivity.

Domino's Pizza, America's largest pizza chain after Pizza Hut, challenges workers by promising customers a $3 discount on any pizza that takes longer than thirty minutes to arrive at their home.

☐ Productivity needs cooperation.

"Of course they're catching us [referring to foreign competition]. They're supposed to catch us. Adam Smith and David Ricardo warned us there would be days like this. It is the way economic adjustment works among nations. As a nation gets successful and rich, it raises its wages and prices. And as this happens, unless it can increase its productivity, it loses business to poorer countries. This process runs its course when the newly rich tend to forget how they became rich and start consuming more than they invest in new means of productivity.

Bill Miller, vice chairman of the board, Bristol-Myers

☐ Automation can dramatically increase productivity.

Take for example that in 1977, 4 percent of America's workers produced more food than 16 percent of the workforce had done in 1947. There were fewer farmers producing more because of automation in planting and harvesting, along with scientific breeding of animals and plants and from better fertilizers, insecticides, and herbicides.

☐ Productivity figures can be misleading.

It is easier for a small company to have a larger increase in sales and profits than a company like General Motors or IBM.

☐ Poor productivity is not always the fault of the worker.

The *Los Angeles Times* reported that James A. Fields, a noted management consultant, said that the average worker is productive only 55 percent of the time. About 15 percent of his effort is lost to "personal time," but 30 percent is lost through scheduling problems, unclear assignments, improper staffing, and poor discipline.

☐ Affluence leads to decreased productivity.

"With industrial maturity and increasing affluence, people like hard work less and work less hard. Therefore, worker's productivity declines. The effect is greatest in industries such as textiles, automobiles, crude steel and ship-building, which are characterized by simple, tedious, and repetitive work."

John Kenneth Galbraith

☐ To increase productivity, you need the proper incentive plan.

Personnel manager to prospective employee: "Oh, we have our own special type of incentive plan, Mr. Smith—we fire at the drop of a hat!"

"Product and service quality as much as price are the keys to customer satisfaction, and therefore productivity."

Robert A. Ferchat, president, Northern Telecom Canada

☐ Productivity lost can't be regained.

It is like a hotel. If a room is not rented for the night, you can't make that money up. We can't inventory idle hours. If people aren't working, the billing opportunity is lost.

☐ To increase productivity, a company may have to do more than just offer incentives.

General Electric's rescue of its old and stagnant circuit breaker business is an example of how production can be increased. GE's $1-billion-a-year electrical distribution and control division in Plainville, Connecticut, makes, among other things, circuit breaker boxes for commercial buildings. When threatened in the early 1980s by the market's slow growth and tough competitors like Seimens and Westinghouse, GE assembled a team of manufacturing, design, and marketing experts that focused on overhauling its manufacturing process. The goal was to cut delivery time form three weeks to three days.

GE was producing circuit breaker boxes in six plants scattered around the United States. They moved all circuit breaker plants to Salisbury, North Carolina, and automated its factory. Time was further saved by the design team that made most of the parts interchangeable, reducing their number to 1,275 while still leaving customers a choice of 40,000 different sizes, shapes, and configurations of boxes.

Results: The plant, which used to have a two-month backlog of orders, now works with a two-day backlog. Productivity increased 20 percent in one year. Manufacturing cost dropped 30 percent. Delivery time went from three weeks to three days.

☐ Too little inventory can hurt productivity.

Ford Motor Company's England plant was threatened with a complete stoppage in their Cortina assembly line, which was producing one-thousand cars a day. A shortage of steering wheels prevented new vehicles from being driven off the line. To get around the problem, the mechanics drove the cars into the parking lot and removed the steering wheels, which they used to drive off other cars.

Even though Ford got around their problem, had they been short parts they couldn't be moved, they would have had to stop the entire plant.

▉ PROFITS

"The superior man seeks what is right; the inferior one, what is profitable."

Confucius

"A business that makes nothing but money is a poor business."

Henry Ford

☐ Profit is like health. You need it, and the more the better. But it's not why you exist.

"We exist to serve the marketplace. The better we do that, the more profits we will make."

Stephen Martin

☐ Profits come after work.

"It is not by gold and silver, but by labour that all the wealth of the world was originally purchased."

Adam Smith, in Wealth of Nations

☐ Profits should be a by-product of what you do.

"Take care of your customers and take care of your people, and the market will take care of you."

John McConnell, chairman, Worthington Industries

☐ Consistency is the key to long-term profits.

"Every business has two financial objectives: One is to make money; the other, more elusive, is to make money consistently."

Dave Linigerr, founder, RE/MAX

☐ If something solves your problem, a profit can be made helping others with the same problem.

A few years ago, Nancy Johnson, a dentist, suffered from itchy, dry hands, thanks to an allergy she'd developed from constant scrubbing. She tried every treatment available, but couldn't find one that worked. She enlisted the help of a chemist who helped her develop a cream. She founded Amera Cosmetics in her basement. Five years later, she had an office and sales had soared to about $12 million.

☐ Letting others share in the profits can create more profits.

In the 1920s, Henry Ford made dealers accept a certain allotment of cars or lose their franchise. They also had to pay cash when the car was delivered. They agreed because Ford allowed the dealers to prosper more than other automobile manufacturers.

Thomas Edison, the creator of the research-lab concept, never forgot that research was fed by funds from profit and that profit came from research. He went so far as to set a weekly quota on the number of inventions he wanted to present to the patent office.

Profits are the reward for doing a better job.

Doc Blakely, humorist

"It is a socialist idea that making profits is a vice; I consider the real vice is making losses."

Winston Churchill

☐ You need a profit to stay in business.

As one midwestern farmer, suffering the plight of agriculture in the 1980s, remarked upon winning a million-dollar lottery and being asked what he planned to do with the money, "I guess I'll just keep on farming until it's all gone."

☐ Profits come second when you put the customer first.

Two often-quoted comments of William Wrigley, Jr., on his business philosophy: Talking about a stick of wood, not a stick of gum, Wrigley said, "In no deal did I ever figure our own profit first. I always mapped out a proposition whereby the dealer or jobber would make a mighty good thing. . . . We must give them the thick end of the stick. No matter how thin our end is, remember we have thin ends coming in from everywhere. And many littles make a lot."

☐ Profits come from doing something right.

"Medicine is for the patients. It is not for the profits. The profits follow, and if we have remembered that, they have never failed to appear."
George W. Merck, founder, Merck Pharmaceutical

☐ High standards can turn high profits.

McDonald's has a restaurant on the eastbound side of the Connecticut Turnpike Interstate 95 in Darien. For years, the place had been an almost unimaginably filthy highway eatery before being converted in 1985 to a McDonald's. Three years later, it was one of the busiest McDonald's in America. In July 1988, it set an all-time monthly domestic record of $604,000 in sales. Same location, just a different standard of quality.

☐ Being too profitable can cause us to miss new opportunities for more profit.

Hertz had been in business for nearly twenty years when Avis started up. Hertz was owned at the time by General Motors, which had plenty of financial muscle to stave off new competition. But Avis decided to rent at airports—a market that Hertz refused to see as profitable.

Because of finding a void in the marketplace, Avid became a major player in the car rental business only because Hertz failed to seize the opportunity first.

☐ Expanding on what you already do can add to profits.

Eastman Kodak, known for its cameras, makes most of its profits from film, not cameras.

IBM sells computers but makes a huge profit on selling secondary items.
General Motors makes a large profit from selling replacement parts.

☐ How important are profits?

"One day the president of a company was having lunch at a downtown restaurant. Halfway through lunch, he realized that four familiar voices came from the next booth. Their discussion was intense enough that he could not resist eavesdropping. He heard each of his managers talking proudly about his department. The chief product engineer said, 'It's no contest. The department that makes the most important contribution to the success of a company is the product division. If you don't have a solid product, you have nothing.'

"The sales manager jumped in. 'Wrong! The best product in the world is useless unless you have a dynamic sales effort to get it sold.'

"The vice-president in charge of corporate and public relations had another opinion. 'If you don't have the proper image inside and outside the company, failure is certain. No one busy a product from a company it doesn't trust.' "

"The vice-president in charge of human relations countered with, 'I think all of you are talking too narrow a point of view. We all know that the strength of a company lies within its people. Minus strong, personally motivated people, a company grinds to a halt.'

"Each of the four ambitious young men continued to debate in favor of his area of primary interest. The discussion continued until the president finished lunch. He stopped by the booth on his way out of the restaurant.

"He said, 'Gentlemen, I couldn't help overhearing your discussion and feel delighted with the pride each of you takes in your department, but I must say that experience has shown me that none of you is correct. No one department of any company is responsible for a company's success. When you get to the heart of the matter, you find that managing a successful company is like being a juggler trying to keep five balls in the air. Four of these balls are white. On one is written PRODUCT. On another it says SALES. The third is labeled CORPORATE & PUBLIC RELATIONS, and the fourth says PEOPLE. In addition to the four white balls, there's one red one. On it is the word PROFIT'

"At all times, the juggler must remember: No matter what happens, never drop the red ball!"

W. Steven Brown, Thirteen Fatal Errors Managers Make

☐ People will not take an idea to market unless they see profit potential.

Robert N. Noyce, who invented the silicon chip, had no illusions about the glories of invention without the ensuing discipline of a profit-driven marketing organization. He founded two companies, Fairchild Semiconductor and Intel.

Noyce said: "Only economically feasible products will become a reality. Where cost can be pushed down rapidly, great new vistas arise."

To cut cost, have each department justify its existence with a profit. Bell Atlantic did this a few years ago after the breakup. When Raymond W. Smith, chairman and CEO of Bell Atlantic Corporation, wanted to set up a series of meetings with the company's 81,000 employees, the communications department of Bell Atlantic agreed to make the necessary arrangements for a mere $64 an hour.

At Bell Atlantic, each department pays its own rent, electricity, office cleaning, and most important, salaries and benefits. If the department can't make a profit, then it suffers layoffs and even could be eliminated and replaced by outside vendors who can perform the service cheaper. Bell Atlantic discovered that this approach forces a department to keep costs down.

☐ Making a profit is really simple.

Take the story of a farmer in West Texas who was asked how he had become rich with only an eighth grade education.

He said, "Well, it ain't hard, really. I just buy things for $1 and sell them for $4. You'd be surprised how fast that 3 percent profit piles up."

☐ PROMOTIONS

A hollywood producer who keeps a goldfish in a bowl on his desk was asked recently why.

He replied glumly, "Because I like to see something around here with its mouth open not asking for a raise."

"Personally, I have never received a promotion in my life that I could not trace directly to recognition that I had gained by rendering more service and better service than that for which I was paid."

Ralph Waldo Emerson

☐ Promotion and responsibility go hand in hand.

"You promote yourself every time you take on a new responsibility."

William Gore, chairman, W. L. Gore & Associates

☐ Promotions are sometimes a matter of timing.

Winston Churchill was a totally unacceptable leader of Great Britain in 1935 and yet in 1940 became England's best choice to lead.

☐ Each promotion requires us to develop additional people skills.

"If one is successful in one's craft, one is forced to leave it. The machine-tool man began in the shops; as V.P. for sales and advertising, he has become an uneasy manipulator of people and of himself. Likewise, the newspaper-man who rises becomes a columnist or desk-man, the doctor becomes the head of a clinic or hospital, the professor becomes a dean, president, or foundation official, the factory superintendent becomes a holding company executive. All these men must bury their craft routines and desert their craft companions. They must work less with things and more with people."

David Riesman

☐ Early promotions can signal long-term success potential.

"The major difference between the goffer and the chief executive officer is that no one works for the goffer, but everyone reports to the CEO. The climb up the ladder from mailroom to corner office really starts the day you are chosen from a group of mailroom boys—and girls—and are appointed head of mailroom operations."

Henry C. Rogers, Rogers Rules for Success

A manager trying to pacify a certain employee who wanted a promotion said, "For many reasons, I simply can't give you a promotion. But I will do this. You have my permission to go back and tell your friends that I offered you the job but you turned it down."

Howard Hess, onetime corporate psychiatrist for Western Electric, said that people are promoted to their level of pain, not their level of incompetence. They get to a level of success that they are not emotionally equipped to function in.

"The best way to get ahead is to teach the person below how to get ahead. You never get promoted when no one else knows how to do what you do now. Most people get promoted because they get pushed up from underneath rather than pulled up to the top."

David K. David

☐ Getting promoted doesn't mean you can slow down.

Poet Robert Frost once observed that if people work faithfully eight hours a day, they may eventually get promoted high enough to work twelve hours a day.

☐ Promoting the wrong person can be damaging.

"It's safer to leave a position vacant than to give it to someone who can't handle it."

David W. Crawley

☐ Every promotion alerts your employees to what you want.

"Every time your superiors promote you, they are in effect saying to your peers and subordinates: 'This person possess the qualities we'd like to see in more of our workers.' "

Donald V. Seibert, CEO, J. C. Penney

☐ A job promotion may result in a person's inability to deal with new responsibilities.

"June Travers was an excellent typist. When an opening for an executive secretarial assistant became available, Teresa Hughes selected June because of her good job performance. In a few days, June seemed to become a different type of person. Instead of being pleasant and good natured, she was irritable, causing associates to dislike her.

"By the second week, June began to complain of having a constant headache and upset stomach. Upon talking to her at length, Teresa found that June was not enjoying her new position. She felt incompetent and ill at ease and was fearful about making errors and learning new skills. June wanted to return to her old job. Although it meant a week of training a replacement, Teresa encouraged June to give up the new job for the sake of her well-being. Teresa then selected another person who was able to accept new responsibilities and adapt to new work situations."

Genevieve Smith, Genevieve Smith's Deluxe Handbook
for the Executive Secretary

□ You may be the only one that appreciates your promotion.

Walter Gifford, former president of AT&T, was a small-town boy who went to work in the big city. A few months after he first left home, he received a promotion. Elated, he wrote his father, a New England Yankee who had wanted the boy to stay home.

His father wrote back, "Any damn fool can make a success in a corporation."

PUBLIC RELATIONS

□ Public relations is telling your story.

As the philosopher Hillel said, "If I am not for myself, who, then, will be for me?"

"Conduct public relations as if the whole company depends on it."
Arthur W. Page

□ The greatest public relations campaign can't turn a flawed product into a great one.

As Yogi Berra once said about a slumping ball club playing to empty seats, "If the fans don't want to come to the stadium, there's no way you can stop them."

Good public relations promotes an all-important image. A case from history is the first televised debate between Richard M. Nixon and John F. Kennedy. People who heard the debate on radio felt that Nixon was the clear winner. But the result among those who saw the debate on television changed history.

☐ A good product is the best public relations.

Debbie Fields, founder of Mrs. Fields Cookies, said that her best public relations approach was a good cookie. When she was twenty years old and newly married, she wanted to sell the soft, chewy cookies that she'd been baking at home. She opened her first cookie store, and by noon nobody had bought any. She filled a tray, stepped out onto the sidewalk, and gave them away. People followed her back—to buy. Even today with over seven-hundred stores, she uses the same technique. At every store, passersby are invited in to sample free cookies.

☐ Some public relations ideas can go awry.

Morris Rotman told the story of Rival dog food's new meatball dinner. Rival's president liked to show visitors how wholesome the product was by eating it in his office. The agency suggested inviting journalists to lunch at which the company president and the pedigree dog would share a table. When the big day came around, the dog either wasn't hungry or was frightened by the lights. He showed total indifference to the meatballs. Desperate, the president reached over into the dog's bowl and ate the meatballs himself.

The following is from an interview in *PR Reporter* with Frank Mankiewicz of the public relations firm Hill & Knowlton:

"The notion of public relations as a profession is as absurd as bartenders calling themselves 'mixologists.' A profession is a skill—PR is not. Lawyers, accountants and doctors can be good PR people. All that's required is a sense of public opinion. A profession has standards and schools. The Public Relations Society of America's PR degrees, all of it's silly. If a person has a PR degree, all it indicates is that he wasted a lot of time that could have been spent studying worthwhile subjects like history or economics. It's about as useful as a degree in astrology. Well, maybe not quite that bad."

▌ PUBLIC SERVICE

☐ You get what you give

"He who sows hemp will reap hemp; he who sows beans will reap beans."
Chinese proverb

"No person was ever honored for what he received. Honor has been the reward for what he gave."
Calvin Coolidge

"Service is the vocation of every man and woman."
Leo Tolstoy

"The service we render to others is really the rent we pay for our room on this earth."

Wilfred Grenfell

"A candle loses nothing of its light by lighting another candle."

James Keller

"To be of service is a solid foundation for contentment in this world."

Charles W. Eliot

"For myself, success is, during this early pilgrimage, to leave the wood-pile a little higher than I found it."

Paul Harvey

"We find our lives in losing them in the service of others."

Anonymous

"Only a life lived for others is worthwhile."

Albert Einstein

"I don't know what your destiny will be, but one thing I know, the only ones among you who will be really happy are those who have sought and found how to serve."

Albert Schweitzer

"No man has ever risen to real stature until he has found that it is finer to serve somebody else than it is to serve himself."

Woodrow Wilson

"There is no higher religion than human service. To work for the common good is the greatest creed."

Albert Schweitzer

☐ It always pays to help others.

N. H. Bronner, founder of the cosmetics company Bronner Brothers, grew up poor on a farm outside Atlanta. The grandson of a slave, he left home after the seventh grade and worked his way through school in Atlanta, selling newspapers door to door. While picking up his sister one day at beauty school, he saw a sign touting the beauty business as "Depression proof." Bronner started selling beauty products on his paper route and gradually built up a business that did $20 million in sales in 1987.

"No community could function without people who consistently give more than they get."

Win Halliburton

☐ We prosper when we put the needs of others first.

AT&T was built with the concept of "Our business is public service."

"I think you have to place the betterment of society, your community, and your profession as one of your goals in life. When you do that, you become more productive in general."

Philip Oxley, president, Tenneco

"A man's true wealth is the good he does in this world."

Muhammad

"Sociologists find that those who volunteer enjoy better health than those that don't."

Eugene C. Dorsey

"The definition of a successful life must include serving others."

George Bush

In 1941, Winston Churchill said, "The destiny of mankind is not decided by material computation. When great causes are on the move in the world, we learn we are spirits, not animals, and that something is going on in space and time, which whether we like it or not spells duty."

Today our duty is to participate in [**mention what the audience is assembled for**].

Kenneth Clark wrote in his book *Civilization*, "I believe that order is better than chaos, creation better than destruction. I prefer gentleness to violence, forgiveness to ignorance, and I am sure that human sympathy is more valuable than ideology. Above all, I believe in the God-given genius of certain individuals, and I value a society that makes their existence possible."

This is the kind of society we must work for. One in which people care about one another. Care enough to be of service.

Eugene C. Dorsey offered the following as examples of how corporations participate in public service: "Workers at Apple Computer Inc. in California help children in hospital wards play computer games and draw electronic pictures. Professionals in Los Angeles renovated the area surrounding a skid-row park. Throughout the country, legions of young professionals assist in programs to eliminate illiteracy. Newspapers around the nation have been recognizing acts of volunteerism by young people."

□ Volunteering can make you live longer.

American Health magazine reported the findings of the University of Michigan's Research Center that says that doing regular volunteer work, more than any other activity, dramatically increased life expectancy and probably vitality.

Philanthropy and volunteerism are part of America's history. After the Pilgrims arrived, people helped people. The formed associations. They formed communities before they formed governments. Out of that spirit came the tradition of giving and volunteering.

Albert Einstein said that it is our obligation to put back into the world at least the equivalent of what we take out of it.

"The more successful someone is, the more time they can find to serve others."

J. Fred Hurt

The following could be used for a call-to-action at the end of a speech on public service.

"Many a floundering ship could be rescued by ideas and energy. A failing business, a scout troop, a church choir, a public school, or a city council. Plenty of struggling organizations are salvageable if they get the right kind of help. Remember: America went from its greatest naval loss (Pearl Harbor) to its greatest naval victory (Midway) in just six months. So plug up the leaks, trim the sails, and get going. Your effort can make a difference."

"All of us are born for a reason, but all of us don't discover why. Success in life has nothing to do with what you gain in life or accomplish for yourself. It's what you do for others."

Danny Thomas, entertainer

Philosopher Christina Hoff said that the replacement of individual good deeds by large-scale public and private charitable institutions resulted in a loss of community. That can lead to self-indulgence and a serious decline in private benevolence.

Participating in public service on an individual basis helps us as much as the people we are helping.

"My theme for philanthropy is the same approach I used with technology: to find a need and fill it."

An Wang, founder, Wang Laboratories

"No one would remember the Good Samaritan if he'd only had good intentions. He had money as well."

Margaret Thatcher

☐ We have to do what is right for us, not what others think we ought to do.

Albert Schweitzer is what service is about. He gave up a prestigious career as a doctor and went to Africa to build hospitals for the poor natives. Many of his friends, who felt that he was throwing away his talents and training, sent a delegation to Africa to attempt to persuade him to come back to his native land.

They asked, "Why should such a gifted man as you give up so much to labor among African natives?"

Schweitzer replied: "Don't talk about sacrifice. What does it matter where one goes provided one can do good work there? Much as I appreciate your kind words, I have made up my mind to stay here and look after my African friends."

He remained there until he died in 1965, at the age of ninety. He worked until the very end, maintaining his zest for living.

"No one, I am convinced, can be happy who lives only for himself. The joy of living comes from immersion in something that we know to be bigger, better, more enduring and worthier than we are."

John Mason Brown

In Lloyd C. Douglas' *Magnificent Obsession*, the plot reveals how a selfish young man leading a useless life was given purpose when he almost drowned. His life was saved by a pulmotor belonging to a famous brain surgeon. The unfortunate tragedy of the story is that the brain surgeon drowned while his pulmotor was being used by the young man.

The story tells how the young man decided to become a brain surgeon to fill the eminent man's shoes. He went on to enrich his life by enriching the lives of others.

Public service is our own opportunity to enrich the lives of others.

In the late nineteenth century, a member of parliament went to Scotland to make a speech. En route, his carriage became stuck in the mud. A Scottish farmboy came to the rescue with a team of horses that pulled the carriage loose. Awed by the great man, the boy would accept nothing in return for helping him out. The grateful statesman asked, "Is there nothing you want to be when you grow up?"

The boy said, "I want to be a doctor."

The man said, "Well, let me help."

True to his word, the Englishman helped make it possible for the Scottish boy to attend the university to graduate as a doctor. A little more than a half century later, on another continent, another world statesman lay dangerously ill with pneumonia. Winston Churchill had been stricken while attending a wartime conference. But a wonder drug was given to him—a new drug called penicillin, which had been discovered by Alexander Fleming. Fleming was the young Scottish lad, and the man who had helped sponsor his education was Randolph Churchill, Winston's father.

□ When we give service to others, sooner or later it will come back to us tenfold.

□ Being involved in public service enriches both the giver and the taker.

John Marks Templeton, who has been called the world's greatest living investor, said that his success as manager of the most successful mutual fund during the 1960s and 1970s, Templeton Growth Fund, was because of his philosophy.

He said, "Success is measured by the degree that one helps and enriches others, even if he helps himself at the same time."

"Strange is our situation here upon earth. Each of us comes for a short visit, not knowing why, yet sometimes seeming to divine a purpose.

"From the standpoint of daily life, however, there is one thing we do know: that man is here for the sake of other men—above all for those upon whose smile and well-being our own happiness depends, and also for the countless unknown souls with whose fate we are connected by a bond of sympathy. Many times a day I realize how much my own outer and inner life is built upon the labors of my fellow men, both living and dead, and how earnestly I must exert myself in order to give in return as much as I have received."

Albert Eistein

Former Speaker of the House Sam Rayburn could be hard and cold on business matters, but a basic gentleness always showed through when he was dealing with his helpers or acquaintances on a personal level. Someone once remarked to him about his extreme politeness to waitresses and bellhops.

He said, "I wouldn't be unkind to a little boy or girl waiting on me for all the gold in Fort Knox. That little girl might be your sister or mine. What we do in this life is often determined by a mighty small margin. I missed being a tenant farmer by just that much"—he snapped his fingers—"but someone was kind to me in my youth."

☐ It's time for us to offer someone else a slim margin.

☐ A public service philosophy is good for business.

James Burke, CEO of Johnson & Johnson, had his staff trace the earnings of companies that had a record of serving the public for at least a generation. They worked with the Business Roundtable's Task Force on Corporate Responsibility in selecting the thirteen companies. They looked at profit performance and rewards to stockholders over a thirty-five-year period.

The conclusion: While the GNP is ten times greater than thirty-five years ago, the net income of those companies is more than twenty-seven times greater. If you were a stockholder and invested $30,000 in a composite of Dow Jones companies thirty-five years ago, it would be worth $219,916 today. If you had invested $2,000 in each of the thirteen companies instead, that $30,000 would be worth 1.4 million.

☐ Public service is a way to express gratitude.

Eugene C. Dorsey, chairman of the Gannett Foundation, when asked how he is, responds, "grateful." He says, "I have been grateful all my life. I do not know the euphoria or stupor of drugs, or the cockroaches and rats of poverty. I have not gone hungry. I've never been homeless. I'm not illiterate or disabled. I've been married to the same woman for 40 years. Our sons are a source of pride and pleasure. Certainly, I've had problems and pain but I have been blessed. I have an obligation to be concerned about others who have not been as fortunate."

"We are here today to salute the staff members.

"In 1987, Hollywood celebrated its 100th anniversary with a special television spectacular hosted by Burt Reynolds. He saluted the Hollywood stunt people who make the actors look good in car crashes, chases, falls and shootups that punctuate most of today's films. I think staff members are the stunt people of the nonprofit sector. Not because they're capable of some pretty creative stunts, but because they make the volunteers look good by taking the falls, making the calls, writing the talks, organizing the meetings and heading for the sidelines when the headlines are written.

"So as Burt Reynolds saluted the movie stunt folks, I salute the professions for making volunteers look like professionals."
Eugene C. Dorsey, chairman, Gannett Foundation

It's a maxim of Hinduism that "he does not live in vain who employs his wealth, his thought, his speech to advance the good of others."

Taoist philosophy says, "The way to heaven is to benefit others."

According to Prophet Muhammad, "A man's true wealth is hereafter the good he does in this world to his fellow man."

Mother Teresa of Calcutta, who was awarded the Nobel Peace Prize in 1979 for her work among the poor in India, put the idea of service into perspective when she said, "We feel that what we are doing is just a drop in the ocean. But if that drop was not in the ocean, I think the oceans would be less because of that missing drop."

Each one of you here today is a drop into the ocean, and without you our project would be less.

☐ One good idea can make a big difference.

The first Key Club was sponsored in 1925 at Sacramento High School in California by the Kiwanis Club of Sacramento. It was the idea of a service organization for the school and community.

The idea slowly spread throughout the country and, by 1939, Florida had enough Key Clubs functioning to call a state convention and form a district. Today, Key Club International is strong in every state and is established in most of the countries around the world.

☐ We cannot ignore the community around us.

Abraham Lincoln used to tell about the wealthy businessman who spent his life so involved in his own affairs that he ignored the community around him.

When the man died, he had inscribed on his tombstone, beneath his name, "Here lies a businessman and a patriot." The first person who saw the inscription said, "A patriot and a businessman . . . what a shame to have to put two men in one grave."

Let's make sure people don't say, "What a shame" about us.

◻ **PURPOSE**

"There's no grander sight in the world than that of a person fired with a great purpose, dominated by one unwavering aim."

Orison Swett Marden

◻ Know your destination.

"That ship which sails by every wind comes never in the harbor."

Finnish proverb

"Having an aim is the key to achieving your best."

Henry J. Kaiser

"The evidence is overwhelming that you cannot begin to achieve your best unless you set some aim in life. What would football be without a goal? You see men play over their heads to reach the goal, whether in sports or throughout life."

Henry J. Kaiser

"There is really no insurmountable barrier save your own inherent weakness of purpose."

Ralph Waldo Emerson

"Man is a stubborn seeker of meaning."

John Gardner

"He who has a 'why' to live for can bear almost any "how.' "

Nietzsche

"The man without a purpose is like a ship without a rudder."

Thomas Carlyle

◻ Have a reason for what you do.

"When a man does not know what harbor he is making for, no wind is the right wind."

Seneca

"The world makes way for a man who knows where he is going."

Ralph Waldo Emerson

"The man who starts out going nowhere, generally gets there."

Dale Carnegie

"Great minds have purposes; others have wishes."

Washington Irving

"Everyone has his own specific vocation or mission in life. Everyone must carry out a concrete assignment that demands fulfillment. Therein he cannot be replaced, or can his life be repeated. Thus everyone's task is as unique as his specific opportunity to implement it."

Viktor Frankl

☐ Everything has a purpose.

"You can do anything with a bayonet except sit on it."

Napoleon

Without a purpose, we are like the man arrested for vagrancy appearing before the judge.

Judge: "When do you work?"
Man: "Now and then."
Judge: "What do you do for a living?"
Man: "This and that."
Judge: "Where do you live?"
Man: "Here and there?"
Judge: "Young man, you are going to jail."
Man: "When do I get out?"
Judge: "Sooner or later."

☐ It's important to know where we are going.

There's a great scene in *Alice in Wonderland* where Alice asks the Cheshire Cat, "Would you tell me please which way I ought to go from here?"
The cat replied, "That depends on where you want to get to."

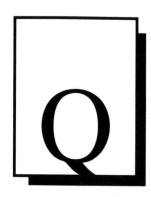

QUALITY

"The quality of your work will have a great deal to do with the quality of your life."

Orison Swett Marden

☐ Quality sells.

"My overcoats sell my overcoats."

Monty Platt, Platt Clothiers

☐ Quality comes from pride.

"I consider a bad bottle of Heineken to be a personal insult to me."

Freddy Heineken

☐ Sell quality to workers.

A sign above each workbench on the production line of a television manufacturing plants said: "Careful, this may be the one you get."

"The quality, not the longevity, of one's life is what is important."

Martin Luther King, Jr.

"Quality is a necessity for survival. It means everything to me, and I know it when I see it."

Richard D. Brogan

Quality is meeting customer expectations at a competitive price.

Thad A. Barrington

"Quality means cultivating a customer that will come to me the next time."

Robert Carlson

"Quality in a service or product is not what you put into it. It is what the client or customer gets out of it."

Peter Drucker

□ Quality must be an obsession.

Ray Kroc was once visiting a Canadian franchise and found a single fly. Two weeks later, the franchisee lost his McDonald's franchise.

"Quality is not an act. It is a habit."

Aristotle

Remember the TV commercial: "At Zenith, the quality goes in before the name goes on."

"Hewlett-Packard support services have long been considered 'products.' "

Hewlett-Packard

"Quality is viewed more as a focus of the organization itself than as an attribute of goods or services."

Warner-Lambert

"At GE, quality is not a spectator sport—everyone's involved."

General Electric

"Good quality is cheap; it's poor quality that is expensive."

Joe L. Griffith

"The surest foundation of a manufacturing concern is quality."

Andrew Carnegie

□ Quality pays in any business.

Alvin Burger had spent much of his life in the pest control business. He grew dissatisfied with the lack of quality in his industry and pledged to do something about it. Most of the industry only wanted to control bugs, but Alvin wanted to eliminate them or give money back. Now Burger has outlets in almost every state and is considered the standard of the industry. All because he wanted to offer more quality.

"There is an old saying in America: 'If it ain't broke, don't fix it.'

"At Xerox, we've replaced that with a saying we have borrowed from the Japanese: 'If it isn't perfect, make it better.' "

D. T. Kearns, annual meeting of Xerox shareholders–1989

☐ There are different levels of quality

If a Cadillac conforms to all the requirements of a Cadillac, then it is a quality car. If a Pinto conforms to all the requirements of a Pinto, then it is a quality car.

☐ Don't ever stop trying to improve.

"I've never been satisfied with anything we've ever built. I've felt that dissatisfaction is the basis of progress. When we become satisfied in business, we become obsolete."

Bill Marriott, Sr.

☐ Quality doesn't come easy; you have to set high standards.

Stanley Marcus's father, the founder of Neiman-Marcus, was always asking how the merchandise offered could be improved. In an effort to eliminate any flaws in the product before it got to the customer, he established an inspection department—unique in the retail business—in which every article of apparel was tried on a model form to determine if it was cut properly and if there were any defects apparent on close inspection.

☐ Concern for quality starts at the top.

William E. Boeing, Boeing's founder, spotted defective parts coming down the line. He swept them onto the floor and cried, "Now make me a good one."

☐ How important is quality?

Westinghouse chairman John C. Marous said, "Total quality is everything. It's a matter of survival. To have it, you're going to have to change your culture."

"Quality is never an accident; it is always the result of intelligent effort."
John Ruskin

☐ The search for quality can cause short-term problems.

Few people realize that Ford Motor Company was Henry Ford's third attempt at making automobiles. He was voted out in one company and went bankrupt in another. Henry Ford was ousted from the Henry Ford Company when he insisted on improving the design of the car instead of thinking of short-term profits. When he was removed by the board of directors, the name was changed to the Cadillac Automobile Company. The Cadillac was originally a Ford. Later, as we all know, Ford's quest for a better car paid off.

Management can communicate its emphasis on quality by paying attention to details. For instance, National Steel requires workers to clean their work stations instead of leaving the task for the janitors. The Japanese co-owners, who suggested the policy, reasoned that if workers have enough pride to take care of their work stations, they might also care more for their product.

☐ Never stop talking about quality.

"If I had a brick for every time I've repeated the phrase Q.S.C.&V. (Quality, Service, Cleanliness, and Value), I think I'd probably be able to bridge the Atlantic Ocean with them."

Ray Kroc, founder, McDonald's

H. L. Mencken, the editor of a magazine, shouted throughout his office, "It's coming in the doors!"

Everybody looked up.

It's up to the bottom of the desk! It's up to the seats of our chairs. It's up to the top of our desk."

Finally, someone asked, "What do you mean?"

"Mediocrity. We're drowning in mediocrity!"

That day, he quit his job as editor.

We should feel that strongly about the lack of quality.

Three people were to be executed: an Englishman, a Japanese, and an American.

The Englishman was asked if he'd like to have a final request. He said, "Yes. I'd like to sing the national anthem."

The Japanese man was asked what his final wish was. He said, "I'd like to give a speech on quality."

When the American was asked what his final request was, he said, "I'd like to be executed before the Japanese so that I won't have to hear another speech on quality."

A man went into a restaurant and ordered breakfast. He told the waiter, "I want two boiled eggs, one of them undercooked so it runs, the other one cooked so hard it looks like rubber. I want my coffee cold and my butter so hard it can't be cut."

The waiter said, "We can't do that."

He said, "Sure you can. You did it yesterday."

☐ We must continually strive to improve. We can't do things today as we did them yesterday and be successful.

☐ A quality product comes from an entire organization committed to quality.

Amana puts out a very expensive microwave oven, but it sells. Why? Because Amana stands for quality workmanship. Quality workmanship may begin on the assembly line, but it is supported in the business office and it is successfully distributed through a sound marketing department and program. Amana and its story rest on a three-legged stool: operations, finance, and marketing.

To be successful, we can be no different.

☐ A reputation for quality can pay big dividends.

Stanley Marcus told of the time that Jack Massey of Nashville was trying to get married in Dallas and the judge asked for some local identification. The bride showed the judge her Neiman-Marcus credit card.

The judge replied: "Well, if your credit is good with them, it's good with me."

☐ Quality is a conviction. It can sometimes cost money.

Debbie Fields, founder of Mrs. Fields Cookies, said "I'm a cookie person, not a business person." She once tossed out $500 worth of cookies and temporarily closed a store because those she sampled were not up to standard.

☐ Make workers responsible for poor quality.

World War II parachute packers had an unacceptable record: nineteen out of twenty parachutes opened. The manager discovered that by allowing the packers the pleasure of testing their parachutes by jumping from a plane, quality rose to 100 percent.

☐ A manager's style should take second place to the quality of each manager's achievements.

Howard Nemerov, the United States' former poet laureate, was asked about his poetic style. He replied that as a young man he smoked a brand of cigars with the motto "All Quality, No Style."

☐ Quality is a way to get and keep customers.

Scott Hallman, CEO of Hospital Correspondence Copiers, a $16-million San Jose, California, company provided medical record-copying services to hospitals nationwide. A key to his sales pitch is the quality of his service—no incorrect records copied, no late delivery. So when monthly customer checks indicate that quality is falling, his salespeople can't take on any new customers for six to eight weeks. Hallman says that he loses some customers, but he has a better record of keeping existing customers than his competitors.

☐ For the quality of your product to improve, top management has to be committed to it.

Levi Strauss & Company designed 501 jeans with copper rivets so that prospectors mining for gold wouldn't tear their jeans on mining tools. The rivets on the back pockets were eventually removed because wearers reported they scratched chair backs. The rivets on the fly, however, remained, although cowboys sometimes voiced complaints about it. In the late 1930s, company president Walter Haas, Sr., was wearing a pair of 501 jeans during a fishing trip. When he crouched close to the campfire one night, the rivet became alarmingly warm. In the heat of the moment, Haas understood with great and urgent clarity the customers' complaints about the rivet. A week later by unanimous decision of the company's board of directors, the rivet was discarded.

☐ When cost reduction becomes priority number one, then quality suffers.

Sometimes doing things that are uneconomical can make more sense than cutting costs, such as the overcommitment to reliability by Caterpillar Tractor who promised "forty-eight-hour parts service anywhere in the world—or CAT pays." Maytag's boast of "Ten years' trouble-free operation," or McDonald's fetish for cleanliness make no economic sense except that they work and have created the leaders in their fields.

RECESSION

A recession is when the three-martini lunch is replaced by the full Coors dinner.

I'll tell you how bad things are. My wife always has an ice-cold double martini waiting for me at the door. Then I catch the bus and go to work.

A recession is when your neighbor is out of work, and a depression is when you are out of work.

A businessperson discussing a recession: "What really worries me is all the unemployed people on my payroll!"

☐ Business is so slow right now, a fellow walked into a store to get change for a $20 bill—and the owner wanted to make him a partner.

☐ We sometimes cause our own recession.

Two farmers were talking over a fence: One farmer, obviously satisfied with the state of things, said "Well, I'm not planting any corn this year, and I'm not planting any wheat either; so all in all I should have a pretty good year."

RESEARCH AND DEVELOPMENT

"I never perfected an invention that I did not think about in terms of the service it might give others."

Thomas Edison

□ Speeding up product development can mean additional profits.

"If you get to market sooner with new technology, you can charge a premium until the others follow."

John Handly, vice president, AT&T

□ A valued trademark name doesn't always assure the success of a new product.

RCA is a well-known trade name for radios and televisions, but when RCA tried to market kitchen appliances in the 1940s, it failed. The consumer didn't connect radios and televisions with refrigerators.

□ You can be successful without spending lots of money on research and development.

Crown Cork and Seal relies on top customer service to succeed, and they do little basic research and don't pioneer new products. Instead, its R&D department is used to solve specific customer problems quickly and to imitate new product innovations created by competitors.

□ It's not enough to develop new products, you also need the money to exploit their potential.

IBM didn't invent the personal computer but had the resources to succeed against those who were early entrants into the market.

□ Companies that create new products often discover that the largest market was not originally known.

When Alfred Nobel was developing dynamite, he was trying to discover a better explosive for the military. As it was, dynamite turned out to be too dangerous for the military but eventually was used by the mining and construction industries, along with the railroad, to replace the pick and shovel.

□ The most successful companies are those that invest in research labs.

The idea of research labs was implemented for General Electric in 1905. Next came Bell Labs, later Du Pont, and then IBM.

"Basic research is what I am doing when I don't know what I am doing."
Wernher von Braun

□ New products don't always come from research and development.

In 1957, Vic Barouh's company made carbon paper. One day he saw a secretary use chalk to erase a mistake. This is how the idea for Ko-Rec-Type was born.

□ Developing a new product is the first step. The second step is getting the potential recognized.

"Xerography, invented by patent attorney and amateur physicist Chester Carlson in his New York City kitchen, was patented in 1937, but IBM, RCA, Remington Rand, and General Electric, among others, rejected it."
Mark Green and John F. Berry, The Challenge of Hidden Profits

☐ Develop products that are needed.

"Competition from the Japanese is just one of a whole bunch of old saws that people use to explain product failure. The key is to find something that will make a difference in your customer's business. Successful products provide instant economic success to the users."

Modesto Maidique, author

☐ New products should improve results for the buyer.

Mark Twain may have been correct when he concluded, "I believe that our Heavenly Father invented man because he was disappointed in the monkey."

☐ New products need to get to market quicker to recoup research and development money faster.

The safety razor took nine years for Gillette to manufacture; television, twenty-two years; radio, eight years; the cotton picker, fifty-three years; nylon, eleven years; the zipper, twenty-seven years.

☐ New products come from companies that encourage new products.

The 3M Company has what they call a "10-percent rule." Employees can spend 10 percent of their time on any project, just as long as it's related to 3M's business.

You know those little yellow stick-on paper slips everyone uses? They were developed with the 10-percent rule and have been a big success at 3M.

☐ When developing a new product, make sure it will fulfill a need.

That's what Betty Nesmith, an executive secretary, did in 1951. The speed of the electric typewriter, new on the market, seemed to multiply typing errors. She concocted a mixture of water-based paint and a coloring agent that blended with the bank's stationery. Soon other employees wanted to use her correction fluid, and by 1956, she was making and selling the product full-time. In 1979, Gillette bought her Liquid Paper Corporation for $47.5 million.

☐ It can be easier to succeed with an improved product than it is with a new product.

It took Polaroid many years to reach $1 billion in sales with their innovative camera because they had to teach people how to use it.

☐ Sometimes technological discoveries occur accidentally.

LTV Corporation's "mistake" occurred in 1958, a landmark year for America's space program. The United States, racing to catch up with the Soviet Union, launched its first satellite. The National Aeronautics and Space Administration was born. And workers at what is now LTV Missile and Electronics Group's Missiles Division in Dallas accidentally left a piece of carbon in a furnace too long.

When LTV workers examined the specimen they nicknamed "burnt toast," they found that instead of burning up in the heat, it was strong. The material, now known as reinforced carbon/carbon, has evolved into key structural material for the space shuttle and may be used on future space vehicles because of its strength and ability to withstand metal-melting temperatures.

☐ We can have more breakthroughs in research if we create an environment that encourages it.

Consider how Montgolfier invented the hot-air balloon. Looking into the fireplace, one of the brothers saw burnt paper scraps rise above the flames and up the chimney. Heated air could make a balloon rise from the earth, he realized.

While working on a better way to make glass, British inventor Alastair Pilkington noticed a film of fat floating in his wife's dishwasher. That idea hook inspired a process where molten glass is floated on a layer of melted metal to provide an otherwise unachievable smoothness.

Dunlop got the idea for the rubber tire by looking at a garden hose. Colt invented the revolver after watching a ship's wheel turn.

☐ When a new product fails, don't let managerial ego keep it on the market.

Remember when Ford produced the Edsel. It was a major failure. All premarket research indicated that the Edsel would be well received, but the public didn't buy it. Ford quickly dropped the Edsel and thereby cut their losses short. Had management's ego been so big they didn't want to admit their mistake, the Edsel could have stayed on the market and could have eventually made Ford Motor Company the failure and not just a product.

☐ The more dominate a company is in its market, the faster they can usually bring out new products.

Black & Decker has a faster rate of new product introduction than any of its competitors in the power tool industry because it has a substantial lead in market share over its competitors.

3M, an office products leader, has over forty-thousand different products.

☐ Instead of developing product families, develop product lines.

For example, When Stouffer's rolled out its Lean Cuisine frozen entrees, what was being sold wasn't frozen food. The company very successfully sold the idea of high-class dieting to an increasingly health-conscious populace. Lean Cuisine wasn't targeted at customers looking for frozen entrees and dinners—it was focused on consumers who would be attracted to the idea that the food was convenient, tasty, and compatible with a healthful weight-conscious life-style. The success of the idea is evident by the booming market for low-calorie frozen dinners.

☐ The more product research develops, the more you will develop through spin-off uses.

3M's brassiere project in the late 1950s was an attempt to borrow from 3M's nonwoven-fiber technology, which already was used to make decorative ribbons for gift packages. The 3M bra offered good support but not much in the way of styling. Even though the bra wasn't successful, it stimulated additional products that were successful. The shape of the bra cups suggested a surgical mask, and the nonwoven fiber had the necessary porous property to let air in but keep germs from going out.

☐ Sometimes a product only has to be improved to increase sales.

Take the fountain pen first introduced in 1884. About sixty years later, after World War II, the ballpoint pen was invented. Then came porous point pens, highlighters, and then mechanical pencils.

No matter how many new word processors or automated office equipment comes to market, pens will always be around in one form or another, as witnessed by the fact that annual sales of pens is near $3 billion.

☐ Give a product a new twist.

The quickest way to create a new product is to give a new twist to one that already exists. This worked for Weight Watchers. There were already hundreds of diets available, but Weight Watchers added the idea of support groups to dieters.

☐ RESULTS

☐ Results require risk.

"Most favorable results were unforeseen by us or anybody else . . . that happens if you drill a lot of wells."

George Galloway, Amoco

☐ Results don't come immediately.

"A journey of a thousand miles begins with a single step."

Chinese proverb

☐ Results are not always accomplished with a frontal assault.

"The only way to lose weight is to check it as airline baggage."

Peggy Ryan

☐ Where you finish is more important than where you start.

"There are two large groups of people in the world—those who start well and finish poorly and those who start poorly and finish well."
A. James Grant

☐ Results come from people who enjoy their work.

"Make it fun to work for your agency. When people aren't having any fun, they don't produce good advertising. Get rid of sad dogs who spread doom. What kind of paragons are the men and women who run successful agencies? My observation has been that they are enthusiasts."
David Ogilvy, founder, Ogilvy & Mather

"Results depend on relationships."
Donald E. Petersen, past chairman and CEO, Ford

"Don't tell me about the labor pains; show me the baby."
Jeanne Robertson, humorist

Management is a lot like golf. It's not how—it's how many. Recently, W. Steve Brown played golf with friends. He had a hole-in-one! He hit the worst golf shot of his life. He skulled; he practically shanked a 7-iron. The ball went out to the right and hit a tree, bounced off, and came back to the fairway; then it hit a rock, rolled up on the green, and went straight into the cup. On the scorecard, he wrote, 1!

☐ Results are good when you do the right thing at the right time.

"Movie tycoon L. B. Mayer and his son-in-law owned a horse together. The horse was considered a good prospect to win the Kentucky Derby. While Mayer was out of the country, the son-in-law entered the horse 'for practice' in a race a few weeks before the derby. The horse won that race; but then it lost the derby. Mayer said, 'He ran the wrong race.' "
Mortimer R. Feinberg, Effective Psychology for Managers

☐ To get the best results, motivate people to do the right thing at the right time.

Knute Rockne, the famous Notre Dame coach, enjoyed whipping his team into a frenzy just before each game. One week, the Irish played Iowa. Rockne told his team, "Iowa is poisoning our water; they're stealing our plays." Notre Dame murdered Iowa. The following week, Notre Dame played Army and lost. Rockne scratched his balding head and said, 'I made the team play the Army game against Iowa. I whipped them up at the wrong time."

"When your work speaks for itself, don't interrupt."
Henry J. Kaiser

"It doesn't matter how a man parts his hair; it's what kind of job he does."
Edgar Speer, chairman, U.S. Steel

☐ It's not what you do but how much you get done.

"It's possible to spend your time working efficiently on unimportant problems which, even if solved, will bring no glory to you and no profit to the company."

Robert H. Henry, humorist

☐ You can get better results with the incentives.

Consultant Edward J. Feeney, who specialized in behavior modification techniques to business, tells of the time he discovered the cost of labor for a typewriter-ribbon manufacturer was only 10 percent of the total product cost. But material was close to 50 percent, and that was quite a bit of waste. Feeney set up a system that allowed employees to measure for themselves how much they were wasting and put in an incentive for reducing waste. As a result, the company's after-tax earnings rose from about 2 percent of sales to 6 percent.

"People who get ahead are those who prove they can get things done."

David Kearns, chairman, Xerox

☐ Don't let rules get in the way of results.

Office manager: "I'm afraid you're ignoring our efficiency system."
Clerk: "Maybe so, but somebody has to get the work done."

☐ A friend of the big boss was visiting him in his office, after an absence of some weeks.

Friend: "Say, what happened to all those 'Think' signs you used to have on walls?"
Boss: "I had to take them down. Everyone sat around all day thinking and never got any work done."

☐ We must channel our energy in the proper direction to get results.

"No steam or gas ever drives anything until it is confined. No Niagara Falls is ever turned into light and power until it is funneled."

John R. Noe

☐ Results come from the results-oriented.

In World War II, the Seabees had a motto: "The difficult we do right now; the impossible will take a little longer."

We don't always see immediate results from our decisions. Like the two veterans of World War II talking, one of them said, "You remember those pills they gave us to help us quit thinking about girls? I think they're beginning to work."

As managers, we are always looking at results. But it is more important to look at what produces results. Appealing to the basic human motivations, produces results. And one of these is love.

As novelist Victor Hugo once wrote, "The supreme happiness of life is the conviction that we are loved—loved for ourselves; in spite of ourselves."

A new salesperson with a large insurance company was ambitious and eager to learn all the techniques of selling. Despite all his efforts, sales were few and far between. Finally, his sales manager told him, "You just aren't cut out to be a salesman."

The salesman sat up in his chair and said, "That's not true. I'm selling all right. It's just that people aren't buying."

☐ No matter how good we seem to be doing, it's results that matter.

☐ Results can be hindered by not being clear about who does what.

Take a young couple who just got married. Once they settle into their new home, the garbage begins to pile up. The bride thinks, "Why doesn't he take it out?" At the same time he thinks "Why doesn't she take it out?" Eventually they start saying something. One accuses the other.

He says, "Taking out garbage is a woman's job."

She says, "Taking out garbage is a man's job."

There is no right answer. But to get results, each has to be clear on who must perform the job.

RETIREMENT

"When a man retires, his wife gets twice the husband, but only half the income."

Chi Chi Rodriquez

The problem with being retired is that you never know what day it is, what time it is, where you're suppose to be, or what you're suppose to be doing. It's a lot like working for the government.

Malcolm S. Forbes, former chairman and editor in chief of *Forbes* magazine said, "Retirement kills more people than hard work ever did."

☐ There is a time to retire.

"It is the nature of a man as he grows older to protest against change, particularly change for the better."

John Steinbeck

The toastmaster said to the guest of honor at a retirement dinner: "As a token of our appreciation, we have created this special gold watch to serve as a constant reminder of your many years with our company. It has to be wound frequently; it's always a little late, and every day at a quarter till five it quits working."

A farewell dinner is where the foreman says, "John Jones will be leaving us after fifty-three years of faithful service, but he'll always be with us in our memories." And the boss says to the personnel manager, "Who?"

◼ REWARDS

"When the number of awards is high, it makes the perceived possibility of winning something high as well. And then the average man will stretch to achieve."

Thomas J. Peters and Robert H. Waterman

"Honor is better than honors."

Abraham Lincoln

☐ It's good management to reward employees with recognition.

The manager of a 100-person sales branch rented the Meadowlands Stadium in New Jersey for the evening. After work, his salesmen ran onto the stadium's field through the players' tunnel. As each emerged, the electronic scoreboard beamed their name to the assembled crowd. Executives from corporate headquarters, employees from other offices, and family and friends were present, cheering loudly.

☐ Reward a deed now, not later.

The president of Foxboro was so pleased with a scientist's solution to a problem and so bemused about how to reward it, he rummaged through most of the drawers in his desk, found something, leaned over the desk to the scientist, and said, "Here!" In his hand was a banana, the only reward he could immediately put his hands on. From that point on, the small "gold banana" pin has been the highest accolade for scientific achievements at Foxboro.

☐ Rewards come from a job well done.

Ray Kroc, McDonald's founder, said, "You should work for pride and accomplishment. Money will come later. It comes only from what's already done. I was brought up to understand that reward will come later."

☐ More suggestions will come forward if they are rewarded.

"At Marion Labs each year, the person who offers the best suggestion receives a week-long, all expenses-paid trip for two to any city in the world, plus an extra week of vacation."

Robert Levering, 100 Best Companies To Work For

☐ Reward employees and they will up your bottom line.

The suggestion box idea works at Kodak because employees receive recognition and rewards for their ideas. If an idea isn't accepted, you receive a written explanation of why action was not taken.

If your idea is used, you are financially rewarded. Kodak has adopted some 700,000 ideas submitted by its employees, who have been rewarded to the tune of $20 million.

☐ Reward those who help build your business.

Joe Girard, "The World's Greatest Salesman," according to the *Guinness Book of World Records,* gives each of his customers his card with the customer's name written on the back. Anytime a new customer comes in with an old customer's name on his card, the old customer gets $25 as a thank-you. In one year, he mailed out $14,000 in checks.

☐ Rewards are needed if you want to continue getting exceptional performance.

The year Scandanavian Air Lines was chosen the best business class airline in the world by its passengers, Scandanavian's chairman Jan Carlzon, threw his employees a special Christmas party. They were given rented limousines to use, and gold watches were freely handed out.

█ RISK

"Behold the turtle. He makes progress only when he sticks his neck out."
James B. Conant

"Nothing will ever be attempted if all possible objections must be first overcome."

Samuel Johnson

"There is only one danger I find in life—you may take too many precautions."

Alfred Adler

"Progress always involves risks. You can't steal second base while keeping your foot on first."

Frederick Wilcox

☐ Sometimes not taking a risk is a risk.

"People who don't take risks generally make about two big mistakes a year. People who do take risks generally make about two big mistakes a year."
Peter Drucker

☐ Risk is necessary for a company to grow and prosper.

Pharmaceutical manufacturers always risk the danger of bringing a killer to market instead of a cure. The Thalidomide drug brought out in the early 1960s left malformed infants. The inoculations in the 1970s for infantile paralysis turned out to be lethal and had to be taken off the market. But because they take these risks, lifesaving drugs have dramatically extended our life expectancy.

☐ Everyone has their own level of risk.

"As far as I'm concerned, nothing is worth going broke for."
Warren Avis, founder, Avis Car Rental

"Excessive caution can stop your potential as much as too much risk-taking."
Robert H. Henry, humorist

☐ It may be better to let others take the risk.

"Never be a pioneer; it doesn't pay. Let the other man do the pioneering and then after he has shown what can be done, do it bigger and more quickly; but let the other man take the time and risk to show you how to do it."
Leo Bakeland, founder Bakelite Corporation

☐ Taking no risk is sometimes the biggest risk.

"Every serious choice that a man or woman makes is a leap, more or less frightening, into contingency. Not to make those choices, not to open oneself to misfortune and the fear of misfortune, is a tempting option, but one gives into it at the risk of never living a fully human life."
Nelson Aldrich, Jr., Old Money

☐ The more we have, the more we have to lose and the less likely we are to take a risk.

Success automatically breeds caution. Listen to some of the sayings: "Don't tamper with success." "If it ain't broke don't fix it." "Don't break up a winning team." "Don't ruin a good thing."

"The people I want to hear about are the people who take risks."
Robert Frost

"Great deals are usually wrought at great risks."
Herodotus

"Take risks. You can't fall off the bottom."
Barbara Proctor

"America is becoming a nation of risk-takers, and the way we do business will never be the same."
Allan A. Kennedy

☐ We can reduce risk by preparation.

Remember the famous saloon scene with W. C. Fields. After watching the canny comedian survey his poker hand, a man asked, "Is this a game of chance?"

Fields replied, "Not the way I play it."

☐ Learning requires risk.

A few years back, I read that Peter Benchley, who wrote the bestselling book *Jaws,* was in Australia observing the filming of his book. In order to observe sharks firsthand, he got into the ocean about thirty yards offshore. He noticed a shark coming dangerously close and apparently coming toward him. He quickly turned around and ran in the water back toward the beach. He described the experience as "dancing on peanut butter."

Somehow odds take most people by surprise. Tennis pro Vic Braden reminds his students that half the people who play tennis *lose*.

☐ Perhaps the biggest threat to a successful business is the willingness to remain comfortable and reject the small risk that could lead to greater rewards.

In the 1960s, Campbell Soup Company produced a comfortable profit almost like clockwork. But a man named Gordon McGovern down in a little-known bakery division wasn't satisfied. Before long, McGovern developed a line of premium cookies. Sales shot sky-high. The brand name was Pepperidge Farm.

A few years later, McGovern was named Campbell's chairman, and he quickly produced a line of gourmet soups that opened new markets. Again sales soared. Perhaps more important, McGovern's creative, take-a-risk attitude soon permeated the company.

☐ Before taking a risk, think of Rudyard Kipling's words:

If you can make one heap of all your winnings
And risk it on one turn of pitch-and-toss,
And lose, and start again at your beginnings
And never breathe a word about your loss . . .

☐ Without risk, there is no reward.

Academy Award–winning actor George Kennedy reached stardom only after he made a difficult decision to change the direction of his life. He was in the army and had completed fourteen years' service—just six short of retirement—when he decided that what he really wanted was to be an actor.

His family and friends advised him not to do it. "Why give up the security of the army and sure retirement benefits for the insecurity of the actor's world? Why trade the certain for the uncertain? At your age, you're crazy to change careers. How do you know you can ever be an actor?"

"Failure didn't fit into my scheme of things," he said. He ventured to Hollywood, won an Oscar for his role in *Cool Hand Luke* and went on to star in a successful television series. He now earns more from one TV commercial than he did in a year with the army.

◼ ROAST

[**Name**] is a miracle worker. It's a miracle when he works.

[**Name**] is a workaholic—mention work and he gets drunk.

[**Name**] had a wreck coming here today. He saw a restaurant with a sign that read, "Drive Thru Window" and he did.

He didn't always want to be [**name of occupation**]. At one time, he wanted to be a pharmacist, but couldn't figure out how to get those little prescription bottles in the typewriter.

The best part about being a vice president [**substitute another title**] is that when you take a two-hour lunch, it doesn't hinder sales.

[**Name**] is the most exciting, charismatic personality around. He recently willed his body to science, and they contested the will.

Did you hear about the accountant who went in for his annual checkup and took his wife along with him? While he was getting dressed, the doctor told his wife: "I don't like the looks of him."
She said: "I don't either. But he's good to the kids."

My boss is very proud of the fact that he became general manager of our company the hard way. He started out as president [**choose appropriate titles**].

Publishing happens to be a difficult business. A very difficult business. I happen to know that a leading medical insurance company now accepts ten years in publishing as legal proof of permanent brain damage. [**Adapt to your field**].

A faith healer had all kinds of successes. Nothing seemed to stop him. His powers were rising, and his popularity was beginning to soar throughout the land.
Once when he was taking a walk, he found a man in tears. He asked him what was wrong.

First man: "I've got this wart on my nose and it's really ugly." (The faith healer touched the wart and it fell off.)

When the faith healer turned the corner, he found another man in tears. He asked the man what his problem was.

Second man: "See this hangnail on my thumb. It's driving me nuts." (The faith healer touched the man's thumb and the hangnail vanished.)

As he continued his walk, he came upon a third man weeping.

Faith healer: "What's the trouble? Perhaps my powers can help you, too."

Third man: "I can't help crying—I'm a professional football player and a team just offered me a contract."

Faith healer: "That sounds all right to me. What's the name of the team?"

Third man: "The [**insert name of the losing team here**]." (The faith healer sat down and cried with him.)

[**Blank**] came home and found his house on fire. He rushed next door and telephoned the fire department.

He said, "My house is on fire."

Fireman: "How do we get there?"

He said, "Don't you have any fire trucks?"

A judge quizzed [**roastee's name**] for running over a beer bottle in the center of the road. "I didn't see it your honor."

"How could you miss a beer bottle in the middle of the road?"

"The guy had it hidden under his coat."

A politician was out of town attending a meeting. He went shopping and admired some material he saw in a store window. The clerk told him he could buy enough material to have a sports coat made. When he took the material home to his own tailor, the tailor suggested: "I think I can also make a pair of pants out of the material, and you'll get a suit, not just a sports coat."

The politician nodded his approval.

Tailor:	"You know I could also make a vest out of the material, and you'd have a nice suit with a vest."
Politician:	"I'm puzzled. When I was out of town, I bought just enough material to get a sports coat made. Now you tell me that I can get a suit with a vest. How could that be?"
Tailor:	"Out of town you could just get a sports coat made. But here in your hometown you're not as big a man as you are when you're out of town."

This story can be used by a boss/manager or anyone else who needs to deflate themselves.

Can be adapted to many professions—brackets indicate where to make the change.

A psychiatrist died and went to Heaven. St. Peter greeted him at the Pearly Gates. He said: "We really need you up here."

Psychiatrist: "Why?"
St. Peter: "Because of the big guy upstairs."
Psychiatrist: "You mean God?"
St. Peter: "No, he thinks he's a [Federal Judge]."

SACRIFICE

"Deferred joys purchased by sacrifice are always the sweetest."
Mike Doyle

H. L. Hunt, the late Texas oil billionaire, once said, "A lot of people know what they want but don't know what they are willing to give up to get it."
That's like saying, "Know thyself."

☐ Personal sacrifice keeps you on top.

Few fell farther than Johnny Miller, who sacked three-quarters of a million bucks for three years on the golf tour. The next year, he tumbled to $61,000, ranking him forty-seventh among golf coin collectors. He said: "There comes a time when you have to realize no job is easy. You have to work at it, and I wasn't willing to do that a while ago. It's a little like a guy playing the slot machines. When he's winning, it's so easy he gets the idea he can keep winning even if he doesn't put any money in the machine. It doesn't work that way."

☐ There is a sacrifice for every success.

The seed dies that the plant may live.
The mountains are barren that the valleys may be rich.
During the building of Boulder Dam, ninety-two men died that the desert might blossom like the rose.

☐ Short-term sacrifice can reap long-term rewards.

In 1937, Tom Murphy went to work for General Motors and later said that he almost refused because the job didn't pay enough. After paying for meals, laundry, and a room at the YMCA, there just wasn't much left of his $100-a-month salary. But Murphy took the job anyway because he thought it was a good opportunity, and eventually he became GM's chairman of the board.

☐ Don't be afraid to sacrifice the present for a future opportunity.

☐ Working with others requires sacrifices.

During World War II, General Eisenhower had to deal with a lot of prima donnas, and one day a young reporter asked him about it.

Reporter: "Ike, how do you do it? You are in constant contact with Patton, Churchill, Montgomery, and De Gaulle. How do you get along with these monumental egos?"

Ike: "It's easy. I just think of how difficult it would be to get along with Hitler."

☐ It's easier to make a sacrifice if you're not alone.

John D. Rockefeller, Jr., said it: "On February 3, 1943, the transport *Dorchester* was torpedoed off the coast of Greenland. As the ship went down, four chaplains—one a Catholic, one a Jew, two Protestants—were on deck passing out life belts. When there were no life belts left, they gave their own away. The chaplains were last seen standing arm in arm praying."

They went to their death, united in the service of a common Lord.

▉ SALES

"The fish sees the bait, not the hook."

Chinese proverb

☐ When someone buys, they want to feel they have something special.

"People will buy anything that's one to a customer."

Sinclair Lewis

Before salespeople sell anything to anyone, they must first sell it to themselves.

☐ The salesperson must believe in the value for the price of the product being sold.

A few years ago, the Manhattan Brook Brothers store was robbed, and the crooks got out with $200,000 worth of clothes. One clerk said: "If they'd come during our sale two weeks ago, we could have saved 20 percent."

☐ Don't overpromise to get the first sale.

Too often salespeople make too many promises. Anyone can get the first order by stretching the truth. The mark of a professional salesperson is getting the reorder.

To paraphrase George Gobel, "A salesman is a fellow with a smile on his face, a shine on his shoes, and a lousy territory."

☐ It isn't easy to be in sales.

"An ideal salesperson has the curiosity of a cat, the tenacity of a bulldog, the friendship of a little child, the diplomacy of a wayward husband, the patience of a self-sacrificing wife, the enthusiasm of a Sinatra fan, the assurance of a Harvard man, the good humor of a comedian, the simplicity of a jackass, and the tireless energy of a bill collector."
Harry G. Moock, former vice president, Chrysler

☐ Too many salespeople blame their territory for their failure.

Have you ever noticed that the most successful salespeople show up in the most unlikely places? The second largest Steinway piano dealer in the country is in Waterford, Connecticut, which has a population of less than twenty thousand.

Salespeople make the territory, the territory doesn't make the salesperson.

You'll make more sales if you remember what management expert Peter Drucker said: "There are no dumb customers."

"The best product must be sold. People won't come to you and take it away from you. You must go to them."
Edna Newman

☐ Why is one salesperson better than another salesperson?

A mediocre salesperson tells. A good salesperson explains. A superior salesperson demonstrates. A great salesperson inspires the buyers to see the benefits as their own.

Sometimes sales can be increased by adding a new product that your existing customers want. For example, in 1971, Avon entered the jewelry business and in less than two years became the largest distributor of fashion jewelry in the world.

☐ To get customers to buy, we have to get them in the mood.

A woman flashing a rather large diamond on her hand told some friends it was her "mood ring." She said, "I had to work like hell to get my husband in the mood to buy it."

☐ Don't overpromise to make a sale.

The new automobile salesman had just joined the agency and had just completed his first transaction. He left the customer in the showroom and cornered his boss.

Salesman: "Look, I gave this customer all of our company offers; I gave him double the book value on his old car, the free new mink coat, the diamond bracelet, and the fifty-dollar-a-week income for four months."

Manager: "We do offer all those things, so what's your trouble?"

Salesman: "He expects a new car, too."

☐ You can increase sales with a sample for the customer to see.

A salesman arrived at a sales fair and the porter asked him how many boxes he had.

Salesman: "I use no boxes."

Porter: "Oh, I thought you were a salesman."

Salesman: "I am. But I sell brains, understand? I sell brains."

Porter: "Well, excuse me, but you're the first traveling man I've seen that isn't carrying any samples."

☐ Good salespeople do not sell the product. They sell the benefits of having the product.

Last year, Americans bought twenty million ¼ inch drills. Not one of them wanted a drill. What they really wanted were ¼ inch holes. But they had to buy the drills to get the holes.

☐ In sales, you must make the prospect remember you.

Victor Kiam, in his book *Going for It!*, tells of the two greatest salesmen he ever knew. Each had an effective gimmick.

John Henry James was 6 feet 6 inches and weighed 245 pounds. He was an expensive dresser who made his rounds in a chauffeur-driven limousine. At each stop, the chauffeur would leap from the car and roll out a red carpet. Then he would enter the store and announce, "Ladies and gentlemen, Mr. John Henry James has arrived!" James would enter, open his sample case, and croon, "I do believe we're going to do some business today." Nine times out of ten he was right.

The second superseller—Bob Englud—wore a raccoon fur coat year round. Kiam asked him why. Englud said, "So you think this is a fur coat, huh? Let me tell you, it's not that at all."

The coat was his icebreaker, his trademark. With it, Englud never had to worry about how to open conversations with clients, and he never had to explain who he was and what he wanted to talk about. When they saw the coat, they were ready for business.

☐ Spreading your sales organization too thin can reduce cost, but it can also reduce sales.

Alloy Rods, spun off from Allegheny International, is the leading U.S. manufacturer of high-quality welding rod, wire, and other welding products.

Its primary products are high-volume, low-value items sold primarily for original equipment manufacturers' use. Alloy Rods also has a line of low-volume, high-value products, which were selling poorly. Sales of these products eroded over eight years from $6 million to $2 million annually. To solve this problem, a separate sales organization was established. Within two years, sales climbed back to $6 million.

☐ Make sure the sales effort supports your business, not the other way around.

Over a ten-year period, Allegheny Ludlum slowly closed down three-quarters of its sales offices, which were once located in important markets. With each closure, sales increased, which is the opposite of most marketing wisdom. This successful change worked because Allegheny Ludlum, a leading producer of stainless steel, started selling standardized products to established customers. It cut costs and increased profits.

☐ Don't just make a sale—make a client.

According to the December 1988 issue of *Success* magazine, Jim Matteson, a New York regional sales director of Data General, is a believer of using seminars to increase sales.

Using seminars, he has boosted the number of contacts his reps make by 50 percent, and sales have gone up accordingly.

☐ Selling is a relationship, and you build relationships systematically, not with a shotgun approach.

☐ Future sales can be increased by properly taking care of today's customers.

A number of years ago, a successful newsletter noticed that their once high profitability was being threatened by a low renewal rate. In an effort to recapture old subscribers, the company instituted an aggressive sales campaign to rebuild their once high subscription rate. Once they did, they noticed that profits were lower than before. After analyzing the problem, they realized that the cost of getting a lapsed subscriber to come aboard again was more than they made from the renewal.

The company shifted their focus from getting new subscribers to keeping the old ones. Eventually the publisher was back to the old high level of profits.

☐ Rising sales figures aren't always positive.

An oil equipment supply company reported a sales increase year after year. Most of the sales were going to repairing old equipment, and the purchase of new equipment was going to the competitors. Eventually the company went out of business.

☐ More important than rising sales is where the sales are coming from.

□ Think of the world without salespeople.

The following was taken from John Hancock Mutual Life:

The salesperson sells cars, tractors, radios, televisions, iceboxes and movies, health and leisure, ambition and fulfillment.

The salesperson is America's emissary of abundance, Mr. and Mrs. High-Standard-of-Living in person.

They ring the billion doorbells and enrich a billion lives. Without them there'd be no American ships at sea, no busy factories, no sixty million jobs.

For the great American salesperson is the great American civilizer, and everywhere they go they leave people better off.

SECRETARIES

There was the Minneapolis secretary who came to work early because her boss had been complaining about her punctuation.

A secretary said: "I sure feel like telling the boss where to get off again."
"What do you mean—again?"
"I felt like it yesterday, too."

Boss: "Do you have a good reason to be late?"
Secretary: "I certainly have, it makes the day seem shorter."

Ideas to drive your boss batty:
A secretary suggested: "Leave that important message he's been waiting for on his desk—in shorthand," or, "Tell your boss, just as he is getting ready to leave for vacation, that you have set up an appointment with an Internal Revenue Service agent to audit his tax returns on the day he returns."

□ Bosses can't survive without a good secretary.

Secretary, taking dictation, to boss: "Do you want the grammatical errors in or out?"

The manager asked his new secretary, "Why don't you ever answer the telephone?"
"Why should I? Nine times out of ten, it's for you."

The Secretary's Day
A.M.
"He hasn't come in yet."
"I expect him in any minute."
"He just sent word he'd be a little late."
"He's been in, but he went out again."
"He's gone to lunch."

P.M.

"I expect him in any minute."
"He hasn't come back yet. Can I take a message?"
"He's somewhere in the building. His hat is here."
"Yes, he was in, but he went out again."
"I don't know whether he'll be back or not."
"No, he's gone for the day."

SELLING

☐ The buyer beware.

Don't take any wooden nickels.

☐ Don't lose a sale by talking too much.

Don't let your tongue cut your throat.

☐ To sell your ideas, you must first get your listener's attention.

A handyman looking for jobs ran this ad in a newspaper: "I can fix anything your husband can. And I'll do it now."

☐ Sometimes it takes time for a new product to develop a following.

Not every customer will buy. Don't let it get to you. If you have a good product, someday they will come around. Coca-Cola Company sold just four hundred Cokes in its first year. McGraw-Hill said that it takes an average of 5.5 visits before a customer says "yes" to a major sale.

☐ Sell the benefit, not the feature.

People don't buy a newspaper. They buy news.

What are you selling? For example, a microwave oven manufacturer doesn't just compete with other manufacturers of microwave ovens for the consumer dollar. It competes with anybody who is trying to find an easier way for the housewife to cook meals.

"Nothing ever happens until somebody sells something."
Red Motley

☐ Sell benefits and you'll sell the product.

"Don't talk machines, talk the prospect's business."
John Henry Patterson, founder, National Cash Register

☐ It's easier to sell to someone who sells to someone else.

"It is always best to sell your product to the jobber because he will, in turn, dispose of it to the retailer."
John North Willys

☐ Figure out a way to get the prospect to call you.

"The chances of selling to a customer are a great deal better if he calls you than if you call him."

William Durr, vice president, Teknetron Infoswitch

☐ We lose sales because we don't ask for the order.

Henry Ford was once asked by an insurance agent whom he had known for many years why he never got any of Ford's business.

Ford replied, "You never asked me."

☐ What are you selling?

"In the factory we make cosmetics, but in my stores we sell hope."

Charles Revson, founder, Revlon Cosmetics

☐ People buy for their reasons, not for ours.

"It is unwise to do unto others as you would have them do unto you. Their tastes may not be the same."

George Bernard Shaw

"Don't oversell. If you do, it's like knocking on a turtle shell trying to get him to stick his head out."

David Crawley

☐ Offer an incentive to buy.

Things are so bad, our local funeral parlor is running a one-cent sale. For an extra penny, you can take a friend.

☐ Successful salespeople never quit selling.

Take the example of Irene Buckley who began selling insurance in the 1930s. She still hasn't stopped. She turned ninety-five recently.

She was slowed up a little one January when she fell and broke a bone in her upper arm. She did go to the doctor's—and while she was there, sold him a $50,000 life insurance policy.

☐ Successful salespeople never quit prospecting.

The number one Century 21 real estate broker in the United States is a Rumanian emigrant named Nicholas Barsan. Every four days, he sells a house. One-third of his commissions come from repeat customers. He still knocks on doors asking homeowners if they are ready to sell.

☐ It pays to stay in touch with your customers.

A florist celebrating his one hundredth year in business, when asked why he was successful, responded, "I have one employee responsible to send out reminders on who-sent-what-to-whom last year at this time and many repeat orders are generated by this simple call."

☐ Some people can sell and some can't.

A man goes with a shop owner into his store basement. He noticed that the walls were lined with sacks of salt. He asked, "You must sell lots of salt."

The shop owner said, "Mister, I couldn't sell a pinch of salt, but the man who sells me salt—can he sell salt!"

☐ You have to find the buyer's hot button.

When former New York Mayor Ed Koch was recuperating from a heart attack, Mother Teresa came to visit him. He invited her in and offered her some freshly made chocolate chip cookies. She refused, saying, "In India when people offer you something in their home, you never take it because they are being kind, and in many cases will starve if you eat their food."

Mayor Koch said: "But Mother, these are the greatest chocolate chip cookies in the world."

Mother Teresa said: "Wrap them up."

☐ The key to selling is to overcome objections.

Joe McGuire knew how to sell. When he was selling Remington Rand electric typewriters in a market dominated by IBM and others, Joe had convinced himself that the Remington Electric was the best typewriter on the market. Whenever a prospect made a comment about his typewriter, he would assume they were praising it. He didn't pretend they were praising it, he believed they were praising it because he believed it to be the best typewriter on the market. He had brainwashed himself to believe that because he knew that every salesman had to learn to sell himself first.

If a secretary would comment, "Gosh, that's a big typewriter," Joe would comment, "I knew you'd like that it's heavy duty and big enough to handle all of your work."

When a prospect would ask how much it cost, Joe would answer, "That's the best part about it—only $635." Some prospects were surprised and would respond, "$635?!" At that time, a manual typewriter cost about half that. But Joe would answer, "I knew you'd be surprised. Most people would expect it to cost a good deal more than that." Joe believed that, and that's why his customers began to see it as a real bargain.

☐ The success of any salesperson is not what the customer believes, but what we believe.

☐ It takes creativity to see some prospects.

Sales consultant Steve Miller said that there were times you had to be creative to get a much needed appointment. He said that once he was about to give up getting in to see one prospect until he went to the airport. He saw the flight insurance machine and took out a policy on his life, making the elusive prospect his beneficiary. He mailed the policy to the potential client with a note that said, "I'm thinking about you." The prospect called him, and he got the appointment.

☐ You'll sell more if you sell what people already want, not what they need.

I overheard a conversation in a restaurant. The waitress was trying to get the customer to try the restaurant's specialty—fried okra. They went on and on, recommending and resisting. Personally, I like fried okra but this story reminds me that you can't get people to believe what they resolutely resist believing.

☐ You can't get a customer to buy something they're determined they don't want.

☐ When it comes to selling, nothing can replace person-to-person contact with the customer.

A few years ago, Blaw Know Food & Chemical Equipment Company had a relatively large sales organization that sold highly engineered products that customers purchased on an infrequent basis. In an effort to lower the cost per sale, their sales reps were prevented from traveling. In a typical month, company airline travel cost was less than $1,000. When sales dropped, the nontravel policy was reversed. Salespeople were ordered to be on the road at least three days a week. Almost immediately the level of incoming orders increased.

It's okay to review travel and entertainment cost, but not at the expense of sales.

☐ To be successful at selling, you have to make the customer like you. People like to do business with people they feel comfortable with.

Burt Reynolds said that the reason why some actors become successful in movies is that the camera likes them. Reynolds said that every day he works in front of a camera, he starts the day off going up to the camera and saying, "I love you. Like me today. Please, like me today."

We need to remember that the customer is like the camera. Make the buyer like you.

☐ Get the customer to say yes to something and then add on to it.

Years ago Mike Nichols and Elaine May had a classic comic routine. A widow (Elaine May) was arranging a funeral for her husband. The funeral director (Mike Nichols) told the grieving widow that he had a $5,000 funeral at the top and a $400 at the bottom. The widow chose the $400 funeral. Nichols congratulated her on the choice and asked, "Do you plan to do the embalming yourself?"

Before she left, she'd spent much more than the $5,000.

☐ You can persuade others to buy if they like you.

Robert B. Cialdini, in his book *Influence: The New Psychology of Modern Persuasion,* said that people often buy because they like the salesperson.

"Let's say you have spent about half an hour with a used-car salesman.

Do you feel as though you like him? If the answer is yes, watch out. You are being manipulated. The question is whether the price on the car is a good deal."

This technique explains the success of such products as Tupperware, Avon, and Mary Kay. The seller of these products is likely to be a friend, or at least an acquaintance.

☐ When selling, explain the benefit to the prospect.

When Michael Faraday invented the first electric motor, he wanted the interest and backing of the British prime minister William Gladstone. So Faraday took the crude model—a little wire revolving around a magnet—and showed it to the statesman. Gladstone, obviously not interested, asked: "What good is it?"

Faraday said, "Someday, you will be able to tax it."

☐ You will sell more if you sell benefits, not features.

Don't sell me books, sell me knowledge.
Don't sell me insurance, sell peace of mind and a secure future for my family.
Don't sell me a house, sell me comfort and pride of ownership.
Don't sell me clothes, sell style, attractiveness, and a sharper image.
Don't sell me a computer, sell me the time saved.

In short, don't sell me things. Sell me ideas, feelings, happiness, and other things I'm interested in.

☐ It's easier to sell a product you love than one you just know about.

Harry Winston, the famous New York diamond dealer, called a wealthy diamond collector about a new diamond he might want to add to his collection. The collector flew to New York, and one of Winston's salesman showed him the diamond. The salesman told the potential buyer about all the technical features of the expensive diamond. The customer said, "It's a beautiful stone but not exactly what I want."

When the customer was leaving the store, Winston himself decided to show him the diamond. When he finished explaining it, the man bought it. When he was asked why he decided to buy now instead of when the salesman offered it, he replied, "Your salesman knows diamonds, but you love them."

☐ Don't talk yourself out of a sale.

Mark Twain once told of the time he listened to a missionary give a sermon. Twain was terribly impressed with his religious zeal. He had real enthusiasm for his message. In fact, Twain was so impressed he decided to contribute five dollars when the collection plate was passed. Instead of stopping, the preacher kept going and going. When he finally quit, Twain was so mad that instead of making a donation he took out a dime.

☐ SERVICE

"Service is often the art of making good on somebody else's mistake."
Cavett Robert

☐ Service is your customers knowing they can depend on you.

Federal Express was founded on dependability. Their motto was to guarantee to "absolutely, positively" get your package there by 10:30 the next morning.

"The trouble with a great many of us in the business world is that we are thinking hardest of all about the dollar we want to make. Now that is the wrong idea from the start. I'll tell you the man who has the idea of service in his business will never need to worry about profits. The money is bound to come. This idea of service in business is the biggest guarantee of success that any man can have."

Henry Ford

"I began slowly to discover that progress, whether of the individual or of a business, depends principally upon giving the largest quality of service for the dollar."

Sebastian S. Kresge, founder, Kresge

☐ Starting a service is less costly than making a product.

"I would say a young man has a better chance if he has an idea for a service. He won't require any machinery to execute his idea."
William P. Lear, Sr.

☐ Service is rewarding.

"The service business is very rewarding. It makes a big contribution to society."

Bill Marriott, Sr.

☐ SMALL BUSINESS

☐ Sometimes small is better.

"Smallness induces manageability and, above, all, commitment."
Mandy Marsh

Aristotle said that young people " . . . have exalted notions because they have not yet been humbled by life or learned its necessary limitations."

☐ Small businesses offer the excitement of youth. Being small, they have the ability to hold exalted notions for employers.

At some point, every small business stood on the brink of disaster. The total sales volume for Coca-Cola was $55 its first year of business.

☐ The smaller a business, the faster they must react.

"Small companies will get killed if they don't adapt. They may even have to change faster, because they don't have the resources to survive otherwise."
Allen A. Kennedy

☐ It's harder today to succeed as a small business.

If you're a small business wondering where all the money goes, be advised that you spend about $4,200 a year in expenses created by government regulation. This means filling out all the forms Washington and state governments require if you want to keep your doors open to customers.

☐ Small businesses offer an environment for new product development.

While 85 percent of all research and development is funded by the top 500 American corporations, more than two-thirds of the really major discoveries have come from individuals and small businesses. Examples: the Apple computer, Nike runners, and, from the University of British Columbia, the rechargeable battery and light pipe.

SOCIAL RESPONSIBILITY

☐ It's our responsibility to share what we have.

"We make a living by what we get. We make a life by what we give."
Anonymous

"The world is a fine place and worth fighting for."
Ernest Hemingway

☐ Popular positions aren't always the right position.

"As long as the world shall last there will be wrongs, and if no man (or woman) objected and no man (or woman) rebelled, those wrongs would last forever."
Clarence Darrow

☐ Businesses owe something back to their community.

Many of the major corporations located in the St. Paul–Minneapolis area tithe to the community. They generously support the arts, symphony, and museum.

"Research shows that generous giving can increase a firm's reputation for social responsibility and even for being a well-run business, factors that can enhance a company's longer-term market position."
Michael Useem, The Loss of Culture

"A recent survey underwritten by Chivas Regal to determine the giving and volunteering levels of working Americans concluded that business and corporations that encourage their employees to volunteer and contribute will benefit if they, themselves, have a reputation for social responsibility. That study revealed a relationship between job satisfaction and the feeling of 'doing good' in the world."

Eugene C. Dorsey, chairman, Gannett Foundation

"Corporations have a responsibility to make a positive contribution to the world."

An Wang, founder, Wang Laboratories

Berkshire Hathaway each year tells stockholders how much the company will contribute to charity and asks them to designate a cause of their choice. One year the company contributed $2 a share.

"The test of our progress is not whether we add more to the abundance of those who have much; it is whether we provide enough for those who have too little."

Franklin D. Roosevelt

"We must listen to public opinion. We must shed our notion that we can counter environmental trends with scientific debate. We must accept that perception and emotion play a large role in shaping society's attitudes. Therefore, we must become better at listening . . . and then better at educating."

Constantine S. Nicandros, president, Conoco

"We have to prove we are willing and able to take more initiative to anticipate environmental problems, plan for their solutions, and share them with society before others demand punitive legislation that prescribes inefficient remedies."

Constantine S. Nicandros, president, Conoco

☐ We all have a responsibility to society.

Ralph Waldo Emerson visited Henry David Thoreau in jail. Thoreau was serving a sentence for not paying his taxes. Emerson said, "What in heaven's name are you doing in jail?"

Thoreau said, "What are you doing out of it?"

☐ We need to sacrifice for what we believe in.

☐ Great businesses and business leaders have a tradition of social responsibility.

Andrew Carnegie preached for and financed the free public library.

Julius Rosenwald, who headed Sears Roebuck, fathered the country farm-agent system and adopted the infant 4-H Clubs.

J. Irwin Miller of Cummins Engine Company based in Columbus, Indiana, has created a vibrant community with the use of corporate funds.

"All of us are proud of our companies. But the good of our entire society here in the U.S. transcends that of any single corporation. The moral order of the world transcends any single nation-state. And you can't be a good businessman—or good doctor or lawyer or engineer—without a just understanding of the place of business in the greater scheme of things.

"Within the past year we've had an incandescent example of a group of men who understood this fact: who saw life steadily, saw it whole, and saw it in a hierarchy—the men who drafted the constitution in Philadelphia 200 years ago.

"What do we remember the oldest of those men—Benjamin Franklin—for? Not for his vigorous advice on how to get up early in the morning, drive a business, make a profit, and win success in the marketplace, though he did all these things with gusto throughout a long life. We remember him and the other men in Philadelphia—and those who signed the Declaration of Independence—because, when it came to the crunch, they did not see winning or self-advancement or even life itself as the only thing. To something greater than themselves—to a new nation 'conceived in liberty and dedicated to the proposition that all men are created equal'—to that concept they pledged all subordinate things—'their lives, their fortunes, and their sacred honor.' And we should never forget their example."

M. John Akers, chairman, IBM

■ SPEECH (Closing)

Comedian George Jessel once advised speakers that "if you haven't struck oil in your first three minutes, stop boring." I'm long past that deadline, and I don't see any oil hereabouts, so good night.

Nowhere have the opportunities been greater than they are in the world today. The challenge to us is to step up the pace of applying today's ideas to tomorrow. We can do this. There is an old saying: "Man can achieve what his mind can perceive."

The time is now, and the person is you.

To know what it takes for us to succeed, listen to the words of basketball great, Larry Bird: "I think hard work is what got me here. I didn't get all the stuff I can do by sitting around. I worked hard for it. I don't think that once you get to one level, you can relax. You've got to keep going and pushing to get to that next level. And that's what I try to do. I feel I owe it to the fans and the Boston Celtics to be the best I can possibly be year after year, and that's why I keep working."

□ We must keep working, and we too will be great.

I'm going to quit before I end up like the medieval knight who returned home to his castle in very poor shape.

He was bruised and battered. His armour was dented in a dozen places, and he was practically falling off his horse. When the king came out to greet him, he asked the knight what on earth had happened to him!

The knight said, "My lord, I merely went out to talk to your enemies in the West."

The king said, "I don't have any enemies in the West!"

The knight said, "Well, now you do."

I'm going to sit down before I make any more enemies.

A high goal can be achieved if we recognize the heights that we can attain. Let me close with the words from a folk song:

"I have flown to star-stained heights on bent and battered wings in search of mythical kings sure that everything of worth is in the sky and not the earth. And I have never learned to make my way down, down, down where the iguanas play."

You and I spend enough time with the iguanas. There are star-stained heights to be attained, if we will reach for them. Now is the time to reach.

☐ Stick with what you know.

Alfred Bloomingdale owned a very successful store but wanted to try his talents at producing a Broadway play. One play after another flopped, and finally one of his friends told him: "Al, close the play and keep the store open at night."

Bloomingdale's grew into being one of America's best-known stores because Alfred Bloomingdale stayed with what he did best. We know what we do best—let's do it.

I want to close now and tell you a superstition about the ocean that one wave comes along greater than the others that came before it. It's called the Ninth Wave. There is no greater force. It's the power of the sea and the wind working together. To catch the Ninth Wave at the right time requires a special skill of timing. Today we see such a powerful wave in our future. Our own Ninth Wave, bringing with it significant change. To benefit from this wave, we must prepare now so that when it's our turn to mount it, we will be able to respond—to catch the mighty Ninth with the best that is in us and ride it all the way to the top.

I once heard a story about a traveler who visited an old Greek monastery that was perched high on a steep mountain. The only way to reach the monastery was in a rope basket.

The traveler got into the basket, and just as he was about to be taken up the steep cliff wall, he noticed that the rope lifting the basket was frayed.

He asked the monk, "How often is the rope replaced?"

Monk: "Every time it breaks."
I'm going to quit before the rope breaks.

Some years after World War II, Winston Churchill was speaking to a group of people seated in a room much like this one. The person who introduced him made a good-natured reference to Churchill's well-known fondness for alcoholic beverages.
He said: "If all the spirits Sir Winston had consumed were poured into this room, they'd reach up to here"—and he drew an imaginary line on the wall some six or seven feet from the floor. When Sir Winston reached the podium, he looked at the imaginary line and glanced up to the ceiling. He then said, "Ah, so much to be done and so little time in which to do it."
There is so much to be done and so little time to do it. We can do what needs to be done because we are committed to our goals.

SPEECH (Opening)

Asking me to speak to you is like the dog walking on its hind legs: It isn't done well, but you're surprised to see it done at all.

"Thank you for that kind introduction. It proves once again that the truth can be likened to a rubber band. That is, if you can't stretch it a little, it isn't very useful."

L. G. Rawl

When Winston Churchill was asked why he had notes during a speech but seldom looked at them, he said, "I carry fire insurance, but I don't expect my house to burn down."

Sometimes I feel like Groucho Marx who said, "Before I speak, I have something important to say."

Being asked to speak reminds me of the minister who told his congregation: "This morning I'm going to speak about the relationship between fact and faith. It's a fact that you are sitting here in the church. It's also a fact that I'm standing here speaking. But it is faith that makes me believe that you might be listening to what I have to say."

Speaking before your peers: Being asked to speak to you is like being the javelin competitor who won the toss of the coin and elected to receive.

That introduction is better than the one a friend got one time. He was guest speaker at a dinner meeting of engineers prepared to sit through the usual longwinded introduction. But before he even had time to collect his thoughts, he was being introduced. The toastmaster announced: "You all know we invited Herb Broker up here to talk to us. He's here, and he's going to."

I hope you will listen to the message and not the messenger.

Charles H. Townes, who won a Nobel Prize for his work in laser technology, opened a talk with a disclaimer: "It's like the beaver told the rabbit as they stared up at the immense wall of Hoover Dam, 'No, I didn't actually build it myself. But it was based on an idea of mine.' "

A speech instructor once advised me that an after-dinner speech should always be short. He said:

Be accurate!
Be brief!
And then be seated!

Ladies and gentlemen, I promise you that I shall be as brief as possible— no matter how long it takes me.

Thank you, Bill. Before the meeting, I thought I heard Bill say to someone that he likes to start off each program with a joke—then he introduced me!

Coming here today, my wife offered me some sage advice. She said, "Don't try to be charming, witty, or intellectual. Just be yourself."

I've always heard that the secret to a good speech is to talk about something that interests the audience.

A Notre Dame football coach was once mistakenly invited to a lecture on campus of SMU. The only thing he knew anything about was football, and it ultimately dawned on him that maybe SMU people didn't want to be lectured on that subject by a Notre Dame speaker. So he went to his dean and asked what he should talk about and he was told, "Pick something noncontroversial—like our religion."

"I can live a month on a good compliment. After that introduction, I can live forever."

Mark Twain

I don't want to be like the successful businessman, invited to deliver the commencement address at a school elected to speak on "How to Succeed." As he entered the door leading to the auditorium stage, he noticed the word *Push* printed in bold letters on it. He thought that would be a good theme for his speech. When he hit the high point of his speech, he said, "I can sum up my message in one word," and he pointed to the door and the students started laughing. Puzzled, the speaker looked at the door. Printed on the inside was the word *Pull.*

When *push* comes to *pull,* I hope my message is clear.

A speaker referring to how he got to be the speaker: "I was asked if I believed in the U.S. Constitution, and I said yes. Then I was asked if I believed in the Bill of Rights, and again I said yes. Then I was asked if I believed in the First Amendment which guarantees free speech, and I replied yes.

He said, "Fine, I want you to come give us a free speech."

That generous introduction reminds me of the man who raised his head up out of the grave on Judgment Day and read the flowing words on his headstone. He said, "Either somebody is a terrible liar, or I'm in the wrong hole."

After that introduction, I'm either the wrong speaker or you are the wrong audience.

Three corporate executives were trying to define the word *fame.*

One said, "Fame is getting invited to the White House to see the president."

The second one said, "Fame is being invited to the White House and while you are visiting the phone rings and he doesn't answer it."

The third executive said, "You're both wrong. Fame is being invited to the White House to visit with the president when his Hot Line rings. He answers it, listens a minute, and then says, 'Here, it's for you!' "

Being asked to speak today is like being in the White House and the call's for me.

Thank you for the generous introduction.

Sometimes I feel like the man who was introduced as a gifted business-man who made a million dollars in Texas oil."

When this speaker rose, he was a bit embarrassed. He said, "The facts he reported were essentially correct but it wasn't oil . . . it was coal, and it wasn't Texas . . . it was California, and it wasn't a million . . . it was only a hundred thousand. Also, it wasn't me . . . it was my brother, and he didn't make it . . . he lost it."

Even though I'm not as good as that introduction implies, I am glad to be here.

A young minister was pacing the floor nervously on the night before he was to preach his first sermon. He told his wife, "I am not worthy of this sacred trust. I am being very presumptuous to think I can point people to a better life."

She answered, "But, darling, remember you are only going to tell about God, not be God."

I hope I don't become like the statistician talking to a Parent-Teacher Association. He was introduced to explain changes in the grading of exams. He began, "Good evening, ladies and gentlemen. The main point to grasp is that not all exams are marked out of 100. In one, the passing mark may be 398 out of 800, in another 170 out of 350.

"To make it easier, we assume that the 800 and 350 both become 100 and that the 398 and 170 both become 50."

After five minutes of this, a hand went up and a parent asked, "Could you explain that bit again?"

The statistician asked, "Which bit do you mean?"

"The bit after 'Good evening, ladies and gentlemen.' "

I hope when I finish I don't have to explain what I said.

An economist was asked to talk to a group of businesspeople about the recession. She tacked up a big sheet of white paper. Then she made a black spot on the paper with her pencil and asked a man in the front row what he saw. The man replied promptly, "A black spot."

The speaker asked every person the same question, and each replied, "A black spot."

With calm and deliberate emphasis, the speaker said, "Yes, there is a little black spot, but none of you mentioned the big sheet of white paper. And that's my speech."

President Eisenhower once admitted to the National Press Club audience that he was not a great speaker.

He once said, "It reminds me of my boyhood days on a Kansas farm. An old farmer had a cow that we wanted to buy. We went over to visit the farmer and asked him about the cow's pedigree.

"The old farmer didn't know what pedigree meant, so we asked him about the cow's butterfat production. He told us he didn't have any idea what it was. Finally we asked him if he knew how many pounds of milk the cow produced each year.

"The farmer said, 'I don't know. But she's an honest cow, and she'll give you all the milk she has.' "

Ike said, "I'm like the cow, I'll give you everything I have."

I don't know if this speech is everything you need, but it's going to give you all I have.

I hope that when I'm finished speaking, I don't experience what Adlai Stevenson did the time he spoke at a small college. When the speech was over, a young man approached him and said, "Mr. Stevenson, that was a wonderful speech—absolutely superfluous."

Stevenson was taken aback but graciously replied, "Thank you. I'm glad you liked it. I intend to have it published posthumously."

The student replied, "Great. The sooner the better."

I hope I say something good and original today. Every speaker dreads the experience I had recently. I was speaking to a group and afterward a member of the audience sent me up a note.

It read: "Dear Mr. [name], your speech was both good and original. Unfortunately, the parts that were good weren't original, and the parts that were original weren't any good."

Being asked to speak reminds me of the experience when Henry Luce, founder of Time Inc. was asked to speak at Harvard. Harvard's president, Laurence Lowell, an aristocratic critic of American society, introduced Luce. As Luce rose to speak, he told Lowell, "Well, I suppose Harvard is still teaching its students that all businessmen are fools."

Lowell replied, "No, Mr. Luce, that's why we invited you here, so they can find out for themselves."

Speaking to you today, I'm violating one of the three pieces of immortal advice from Winston Churchill, who said: "Never try to walk up a wall that's leaning towards you. Never try to kiss a person that's leaning away from you. And never speak to a group that knows more about a subject than you do."

◻ STRESS

A diamond is a chunk of coal that made good under pressure.

☐ Layoffs or threats of layoffs can increase employee stress.

In the late 1960s when Boeing was reducing its work force, there was a saying going around Seattle: "An optimist who works at Boeing brings his lunch. A pessimist leaves his car running."

"Stress can be caused by the parental voice saying, 'Succeed or no one will love you, for there is no room for failure in this world.' "

Dr. Hilary C. Olson

"The American people are so tense that it is impossible to put them to sleep—even with a sermon."

Norman Vincent Peale

"Former President Eisenhower explained his 1955 heart attack on the golf course in terms of tension. He told an interviewer that he received notice of a telephone call on the fourth hole, and drove back to the clubhouse in his cart. Then he learned that the State Department had been trying to reach him but would not be ready to talk for about an hour.

"So he returned to his game. A few holes later he received notice of another urgent call. He discovered, when he got back to the clubhouse a second time, that it was still the first call. He returned again to his game.

"Some time later he returned to the clubhouse and completed the call. Then he started on the second nine, only to be interrupted by still another call. This was from someone who did not know that he had already completed the business involved.

"He said, 'I always had an uncertain temper, and by this time it had gotten completely out of control. One doctor said that he'd never seen me in such a state—and that's the reason I had the heart attack. So I've never gotten angry again.'"

Mortimer R. Feinberg, Effective Psychology for Managers

☐ Stress can be improved by simplifying a job.

"Betty Mullins, a top-level secretary for an insurance firm, was assigned the responsibility of getting out a monthly mailing of personalized sales letters. She became discouraged because the job was never completed on schedule. Originally, three stenographers were each assigned parts of the job to be completed during a three-day period. Because of other unexpected 'crisis' jobs, at least one of the three stenographers always failed to complete her part of the job on time.

"Betty revised the procedure by concentrating the entire efforts of two stenographers on the job, leaving the third stenographer to the 'crisis' jobs. Stenographer 1 set up the letter and envelopes on the automatic typewriter while Stenographer 2 duplicated the enclosures, folded and stuffed the letters and enclosures, and sealed the envelopes. With no interruptions, Stenographers 1 and 2 were able to finish the work in one day. From then on, the mailing went out on schedule, and two workdays were saved."

Genevieve Smith, Genevieve Smith's Deluxe Handbook
for the Executive Secretary

☐ Stress can be caused by having to make decisions.

"Assume you are an individual torn between purchasing one of two or three medium-sized cars. On a Saturday, you rush first to the Ford dealership and then across the street to the Chevy dealership and eventually down the street to the Plymouth dealership. Because you are a value-conscious buyer, you compare the features and prices of each car but after the comparison you are still undecided on the best value. Finally, as the Saturday wears on, and your need for a car increases, you make a commitment with one of the three car dealers (the one you trust). For you it was a difficult decision."

Joseph R. Mancuso, How to Prepare and Present a Business Plan

Columnist Sydney Harris shared the story of a friend who was treated very gruffly by a vendor with whom he had been most cordial. Harris expressed surprise at his friend's pleasant response when treated with such rudeness.

The friend replied kindly, "Why should I let his actions determine my behavior?"

This man would undoubtedly live a long, relatively stress-free life, because he had placed the focus of control directly inside himself, instead of reacting as if others and external events caused him to think, feel, and act in certain ways.

☐ You can control stress by not taking your work home.

"Marshall Rinker Sr., president of Rinker Materials Corp., was on a golfing vacation when a subordinate telephoned. Rinker returned the call from the clubhouse at the end of the ninth hole. He listened carefully as the subordinate explained the sticky situation. Then Rinker asked one question: 'Are the others worrying?'

"The subordinate said: 'They certainly are.'

"Rinker responded in a relaxed tone, 'That's fine. If they're worrying, then I can go back to my golf. I'll be in the office next week, and then I'll worry while they play.' "
Mortimer R. Feinberg, Effective Psychology for Managers

▮ SUCCESS

☐ You get what you deserve.

"No one is either rich or poor who has not helped himself to be so."
German proverb

☐ You need help to become successful.

"Few people are successful unless a lot of other people want them to be."
Charlie Brower

"The virtue you would like to have, assume it as already yours, appropriate it, enter into the part and live the character just as the great actor is absorbed in the character of the part he plays."
Ralph Waldo Emerson

"Let us be thankful for fools. But for them the rest of us could not succeed."
Mark Twain

"Eighty percent of success is showing up."
Woody Allen

The key to success is setting aside eight hours a day for work and eight hours for sleep and making sure they're not the same hours.

John D. Rockefeller, Jr., was once asked for the secret of success. Rockefeller thought for a minute, then replied: "Get up early, work late—and strike oil."

☐ Success is a slow process.

"Grain by grain—a loaf; stone upon stone—a palace."

George Bernard Shaw

☐ You become the people you are around.

"Who keeps company with a wolf will learn to howl."

Henry Cannon

☐ There is no road to success unless it's just doing what needs to be done.

For every person who climbs the ladder of success, there are a dozen waiting for the elevator.

Kathy Griffith

"To succeed, jump as quickly at opportunities as you do at conclusions."

Benjamin Franklin

☐ Success is timing.

"I was in the right place at the right time and nobody ever knew any better."

Durward Kirby

"Many a man owes his success to his first wife and his second wife to his success."

Red Buttons

"Success has ruined many a man."

Benjamin Franklin

"Why are there so many best-sellers about how to dress or plan or eat for success—and so few on how to work for it?"

Arch Napier

☐ Success stops when you do.

"You'll die if you sit on your laurels."

Pindaros Roy Vagelos, president, Merck Pharmaceuticals

"To be a success in business, be daring, be first, be different."

Henry Marchant

"If you wish success in life, make perseverance your bosom friend, experience your wise counselor, caution your elder brother, and hope your guiding genius."

Joseph Addison

You may recall the television commercials for Eastern Airlines several years ago, in which the closing line was, "We have to earn our wings every day."

We also have to earn the right to be in business every day.

☐ Success often goes to the steady player.

"A man who makes a big splash may be a man who has gone overboard."
Parkes Robinson

"Success is a journey, not a destination."

Ben Sweetland

"Never tell anyone what you are going to do till you've done it."
Cornelius Vanderbilt

You can't get too much of success. To quote Mae West, "Too much of a good thing is wonderful."

☐ Don't expect success to come overnight.

Ray Kroc, who built McDonald's Corporation from a handful of hamburger stands into the world's largest food chain, didn't sell his first hamburger until age fifty-two.

☐ Success breeds success.

"One you've had a good opening night, you can't wait to do the next night. An initial success causes you to be more confident and pleased with yourself the next time around."

Ed McMahon

"There is a fine line between success and failure.

"In baseball, the difference between a .350 hitter and a .250 hitter is only a quarter-inch up or down on the bat."
Mortimer R. Feinberg, Effective Psychology for Managers

☐ Even though there is a small difference in performance, it can mean as much as a million dollars a year to be a .350 hitter instead of a .250 hitter.

"Success comes when you take responsibility for yourself.

"Responsibility, points out Joe Crail, president of Coast Federal Savings and Loan Association, is 'the feeling that the individual is personally responsible for the success of all activities with which he is associated. It is the urge to do or get done what ought to be done. Believing in Santa Claus, luck, a minister, a superior, or anyone else to solve one's problem is a sign of immaturity. Believing in personal responsibility in one's own life is necessary for security and happiness.' "
Mortimer R. Feinberg, Effective Psychology for Managers

"You have removed most of the roadblocks to success when you have learned the difference between movement and direction."
Joe L. Griffith

"It's not enough that we should succeed, but our friends must fail as well."

La Rochefoucauld

"Success isn't how far you got, but the distance you traveled from where you started."

Peter Frame

"People can make or break a company. Management can do whatever it wants with the banks and borrowing and manipulating and everything else. If the spirit of the people isn't in everything they do, it's going to fail."

Vic Barouh, founder, Barouh-Eaton Allen

"So many smart people stop their own success. There is a strong element of luck in both success and failure, but I believe there are no 'secrets' to success. People fail quite often because they shoot themselves in the foot. If they go a long time without shooting themselves, others begin calling them a genius."

An Wang, founder, Wang Laboratories

☐ You can't change what you have, so make the best of it.

"Success in life comes not from holding a good hand, but in playing a poor hand well."

Warren G. Lester

☐ Success requires work.

A well-known baseball umpire was once asked if there was such a thing as a "natural" umpire. He responded, "Yes, but no one starts out that way." In this regard, managers, umpires, and surgeons have much in common.

A broadway actor said, "Acting is pretending, and the most difficult part is pretending you're eating regularly."

☐ Success is hitting singles and doubles, not home runs.

In Arthur Miller's famous play, *Death of a Salesman,* Willy Loman was always going to make the "big sale" that was going to make him rich and famous, but he died a pathetic, defeated person.

☐ Success in one area doesn't ensure success in another area.

Two men were commenting on a friend's bad luck at the horse races.

First man: "It's amazing how lucky he is at cards and how unlucky he is at the track."
Second man: "Well, the trouble is they won't let him shuffle the horses."

☐ Success is a steady process.

Motto on wall of auto agency sales manager's conference room: "The elevator and escalator to success are out of order. You'll have to use the steps—one at a time."

To laugh often and much;
To win the respect of intelligent people and affection of children;
To earn the appreciation of honest critics and endure the betrayal of false
   friends;
To appreciate beauty,
To find the best in others;
To leave the world a bit better, whether by a healthy child,
a garden patch or a redeemed social condition;
To know even one life has breathed easier because you have lived.
This is to have succeeded.

Ralph Waldo Emerson

☐ Don't coast on your past success.

   When Louis L'Amour was asked how he could finish one book and
instantly start another one, he said: "I'm like a big old hen. I can't cluck too
long about the egg I've just laid because I've got five more inside me pushing
to get out."

Six Guidelines to success:

1. Do something you enjoy.
2. Don't expect or ask for something for nothing.
3. Give more than you get.
4. Never be satisfied.
5. Don't feel sorry for yourself.
6. Learn your abilities and your limitations.

☐ It's very important to pick the right mentor who will guide you properly.

   "Very few people get to the top without being taken under the wing of
an older person somewhere along the way."

Jean Paul Lyet, former CEO, Sperry

☐ Success is being willing to go that extra mile because most people won't.

   Jeffrey Feinman, president of Ventura Associates, promotional consultants, told about the time a salesman had a problem with a key account. When
Feinman asked him to return from Key West where he was vacationing, to see
a client, the salesman complained that there was only one flight a day.

   Feinman said, "Look, there are connecting flights and ways to do it.
Suppose I said, 'If you're there at noon tomorrow, I'll give you $100,000?'
Would you be there?"

   The salesman replied, "Yes."

   Feinman said: "What you're telling me is that it's not important enough
to you to see the client, which I can accept, but let's not con me or con yourself
that you can't make flight arrangements."

☐ Success breeds success.

Victor Kiam took the Remington Electric Shaver from obscurity to worldwide prominence because of what he learned in previous jobs. First he was successful selling toothpaste for Lever Brothers, then he went over to Playtex and sold girdles. After being made marketing director at Playtex, he was asked to enter a new market and that was selling brassieres. Taking an old idea from his toothpaste days, he offered a free bra to anyone who mailed in a coupon, plus a dollar for shipping. Thousands of women took the offer, and Playtex was suddenly successful in the brassiere business.

☐ The slim margin of success can make a big difference.

One year, Jack Nicklaus accumulated winnings of 228,000, with an average of 70.34 strokes per round. The same year, Bob Charles won only $48,000, with an average of 70.90—a difference of one-half stroke per game under Nicklaus.

In a horse race, first place may pay $15,000 and second $5,000. The horse that wins isn't three times faster than the second-place horse.

One of the most popular presidents of this century, John Kennedy, defeated Richard Nixon by less than one percent out of the 68 million votes they shared. And Nixon overcame Hubert H. Humphrey by a similarly narrow margin—0.4 percent.

George Sand, the nineteenth-century novelist, offered five parts for enjoying success:
1. Simple taste
2. A certain degree of courage
3. Self-denial to a point
4. Love of work
5. A clear conscience

■ SUPERVISION

"A supervisor has to regard those on the line as 'our people,' not a part of the fixtures. If you're not capable of doing that, I can't use you. The last thing I need is the Marine-sergeant type, hassling the troops, It's got to be somebody who can empathize and relate to people. Other kinds of skills we can teach you."

Donald Port, personnel, Gillette

☐ Don't forget that supervisors need people skills.

"You can't get to the point where you're so demanding of people that you think every time you press a button the whole world's going to jump. On the other side of the button, there's a human being."

Wallace Timmeny, former associate director, Securities & Exchange Commission

"The function of a supervisor is to analyze results, not try to control how the job is done."

Garry Jenkin, management consultant

"Sometimes you must be willing to listen to some really bad opinions from subordinates. You can't put down what they say because if you do they'll quit telling you what they think, and it's like working with a puppet on a string."

John Bryan, chairman, Consolidated Foods

"A good supervisor is a catalyst, not a drill sergeant. He creates an atmosphere where intelligent people are willing to follow him. He doesn't command; he convinces."

Whitley J. David

☐ Some people only work when they are being watched.

An employer who believed in supporting all efforts to introduce a new spirit into industry had called his men together to present his plans for bettering working conditions.

He said, "Now, whenever I enter the plant, I want to see every man cheerfully performing his task and, therefore, I invite you to place in this box any suggestions as to how that can be brought about."

A few days later, he opened the suggestion box and found this: "Take the rubber heels off your shoes."

☐ Some people need to be supervised.

A salesman rang a doorbell at a house. He saw through the window that a young boy was practicing the piano. The young boy answered the door and the salesman asked, "Is your mother home?"

The boy answered, "Now what do you think?"

"Father Theodore Purcell of Loyola University points out that the mark of a successful supervisor is that 'he listens.'

"He provides the following illustration:

"Skilled craftsman Terry O'Boyle, very proud of his work, says: 'Things are going pretty good in our shop. We have few grievances. And you can talk to the foreman. . . . The foreman has been right with me. And the former division man would stop and talk anywhere with you.' "

Mortimer R. Feinberg, Effective Psychology for Managers

One supervisor more concerned with his power than results called in one of his workers.

Supervisor: "Jones, I've heard you have been praying for a raise. Is that right?"

Jones: "That's right, sir."

Supervisor: "I'll have you know that I will not tolerate anyone going over my head."

T

TACT

"Whatever you have to say to people be sure to say it in words that will cause them to smile and you will be on pretty safe ground."

John Wanamaker

"Cultivate the art of pleasing—say the right thing or say nothing."

Warren Lester

"Advice is not disliked because it is advice, but because so few people know how to give it."

Leigh Hunt

Tact is telling someone to go to hell and having them look forward to the trip.

"Tact is the art of making a point without making an enemy."

Dr. Jon Olson

Sometimes when it comes to tact we're like Mark Twain, who said about Richard Wagner's music, "It's not as bad as it sounds."

"Tact is the art of seeing people as they wish to be seen."

Dr. Michael LeBoeuf

Tact wins friends; the lack of it often loses them. Tactful people make friends rapidly because they have a way of drawing people out and inducing them to express the best within them.

I'll tell you what tact isn't.

Customer: "I want to buy the cheapest suit in the house."
Clerk: "You're wearing it."

Psychiatrist: "What seems to be your problem?"

Patient: "All my life, I've had trouble getting along with people. I never say the right thing. Can you help me, you no-good, money-grubbing quack?"

☐ TAXES

You have to admire the Internal Revenue Service. Any organization that makes that much money without advertising—deserves respect.

"I feel very honored to pay taxes in America. The thing is, I could probably feel just as honored for about half the price."

Arthur Godfrey

Will Rogers overpaid his income tax one year but was unable to collect the money due him. After endless queries had been ignored, Rogers evened the score on his next year's return by listing under deductions: "Bad debt, U.S. Government—$40,000."

Next to surviving an earthquake, nothing is quite as satisfying as getting a refund on your income tax.

"No man's property is safe while Congress is in session."

Mark Twain

"We don't seem able to check crime, so why not legalize it and then tax it out of business."

Will Rogers

The Grace Commission organized during President Ronald Reagan's first term in office reported that "100 percent of what is collected" in personal income taxes "is absorbed solely by interest on the federal debt and by the federal government's contributions to transfer payments."

"If I have caused just one person to wipe away a tear of laughter, that's my reward. The rest goes to the government."

Victor Borge

Deductions can't always be used. A man was called in by the Internal Revenue Service to explain his return. He was disputing the rule that a baby born in January couldn't qualify as an exemption for the previous year.

He asked: "Why not? It was last year's business."

To take advantage of the lower income tax paid by a partnership, a man set up a partnership to include not only his wife but their small children as well. His wife was being cross-examined in connection with this in a federal court.

The prosecutor asked, "Do you participate in the management of the business?"

She replied, "No, I've been too busy recently to participate."

The prosecutor demanded, "Too busy doing what?"

The wife said, "Producing partners."

The IRS can put real fear in some people.

IRS Agent: "First time you've been audited?"
Taxpayer: "Yes, how did you know?"
IRS Agent: "You don't have to spread eagle."

TEAMWORK

"A company is like a ship; everyone ought to be prepared to take the helm."

Morris Weeks

"We won't try anything unless we find a user who will cooperate with us in an experiment."

Allen-Bradley executive

"The achievements of an organization are the result of the combined efforts of each individual."

Vince Lombardi, football coach

"It is better to have one person working with you than having three people working for you."

Dwight D. Eisenhower

"One hundred organized men can always defeat one thousand disorganized ones."

Lenin

"Team spirit is what gives so many companies an edge over their competitors."

George Clements

"A house divided against itself cannot stand."

Abraham Lincoln

"They said you have to use your first-best player, but I found out you win with the five that fit together best."

Red Auerbach, coach, Boston Celtics

"No one can play whatever position they choose. If that happened in baseball, there'd be nine pitchers."

Billy Martin

When General Eisenhower was asked how he managed to keep the diverse elements together in the battle of Europe, he said, "Sir, it is one team or we lose."

"It takes two wings for a bird to fly."

Jesse Jackson

Every employee is a valuable member of the team. They are as country music singer Lee Greenwood sings so grandly, "the wind beneath my wings."

"Very few people are such complete self-starters that they can make it without any help."

Robert Beck

Lee Iacocca said when he took over Chrysler, "People in engineering and manufacturing almost have to be sleeping together; these guys weren't even flirting."
For our team to be successful, we have to start flirting with each other.

☐ Every member of the team is valuable.
"No baseball pitcher would be worth a darn without a catcher who could handle the hot fastball."

Casey Stengel

Sign on Ted Turner's desk: "Either lead, follow or get out of the way!"

As the mouse said to the elephant as they walked across a bridge. "Together we're shaking this thing." That's the way every team member must feel, that they are doing their part.

There is an idiom in Japan: "to eat from the same pot." Anyone associated with a business enterprise "eats from the same pot" whether he is a welder, a switchboard operator, a chemist, or an accountant. If the pot were to disappear, everyone would go hungry. But when the pot is full, the fruits of labor are shared by all.

☐ Teamwork is cooperation.
In World War II, bombers learned to fly close together so that they could take advantage of multiple air defense systems. There was no room for showboating in the sky. Basketball players who take shots indiscriminately won't get the ball much. The hunter who scares the game away will not be invited to hunt again.

"Team spirit is what gives so many companies an edge over their competition."

George L. Clements

☐ Putting each team member in the proper place ensures that the team will be more successful.

In a scene from the movie *Ben Hur*, Judah Ben Hur was trying to get a team of horses to pull a chariot. They were magnificent, high-spirited animals—yet they were pawing the ground, balking at his commands, and scarcely moving the chariot, despite his strong voice and the constant cracking of his whip. A skilled old horse trainer approached and instantly put his finger on the problem. He told young Judah Ben Hur, "They are not pulling together as a team!"

The old man adjusted the rig, carefully aligned the horses, and climbed into the chariot. He cracked his whip; and instantly—four horses started as one. Around the track they went at breathtaking speeds.

As he handed the reins back to Judah, the old man said, "They are beautiful babies, but you must make them work together as a team."

"A well-run restaurant is like a winning baseball team; it makes the most of every crew member's talent and takes advantage of every split-second opportunity to speed up service."

Ray Kroc, founder, McDonald's

☐ Every team member is important.

There's always some argument, you know, about which is the most important to a song's success—words or the music. Well, the story goes that after the success of the musical *Showboat*, the wife of Jerome Kern, who wrote the music, and the wife of Oscar Hammerstein II, who wrote the lyrics, were at a party.

A lady came up to Mrs. Kern and gushed, "Oh my goodness, your husband is the man who wrote that wonderful 'Old Man River.' "

And Mrs. Hammerstein spoke up and said, "No dear—my husband wrote 'Old Man River.' Her husband wrote, 'Dum-dum-dum-dum, da-dum-dum-dum-dum . . . ' "

At Donnelly Mirrors, employees work as a team. If you don't do your work you have to answer to the team, not the company. Each team member is responsible to the other members of the team.

☐ We need to realize that we can do our best by working together.

A textile worker got caught up in some yarn, and he tried to get himself untangled. The more he tried to untangle himself, the more tangled he became. Finally, he called the foreman, who asked, "Why didn't you call me."

Worker: "I was trying to do the best I could."

Foreman: "You could have done your best by calling me."

☐ Teamwork requires unselfishness.

Bees live through the winter by mutual aid. They form into a ball and keep up a dance. Then they change places; those that have been out move to the center, and those at the center move out. Thus they survive the winter. Should those at the center insist on staying there, keeping the others at the edges, they would all perish.

Too many people see business as a dog-eat-dog world in which the most important thing is looking out for number one. Like the cannibal who told Mark Twain, "We understand Christianity; we ate the missionaries," I think they miss the point.

☐ We must learn to set aside our differences for the good of the team.

☐ Teamwork breeds more productivity.

Recently, a minister noticed a flock of geese flying in their traditional "V" formation, heading for Canada.

It reminded him of a study he had read about. Two engineers learned that each bird, by flapping its wings, creates an uplift for the bird that follows. Together, the whole flock gains something like 70 percent greater flying range than if they were journeying alone.

It's the same in any organization. When we combine our efforts, our talents, and our creativity, we're far more productive than when we all go in different directions.

A few years ago, a group of music legends assembled in Los Angeles to record the song "We Are the World." Lionel Richie, the popular musician, organized the event. On the entrance of the recording studio, he posted a sign saying, "Check your ego at the door." Although every singer was a star, not everyone had a solo.

The eventual success of the song was because of cooperation, not competition.

☐ Unfair compensation can destroy teamwork.

Over eighty years ago, J. P. Morgan & Company discovered that their clients who did poorly had one thing in common. Each company's top executives were paid more than 130 percent of the compensation of the people on the next level, and those people were paid 130 percent more than the next level, and so on. This out-of-balance compensation created an adversarial situation instead of a teamwork atmosphere.

"There is nothing that can't be accomplished when the right people are swept up in a worthy cause, divorced from who gets credit for what. Ask yourself!

"Are you an active member, the kind that would be missed?
Or are you satisfied just to have your name upon the list?

Do you go to the meetings and mingle with the crowd?
Or do you stay at home and bellyache long and loud?
Do you get involved and help your group along?
Or are you satisfied to be the kind to just-belong?"
Cavett Robert, founder, National Speakers Association

A story going the rounds has a moral for executives who rely on tests in hiring employees:

A firm needed a researcher. Applicants were a scientist, an engineer, and an economist. Each was given a stone, a piece of string, a stopwatch—and was told to determine a certain building's height. The scientist went to the rooftop, tied the stone to the string, lowered it to the ground. Then he swung it, timing each swing with the watch. With this pendulum, he estimated the height at 200 feet, give or take 12 inches.

The engineer threw away the string, dropped the stone from the roof, timing its fall with the watch. Applying the laws of gravity, he estimated the height at 200 feet, give or take six inches.

The economist, ignoring the string and stone, entered the building but soon returned to report the height at exactly 200 feet. How did he know? He gave the janitor his watch in exchange for the building plans. He got the job.

◼ TECHNOLOGY

☐ No matter how technical we become, the customer must be number one.

"IBM is customer- and market-driven, not technology-driven."
Buck Rogers, former IBM V-P, Marketing

"Television is the triumph of machinery over people."
Fred Allen

"Automation may be great, but nothing speeds up work like a wastebasket."
Frank Hodur

☐ Technology is no better than the user.

As one manager said: I don't like this darn computer, I wish that they would sell it; it never does what I want it to, only what I tell it.

☐ You can't stop progress.

"Once technology is out of the jar, you can't put it back in."
Ervin L. Glaspy

☐ Technology doesn't have to be based on the space age to be useful.

Ray Kroc built McDonald's with the latest technology for making better hamburgers. Because of technology, he built his fortune in a business, eating out, that was already overcrowded.

☐ Technology can save money and boost productivity.

Burger King put TV terminals in their kitchens so that the chefs could read their incoming orders from a screen that were taken from the cash registers out front. As a result, the cooks made fewer mistakes and wasted less food.

☐ We can't always see the development of technology until after it occurs.

Thomas Watson, founder of IBM, started out in the 1920s designing, selling, and installing punch-card equipment. He had no idea that technology would take IBM to the forefront of the business world.

☐ Technology can give you a competitive advantage.

The radial tire allowed Michelin to challenge Goodyear and Firestone. In typewriters, electronics was the undoing of Underwood and other mainstays.

☐ New technology keeps you from sitting on your laurels.

Years ago, Dictaphone was so far ahead in the dictaphone industry they made the mistake of assuming nobody could catch up. Then IBM bought Dictabelts, which had an advanced magnetic tape technology, and suddenly Dictaphone had to catch up.

Thomas Edison once said that his greatest discovery of all was the discovery of what people wanted to use.

"Technologies that are emerging today will give us the ability to explore, convey, and create knowledge as never before. This has enormous implications for us as individuals, as well as for our institutions. We have an opportunity that is given to few generations in history. I believe that if we respond with our best creative energies, we can unleash a new renaissance of discovery and learning."

John Scully, chairman, Apple Computer

☐ Technology is what allows people to do things that otherwise would not be possible.

"Technology is how to make and use a knife—how to weave cloth—how to make and control a fire—how to preserve food—and millions of other things, some that seem astounding, and others that are so familiar that they are simply taken for granted as being self-evident."

Jerrier A. Haddad

"Most economists concur that 50 to 60 percent of our economic growth can be attributed to technological innovations."

Ian M. Ross, president, AT&T, Bell Laboratories

☐ New technology can quickly get outdated.

Technology progresses so fast that sometimes companies spend millions of dollars on equipment that is quickly replaced with new technology. As one executive put it, "It's like building an awesome horseshoe factory after Henry Ford has his insight into the automobile assembly line."

Demand is often waiting for the technology to make it possible. For example, America has been a national society for about twenty-five years, largely because of television. But it never had a national newspaper until *USA Today* appeared, and it filled the demand only after technology made it possible.

☐ Technology can achieve total domination or total freedom.

On February 8, 1984, U.S. astronaut Bruce McChandless walked in space . . . totally free of any connection to earth. No ropes to the spacecraft, no planet beneath his feet. For the first time ever, a human being was completely on his own, an individual satellite drifting in space. He was quite literally set free by technology.

☐ Some companies profit by sharing their technology.

Kodak licensed their camera technology to numerous competitors to help them sell more cameras. Kodak did this to stimulate sales of Kodak film.

Intel licensed IBM and Commodore to make the 8088 microprocessor. This made buyers competitors, but it also scared off more competition in the process.

"Change brought about by new technology is never seen as important as it may become.

"For example, when the telephone was invented, the chief engineer of the British Post Office said it might be useful in America, but in England, there was no need for telephones, since 'we have plenty of messenger boys.'

"A similar view was taken by an officer of Western Union, who expected the phone primarily would be used to help telegraph operators communicate with each other. He simply could not visualize the elimination of telegraphers by universal telephone service."

James H. Rosenfield, senior vice president, CBS Broadcast Group

☐ Technology can bring about a loss of worker pride.

Think back to the days when most workers were craftsmen. They took pride in their work. Let's follow a man named Jones. Jones was a carriage maker, and one day, out of a job, he appeared at a wagon factory looking for work. Instead of asking him to make the whole wagon, he was asked to only make wagon wheels.

The bigger the company got, the less part Jones played in making the wagon. Eventually he only made a part of the wheel. He became detached and lost pride since he played such a small part.

"There has always been at each decisive period in this world's history some voice, some note, that represented for the time being the prevailing power. There was a time when the supreme cry of authority was the lion's roar. Then came the voice of man. After that it was the crackle of fire. . . . And now, finally, there was heard in the streets of Detroit the murmur of this newest and most perfect of forces, the automobile, rushing along at the rate of 25 miles an hour.

"It was not like any other sound ever heard in this world. It is not like the puff! puff! of the exhaust of gasoline in a river launch; neither is it like the cry! cry! of a working steam engine; but a long, quick, mellow gurgling sound, not harsh, not unmusical, not distressing; a note that falls with pleasure on the ear. It must be heard to be appreciated. And the sooner you hear its newest chuck! chuck! the sooner you will be in touch with civilization's latest lisp, its newest voice."

Robert Lacey, Ford

TIME MANAGEMENT

☐ Make time management a priority.

"Time is the scarcest resource, and unless it is managed nothing else can be managed."

Peter Drucker

"Remember that lost time does not return."

Thomas à Kempis

"Waste neither time, nor money, but make the best use of both."
Benjamin Franklin

☐ You can't get back lost time.

Hours misspent are wasted: How we wish we could live them over again. But, as the Japanese proverb says: "Spilled water never returns to the cup."

"Most misfortunes are the results of misused time."

Napoleon Hill

"Why kill time when one can employ it?"

French proverb

Tomorrow is often the busiest day of the week.

☐ Don't waste time.

"The only person to succeed while horsing around is a bookie."
Bob Murphey, humorist

The Greek philosopher Theophrasteus said more than two thousand years ago that "time is the most valuable thing a man can spend."

When Lenin took over in Russia, he preached that time must be preserved and used effectively.

"Poor delegation is a major cause for lost time."
Margaret McElroy

"Father Time is not always a hard parent, and, though he tarries for none of his children, often lays his hand lightly on those who have used him well."
Charles Dickens, Barnaby Rudge

☐ When you practice time management, the rest of the world conforms to your schedule.

Former Secretary of State Henry Kissinger once said when looking at his calendar, "There can't be a crisis next week. My schedule is already full."

" 'If you knew Time as well as I do, you wouldn't talk about wasting it,' said the Mad Hatter."
Lewis Carroll, Alice in Wonderland

"Everything requires time. It is the only truly universal condition. All work takes place in time and uses up time. Yet most people take for granted this unique, irreplaceable, and necessary resource. Nothing else, perhaps, distinguishes effective executives as much as their tender loving care of time."
Peter Drucker

"People who make the worst use of their time are the same ones who complain that there is never enough time."
Anonymous

"Time is money, especially overtime."
Evan Esar

"Time is everything. Anything you want, anything you accomplish— pleasure, success, fortune—is measured in time."
Joyce C. Hall, chairman, Hallmark Cards

"You can only manage time in those moments when you are alert to what is going on within you and around you."
James T. McCay

☐ You are the only one who can waste your time.

What do you do when you are caught in a traffic jam? Noel Coward didn't fuss and fume; he took out a piece of paper and wrote his popular song, "I'll See You Again."

☐ Work smart. Use your time wisely.

Dale Carnegie told the story of two men who were out chopping wood. One man worked hard all day, took no breaks, and only stopped briefly for lunch. The other chopper took several breaks during the day and a short nap at lunch. At the end of the day, the woodsman who had taken no breaks was quite disturbed to see that the other chopper had cut more wood than he had.

He said, "I don't understand. Every time I looked around, you were sitting down, yet you cut more wood than I did."

His companion asked, "Did you also notice that while I was sitting down, I was sharpening my ax?"

A business executive arrived at his office one morning, looked at the stacks of papers on his desk and sighed: "Life is a sequence of things you meant to get done yesterday."

☐ Don't let others waste your time.

Cartoon lines in the *Wall Street Journal:* Boss to employee: "It's lonely at the top, Harris, but not so lonely that I want you walking into my office twenty times a day."

H. L. Hunt gave up smoking cigars, which he loved, in the 1950s. But it wasn't for reasons of health. It was the profit motive.

The way H. L. figured it, just the time he took to unwrap his cigars— time he otherwise could have spent concentrating on his work—was costing him $300,000 a year.

What are we doing that's costing us money?

☐ Don't do things that waste your time.

Football coach George Allen's wife, Etty, said, "His favorite food is ice cream because he doesn't have to chew it."

Ivy Lee, a management consultant, was called in by Charles Schwab, chairman of Bethlehem Steel Company, to give him advice on how to better manage his time. Lee told him to write down every evening the six most important things he had to do the next day and to list them in the order of importance.

Schwab asked Lee how much he wanted for this advice and Lee said, "Use the plan for several months and send me a check for how much you think it is worth." Eventually Lee received a check for $25,000—not a bad sum sixty years ago.

A little boy, late for school, asked God to help him get there on time. He ran, stumbled, and breathlessly said, "God, I asked you to help me, but don't push me." Don't let your job push you; you'll stumble if you do. Discipline your time.

☐ Preparation can save time.

A salesman from Mississippi once told me about this incident early in his career. He was having the biggest day of his life in a little clothing store on the outskirts of Jackson. They loved him. The more he talked, the more they ordered, much more than was normal for a store that size. He left thinking he was a world-beater—until he phoned in his order.

At the name of the client, his boss burst into laughter. He guffawed, "You sold what to who?"

The salesman told him again. He said, "It's a great order. The best I ever had."

The boss asked, "Did you check the credit book?"

The salesman's bubble collapsed. No wonder they had been eager to order from him. His "great" customer never paid his bills.

A little preparation—in this case just checking the credit book—would have saved him a day of work. It was a costly but effective lesson.

☐ Time is money.

This story about Ben Franklin applies even today.

One day, Ben Franklin was busy preparing his newspaper for printing when a customer stopped in his store and spent an hour browsing over the various books for sale. Finally, he took one in his hand and asked the shop assistant the cost.

The assistant answered, "One dollar."

The customer said, "A dollar. Can't you sell it for less?"

The assistant replied, "No, the price is a dollar."

The customer said that he wanted to see Mr. Franklin. When Franklin appeared from the back room, the customer asked how much he wanted for the book.

Franklin said, "One dollar and a quarter."

The customer was taken aback. "Your assistant only asked for a dollar."

Franklin said, "If you had bought it from him, I could sell it to you for a dollar. But you have taken me away from the business I was engaged in."

The customer pressed on. "Come on, Mr. Franklin, what is the lowest you can take for it?"

Franklin said, "One dollar and a half. And the longer we discuss it, the more of my time you are taking up and the more I'll have to charge you."

☐ We need to have a sense of what our time is worth for others to value our time.

☐ Only you can waste your time.

Years ago, while serving in the U.S. Navy, I was stationed aboard an aircraft carrier. I was faced with the prospect of wasting two years of my life floating around on the Pacific Ocean. It was during these two years that I learned a valuable time-management tool. After complaining to a fellow sailor, he said, "You are the only one who can waste the two years."

This advice has served me well. I always try to find a way to productively use my time no matter where I am. For example, I edited the bulk of this book at 30,000 feet when other passengers were staring out the window.

☐ We should value our time, for we may have less of it than we think.

In 1939, Frank Whittle and Hans von Ohain were both working on the idea of the jet engine. Von Ohain was in Germany and Whittle was in England. Both were in different geographic and political arenas but were separately working toward the same goal.

No matter how original our ideas may seem to us, someone else may also be racing to the finish line with the same idea.

∎ TRAINING

"A company has an obligation to provide training and the opportunity for development of its people who want to improve their skills, expand their career opportunities or simply further their general education."
Dana Corporation's philosophy

"Money spent on the brain is never spent in vain."
Joe L. Griffith

"The only companies that grow are those that expect their people to grow, and spend time and money and understanding to help them do it."
William Marsteller

☐ Employee training is the key to a better economic future.

"Better-trained managers and continued research will lead to higher-quality and low-cost goods and services, and will double the standard of living in the next thirty years."
John Templeton, founder, Templeton Funds

☐ Your business will grow to the same degree that your employees grow.

Forrest Ford, president of Forrest Ford Consultants in St. Louis, has sent over half his work force through a Dale Carnegie course to create more productive employees. He feels that this training is one of the reasons his company is growing so rapidly.

☐ Training costs but it also pays.

Stew Leonard's Norwalk, Connecticut, store became well-known for customer service after being written up in Tom Peter's *In Search of Excellence*.

Leonard's one store does as much business as about ten average super-markets. He attributes much of his store's success to having sent his entire 630-member staff to Dale Carnegie courses, and the results show in the smiles that beam on every face in the store.

□ There is a direct relationship between the successful companies and those that emphasize training.

Top high-tech companies like IBM, McDonnell Douglas, Boeing, and Xerox spend between 2.5 percent and 3.5 percent of sales on training.

□ The companies that get the most from training are those that invest their training dollar wisely.

Companies like IBM, Hewlett-Packard, and Merrill Lynch develop training to help them excel, not just get by.

"In the long run, training our people may be as important as anything we do."

Joseph Murray, Security Pacific Leasing

□ Good training can help you overcome your shortcomings.

When NFL running back Herschel Walker was in junior high school, he wanted to play football but the coach told him he was too small. He advised Herschel to go out for track. Instead of taking the coach's advice, he under-took a training program to build himself up. A few years later, he won the Heisman Trophy.

□ Never stop learning.

"Do your homework! Nothing helps success more than knowing what you're doing. It reduces the risks and works like an insurance policy for your own ability."

Philip Oxley, president, Tenneco

□ Hands-on training is the most productive.

"Trainees learn only 16 percent of what they read; 20 percent of what they see; 30 percent of what they are told; 50 percent of what they see and are told and 70 percent of what they see, are told and respond to; and 90 percent of what they do."

Joe L. Whitley

□ Training is important to any company's success.

When Mary Kay Ash started Mary Kay Cosmetics in 1963, she had retired as a national sales director of a large company. With this knowledge of training, she was able to build a company with $400 million plus in annual sales.

Some years ago, Alfred North Whitehead, looking back over centuries of human progress, counseled: "In the conditions of modern life, the rule is absolute, the race that does not value trained intelligence is doomed."

Likewise for the individual or company. The one that doesn't continually train is eventually doomed.

☐ Training is only the first step.

"A teacher can only lead you to the threshold of your own mind."
Kahlil Gibran

"To improve a company fast, develop people fast."
Andrall E. Pearson, past president, PepsiCo

"We need to train our people further so that they themselves have the necessary skills and tools to enable them to suggest valuable improvements in process and even in design."
Thomas Horton, president, American Management Association

☐ The right training should be given to the right person.

Some very astute soul is alleged to have remarked, "Never try to teach a pig to sing. It just wastes your time and annoys the pig."

Consider this conversation between a young woman and her counselor:

Counselor: "You feel that to get what you want out of life you'll have to get a master's degree?"

Young woman: "Yes, but by the time I could get that degree, I'd be thirty years old! I can't afford to wait that long to get started in a career."

Counselor: "But won't you be thirty years old, even without the degree?"

☐ It's never too late to grow.

☐ Are your people trained to help the customer?

Recently, the *Wall Street Journal* ran an article about Sears' current reputation. Robert Kelly, who teaches management at Carnegie-Mellon, told about his experience at Sears. Sears advertised a special sale on its new top-of-the-line vacuum cleaners. Kelly called to buy one. The salesclerk had never heard of the product and was unaware of the sale.

Her boss suggested that Kelly call other Sears stores to find the item, but refused to do the calling for him on the grounds that she was "too busy for that kind of service."

Kelly called the customer service department, where a representative offered to order the vacuum cleaner but said that it would have to be picked up at a distant Sears warehouse.

Kelly then asked to speak to the store manager, who said he would look into it and get right back to Kelly. He didn't.

Four days later, a Sears salesclerk called Mrs. Kelly independently to inquire whether she might be interested in a vacuum cleaner.

This kind of nonsense isn't limited to Sears. Salespersons at many stores appear ignorant of both their merchandise and the rudiments of customer service.

☐ In addition to technical training, organizations should include personal enrichment training.

Successful companies like Marriott invest over $20 million a year on training. They give their 140,000 plus employees the chance to grow personally as well as technically.

☐ Training can modify behavior, develop skills, and reduce turnover.

Author-speaker W. Steven Brown told the story of a Fred Miller, who is in the insurance business in Birmingham, Alabama. Brown never quite understood why, but for a number of years Fred experienced a sizable turnover in clerical positions in his small company. Brown was most impressed with one of the new employees. At the first opportunity, he complimented Fred on her. His response was that he planned to terminate her. Shocked, Brown asked, "Why?"

He said, "She's stupid!"

Brown said, "I thought she was super. How could you feel that way?"

He replied, "Part of her job was to do mathematical calculations. She was doing them by hand, while a calculator sat idle on her desk."

Brown said, "Fred, she doesn't know how to use the calculator."

He snapped, "She does!"

"She can't!"

"She does know how to use the calculator."

"How do you know?"

Indignantly he responded, "I spent ten minutes training her."

Obviously, Fred did not have an understanding of what it required to develop such a skill or the patience to train.

☐ Our training determines what we will become.

Two thousand three hundred years ago, a wise father chose the greatest scholar of his age to tutor his young son in liberal arts. Aristotle instructed the boy in architecture, music, literature, politics, and the natural sciences.

A few years later, the boy, barely in his twenties, set out to conquer the world. He did. It took him just eleven years. He became the greatest leader, the most visionary strategist, the finest administrator the world has ever known. He became Alexander.

If we want to prepare leaders for tomorrow, we must give them the proper training today.

◼TURNOVER

☐ To avoid turnover, put the right person in the right job.

"The man who is born with a talent he is meant to use finds his greatest happiness in using it."

Johann Wolfgang von Goethe

☐ People don't quit jobs they love.

"I wanted to be a football coach since I was eleven years old. It's all I ever wanted to be. I work sixteen hours a day at it, but I feel I've never worked a day in my life. I get up in the morning wanting to go to work because it's not work."

John Ralston, former NFL coach

☐ Turnover is costly to the employer.

Tom Gerrity, a founder of Index Systems, said that it cost his company about $20,000 to replace one employee. Turnover alone was taking $500,000 from the bottom line.

☐ Turnover can be reduced if employees have clear definitions of who they are.

Index Systems, a multimillion-dollar programming firm, once had a turnover rate of 15 percent jump to over 30 percent. The problem was traced to the fact that the company wasn't overconcerned about titles, lines of authority, or formal structure. By implementing this, employees doubled from one hundred to two hundred, sales increased 40 percent annually, and the turnover rate dropped from 30 to 15 percent.

☐ One way to reduce turnover is to give employees a reason to stay with the company.

Bill Danner, president of Trak, had always thought that his employees were happy. He took them for granted. Then suddenly many of his key people began to quit. He asked some of his top people what would keep them from leaving, and several of them said they wanted to develop management skills outside of their functional areas. He let them develop as they wished, and they all stayed.

☐ People change jobs for different reasons.

A woman applying for a new job was asked why she had left her old job: "I worked for a nudist camp and I needed a change of scenery."

U

UNEMPLOYMENT

"Millions of Americans aren't working. Thank God they've got jobs!"
Joe L. Griffith

"When more and more people are thrown out of work, unemployment results."

Calvin Coolidge

☐ Sometimes trying to save a few jobs can cost more jobs.

". . . a country, an industry or a company that puts the preservation of blue-collar manufacturing jobs ahead of international competitiveness (which implies a steady shrinkage of such jobs) will soon have neither production nor jobs. The attempt to preserve such blue-collar jobs is actually a prescription for unemployment."

Peter Drucker

As Terry Bradshaw once said about the requirements of the speaking circuit he was pursuing after his retirement from professional football, "When you're unemployed, you have to work all the time."

☐ There are plenty of jobs, but they're not always desirable.

Miami, as you may or may not know, is getting a reputation as a crime center. This man was looking for a job and was told by another man to go to Miami.

First man: "I don't want to go to Miami. It's dangerous down there."
Buddy: "Listen, that's all exaggeration. I know a guy who went to Miami and he got a job right away."
First man: "What kind of job?"
Buddy: "He's a tail gunner on a milk truck."

☐ There's more than one way to solve the unemployment problem.

Husband: "I found a great job! Good salary, paid holidays, free health insurance, and four-week vacations."

Wife: "Whee! That's wonderful, dear!"

Husband: "I know you would be pleased. You start Monday."

V

▢ VALUES

"The institutional leader is primarily an expert in the promotion and protection of values."

Philip Selznick, Leadership and Administration

"If you want to know a good company's shared values, just look at its annual report."

John Stewart

"The noblest question in the world is, 'What good may I do in it?'"

Benjamin Franklin

It has been disparaged broadly, mostly by the young, but tradition can be important to the success of a company by reinforcing important values. As G. K. Chesterton once put it, "Tradition does not mean that the living are dead, but that the dead are living."

"What you really value is what you miss, not what you have."

Jorge Luis Borges

When it comes to the value of something, too many of us feel like Will Loman in *Death of a Salesman.* He said, "Once in my life I would like to own something outright before it's broken. I'm always in a race with the junkyard!"

"Everybody in the world is good for something. At least they can be a bad example."

Cavett Robert

☐ A value-oriented business reputation is priceless.

Tony, the Maytag repairman, sells more washing machines than anybody else because people think they don't need him, but he is there in case they do.

"Value is in the doer, not the deed."

Denis Waitley

☐ Value is sometimes in the eyes of the holder.

A minister selected a 50-cent item at a convenience store, then discovered he didn't have any money with him.

He said, "I could invite you to hear me preach in return, but I'm afraid I don't have any 50-cent sermons."

The clerk said, "Perhaps I could come twice."

A farmer left all his land to his three sons, telling them of a great treasure buried within it. When the man died, the boys dug up every square inch of soil, searching in vain for hidden riches. It was only after they planted the ground and their harvest bore fruit that the sons came to understand the nature of their father's legacy. They learned the values of patience and hard work.

☐ A good value system keeps you from losing sight of why you are in business.

Examples of businesses that serve their needs first are everywhere: hospitals that focus on payment rather than pain; car repair operations that are concerned with warranty rather than repair; computer departments that are too concerned with machinery and methods than timely information.

☐ Values are sometimes determined by public perception.

Gordon Getty said that when he was a teenager, he asked his father, the legendary J. Paul Getty, about the merits of the family brand. When he asked his father what the differences between the various brands of gas were, his father replied, "Frankly, none, son."

☐ There isn't much difference between our product and our competitor's other than the perceived value.

☐ With a set of values, it is easier to make decisions.

When President Dwight D. Eisenhower was a general in World War II, a reporter asked him how he could order hundreds of young men to battle knowing that so many of them would be killed. He pointed to a book on his desk and said, "See, that's the book on how to fight a war. I just go by the book. It tells me what to do."

☐ In business, we need values to give us guidelines that help us make tough decisions.

The public perceives value differently with each product. For example, Arm & Hammer's detergents have been perceived better than the competition because the box is heavier even though it yields the same number of washes.

Because of perceived value, a paint job on a medical instrument may have an important impact on the purchaser even though the paint has no impact on the instrument's performance.

In 1985, *Chain-Age* magazine did a survey of what customers believed to be the value of a product. The results were broken down as follows:

Workmanship	23 percent
Price	21 percent
Materials	14 percent
Looks	13 percent

◻ VENTURE CAPITAL

◻ It's easier to attract venture capital when you have contributed your own risk money first.

Fred Smith put up $4 million of his own money when he started Federal Express in 1971. This sweetener helped persuade a handful of venture capitalists to put up over $80 million. At that time, it was the largest venture capital package ever assembled.

◻ Sometimes getting enough money to get started is the hardest part.

"Money is the seed of money, and the first guinea is sometimes more difficult to acquire than the second million."

Jean-Jacques Rousseau

◻ To obtain venture capital you will have to give up some ownership.

"I've learned that it's always better to have a small percentage of a big success, than a hundred percent of nothing."

Art Linkletter

Venture capital is always a risk. Listen to the words of a veteran venture capitalist: "I've been funding entrepreneurs for twenty-five years. When I started, my record was fifty-fifty. And today my record is still fifty-fifty."

◻ Getting capital is sometimes being in the right place at the right time.

One venture capitalist said: "If I have been successful funding ten Chinese and you walk into my office and you're Chinese, then it's more likely to have a positive impact on me. It gives me a good gut feeling."

☐ Every idea isn't a good idea.

Once upon a time, so the story goes, in this little town in West Virginia, an old Civil War cannon sat in front of the county courthouse.

A cousin of one of the county commissioners was employed to keep the cannon polished. Each morning, he picked up his polish and his rag, marched out of the courthouse, and spent the day polishing the gun.

This went on for several years. But then the cannon-polisher's cousin, the commissioner, got involved in a factional political fight and was defeated at the next election. The cannon polisher lost his job.

The next day, he showed up at the bank. He wanted, he said, to take out a loan.

The banker said, "For what purpose?"

The cannon-polisher said, "Well, sir, it's this way. You know for the last twelve years I've been polishin' that cannon in front of the courthouse. And I done a good job. Nobody can say different. Well, I got twelve years of on-the-job experience. Now I want the money to go buy my own cannon and polish so I can go into business for myself."

☐ There's more than one way to raise capital.

A young reporter was interviewing a successful businessman.

Reporter: "What's the secret of your success?"
Businessman: "A strong will."
Reporter: "Can you elaborate on that?"
Businessman: "Yes. A strong will that left me $1 million."

☐ For venture capital to be profitable, you need to know when to sell.

In 1955, Ray Kroc bought the franchise rights to McDonald's. Desperate for money, he offered several potential investors half the stock in his company for $25,000. Today that stake would be worth more than $5 billion.

Seven years later and still strapped for cash, he bought the entire company for $2.7 million, financing the deal at exorbitant interest rates that brought the total purchase price to $14 million.

While all venture capitalists acknowledge that funds invested into research and development are risk capital, none makes investments without the reasonable expectation of discoveries and information that can lead to future profits.

When Queen Isabella hocked her jewels and footed Columbus' bills, you can bet she wasn't doing it just to prove the earth wasn't flat. She expected profitable trade to result from the trip.

Venture capital is risky. For instance, the typical venture source with ten investments of $100,000 each will have committed $1 million to their portfolio. If all the investments eventually turn sour save one, the batting average will be 10 percent. However, if the one success produces a $2 million gain on the original $100,000 investment, or a 20 times return, the slugging average would be calculated as 2:1 or $2 million returned on the $1 million invested. This, according to one of the venture capitalists in Boston, accounts for the confusion in analyzing the industry. One success could actually count much higher than a grand-slam home run.

Some venture capitalists want to take debt with option to buy stocks later. A classic example of a debt with warrants-type of investment occurred in the mid-1960s. Fred Fideli of the Worcester-based firm, State Mutual Life Assurance Company, traveled to Chicago in order to evaluate a growing chain of hamburger stands. Although only one hundred units were operating at this time, after personally visiting about seventy-five of the chains, Fideli offered a loan of $750,000 with an interest rate of 7 ½ percent to this business now headed up by the famous entrepreneur, Ray Kroc. In addition, to sweeten the financial attractiveness of this loan, Fideli obtained warrants to purchase 10 percent of the common stock of the chain.

About ten years later, State Mutual had received full payment for its loan, exercised the warrants on the company, and sold the stock in the public market. Rumor had it that this conservative life insurance company realized about $12 million in turn for making this loan. The McDonald's Corporation was the most successful of all of State Mutual's investments.

David Silver, a columnist for *Venture Magazine* said that the three ingredients for a successful investment of venture capital are:

1. A big market
2. A good product
3. A good management team

According to Silver, the most successful venture capital investment ever made was not in a product but in the service industry. A twenty-eight year old man named Fred Smith raised $94 million to launch Federal Express. He still maintained 4 percent of the business while putting up less than 1 percent of the capital.

WEALTH

"Wealth is largely a result of habit."

John Jacob Astor

☐ Easy come, easy go.
"Wealth which comes in at the door unjustly, goes out at the windows."
Egyptian proverb

"The way to wealth is as plain as the way to market."
Benjamin Franklin

"A man is rich in proportion to the things he can afford to let alone."
Henry David Thoreau

☐ Work for yourself.
"It is most unusual for someone to become wealthy by working for a rich man."

Carl Riblet

"If you can actually count your money, then you're not rich."
Joseph P. Kennedy

"Wealth can't buy health, but health can buy wealth."
Henry David Thoreau

A millionaire in money is nothing compared to being a millionaire in friends.

☐ The wealth of a nation is worth preserving.
"You may try to destroy wealth and find that all you have done is increase poverty."

Winston Churchill

☐ What is wealth if you can't enjoy it.

"Wealth is not his that has it, but his that enjoys it."

Josh Billings

"A man who has a million dollars is as well off as if he were rich."

John Jacob Astor

"The sole purpose of being rich is to give away money."

Andrew Carnegie

"Reservoirs of wealth in the hands of individuals are just as necessary as in the hands of banks and insurance companies, because individuals can take risks and undertake enterprises which such institutions cannot."

James Duke, founder, American Tobacco and Duke University

"Remember, wealth is not only what you have, but also what you are."

Garry Jenkin

"In the race for wealth . . . he may run as hard as he can and strain every nerve and muscle, in order to outstrip all his competitors. But if he should jostle, or throw down any of them, the indulgence of the spectators is at an end. It is a violation of fair play, which they cannot admit of."

Adam Smith, Wealth of Nations

"American wealth began with personal austerity and self-denial."

Richard M. Huber, The American Idea of Success

"I been rich and I been poor. Rich is better."

Sophie Tucker

"Let me tell you about the very rich. They are different from you and me. They possess and enjoy early, and it does something to them, makes them soft where we are hard, and cynical where we are trustful, in a way that, unless you were born rich, it is difficult to understand. They think, deep in their hearts, that they are better than we are because we had to discover the compensations and refuges of life for ourselves. Even when they enter deep into our world or sink below us, they still think that they are better than we are. They are different."

F. Scott Fitzgerald

"The first wealth is health."

Ralph Waldo Emerson

☐ The hardest part of wealth is getting started.

"To turn $100 into $110 is work. To turn $100 million into $110 million is inevitable."Edgar Bronfman, chairman, Seagram

☐ The hardest part of wealth is getting started.

John Jacob Astor said that the first thousand dollars cost him more effort than all of his millions. Youth who are careless with their dimes and quarters never get this first thousand, and without it no fortune is possible.

☐ The chief reward of a job well done is not the wealth it brings but the satisfaction derived from having done it.

Once there was a man who liked his job but whose family clamored for more and more money. The man resisted them for a long time but finally gave in and found a job that paid more but that he liked less. He worked long and hard. He changed jobs frequently and badgered his employers for higher salaries. Soon, his children enjoyed the best of everything. Yet they still made him miserable with their clamor, and the father saw that they were no happier than they had been before. Outraged, he stripped every child of its belongings. He took back the clothes and the cars. He fired the maid and the cook. He made sure they had enough to eat but spent nothing on delectables. "If you can't be happy eating beans, you won't be happy eating steak."

Luckily, our steak still lies ahead of us. But it is important while we are still a young company, while we are still eating beans, that we find value and joy, that we find happiness, in our work.

"Of what use would great wealth be to me? My wants are simple. I could spend no more than my income. Leave it to my children? The last wish in my heart would be to handicap them with great riches and steal away their fund of individual initiative. Any man should think a long time before he bars his children from the opportunity of creative effort or the fashioning and determination of their own lives and happiness."
A. P. Giannini, founder, Bank of America

WINNING

"Winning is a habit. Unfortunately, so is losing."
Vince Lombardi, football coach

"The lesson that most of us on this voyage never learn, but can never quite forget, is that to win is sometimes to lose."
Richard M. Nixon

"The only thing harder to handle than winning too much is losing too much."
John Wooden, basketball coach

"Anyone can win—unless there happens to be a second entry."
George Ade

"To me a winner is someone who recognizes his God-given talents, works his tail off to develop them into skills, and uses those skills to accomplish his goals. Even when I lost, I learned what my weaknesses were, and I went out the next day to turn those weaknesses into strengths."

Larry Bird

"Winning companies focus on rewarding stars, cutting dead wood."

Andrall E. Pearson, former president, PepsiCo

"I don't see any virtue in losing. This society rewards people who win."

Robert Crandall, chairman, AMR, parent to American Airlines

"Winning isn't everything, but the will to win is everything."

Vince Lombardi, football coach

Winners:	Losers:
Always have an idea	Always have an excuse
Always say, "I'll do it!"	Always say, "It's not my job!"
See an answer for every problem	See a problem for every answer
Always say, "I can"	Always say, "I can't"
Look for a way to do it	Look for a way to get out of it

☐ We become winners when everything but first place is losing.

Richard Petty has won more prize money than any other stock car driver in history. His story about what happened when he reported the results of his first race to his mother is an intriguing one.

He shouted as he rushed into the house, "Mama, there were thirty-five cars that started, and I came in second in the race!"

His mother replied, "You lost!"

He said, "But, Mama, don't you think it's pretty good to come in second in my first race—especially with so many starters?"

She said, "Richard, you don't have to run second place to anybody!"

For the next twenty years, Richard Petty dominated stock car racing. He never forgot his mother's challenge—"Richard, you don't have to run second to anybody!"

"Some say the will to win is a bad thing. In what way? Education is supposed to prepare a young person for life, and life is competition. Success in life goes only to the person who competes and wins. A successful lawyer is the one who goes out and wins—wins law cases. A successful physician is one who goes out and wins—saves lives and restores people to health. A successful sales manager is a man who goes out and wins—sells the goods. The successful executive is the man who can make money. There is no reward for losing. So that leaves living life only one way—with the will to win!"

Knute Rockne

Larry King wrote in *USA Today* about the late Edward Bennett Williams who owned the Baltimore Orioles. While sitting at an Orioles game with Williams during the 1983 World Series, Larry told of the following event:

"It was the last inning of the fifth game; I don't think I'd ever seen anyone as excited as Ed. The Orioles led 5–0 with two outs, and still he whispered to me, 'I don't like this, Larry. It's going too well. We are going to lose this thing.'

The Orioles did win the World Series, but the story makes the point that the real winners in life are those who no matter how far ahead they are realize they could still lose it.

☐ We can't sit back on our lead and expect to be long-term winners.

☐ You don't always win with size.

In the War of 1812, the American general William Winder had a four-to-one troop superiority over the British, but he led his army to defeat and was taken prisoner. The British later let him go, realizing that the general's incompetence made him an ideal opponent, so they returned him to the American army. They made the right decision. The British later attacked our nation's capitol and burned most of it to the ground. Winder was in charge of defending it.

The British were greatly outnumbered but won on competence, not on numbers.

Winning is sometimes just intimidating your competition. Muhammad Ali was a brilliant practitioner of this technique. Ali was a genius at psychological warfare. He said over and over, "The bear will fall in five." Sure enough, when the fifth round came, the bear fell, exactly as Ali had convinced him he would.

☐ Attention to detail can make you a winner.

"Ara Parseghian, the great Notre Dame football coach who successfully reversed the school's football fortune, is a fanatic for detail, training, preparation, and practice. I quote from an article in *Time*: 'For Ara Parseghian, the man who cannot stand to lose, the day begins at 5:30 a.m. with four cups of coffee, usually ends with a tranquilizer and the late late show. Even when he eats, he has a pencil in the other hand, diagramming a play. Is there something he has forgotten, some minuscule detail he has overlooked, some new way to win?' "

Mortimer R. Feinberg, Effective Psychology for Managers

"A winner . . . knows how much he still has to learn, even when he is considered an expert by others;

"A loser . . . wants to be considered an expert by others, before he has even learned enough to know how little he knows."

Sydney Harris

At Harvard Square, a friend and I watched as a chess expert took on all comers and then collected money from his defeated opponents. After exchanging pleasantries, my friend sat down at the board and soundly defeated him.

I commented to my friend as we walked off, "I didn't know you were such a fine chess player."

He confessed, "I'm not. Before we started, I told him that I worked for the IRS."

☐ WORK

☐ Work gets results.

"Words do not make flour."

Italian proverb

"He that wishes to eat the nut does not mind cracking the shell."

Polish proverb

"Anything in life worth having is worth working for!"

Andrew Carnegie

"He who is afraid of doing too much always does too little."

German proverb

"There is nothing better for a man than to rejoice in his work."

Ecclesiastes 3:22

There are many formulas for success—but none of them works unless you do.

There's no better way to get a day's work done than to work a day.

Work is the least expensive way to occupy your time.

"Hard work is an accumulation of easy things that should have been done last week."

Kathy Griffith

☐ Pace yourself.

"There is nothing quite so valuable as work. That's why it's a good idea to leave some for tomorrow."

Marian Dolliver

"Work is the easiest activity man has invented to escape boredom."

Anonymous

Paddle your own canoe.

Maurice Kirkpatrick

☐ If you are willing to work, others will let you.

Be first at your desk in the morning and that's where they'll dump all the day's work.

"Miracles sometimes occur, but one has to work terribly hard for them."
Chaim Weizmann

☐ There is only one way to reach the goals that we have set.

"The common denominator for success is work."
John D. Rockefeller

☐ Whom do we work for? The boss or the products we sell?

"It is not the employer who pays wages—he only handles the money. It is the product that pays wages."
Henry Ford

☐ You can't get by on talent alone.

"Nobody should think they can just coast through life on the basis of gifts that they have nothing to do with in the first place. You have to pay your dues and do your homework."
Steve Allen

☐ It's the work that is not required that will get you to the top.

Andrew Carnegie, still in his teens, rose to a position of prominence with the Pennsylvania Railroad. The reason was because of the extra work he did.

"I have always found, when I was worrying, that the best thing to do was put my mind upon something, work hard and forget what was troubling me."
Thomas Edison

"I go on working for the same reason that a hen goes on laying eggs."
H. L. Mencken

☐ We are quite often known by what we do.

"As soon as a stranger is introduced into any company, one of the first questions which all wish to have answered is, 'How does that man get his living.' He is no whole man until he knows how to earn a blameless livelihood."
Ralph Waldo Emerson

"If one is not constrained to labor, one is not constrained to accomplish."
Mark Camp

"If the power to do hard work is not talent, it is the best possible substitute for it."

James A. Garfield

☐ The trouble is too many people want to put their feet up before they work.

"If you work hard and keep both feet to the ground, you'll eventually reach a point at which you'll be able to put both feet on a desk."

Myron Cohen, comedian

"Nobody ever drowned in his own sweat."

Ann Landers

"I feel every person can have everything if they are willing to work, work, work."

Estée Lauder

Sherlock Holmes to Dr. Watson: "I never remember feeling tired by work, though idleness exhausts me completely."

"The object of living is work, experience, happiness. There is joy in work. All that money can do is buy us someone else's work in exchange for our own. There is no happiness except in the realization that we have accomplished something."

Henry Ford

"Work is so much more fun than fun. It's improperly called work."
Trammell Crow

Henry Ford said that no work with interest is ever hard. If a person tends to remain always a manual laborer than he should forget about his work when the whistle blows, but if he intends to go forward and do anything, the whistle is only a signal to start thinking.

Ralph Waldo Emerson said to an aspiring artist, "There is no way to success in our art but to take off your coat, grind paint, and work like a digger on the railroad, all day, every day. When I was a boy, my mother often said to me, 'If it is to be, it is up to me.' "

Harry S. Truman was a no-nonsense president whose attitude toward life was summed up in this sentence: "I found that the men and women who got to the top were those who did the jobs they had in hand with everything they had of energy and enthusiasm and hard work."

☐ If you work hard, you will do well.

☐ It's the extra work you do that is the difference between success and failure.

Curt Carlson, CEO of the Carlson Companies, is estimated by *Forbes* magazine to be worth $500 million. He said that the first five days of the week are when you work to keep up with the competition. It's on Saturdays and Sundays that you get ahead of them.

◻ WORK ETHICS

Japanese executive: "The Japanese are very different from the rest of the world. Their only natural resource is the hard work of their people."

Employee: "there's no point in working late to impress management. They all go home early."

"Never itch for anything you aren't willing to scratch for."
                                                                          Ivern Ball

Robert O. Anderson, the largest landowner in the United States, said, "I don't think the important traits for good managers have changed very much . . . hard work."

"Too many people today only want to put in a 40-hour week. I always told my managers that you can't be successful unless you tell your wife not to expect you home for dinner."
                                        C. Kemmons Wilson, founder, Holiday Inns

"If I find people who can tell me what's on TV at 8:15 on Thursday night, then I'm not interested in hiring them."
                                    Rene C. McPherson, former chief executive, Dana

"If you can't beat the Germans or the Japanese, and you can still sleep soundly at night, you're not right for the job."
                                                                          Ross Perot

"The man who will use his skill and constructive imagination to see how much he can give for a dollar instead of how little he can give for a dollar is bound to succeed."
                                                                         Henry Ford

◻ The world doesn't owe you a living.

"The boy who believes that his parents, or the government, or anyone else owes him his livelihood and that he can collect it without labor will wake up one day and find himself working for another boy who did not have that belief and, therefore, earned the right to have others work for him."
                                                                      David Sarnoff

Donald M. Kendall, former chief executive of PepsiCo, said, "Start at the bottom. My biggest problem with business school graduates is that too many don't want to start where you learn the business. They want to get into planning, a desk job, more money, instead of getting into a Pepsi plant or on a truck route. When they are forty or so, they should be headed for top management, but at that point others just pass them by.

"One brilliant marketing man didn't make it all the way to the top because he had never worked at or understood the nature of the jobs basic to the business. That man became the butt of company jokes. We used to say that he didn't know one end of the soaker from the other."

Index